THE ROAD ON WHICH WE CAME

Po'i Pentun Tammen Kimmappeh

THE ROAD
ON WHICH
WE CAME

A History of the Western Shoshone

STEVEN J. CRUM

University of Utah Press
Salt Lake City

♾ Printed on acid-free paper

LIBRARY OF CONGRESS CATALOGING-IN-PUBLICATION DATA

Crum, Steven J. (Steven James), 1950–
     The road on which we came = Po'i pentun tammen kimmappeh : a
history of the western Shoshone / Steven J. Crum.
        p.   cm.
     Includes bibliographical references and index.
     ISBN 0-87480-434-5 (alk. paper)
     1. Shoshoni Indians—History.   2. Shoshoni Indians—Social life
and customs.   3. Shoshoni Indians—Government relations.   4. Great
Basin—History.   I. Title.   II. Title: Po'i pentun tammen
kimmappeh.
E99.S4C78   1994
973'.04974—dc20   93-39441

CONTENTS

Maps   vi

Preface   vii

1. The Native Way of Life   1

2. Warfare and Adjustment:
   The Western Shoshone and the Americans, 1848–1880   17

3. The Western Shoshone Reservation (Duck Valley), 1880–1933   43

4. The Nonreservation Shoshone, 1880–1933   59

5. The Western Shoshone and the New Deal, 1933–1941   85

6. From the New Deal to Termination, 1941–1960   119

7. Recent Western Shoshone History, 1960–1990   149

Epilogue   185

Notes   189

Bibliography   223

Index   233

MAPS

Aboriginal Western Shoshone Territory   3

Duck Valley Indian Reservation   45

Lands Allocated for Western Shoshone (1910–1931)   61

Western Shoshone Reservations and Colonies   87

Present Land Base of the Western Shoshone   151

PREFACE

This history of the Western Shoshone people of the Great Basin is the result of fourteen years of research, an undertaking begun in 1978 when I was a graduate student in history at the University of Utah. My doctoral dissertation, which focused upon the impact of the New Deal on the Basin Shoshones, reflected an early phase of my deep interest in tribal history. Upon completing the dissertation in 1983, I kept alive the idea of writing a comprehensive history of the Western Shoshone. This study represents the culmination of that drive.

In writing this general history of the Western Shoshone people of the Great Basin, I was influenced by recent scholarship in western American history. I was deeply affected by Patricia Limerick's *Legacy of Conquest* (1984). She accurately points out that historians have too often portrayed Indians as "passive," relegating them to the role of "supporting actors." Limerick refutes this old frame of reference by showing that tribal people for centuries have been an active force in shaping their history, even after European contact. She writes that Indians played an "active role . . . in shaping history" and notes that they also represent the "power of cultural persistence," since they have sought to preserve their cultural heritage.[1]

I was also moved by two other works. One of these is Todd Benson's 1991 article, "The Consequence of Reservation Life: Native Californians on the Round Valley Reservation, 1871–1884."[2] He too concludes that Indians have actively shaped their own history. Benson provides ample evidence that the tribes that settled on the Round Valley Reservation in northern California determined their own course of action to varying degrees, despite their subjection to the paternalistic policies of the federal government. The second work is Robert Berkhofer's "Cultural Pluralism versus Ethnocentrism in the New Indian History" (1987). Berkhofer maintains that historians must place the "Indian actors in the forefront of the action."[3] These three authors, along with others, believe that the academic community needs to adopt a new approach to Indian history.

I agree with the major argument made by these scholars, and I include in my study numerous examples of the Shoshone people as an active force in shaping their own history. For example, they created their unique way of life before European contact, effectively adapting to the dry physical environment. They reacted to the intruders by defending their home territory in the mid-nineteenth century. After contact, they accepted some federal government policies but opposed others until the government modified its position to accommodate Shoshone demands. At times, some Shoshones rejected federal objectives altogether. On occasion, the Shoshones disagreed among themselves over federal initiatives. To varying degrees, all the Basin Shoshones accepted the changes brought about by the dominant society. Yet, at the same time, they actively sought to preserve different aspects of their native culture—an effort that persists even today.

I was driven to write this history of the Western Shoshone for at least three reasons. First, no comprehensive history of the Basin Shoshones has previously been written. There has been only one short tribal history, *Newe: A Western Shoshone History*. This brief study, published in 1976, was the work of the Inter-Tribal Council of Nevada. Its major strength is the focus on nineteenth-century Shoshone history. Roughly two-thirds of the book deals with the pre-1900 period.[4] Its weakness is the limited treatment given to the twentieth century. Second, as a historian, I found the history of the Shoshone fascinating. Third, I myself am a Shoshone. My ancestors were born and spent their lives in northeastern Nevada. My paternal great-grandparents, Dick and Emma Crum, lived in Battle Mountain. Their son (my grandfather) Jim Crum moved to the Duck Valley Reservation in the mid-1930s to secure employment. My maternal grandmother, Anna Premo, was born in Ruby Valley. Her husband, Thomas Premo, and his ancestors came from the Jarbridge Mountains and settled on the Duck Valley Reservation before 1900. My tribal enrollment (7/8 degree Shoshone) therefore lies on this reservation where I grew up. As a tribal member, I believe I can offer a unique perspective on the history of the Western Shoshone people.

The approach taken in this study is historical and to a certain extent ethnohistorical. Ethnohistory combines anthropology with history, and the outcome is cultural history. I have made use of anthropological sources and oral interviews with tribal members to emphasize the cultural side of Shoshone history. I also draw upon the traditional historical sources, mainly the unpublished correspondence of the Bureau of Indian Affairs (BIA) filed in the National Archives and its regional branches. My study proceeds chronologically. Most chapters are divided into subsections that treat specific time periods, themes, and topics. Much of my study focuses on dealings of the federal government with the Western Shoshone and on the relations between the Western Shoshone people and the dominant U.S. culture from the mid-nineteenth century to the present. At first glance this approach might appear to be old-fashioned, since it is largely a history of Indian policy. However, my study is different from traditional studies in two ways. First, I deal with events up to 1990, unlike previous works, which end at an earlier period. Second, mine is a kind of "grass roots" study since it considers Shoshone reactions to federal policies.[5] To a degree, it is a reversal of older works in its presentation of Shoshone history from local, native points of view.

I focus on the twentieth century because most tribal histories give only scant attention to this period. For example, Peter Iverson wrote that "few tribal historians considered the twentieth century in much detail."[6] More recently, Colin Calloway noted that "historians and the general public alike seem to have been comfortable with the notion that Indian history ended in 1890 with Wounded Knee and the official closing of the frontier."[7] The older works have been deeply influenced by the "frontier thesis" made popular by Frederick Jackson Turner in 1893. He impressed upon the historical profession the notion that Indians were an insignificant and unimportant element when the so-called "frontier" ended around 1890.[8] Historians for a long time accepted this thesis, and in their tribal histories, they took the chronology up to the closing years of the nineteenth century and then dropped the subject. It is important for historians to recognize that Indians have continued to be an active historical force since 1890 and into the twentieth century. For this reason, roughly three-fourths of my study focuses on this century. Chapter 5 is for the most part a condensation of my dissertation on the New Deal period.

The good news is that, since 1970, a handful of scholars who have written tribal histories have broken free from Turner's influence. In their publications, the following individuals give full treatment to tribal history, including the post-1890 period: Edmund Danzinger, Jr., *The Chippewas of Lake Superior* (1978); Patricia Ourada, *The Menominee: A History* (1979); Peter Iverson, *The Navajo Nation* (1981); John Finger, *Cherokee Americans: The Eastern Band of Cherokees in the Twentieth Century* (1991); Morris Foster, *Being Cherokee: A Social History of an American Indian Community* (1991); and Veronica Tiller, *The Jicarilla Apache Tribe: A History, 1846–1990* (1983, 1992).

Concerning the nature of tribal history, I am one of those who maintain that there is no such thing as a monolithic Indian viewpoint. Perhaps Tiller said it best when she wrote that "there is no composite Indian

Colony; Richard Clemmer, professor of anthropology at the University of Denver; and my aunt Naomi Mason who is an enrolled member of the Duck Valley Reservation.

I am also grateful to several Western Shoshone individuals who allowed me to record interviews with them, and to others who allowed me to ask questions and take notes during informal visits. Those with whom I conducted recorded interviews include Pauline Esteves of Death Valley, California; Whitney McKinney of the Duck Valley Reservation; Bud and Isabelle Decker and their daughter Berdine Ramos, all of the Battle Mountain Colony; and Bert Tybo of Duck Valley. Others who allowed me to ask questions and to take notes were Irene Adamson of Battle Mountain, Marie Allison of Fallon, Gracie Begay of Wells, Delores and Earl Conklin of Battle Mountain, Lillian Garcia of South Fork, Ernest Hooper of Fallon, Alta McQueen of Wells, Jerry Millett of Duckwater, Henry Sam of Elko, Alfred Stanton of Ely, Frank Temoke, Sr., of Ruby Valley, Pansy Weeks of Fallon, Jack Woods of Elko, the late Glenn Holley of Battle Mountain, and the late Brownie Sam of Elko. I give my deepest apology if I have overlooked other names. I should stress that the interpretations and the emphasis on certain topics presented in this study do not reflect the views of the persons listed here. I take full responsibility for my work.

I wish to thank the many archivists and their staffs who assisted me with my research at the National Archives in Washington, D.C.; the Federal Archives and Records Centers at Denver, Fort Worth, Laguna Niguel (California), and San Bruno (California); the Special Collections at the University of Nevada at Reno and the University of Utah; and the Nevada Historical Society, Reno. Dan Nealand and Kathleen O'Connor, both archivists at San Bruno, were especially helpful.

I also thank the organizations that granted financial support for this undertaking. The Marriner S. Eccles Graduate Fellowship in Political Economy (1981–1983) enabled me to finish a good portion of my research in the early 1980s. The fellowship under the Charles Redd Summer Fellowship program at Provo, Utah, in 1988 enabled me to conduct research on recent Shoshone history. My acceptance in the 1988 National Endowment for the Humanities Summer Seminar, entitled "New Directions in Native American History," and in the 1990 NEH Summer Institute, "Myth, Memory, and History," allowed me to write chapters 1 and 6. A postdoctoral fellowship under the University of California President's Fellowship Program (1989–1990) allowed me to finish most of this study. Under the UC fellowship, Kelly Crabtree of the Native American Studies Program entered this work on computer, and I thank her for this effort. Douglas Van Lare, a student at the University of California at Davis, drew the maps.

viewpoint because of the multiplicity and diversity of Indian cultures throughout the United States."[9] Taking this position a step further, even within a particular tribe, there is diversity with regard to dialect; regional history, if a tribe lives over a vast area; and philosophies concerning government policies applied to Indians after contact. It is more appropriate, then, to use the plural form in referring to viewpoints, perspectives, and native voices. This is certainly true for the Western Shoshone people of the Great Basin.

Throughout my study, I use the terms *Indian* and *Native American* interchangeably. Both are now used to identify this nation's first inhabitants. The older term, *Indian*, has been around for 500 years. However, in recent decades, an increasing number of native persons have become critical of this label, calling it a misnomer placed upon tribal peoples by Christopher Columbus. In rejecting this general term, they suggested a new one, *Native American*. This new label has gained popularity in recent years, and the major U.S. newspapers adopted it in 1988. But the older label is still used frequently, especially in rural areas and on reservations. For this reason, I have chosen to use both interchangeably in my references to the native people of the Great Basin. In the early chapters I use the name Newe, or "people," to refer to the Great Basin Shoshones since it was their indigenous name for themselves before contact. For much of my study, however, I rely upon the historic name Western Shoshone or Shoshone because it has been widely used and accepted by both Indians and non-Indians after contact. The origin of the word *Shoshone* is a mystery to the Newe themselves. Without doubt, it originated with white Americans when they came into contact with the indigenous Newe before the mid-nineteenth century.

Another problematic name is that of the Bureau of Indian Affairs (BIA). This federal agency was created in 1824 but did not receive that name until the late 1940s. Its original name was the Office of Indian Affairs. It was also called the Indian Bureau or the Indian Office. I use all these labels, according to the time period under discussion.

I am grateful to all those who helped me with this project over the years. First I thank those who reviewed the entire study and commented on it: Frances Minton of Salt Lake City, who examined each chapter with a critical eye; my parents Earl and Beverly Crum of the Duck Valley Reservation in Nevada; Dr. Elmer Rusco, professor emeritus at the University of Nevada at Reno; and my wife Annette Reed Crum who is Tolowa-Yurok, enrolled on the Smith River Rancheria in northern California. Additionally, I thank those who read one or more chapters: Jack D. Forbes, professor of anthropology and Native American studies at the University of California, Davis; Felix Ike, a Shoshone from the Elko

I dedicate this history to my parents Beverly and Earl Crum and also to the Western Shoshone (Newe) of the Great Basin. As fluent native speakers, my parents were extremely helpful. They translated the Shoshone songs, words, and sentences included in this study.

1

THE NATIVE WAY OF LIFE

The Western Shoshone people of the Intermountain West called themselves the Newe (people). They occupied a large area in the Great Basin region, from southern Idaho (north) to Death Valley, California (south), and from the Smith Creek Mountains in central Nevada (west) to the area around present-day Ely, Nevada (east). The Newe called their homeland Pia Sokopia (Earth Mother). They developed a distinctive way of life before white contact, one that continued to exist even after white people entered the Great Basin.[1]

According to their oral tradition, the Newe were placed in their homeland by the Creator (Uteen Taikwahni), whose complexion was the same color as that of the natives. Once placed on the land, two native women instructed the coyote to carry a large, pitched water-basket with him on his journey into the Basin area. Coyote was specifically told not to open the lid. Moved by irrepressible curiosity, he periodically opened the basket during his trip. The beings concealed inside jumped out here and there. The Newe believe this explains why they live over a large area. Today, family groups can be found in Death Valley, the Reese River Valley, Ruby Valley, the South Fork Valley, and numerous other places, primarily in Nevada.[2]

Earth Mother consists of high desert country with a low annual rainfall, averaging 5–10 inches. Typically, valley floors lie at 4,000–6,000 feet elevation; the surrounding mountain ranges, usually running north-south, are 9,000–10,000 feet high. Summer months are hot and dry, and winters are cold. The most visible vegetation is sagebrush. At higher elevations juniper and pinyon pine are abundant. Varied plant life flourishes in the fertile valleys along creeks and wherever marshes and small, shallow lakes formed. There is no natural drainage in the Basin.[3]

The limited natural resources of the Great Basin meant that the Newe

1

could not overpopulate their country, nor could they concentrate in large numbers in one particular place over a long period of time. Instead, they formed small, extended family groups, each of which inhabited a particular place, or valley, where their ancestors had lived since time immemorial. The family groups had different names, usually based upon a local food resource or a particular occupation or a geographic feature. Those in Big Smoky Valley were the *wi yimpihtikka* (eaters of buffalo berry); those in Pine Valley, the *pasiatekka* (eaters of redtop grass); those in Ione Valley, the *waitekka* (eaters of rice grass); those in Ruby Valley, the *watatekka* (eaters of rye grass seeds); and those in Duckwater Valley, the *tsaitekka* (tule eaters). Those who lived north of Battle Mountain were the *tosa wihi* (white knives) because they made arrowheads and knives from a local white rock quarry. Those in Death Valley called themselves the *timbisha* (or *tempisa*) after Furnace Creek.[4]

An extended family consisted of the entire nuclear family along with the grandparents, uncles and aunts, and first cousins. It was a cohesive and close-knit unit. First cousins were considered to be brothers and sisters, and uncles and aunts were recognized as second parents. The grandparents were venerated because of their knowledge and wisdom. Each extended family had rules governing human behavior and relationships. For instance, they forbade the marriage of close relatives, so that first cousins could not marry. Instead, the young people had to find mates outside their extended family group.[5] Individuals identified potential mates at the large regional pine nut festivals or dances. Sometimes parents arranged marriages after they concluded that a person would most likely be a good provider for a son or daughter.

One notable aspect of the Newe was their peaceful way of life. This development was the result of extended families living over a large area. There was no competition over land. The Newe shared the available resources, and their hunting and gathering areas overlapped. The Newe also maintained cordial relations with their tribal neighbors, including the Numa (Northern Paiute) who lived to the west. Brief periods of ill feeling arose when one tribe intruded into the land of the other, but there was no organized warfare between tribes.[6]

Like other native peoples of North America, the Newe did not have a written language before European contact, but they had developed an exceedingly rich spoken language. For example, the Newe language distinguishes many degrees of relationships: an older sister is called *patsi,* a younger sister is *nammi;* a paternal grandmother is *huttsi,* a maternal grandmother is *kaku;* a paternal grandfather is *kenu,* a maternal grandfather is *toko.*[7]

The Newe were able to survive in an arid environment by eating a

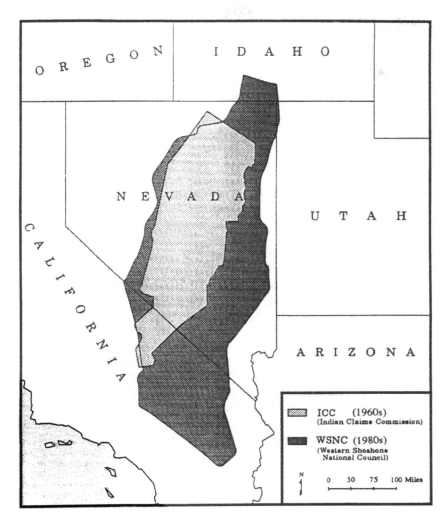

Aboriginal Western Shoshone Territory

wide variety of available foods. Animal foods included jackrabbit, cotton-tail rabbit, ground squirrel, ground hogs or woodchucks, sage hen, antelope, and deer. Plant foods included chokecherries, yumpa roots, and pine nuts (or pinyons), among others. The Newe were a hunting and gathering people who "took care not to upset the delicate balance of their unique environment."[8]

Without doubt the most important overall plant food source for the

Newe was the pine nut. The nuts grow on pinyon trees, which flourish at elevations from 5,000 to 9,000 feet. The trees become fully mature after 75 years and continue to produce for as long as 300–400 years. A single tree produces nuts irregularly, at intervals from three to seven years, and the nuts take two years to fully mature in the cones.[9]

In the early fall, when the pine nuts were ripe, the Newe families met to harvest the nuts communally. They used long poles to remove cones from the trees. They then roasted the nuts, which have a good food value: 10 percent protein, 23 percent fat, 54 percent carbohydrate, and 14 percent other nutrients. In addition to eating them like any other nut, the Newe also ground pine nuts into meal, which they made into gravy and mixed with deer meat. With the addition of the other foods available to them, the Newe had a wholesome diet.[10]

The Newe held prayers, ceremonies, and dances both before and after the pine nut harvest. The person in charge of the harvest started the activities by tossing some pine nuts in the four cardinal directions. He or she then gave a prayer, thanking the Creator for having created life on earth and paved the way for a good pine nut harvest. Once this was done, the Newe underwent a cleansing ceremony: "They crossed their arms over their chest, gently striking themselves; then they raised their arms and brought their hands and blew between them. Some moved their hands over their entire bodies in waving motions . . . These symbolic gestures were made to signify cleansing."[11] They cleansed to feel good about themselves and to reassure physical and mental well-being. After the cleansing ceremony, the Newe held round dances for five days, dancing in a circle in a shuffling motion, led by a singer. The purpose of the dance was to express appreciation to Pia Sokopia for having brought forth an abundance of pine nuts. One round dance song had the following words:

Imaa Hupia

Tsaan napuni, tai sokopin,
tsaan napuni, tai sokopin,
oyo paam paan kematu
tsaa napuni, tai sokopin.

Tsaan napuni, tai sokopin,
tsaan napuni, tai sokopin,
Soko tontsiyama, paan kematu
tsaan napuni, tai sokopin.

(The Early Morning Song)
How beautiful is our land,

how beautiful is our land,
forever, beside the water, the water,
how beautiful is our land.

How beautiful is our land,
how beautiful is our land,
Earth, with flowers on it, next to the water
how beautiful is our land. [12]

Owing to its primary importance in the Newe diet, the pine nut found its way into the oral tradition. Although the accounts vary, depending on the storyteller and the location of his or her Newe group, all agree upon one thing: that the pine nuts came to the Newe from a northern location. Here is one account told by the Newe of the South Fork Valley in northeastern Nevada:

In the extreme southern part of the state, the people were playing handgames and while Crow was watching the game he started to choke. He couldn't stop so the Indian doctors started doctoring him but nothing helped and they were unable to help him.

From the North, the North wind was blowing as it was in the Autumn. While the doctors were puzzled over what was choking Crow, Coyote came over and told them that his powers had revealed to him that Crow had come under the spell of "two-pointed sides" and that Crow's keen sense of smell had smelled the odor of roasting pine nuts on the North wind.

When Coyote revealed the cause of Crow's strange choking, they decided to journey to the North to see this "two-pointed sides" and to get the Main Seed of the pinetree as they wanted to have the tree growing here too . . . They went further North and went through Owyhee and they passed through Boise [Idaho]. Somewhere near the present town of Boise their destination was reached and the place they came to is called "Sahme ii." This means Place of Junipers which once were pine trees.

The Pinenut Eaters made them welcome and invited the people to play handgames and dance with them. Coyote thought that one night was too short so he made two nights into one . . .

Meanwhile, Field Mouse was looking all over for the Main Seed and he couldn't find it. He climbed over people, logs, rocks, and finally he climbed on a tree. There, not very far away was the Main Seed hid on the highest tree. But he couldn't climb the tree as a very old woman was guarding it. Whenever he started to climb she would open her mouth to shout a warning and Field Mouse would have to close her mouth for her. He finally succeeded in stealing the Main Seed and half of the visitors ran off with the Main Seed.

The Pinenut Eaters were exhausted from the long, long night of fun and were fast asleep but someone aroused the camp to tell them about the visitors stealing the Main Seed and sleep was forgotten while the chase was on . . .

They entered Smoky Valley [central Nevada] and there the Pinenut Eaters caught up with them. Coyote was very brave and he held them off from the others. Coyote was finally shot and somewhere in Smoky Valley there is a buckberry tree which grew on the spot where Coyote was killed. It is very bitter and cannot be eaten. The other buckberry trees which are edible are the fallen companions of Coyote. Crow hid the Main Seed in his thigh and before he was killed he wished his thigh into becoming infected and also that Crane would kick it and temporarily lose his mind.

Crane's power told him that Crow had hidden the Main Seed in his thigh and when he came to Crow's body he kicked his thigh as Crow had wished. Crane became so dizzy and confused he sat down facing the North. Crane's friends came to him and when his mind became clear he told them that Crow's thigh flew off and they all started looking for it but all they found were tracks leading up into the mountains.

Even as they looked at the mountains they could see a dense growth of pine trees and the people were already burning wood to roast pinecones in. Crane and his friends decided to go and see what was happening and found the people already pouring the pinecones into the ashes . . . Perhaps you may have seen a red coloring in the mountains which looks like blood flowing down somewhere in the Southern part of the State. We are told it is there because when Crow was choking he vomited blood.

To this day we are warned to sit quietly and not to laugh and talk loudly while we are eating pinenuts because it would choke us and kill us.[13]

Like many folk tales, this Newe pine nut story served several purposes. In addition to celebrating an important food source, it explained an existing condition: the scarcity of pine nuts in southern Idaho and their abundance in central Nevada. Because the pine nuts, according to myth, were stolen from southern Idaho, very few can be found in that region now. Because the stolen pine nuts were brought to central Nevada, they are abundant there, especially around the Reese River Valley mountain area. In fact, the Newe living north of the Humboldt River traveled to central Nevada to harvest the nuts.

The Newe knew that the pine nut crop might fail in some years. In such a case, they were able to fall back upon other important foods. One was the desert black-tailed jackrabbit, a common species in the Great Basin. The Newe hunted rabbits communally in rabbit drives staged by men from closely related extended families. They drove the rabbits into a long net, and the hunters clubbed what they needed for their winter food supply. The drives usually lasted several days and were held either in conjunction with the annual pine nut harvest or later. If the drive took place during the harvest, the women gathered nuts while the men drove and hunted. The rabbits provided more than food, for the Newe used the skins and fur for blankets and clothing.[14]

The Newe also hunted large game animals, such as antelope and deer. Antelope were difficult to kill because of their swiftness, so the natives relied upon the spirit world for assistance. A medicine person—who could be a man or a woman—prayed and asked for power over the animals. The next day the Newe conducted an antelope drive, chasing the swift animals into a V-shaped funnel constructed of sagebrush. The entrance of this fencelike structure could be several miles wide, narrowing to a small opening into a corral. Once the hunters had herded the antelope inside, they killed a few of them for food and skins and released the remaining animals. They hunted antelope throughout the year. The Newe hunted deer in the fall when they were fat. They made use of all parts of these large animals, turning the hides into clothing and footwear, and the antlers and bones into eating utensils and digging instruments.[15]

The Newe had deep respect for all living things, including animals, so they hunted only for food and to supply their other needs. They did not overkill, nor did they hunt for sport. Their respect for the animals was expressed in the lyrics of round dance songs. For example, the following songs were sung in recognition of the antelope and other antlered animals:

Antelope Song

Pia wantsipe toowenennÅten
Pia wantsipe toowenennÅten
Pennan tapai tatawentun toowenennÅten.

Buck antelope slowly grazing about
Buck antelope slowly grazing about
Sun beams flickering as he stands grazing about.[16]

The Antlered One (Wantsi)

Wantsi manniyu, hainna,
Wantsi manniyu, hainna,
Wantsi manniyu, hainna.
Wantsi yehnen kahni kematu, hainna,
Wantsi manniyu, hainna.

Antlered one, crossing over the water,
Antlered one, crossing over the water,
Antlered one, crossing over the water.

Antlered one, next to the dwelling place of the Porcupine,
Antlered one, crossing over the water. [17]

Because of their hunting and gathering way of life, the extended
families moved about inside their larger tribal territory. In the summer,
they resided in temporary camps located where ripened seeds and other
foods could be found. Summer houses consisted of branch structures tied
together and covered with leaves and grass to ward off the hot summer
sun. Over the winter, the Newe settled down for several months. Winter
houses, much more elaborate than summer camps, were built of willow
shaped in a conical frame and covered with grass and skins to keep out
the snow and wind.

Although the Newe moved about throughout the year, they still had a
strong sense of place. In fact, they were deeply attached to particular
valley areas and the nearby mountain ranges. They did not wander
aimlessly but remained within niches inside the larger tribal territory. [18]

For the Newe, time passed in a cycle divided into four seasons:
Tahmani (spring), Tatsa (summer), Yepani (fall), and Tommo (winter). Each
season had its appropriate activities. In the spring the men hunted
groundhogs and squirrels while the women dug camas roots and other
edibles. During the summer the men hunted sage hens and ducks while
the women wove collecting and winnowing baskets in anticipation of fall
harvests. The fall was the busiest time of year, when both men and
women harvested pine nuts and the men conducted rabbit drives. Round
dances marked the cycle of time. Spring dances were held with the
expectation that plants would grow abundantly. Summer dances were a
time to celebrate the ripening of plant food. And the fall dances were
directly connected to the harvesting of pine nuts and the rabbit drives.
Led by a singer, who was a highly respected member of the group, the
dances lasted five nights, from early evening to sunrise. [19]

Like their Northern Paiute neighbors to the west, the Newe did not
have a centralized political organization involving all the extended family
groups. The sparse population and sustainable way of life did not demand
a central organization. On the other hand, the Newe periodically came
together and held large gatherings. The families living in the same area
convened for stick (hand) games, which were both a social activity and a
form of gambling that involved guessing. Larger groups assembled for
antelope and rabbit drives and the accompanying round dances. [20] Although some Newe were separated by hundreds of miles, they still shared
a culture and language.

Like the other tribes of the Great Basin, the Newe were noted for
their basketweaving, a craft and art form practiced by the women. Baskets

were made of various plant fibers, primarily willow branches. They varied in size and were used for different purposes, such as collecting, carrying, and storing. Relatively flat winnowing baskets served to sift seeds, nuts, and other small edible foods. Cradle boards were another form of basketry. The board frame was constructed of thick willow shaped into an oval and backed with small willows laid crosswise. The entire surface was then covered with buckskin. A woven basket sunshade was placed near the top of the frame to protect the baby's head. This cradle board, or baby basket as some called it, represented protection and security; the Newe saw it as an extension of the "womb environment." In the words of one commentator, the cradle board "kept [the baby] close to his mother and bonded him to his heritage of deep spiritualism and respect for all life."[21] Unlike baskets, pottery was not much used in the Great Basin. Basketry suited the Newe way of life because it was both durable and lightweight, ideal for people who were hunters and gatherers.

Besides basketry, the Newe also collected and made other utilitarian items. The women sought out large, smooth lava stones to use for grinding chokecherries, pine nuts, and other seeds and berries. The men made bows and arrows out of straight branches and crafted bowstrings from strips of animal skin. Both men and women shaped animal bones and antlers into eating utensils and digging instruments. The Newe relied upon the environment for all the elements of survival. This explains why their reverence for the land and for all the living things it provided.[22]

The Newe were a deeply religious and spiritual people. They were led by spiritual or medicine leaders, both men and women, who were highly regarded and respected for their knowledge of plants used for medicine and their understanding of other living beings, both human and animal. These medicine persons led healing ceremonies for those who were physically or emotionally ill. They also led the group in prayers at large gatherings, such as the annual pine nut harvest, round dances, and antelope drives. They used the tail feathers of the eagle (Pia kwi'naa), a highly regarded bird.[23]

Newe medicine people understood the use of plants for medicinal and healing purposes. Among their remedies were the following: Oregon grape *(sokoteheyampehe)* was used as an eye medicine; cedar pitch *(waappittan sanappin),* after it was ground to a mash, was used for cuts and wounds; and snakeweed *(kwitawoyampeh)* was used for diarrhea.[24] So rich was their use of plants for medicine that some white scholars wrote that "the Shoshones . . . certainly were found to possess a much greater medicinal plant lore and used more native medicines than either of the other [Basin] tribes."[25]

Other plants were used for spiritual cleansing. For example, rabbit brush *(tapai sipappin)* was rolled into a tight bundle and burned for purification, so that the smoke would ward off the ghost or spirit of the deceased in a dwelling where someone had died.[26]

Lacking a written language, the Newe relied upon oral tradition to pass along tribal knowledge. The round dance songs were one way to do this. The songs tell how the Newe lived in unison with nature. Animals, including wolf and deer, are principal characters in many of them. Many of the songs also stress the beauty of the natural world (Pia Sokopia), while others emphasize proper human behavior. One of the latter type went like this:

> Pia isam pentsi,
> pennan kwasin kasunka
> piyaahteki,
> piyaahteki,
> piyaa tua nooten.
>
> Furry Wolf,
> On his tail he carries him away,
> Carries him away,
> Carries him away,
> Upon his tail he carries the child away.[27]

This song warned children that if they misbehaved, they would be carried away by the wolf. Wolf was the principal father figure in Newe mythology. Over time the Newe modified this story to include Coyote, Wolf's younger brother. Parents used to tell their children, "Hai entenankanhu Itsappe en hwasi pinookkwanto'i [if you don't behave yourself, Coyote will carry you off on his tail]."[28]

The role of women was recognized in some songs. Here are two songs that focused upon women and their valuable contribution to Newe life:

Song One

> Hupia waimpentsi
> Hupia wentsetuih hainna,
> Hupia waimpentsi
> Hupia wentsetuih hainna,
> Pennan napaatuintsi
> Okwaitemmayenten,
> Hupia wentsetuih hainna,
> Hupia wentsetuih hainna.
>
> Song Woman
> Sits beating the rhythm of her song,

Song Woman
Sits beating the rhythm of her song,
There in a distant place
Next to her cousin, the water,
Beating the rhythm of her song,
Beating the rhythm of her song.[29]

Song Two

Uppi katete hunumma,
tepi yantumma, hain.

Upi katete hunumma,
tepi yantumma, hain.

Ainka tempin huutepenna,
tepi yantumma, hain.

There, in a distant place, she sits in an arroyo,
winnowing the pine nuts.
There, in a distant place, she sits in an arroyo,
winnowing the pine nuts.

By the red-rock-wooded place,
winnowing the pine nuts.[30]

Newe tradition was also passed down during winter storytelling. Once the people had settled into their winter camps, storytelling was a favorite activity. The principal characters of the Newe stories were animals, including Wolf and his brother Coyote. Wolf was a positive force, but Coyote was a trickster, a contradictory being who represented both good and bad. Cottontail Rabbit was also a popular figure.[31] Like the dance songs, the stories also served various purposes. They explained why conditions existed in real life, as in the pine nut story. They also served as entertainment, since many stories were humorous. And like the dance songs, stories also taught proper behavior for human beings. One "explanation" story tells why human beings have five fingers:

> Once upon a time a fox and lizard had a quarrel. The fox said man should have four fingers just as he had. The lizard said man should have five fingers like he had. The fox became angry and chased the lizard. The lizard ran into a bush and the fox set fire to it . . . At last the lizard ran into a crack in a rock and the fox couldn't do anything about it so the lizard won the quarrel and that is why man has five fingers like a lizard.[32]

The following story about coyote and sage hen focuses on proper behavior, showing that people who are not good to others must pay the price for inappropriate behavior:

Coyote came to the Sage Hen's children while their mother was away. Coyote said, "Where is your mother?" The children said, "Our mother has gone out after locust for us to eat." So Coyote teased those sage hen children. He urinated on them. When the mother came home they told her Coyote had been there and what he had done to them . . . Sage Hen went looking for Coyote. She was angry at what he had done to her children. When she got to him, she flew up and scared him. He was so frightened he jumped into the water. Sage Hen went away for awhile. Coyote got out and was trotting along when Sage Hen flew up and scared him again. She was getting even with him for tormenting her children. She kept on scaring him for a long time, then she let him go.[33]

Because of his cunning ways, Coyote was often portrayed as the bad guy in Newe stories. Thus the Newe told their children, "Don't be like Coyote."

Long before the coming of the whites, the Newe had developed their own distinctive way of life, characterized by the concept of living in harmony with the natural environment. Because Earth Mother provided for their needs, the Newe had a strong regard for the land. This aspect of their life was noted by nineteenth-century observers who wrote about the Basin area. Historian Hubert Howe Bancroft wrote that "they are lovers of their country; lovers not of fair hills and fertile valleys, but of inhospitable mountains and barren plains."[34]

After centuries of isolation, the Newe eventually came face to face with European explorers. Beginning in 1492 Spain entered the Western Hemisphere and claimed much of the land by the so-called "right of discovery."[35] This included much of the southwestern United States, including the Great Basin. But the Spanish settlers never colonized the homeland of the Newe.

Spain was followed by other European nations, and the newcomers competed for the lands occupied and claimed by the native peoples. One conflicting claim was resolved in 1819 when the United States and Spain negotiated the Adams-Onis Treaty, called the Transcontinental Treaty. This agreement recognized Spanish ownership of the Southwest to the 42nd parallel, or the modern day Idaho-Nevada border. In this way, Newe land in the Great Basin officially fell under Spanish jurisdiction, although Spain had claimed the region much earlier. When Mexico won independence from Spain in 1821, the Great Basin became Mexican territory.[36] As for the Newe, they were completely unaware that Spanish-speaking people had claimed title to Newe Sokopia.

Although Mexico claimed the Great Basin from 1821 to 1848, its citizens, like the Spanish, failed to settle this region. Rather it was

English-speaking individuals who took the initiative, without Mexican approval. The earliest intruders were fur trappers involved in the lucrative business of trapping beaver. The pelts were used in the fashion industry for making felt hats, a popular dress item in the eastern United States and Europe in the early nineteenth century.[37]

Trappers employed by British-owned companies operating out of Canada and American companies competed for the beaver trade in the trans-Mississippi West. Perhaps the first trapper to enter Newe Sokopia was Jedediah Smith. Employed by the Rocky Mountain Fur Company, headquartered in St. Louis, Smith crossed central Nevada in 1827 in his quest for beaver, a trip that extended into California. He missed the Humboldt River to the north and found no beaver in Newe territory.[38] This explains the rapidity of his journey across the Basin. Smith described the few natives he encountered, indicating that they were the "most miserable of the human race having nothing to subsist on (nor any clothing) except grass seed, grasshoppers, etc."[39]

Jedediah Smith's 1827 trip is significant for two reasons. First, he was the first white seen by the Newe. Second, Smith's low opinion of the Indians established the reputation of the Great Basin tribes, including the Newe, as the lowest form of humanity—a negative stereotype that persists today. Since the whites considered the Newe and other Basin groups as nothing more than lowly and simple gatherers who spent their time digging for edible roots, they later gave them the derogatory label of "diggers."[40]

If Jedediah Smith's sojourn of 1827 had no immediate impact on the Newe, the same cannot be said of Peter Skene Ogden's expedition of late 1828 and 1829. Ogden worked for the British-owned Hudson's Bay Company. Fully aware of its American competition, the company instructed its employees to carry out a "scorched earth" policy of depleting the beaver population in the Far West. The American trappers, the British reasoned, would thus lose the war for beavers and have no motive to reconnoiter the rivers of the West.[41]

In November 1828 Ogden and his men became the first whites to locate "Mary's River" (later renamed the Humboldt), which flows across the northern Great Basin. They found many beavers, and they quickly trapped out the area. Their activities affected the Newe living along the Humboldt, who relied upon the beaver for winter clothing. In retaliation for this loss, the Newe took some of the metal traps intended for the beaver.[42]

Ogden's stock animals ate the late fall/early winter grass seed the Newe depended upon for food. Combined with the near elimination of the beaver, this meant that Ogden's expedition seriously disrupted the delicate balance of the environment in which the Newe had lived for generations. The Newe understood that the newcomers, whom they called Taipo (white), were responsible for the changes. As a result, when Ogden's expedition returned to Newe country in the spring of 1829, the Newe were generally cool toward the whites.[43]

Ogden took note of the Newe, whom he described as wearing rabbit-skin clothing, eating plant foods, living in settlements along the Humboldt River, and being of a peaceful disposition. Only a few Newe possessed American guns and metal knives, most likely used for hunting. Like Jedediah Smith, Ogden painted a derogatory picture of the Newe, noting that they were "miserable looking wretches."[44]

The depletion of some of the area's natural resources was clearly evident in 1833 when American fur trapper Joseph Reddeford Walker traveled along the Humboldt River. He found little if any beaver and assumed that the Indians had taken most of the fur-bearing animals. Walker did not know of Ogden's earlier "scorched earth" mission. Walker found the Newe unfriendly, since his trapping expedition was a reminder to them of earlier negative developments. Some Newe demanded food and horses in payment for right-of-way through Newe Sokopia. Frustrated by their failed beaver quest, some of Walker's men killed a half-dozen Newe individuals, perhaps more. They also stole an Indian beaver robe found in a dwelling. These incidents caused the Newe to hate the Taipo. The Walker expedition began the loss of lives that continued through the mid-nineteenth century.[45]

As time passed the Newe had to deal with a different kind of Taipo: the European American emigrant from the East. In the 1840s groups of white Americans from the East and Midwest left their homes to build new lives in what they believed to be the earthly paradise of California. The emigrants, seeking the shortest possible route westward, followed the already known Humboldt River across Newe country.[46]

One of the better known emigrant groups was the Bidwell-Bartleson party of 1841. It traveled the Humboldt River route and entered Newe Sokopia. Finding it difficult to hunt the swift antelope, members of the party purchased food from the Newe, whom they characterized as friendly. Unlike their attitude toward earlier trappers, the Newe were not hostile to these newest comers. They knew that the emigrants were simply passing through and would not stay to further deplete Newe food resources.[47]

By the late 1840s the Newe living along the Humboldt River were in the midst of a visible cultural change. The emigrant groups and their stock animals had continued to deplete the natural resources along the river. Some Newe had secured horses and guns from the emigrants—possessions that may have helped them to become more effective hunters but also accelerated the depletion process. The Newe now had to travel farther in the quest for food. Despite these changes, however, the deep-rooted culture of the Newe remained largely intact in this early period of Indian-white contact. For example, the Newe seldom used English words for their new acquisitions. Instead, they gave native names to the new things: *punku* (from *punhuttsi*, or "pet") became the word for "horse," and *aiti* the word for "gun" (*huu aiti* is the word for bow). The Newe survived the depletion of resources along the Humboldt River by focusing on other native foods hardly touched by the whites and their livestock. These included pine nuts, and also deer and antelope, which the emigrants found to be an elusive quarry. In this way the Newe adapted to the stresses of contact with European culture.

2

WARFARE AND ADJUSTMENT: THE WESTERN SHOSHONE AND THE AMERICANS

1848—1880

During the third quarter of the nineteenth century the Newe (Shoshone) of the Great Basin experienced the greatest changes of their history. This was the result of the massive influx of Anglo-Americans passing through Newe country on their way to the West Coast, followed soon after by settlers. The federal government, which claimed jurisdiction over all Indian tribes in the United States, insisted that the Shoshones conform to new federal Indian policies. This brought about a state of chaos and warfare that lasted for several years, followed by a period of adjustment. Although the native life-style had been permanently disrupted, the Newe continued to adhere to their own culture even after white contact.

1848—1863

In the mid-nineteenth century, developments even more dramatic than those of the earlier period affected the Newe. The first was a major jurisdictional change, when the Great Basin became part of U.S. territory in 1848. Earlier, Newe land had been claimed by Spain and then Mexico. However, when Mexico lost the war of 1846–1848, it was forced to cede its vast domain to the United States. Under the Treaty of Guadalupe Hidalgo, the Great Basin and most of the Southwest became U.S. territory. Unlike the Mexican government, the U.S. government quickly asserted strong and paternalistic control over its new acquisition.[1]

The second major development was the California gold rush. In early 1848 gold was discovered in the foothills of the Sierra Nevada along the American River at a place called Coloma. This discovery created a national "mass hysteria" that caused hundreds of thousands of people to flock to California in search of wealth. To reach their destination the gold seekers took one of three main routes: the Overland Route along the Humboldt River in the Great Basin. In 1849 alone, 100,000 individuals traveled to California, and approximately three-fifths of them took the Overland Route through Newe country.[2]

This mass movement across the Great Basin, which continued into the early 1850s, had a dramatic impact on the Newe. The emigrants and their livestock seriously depleted many of the food resources along the Humboldt River. This left less for the Newe, and famine was the result. As early as 1852 one observer pointed out that "game" was "scarce" and that the Indians were in a "state of starvation."[3] In 1855 the Newe were reported to be "very destitute," and "they all complained of being hungry."[4] The gold seekers and their stock markedly affected the Basin environment along the Humboldt River, permanently altering the balance of life between humans and the land.

Worse, unscrupulous gold seekers and other emigrants maltreated the Newe, whom they regarded as beings of a lower order. They used the Indians for target practice and sexually abused the women. Countless native lives were lost within a few short years.[5] Such malicious behavior persisted throughout the 1850s. One white observer in 1858 stated that "I have learned sufficient since in the Territory, to leave no doubt in my mind, that the Indians along the Humboldt, have been imposed on, and ill-treated by emigrant parties."[6]

The Newe did not passively suffer abuse from unruly whites. Instead, they retaliated by conducting guerrilla warfare and taking white-owned horses and weaponry. To carry out raids, the Newe had to organize into bands larger than their traditional, extended family groups. Each band consisted of several extended families from a particular region. The band leaders were those influential individuals who had traditionally conducted rabbit drives and led the round dances. Nearly all the organized bands took on the names of the leaders. They relied upon the newly acquired guns and horses to fight the invading whites. These bands represented the Newe's effort to shape their own history by finding a more effective way to deal with the newcomers. Several bands existed in the second half of the nineteenth century, and at least two continued into the twentieth.[7]

The best known of the newly formed band organizations in northern Nevada in the 1850s was the White Knife (Tosa wihi). As noted in chapter 1, the Newe living along the Humboldt River and to the north utilized the white rock quarry near Tuscarora, Nevada, to produce white arrowheads and knives. In the early 1850s the Tosa wihi Newe quickly shifted their weaponry from game to defense. They were such skillful and persistent fighters that the whites who traveled along the Humboldt acknowledged the threat of the Tosa wihi. By the mid-1850s this band possessed a sizable and powerful organization and had declared "open war" against the whites. More than any other Newe band, the Tosa wihi became known for their aggression against the whites.[8]

A third major development was permanent settlement in the Great Basin. In 1847 members of the Church of Jesus Christ of Latter-Day Saints, popularly called Mormons, settled the area of Salt Lake City. As their numbers increased, the federal government created the Utah Territory, which encompassed much of the Basin, including both Utah and Nevada. Although the center of Mormon settlement was some 350–400 miles east of Newe country, the white settlers slowly moved westward. Both Mormon and non-Mormon settlers entered Newe homelands in the late 1850s and early 1860s, further disrupting the traditional way of life.[9]

A fourth development was the emergence of federal government relations with the Newe. The U.S. government had always considered itself as having authority over the Indian tribes. This kind of thinking was best expressed in an 1831 Supreme Court decision that declared the federal government to be the "guardian" of its Indian "wards." When the Utah Territory was created in 1850, Mormon patriarch Brigham Young was made territorial governor and was also chosen as ex-officio superintendent of Indian affairs for Utah. Newly created territories worked in conjunction with the Office of Indian Affairs (today the Bureau of Indian Affairs), a federal agency created in 1824 to look after the affairs of Indian tribes. The agency was based in Washington, D.C.[10]

Federal officials under the Utah Indian Superintendency of the Office of Indian Affairs attempted to deal with the warfare between the Newe and the emigrants. The first federal agent to establish contact with the Newe was Jacob Holeman. In 1852 he visited the Newe along the Humboldt River to determine the underlying cause of conflict between the Indians and whites. After talking to both sides, Holeman concluded that the source of conflict was "the bad conduct of the whites": White emigrants would shoot Indians while they were hunting and gathering. Whites also lured the "Indians into their camps," proclaimed friendship, then killed them. Holeman gave the Newe gifts and presents to soften their hatred "towards the whites." He also worked hard to convince the Newe that the "great [white] Father" (the federal government) was a friend of the Indians and not like the unruly white emigrants.[11]

In 1853 Holeman paid a second visit to the Newe. By this time he understood that they were organized into bands, and he made it his objective to meet the band leaders since they had influence over their followers. He made contact with one Newe leader, Ne-me-te-kalt (Neme tekkate), who lived along the Humboldt. Between Holeman's two visits some unruly California-bound traders had murdered Ne-me-te-kalt's son. The leader and his band were preparing to attack any whites they could find. But before the attack took place, Holeman convinced Ne-me-te-kalt that not all whites were bad, that there were different types of whites, and that the white men who had killed his son were malicious traders and not peaceful emigrants. Holeman calmed Ne-me-te-kalt by giving him presents and promising future gifts and concessions.[12] The agent's tactic of meeting with native leaders set a precedent, followed by later government agents and officials, of dealing with Newe band leaders as representatives of their people.

Holeman's tenure as government agent was brief. Before leaving office, however, he made some shrewd assessments. He concluded correctly that the whites were the cause of the warfare and unrest that characterized the 1850s. To initiate peace Holeman recommended that an Indian agency be created to protect the Newe, that military forts be established to maintain the peace, and that a peace treaty be negotiated with the Newe.[13] Although not taken seriously in the early 1850s, Holeman's recommendations were later carried out.

The next Utah territorial agent to deal with the Basin Newe was Garland Hurt, who honored Holeman's earlier promises to give the Indians gifts. Hurt concluded that warfare between the Newe and whites would continue as long as the emigrants passed through the lands "claimed" by the natives. To deal with this problem, he decided to negotiate a peace treaty with the Newe living along the Humboldt River.[14]

On August 7, 1855, Hurt met and negotiated a treaty with hundreds of Newe, including Ne-me-te-kalt and other leaders. The Newe, who had lived in peace before white contact and were tired of fighting, agreed to end the warfare against the whites who passed through and promised to be friendly to those who settled on their lands. According to government report, they also agreed to subordinate themselves to the "laws of the United States." This provision, obviously, was the work of Hurt who wanted the natives to accept government paternalism. For making these concessions, the government agreed to give the Newe $3,000 worth of goods, including "clothing" and "farming implements."[15] The treaty of 1855, however, was not approved by the Office of Indian Affairs, and it was never ratified by the U.S. Senate. There were at least two reasons for its failure. First, Hurt had no authority to negotiate such a treaty. Second, the treaty did not transfer Newe land to the Americans, something that the whites wanted. The treaty was not a binding compact, and as a result the Indian-white warfare continued in the Great Basin.[16]

The whites did allow the Newe to express their native culture during the 1855 treaty negotiations. Once an agreement had been reached, approximately fifty to sixty Newe leaders sang round dance songs while many others danced to celebrate the occasion. This event was the first time in Newe history when traditional round dances were held at a Newewhite gathering. At the same time, Newe culture was already changing;

by the mid-1850s some individuals were wearing American-style clothing, including caps, coats, and pants.[17]

Other factors contributed to the continuous warfare between the Newe and the whites. One was the Indians' practice of taking white-owned cattle and food supplies. The whites had killed much of the wild game, and their cattle had eaten or destroyed large amounts of roots and seeds. In a state of near starvation, the Newe often caught the white emigrants off guard and raided their food supplies. Of course, the whites retaliated, and the Indian-white strife persisted.[18]

The Newe's acquisition of firearms by the early 1850s was still another source of conflict. Because the white man's weapons proved more efficient than the native bow and arrow, the Newe used the firearms first for hunting and later to shoot at invading whites. By the mid-1850s, guns were common in the Great Basin. Garland Hurt reported that the Tosa wihi "were well supplied with guns and horses and were anxious to trade for ammunition." Many whites refused to sell guns or powder to the Indian, afraid the natives would use the weapons against them and not solely for hunting game. Those Newe who declared themselves friendly to the whites, including the followers of Ne-me-te-kalt, also became angry when "the Americans wouldn't sell them any powder."[19] Raiding white emigrants was one way to secure needed supplies, both food and weapons.

In 1857 Jacob Forney became the new superintendent of Indian affairs for the Utah Territory, replacing Brigham Young who had had only minimal contact with the Newe. Forney agreed with the observations of both Holeman and Hurt, stressing that the Newe had been badly treated by some "emigrant parties." He also acknowledged that the whites were no longer passing through Newe territory but were now establishing permanent settlements, which severely depleted native food supplies. Forney concluded that the Shoshones must acquire a new life-style to survive: They must be placed on a reservation and become farmers. He recommended that one locality should be set aside as a reservation before the white settlers claimed all the good land. In February 1859 Forney instructed Robert Jarvis, one of his subordinates, to set aside a reservation in Ruby Valley, northeastern Nevada, for the Shoshones living along the Humboldt River and the main Emigrant Road (Overland Route). Ruby Valley was a fertile spot, some "ninety miles long" and "six to ten miles wide."[20]

In March 1859 Jarvis established a "six miles square" reservation in Ruby Valley, the first of its kind for the Newe, and he himself became the local federal agent. His main goal was to teach the Newe to farm. A few months later, in June 1859, Jarvis resigned, and the responsibility to make the Indians into farmers fell to his successor, Benjamin Rogers.

Rogers acquired some farm implements and began teaching the Indians farming techniques. Many of the Newe who moved to the Ruby Valley Reservation were under the influence of Sho-kub (Tsokkope), a band leader known to be friendly to whites. He needed little encouragement to learn the ways of agrarian life. As early as 1856, with the assistance of friendly settlers, Sho-kub had harvested fifteen acres of "wheat, potatoes, and squashes." As a Newe leader, he was fully aware that the native food sources were rapidly diminishing and knew that the Newe needed a new food source to sustain life.[21]

The Office of Indian Affairs neglected to carry out proper maintenance and upkeep of the newly established reservation. For example, although the reserve was proclaimed to be "six miles square," it was never surveyed, so its boundaries were arbitrary. Further, the Indian Office failed to provide needed material goods for the Newe who moved there. In 1860 Agent Rogers requested that the Indians be given additional cattle and farm implements so they could expand their infant economic enterprises. The government did not respond to this request. If necessary supplies were not forthcoming, neither was Rogers's salary. He filed a suit against the government in an attempt to receive his back pay and eventually resigned from his position. Without a local agent to act as a guide, and lacking financial and material support from the Indian Office, the Indians grew no crops after 1861.[22]

In 1861 Benjamin Davies, then superintendent of Indian affairs for the Utah Territory, visited the Ruby Valley Indians. Sho-kub asked Davies if the government intended to revive the reservation farm. Davies was noncommittal, but he did make an interesting recommendation to the Indian Office. Realizing that white settlers would soon occupy all of the fertile Ruby Valley, and that the "six miles square" reservation was "too small" for all the Shoshones of the area, Davies recommended "that the whole valley be declared" as a reservation for the Newe and "that farming operations be commenced there at once."[23] The Office of Indian Affairs did not listen or respond.

The area of Ruby Valley fell within the boundaries of the Nevada Territory when it was established in 1861. In the next few years government officials of both Nevada and Utah dealt with the affairs of the Basin Newe. Eventually, the Nevada Indian Superintendency assumed total responsibility for the affairs of the Newe.

Sho-kub died in late 1861, and after his death the war between the Newe and whites escalated in northeastern Nevada. Sho-kub had selected Buck, a young subchief, as his successor. Upon assuming leadership, Buck did not follow the friendly course established by Sho-kub. He hated the whites because they had settled or were in the process of settling on the lands of the Newe. But not all the Newe living in Ruby Valley shared Buck's unfriendly stance. The followers of Temoke, another band leader of Ruby Valley, chose the late Sho-kub's friendly path. Since two bands with opposing views could not live side by side, Buck and his supporters left Ruby Valley and joined the Tosa wihi north of the Humboldt River.[24]

Governor James Nye of the Nevada Territory regarded Buck as "a troublesome Indian, whose policy" was to "drive" the whites from northeastern Nevada. Although Buck did not rid Newe country of the whites, he made life uncomfortable for the settlers in the early 1860s. Soon after Sho-kub's death, the Tosa wihi and Buck's band attacked emigrant parties, took cattle belonging to the white settlers, and attacked white settlements, including the Overland Mail stations.[25]

Intermittent warfare against the whites prompted the federal government to establish a military fort in Ruby Valley in 1862. The fort was staffed by Colonel Patrick E. Connor and his California Volunteers, who had instructions to protect white emigrants and also to patrol the Overland Route.[26] But Connor did more than this: He ordered his troops to hunt down the Newe and kill them indiscriminately. He instructed his troops to "leave their bodies thus exposed as an example of what evildoers may expect . . . you will also destroy every male Indian whom you may encounter . . . this of course may seem harsh and severe, but I desire that the order may be rigidly enforced, as I am satisfied that in the end it will prove most merciful."[27] Many of the Newe were killed, and the survivors came to fear the troops, whom they called *tuukkwasu'unneen* because of the "black shirts" they wore as uniforms.[28]

In the end Connor's troops did not kill all the Newe men. Instead, they captured various leaders and held them hostage. According to oral tradition, the Newe received the following ultimatum: "Are you able to become scouts? If you don't do that, we will kill all of you." Facing death, the Newe leaders reasoned that "we should become scouts in order to save ourselves."[29] Several leaders therefore became army scouts and helped the troops identify Newe who were hiding or resisting the army. As a reward they were given the title of captain. After the early 1860s one could find Newe named Captain Buck, Captain Sam, Captain Charlie, and Captain Bob, to list only a few.

Although most of the Newe-white battles in the 1850s and early 1860s took place along the Humboldt River in northern Nevada, the conflict eventually moved south to central Nevada, also part of the traditional lands of the Newe. This region became a popular travel route after Captain James Simpson and Howard Egan, two explorers hired by the federal government, marked out the so-called Central Route across the Great Basin in 1859. Easterners soon heard of this new route; it was used by the Pony Express from April 1860 until October 1861 when its operation ended. The noted Butterfield Overland mail company also used the central route after March 1861.[30]

By 1861 the violence that had surfaced in northern Nevada a decade earlier repeated itself in central Nevada. The Newe of this region also organized into bands to fight the whites. The largest and best known band, consisting of 300–400 individuals, was led by Tu-tu-wa (or Toi-Toi) of the Reese River Valley. As was the case up north, the Newe of central Nevada fought to preserve human lives and to maintain the native lands and food sources that were seriously threatened by the influx of emigrants.[31]

To secure peace between the Newe and the whites, James Nye, Nevada territorial governor and ex-officio superintendent of Indian affairs, sent federal agent Warren Wasson to central Nevada. In December 1861 Wasson visited Tu-tu-wa in the Reese River Valley. According to the native oral tradition, the two men negotiated a treaty in which Wasson acknowledged native ownership of the land and the natural resources. For his part, Tu-tu-wa agreed to be friendly to the whites and told his followers not to attack the emigrants. He also agreed to allow the whites to use the natural resources as they passed through Shoshone country, including wood and wild game. But Tu-tu-wa did not surrender any of his land to the Americans because the Newe wanted to continue to live and hunt as their ancestors had always done. In any case the Tu-tu-wa Treaty, as the Newe called it, never became a legally binding pact, since the U.S. Senate did not ratify it, and the whites did not view it as a treaty.[32]

By the early 1860s both the Newe and the Americans were ready for peace. The Newe wanted peace because they now knew that the whites were more numerous, and hence more powerful, than the Indians. They also understood that the whites possessed an organized army that would fight the tribes; Colonel Connor's expedition of 1862 was a vivid reminder of this fact. At the same time the federal government also wanted peace. Beginning in 1861 the United States was engrossed in its own Civil War; to keep its soldiers and resources back east, the Union looked for ways to pacify the Indian-white conflicts in the far western region. The U.S. government wanted a treaty with the Newe for another reason as well: the Newe occupied and claimed a vast land base in the Great Basin, and the government needed to secure their permission in order for the whites to legally build railroads and other travel routes across Newe land. One way to secure rights-of-way was by treaty.

In 1862 Congress passed the Pacific Railway Act, which paved the way for the construction of the "transcontinental" railroad. When completed in 1869, this railroad followed the Humboldt River across Nevada.[33] In mid-1862, the federal government prepared to negotiate a compact with all the Shoshonean-speaking people living in the Rocky Mountain West. Congress appropriated $20,000 to finance the negotiations. Federal officials were given discretionary authority in their dealings with the Indians. One of those officials was James Doty, the superintendent of Indian affairs for the Utah Territory and one of the individuals who later negotiated with the Shoshones.[34] Because the Shoshonean speakers lived within an exceedingly large area, stretching from central Wyoming to central California, the officials decided to negotiate five separate treaties with the various Indian groups. One treaty would be with the Great Basin Newe living in northeastern Nevada. The government labeled the Newe of this area the Western Shoshone.

On October 1, 1863, Doty and Governor Nye of Nevada met in Ruby Valley with many northeastern Nevada Newe (Shoshones) and concluded a treaty with them. The federal government and the Shoshones agreed to establish peaceful relations. The Indians agreed not to attack white settlers and emigrants. Offenders would be punished if they did not abide by this provision of the pact. Although the treaty was basically one of "Peace and Friendship," it had additional provisions. The Indians agreed to permit the whites to build military forts, mail stations, and settlements on their lands. They also granted the whites the right to explore and extract mineral wealth from their lands. The Shoshones "defined" the area of their territory, which is "described" in the treaty. They consented to move to reservations established within their treaty territory "whenever the President of the United States shall deem it expedient for them to abandon the roaming life . . . and become herdsmen or agriculturalists." The white negotiators realized that the influx of settlers had destroyed or depleted many of the Indians' food sources. To "compensate them" for this loss, the government agreed to provide the Indians an annuity payment of $5,000 (in the form of goods) for a twenty-year period. The U.S. Senate ratified the treaty in 1866, and in 1869 President Ulysses Grant confirmed it.[35]

In examining the Treaty of Ruby Valley, as it is called, one sees that compromises were made. For example, the Shoshones were willing to live on reservation land in the future, but they were unwilling to leave their valley regions. For this reason the government agreed to establish several reservations at different locations. This was why the word *reservations* was inserted in the treaty.[36] The government wanted the Shoshones to become cattlemen and farmers, and it intended to establish large reservations so the Shoshone could conduct these enterprises effectively.

Although some twentieth-century commentators have argued that the Shoshones gave up their land under the treaty, this was not the case. On the contrary, the treaty negotiations recognized the Western Shoshone people as the legal owners of a vast area in the Great Basin. Jacob

Lockhart, Indian agent for Nevada, who witnessed the treaty negotiations, reported to the *Reese River Reveille* that "the treaty is in no instance considered as extinguishing the Indian title to the land described in their limits."[37] Although Lockhart was actually referring to the Shoshoni-Goship Treaty of western Utah, negotiated eleven days after Ruby Valley, the same principle of not surrendering title to the land also applied to the Western Shoshones in the Ruby Valley treaty because the two treaties are parallel in content and purpose. It appears that the government intended to negotiate a second treaty, or conduct another form of negotiation, to secure title to Shoshone land at a later date. But this process never took place.

By recognizing the Shoshones as the owners of a land base, the federal government gave them an implied right to continue to hunt and gather, although this was not explicitly stated in the treaty. Apparently, during the treaty negotiations, one or more officials told the Shoshones they could continue to hunt and gather as their ancestors had done. Thus, in the years after 1863 the Shoshones in many places in the Great Basin continued to maintain their traditional way of life. Later they argued that the treaty guaranteed them this right.[38]

Not all the Great Basin Shoshones participated in the treaty process. Only the bands living in northeastern Nevada were directly involved, including the White Knives (Tosa wihi), who lived north of the Humboldt River, and Chief Temoke's band of Ruby Valley. Temoke was the major chief of the twelve who signed the treaty.[39]

The treaty negotiators realized that only one-fourth of the Basin Shoshone population was involved in the treaty process. To secure the endorsement of the other three-fourths, Doty, as one of the two principal treaty officials, intended to "meet some of them at Reese River" after leaving Ruby Valley.[40] But no meeting ever took place. Thus, the Ruby Valley treaty did not include those Shoshone living in central and southern Nevada, or those living in eastern California. On the other hand, all the Basin Newe became known as the "Western Bands of Shoshones" or "Western Shoshones" because of the Ruby Valley treaty. The Newe now call themselves by this name.

Although the negotiators left behind no accurate map, it appears that the treaty territory was roughly conterminous with the northern half of the aboriginal Newe territory, extending from the Snake River Valley on the north, to the Smith Creek Mountains on the west, to the northern portions of the Duckwater and Reese River valleys on the south, and to the Steptoe Valley on the east.[41]

1863–1879

The period after the signing of the Ruby Valley treaty marked a new era in relations between the government and the Western Shoshones.

Generally speaking, the Shoshones kept their side of the treaty bargain: They cooperated with the government and became peaceful. In November 1863 Chief Temoke gave his permission to Colonel J. B. Moore of Fort Ruby to hang a Shoshone who had killed some emigrants before the signing of the treaty. The officers of Fort Ruby gave Buck the title of chief (or captain) for cooperating with the whites in putting down an Indian attack that occurred after 1863. The White Knives, whose assertiveness had been mellowing since the late 1850s, also became peaceful after the treaty was signed.[42] Clearly, the Western Shoshones were seeking to adjust to the new reality of life in the Great Basin.

Many non-Indians commented on the cooperative behavior of the Basin Shoshones after 1863. In September 1864, Governor Nye reported that "since the making of the Treaty" the Shoshones "have been quiet and have conducted themselves peaceably and commendably." Indian Agent Franklin Campbell wrote in 1866 that the "behavior" of the Shoshones has "been excellent." Captain James Biddle of Fort Halleck, Nevada, remarked in 1872 that the Shoshones were "peaceable." In February 1874, a non-Indian of Eureka, Nevada, noted that the Shoshones "have never taken up arms as a tribe against the whites at any time to my knowledge." Throughout the 1870s Levi Gheen, the local government agent who served the Western Shoshones, reported time after time that the Shoshones were "peaceable" and "obedient."[43]

Sporadic conflicts did occur between the Shoshone and whites after 1863. Quarrels over water rights arose when the two groups established small farms adjacent to each other. Conflict also resulted from some Indians acquiring liquor and making threatening gestures toward whites. Some Indians continued to steal livestock from the whites when they had nothing to eat. A few Indians died in these conflicts.[44] The records of the Office of Indian Affairs do not indicate whether any whites were killed by the Indians from 1863 to 1880. After 1863 violent conflicts between Indians and whites were isolated and infrequent, in contrast to the general warfare that existed before the signing of the treaty.

Unfortunately, the Shoshone were the focus of mass hysteria among the white people in Nevada in the 1860s and 1870s. An example of this anti-Indian feeling occurred in September 1875 when the so-called White Pine War took place in eastern Nevada. It began on September 1, when a Shoshone-Goshute named Toby killed a white mining prospector named James Toland, after the miner failed to pay him for prospecting services rendered. The crime, along with other closely related events, led the whites of eastern Nevada to assume falsely that the Goshute Tribe, along with the Shoshones, had planned an all-out war against the whites. They immediately sent a telegram to General John M. Schofield, who was commander of far western U.S. military forces with headquarters in San Francisco. Within a few days a military expedition arrived in White Pine

County to investigate the rumored Indian-white conflict. By September 14, the military had captured Toby and were holding him prisoner. But the local white ranchers demanded that the military punish him. The officer in charge gave in, and the whites quickly hanged Toby. The White Pine War ended before it began.[45]

The rumor of an Indian-white war in eastern Nevada in September 1875 was a result of hysteria among whites. Their insecurity was fueled by beliefs that had no foundation in fact. First, they believed that nearby Mormons, who disliked the gentile white settlers, had encouraged the Indians to attack the settlers. Second, the whites regarded the Indians as unruly "savages" who were sure eventually to attack the white population. Third, the whites assumed that the Indians banding together to harvest pine nuts were actually planning a major offensive against them. In addition, the whites were already feeling uneasy about the Indian-white warfare taking place around the Far West. They concluded that the Indians were now instigating warfare in the whites' own back yard.[46] All these beliefs were completely groundless.

This white hysteria of September 1875 led the newspapers of the Far West to maintain that a war was taking place along the Nevada/Utah border, primarily in eastern Nevada. On September 7, the *San Francisco Chronicle* reported "a general uprising of the Indians in eastern Nevada." On the same day the *Salt Lake City Tribune* stated that the Indians along the Utah/Nevada border were "preparing for war." The *Pioche Daily Record,* published in southeastern Nevada, reported that "all the Indians in Eastern Nevada are on the warpath" and that "several whites have been killed."[47]

Although these newspapers were for the most part referring to the Goshute Tribe of eastern Nevada and western Utah, some articles did take note of the Shoshones. The *San Francisco Chronicle* reported on September 8 that Shoshones had raided a mining camp near Battle Mountain. Two days later, it stated that the Shoshones around Austin were quitting their ranch jobs and moving eastward to join the Goshutes. All these stories were false, and the Nevada newspapers quickly retracted their earlier statements about an uprising in eastern Nevada.[48]

Before this entirely fabricated war ended in September 1875, five persons had lost their lives: Toland, who was murdered by Toby; Toby, who was hanged by the whites; Solomon, an innocent Shoshone, who sought to help the whites but was shot and killed by some ranchers who suspected him of being an enemy; and two other innocent Indians, who became the final victims of this senseless hysteria. The clamor quickly died down after the whites realized their blunder.[49] Thus it could be said that the whites to some extent maintained a state of war against the Shoshones after 1863.

The Western Shoshones were also indirectly affected by the so-called Bannock War of 1878. This war was a series of military skirmishes in southern Idaho and eastern Oregon between the Indians and whites. Led by Buffalo Horn, the Bannocks sought recruits from nearby tribes and received support from Chief Egan and other Northern Paiutes of Oregon, who were already angry with the Americans. Buffalo Horn began this warfare because of white injustice. Under the Fort Bridger Treaty of 1868, the Bannock were promised the rich "camas prairie" country in southern Idaho, an area abundant in camas roots, an important food source. However, the whites did not honor the Indians' title to the land. Instead, in the 1870s, the Bannocks were required to move to the Fort Hall Reservation. When the Indians were given only meager rations, the local reservation agent allowed them to secure native food sources off-reservation. Upon returning to the "camas prairie" country, the Indians were deeply angered over white domination of the land. The war lasted four months, from June to September. Both Buffalo Horn and Egan lost their lives in the conflict, and their followers were eventually confined, primarily at Fort Hall.[50]

While the Bannock War was in progress, the white Nevadans spread rumors that the Basin Shoshones either sympathized or had actually joined forces with the Bannocks. In mid-June the *Reese River Reveille* reported that the Shoshones around Austin had purchased large amounts of ammunition and then sent the powder and other material to the Bannocks. A few days later the *Elko Weekly Post* wrote that the "Shoshones have left Smoky Valley . . . it is thought to join the hostiles."[51] To counter these unfounded rumors, the Shoshones of central Nevada held an important meeting in Belmont on June 25, 1878. With the support of sympathetic whites, they drafted a statement to the effect that the Shoshones were friendly people and had no intention of joining the Bannocks. Signed by ten leaders, it read in part: "The Indians of Belmont, Tybo, Reveille, Hot Creek, Ione, Ellsworth, Eureka, White Pine in particular, and in fact all of the Indians south of the C.P.R.R. [Central Pacific Railroad], both Shoshones and Piutes, are friendly with the whites and hope to remain so."[52]

Unfortunately, some whites still did not believe the Shoshones. After the Belmont gathering, the *Reese River Reveille* reported that Shoshones had threatened white cowboys in the isolated country between Tuscarora and Battle Mountain. The newspaper claimed that this action was "proof" that the Shoshones were going north to join the Bannock. Additionally, there were stories that Shoshones had killed white-owned cattle near Tuscarora. But when Levi Gheen visited the scene, he found the rumor to be false. Although excited by the war, the Shoshones remained neutral in 1878 and did not join the Bannocks.[53]

Regardless of the hysteria, the Western Shoshones continued to honor the Ruby Valley treaty by permitting the whites to settle, to explore, to mine mineral resources, and to improve their lands. In the 1860s several Nevada towns, including Austin, Carlin, Elko, and Eureka, were founded within the Western Shoshones' treaty territory. By 1870 Austin had a population of 1,324, and Elko's population was 1,160. Miners were extracting copper and lead from the Shoshones' land, and in 1869 the Central Pacific Railroad had completed its tracks across Shoshone lands.[54]

The establishment of permanent settlements in Nevada further altered the native environment, especially in the fertile valley regions, including Ruby Valley, Reese River Valley, and Duckwater Valley. White settlers introduced the cattle economy; their stock further depleted the grasses and seeds the Shoshones had traditionally relied upon. The Indians had to travel farther to find native foods, and they also had to rely on the new foods and new kinds of work introduced by the whites.[55]

Even more devastating to the environment was the mining industry in the Reese River Valley and other places. To separate worthless ores from iron, silver, and other valuable metals, the miners smelted the ores with charcoal, considered a highly efficient fuel at that time. Because of the expense of importing coal and other fuels, native pinyon wood was converted into charcoal. The mining industry thus was heavily dependent upon the thick pinyon groves that thrived in the Basin region. Unfortunately, within a few years entire areas were completely deforested, especially around the mining settlements of Austin, Eureka, and Ely.[56] This in turn meant a severe reduction in the supply of pine nuts, a major food source for the Shoshones. Again, the Shoshones had to travel farther for their harvest.

No longer able to follow their native way of life completely, the Shoshones had to adjust—for example, by engaging in money-making activities. Some sold native food products to the whites during the years when there was an abundant supply or bumper crop. The Austin Shoshones sold currants in 1864, and pine nuts in 1865, 1875, and 1877, when the harvest was especially abundant. In 1873 one enterprising Shoshone caught salmon in the Owyhee River in the vicinity of today's Duck Valley Reservation and then sold his catch.[57] During average or poor years, the Shoshones harvested native foods for their own survival and sold nothing to whites.

Having observed the activities of whites, some Shoshones began practicing agriculture in the late 1860s, another example of Shoshone adjustment to the new reality. In 1867, those living near the White Pine Mountains in eastern Nevada grew sunflowers as a new food source introduced to them by white settlers. Shoshone agriculture expanded in 1869 when Levi Gheen was hired as "Farmer-In-Charge of the Western

Shoshone." By the early 1870s the Shoshones of Ruby Valley, Spring Valley, Steptoe Valley, and Duckwater Valley all were tending small subsistence gardens. Some became so enthusiastic about their new enterprise that in March 1873 Chief Temoke of Ruby Valley sent two representatives to meet Gheen to secure more seeds. In August 1875 the Duckwater Shoshones asked for a new plow; they received one and continued to cultivate grain. When some Shoshone groups had produced more than enough for their own consumption, they sold the surplus to the whites. Some Austin whites purchased Indian-produced barley in August 1877.[58]

Many Shoshones ended up as laborers for the whites. Most worked on ranches, where the men served as cowboys and haycutters and the women as household servants. A few individuals eventually acquired the surnames of their ranch bosses. By the mid-1870s there was considerable demand for Shoshone labor, and some whites became dependent upon Indian labor. It was reported that "many ranchers have had the same Indians working for them for years."[59] White employers understood that the Shoshones still relied largely upon native food sources and accordingly, around September of each year, they allowed their Indian workers to leave the ranches temporarily to harvest pine nuts.

Other Shoshones engaged in different types of money-making activities. For example, in 1865 the Shoshones around Austin made straw hats, no doubt for sale to the whites. Some cleaned the streets of Austin for pay. Knowing that the whites were searching for mineral wealth, a few became mining guides and prospectors. The Ruby Valley Shoshones became cattle owners when the government provided them with cattle after the signing of the Ruby Valley treaty.[60] The cattle were later removed from Ruby Valley and taken to Duck Valley when a reservation was established there in 1877.

Although the Western Shoshones honored the treaty by remaining peaceful and by permitting the whites to settle on their lands, the federal government did not uphold its side of the agreement. It had promised to establish more than one reservation within the described treaty territory and to give the Indians an annuity, paid in the form of goods valued at $5,000 each year for twenty years. The government fell short on both these pledges, and its failure is worthy of examination.

When the government promised in the treaty to establish more than one reservation for the Western Shoshones within their defined territory, it failed to specify locations. Government officials knew that the Shoshones lived over a large area of the Great Basin. In 1862 Governor Nye of Nevada had noted that the Shoshones were "a heterogeneous" people "consisting of a number of different bands."[61] He must have realized that it would be difficult to place all the Shoshones on a single reservation, and he was probably responsible for writing Article 6 of the treaty, which stated that "such reservations" (that is, more than one) would be set aside for the Indians in the years after 1863. Additionally, the Indians themselves wanted the reservations to be established in their native valleys, where their ancestors had lived for countless generations.[62]

Federal officials considered Ruby Valley a prime location for several reasons. First, it had abundant natural resources. Second, the 1859 unsurveyed reservation was located there. Third, since 1859 a large number of Shoshones had occupied the valley. Fourth, the treaty of 1863 had been negotiated in Ruby Valley. Fifth, after the signing of the treaty, Governor Nye had "reoccupied" the unsurveyed "six miles square" tract as a possible reservation site. Sixth, the valley lay within the boundaries of the Western Shoshone treaty territory.[63]

Based on these factors, the Office of Indian Affairs in 1864 selected Ruby Valley as a reservation site for the Shoshones. Jacob Lockhart, the Indian agent for Nevada, was instructed to survey the unsurveyed "six miles square" tract. In fact, Lockhart in 1864 intended to have all the Nevada Indian reservations surveyed. These included the Walker River and Pyramid Lake reservations, both located in western Nevada and designated for the Northern Paiutes, and the Ruby Valley Reservation. Lockhart found it difficult to hire a surveyor at this time because surveyors could profit more by surveying land tracts in the gold fields of the West than by surveying Indian reservations. By late 1864 Lockhart had hired a surveyor who mapped the Walker River Reservation and partially mapped the Pyramid Lake Reservation. He did not survey the Ruby Valley Reservation because of its distance from Carson City, where the Nevada Indian Agency was located. By mid-1865, the Ruby Valley Reservation was still not surveyed. Lockhart explained, "I did not succeed in getting the 'Ruby Valley' Reserve surveyed as it is far from the other Reserves and not having funds to go there it is yet unsurveyed."[64]

After the mid-1860s, many white settlers began to farm and ranch in Ruby Valley. In 1866 Indian Agent Franklin Campbell noted that the "reserve in Ruby Valley, which was formerly intended for [the Indians'] use, is now occupied by settlers and the Overland Mail company's farm."[65] He recommended "that another [reservation] be set apart for them upon the headwaters of the Humboldt River" or near Ruby Valley.[66] The unsurveyed tract was no longer available as a reservation site.

Even though the "six miles square" tract was never surveyed as a permanent reservation for the Shoshones, those of them who lived in Ruby Valley continued to regard it as their home. In 1874 an Indian agent remarked that the land "near the Overland farm in Ruby Valley is considered by the Indians their capital or centre place" and noted that "their great chief [Temoke] resides there."[67] However, with further encroachment of the white settlers, the federal government no longer considered Ruby Valley a practical choice for a reservation site.

By 1869 and 1870 the Indian Bureau was inconsistent on the subject of a reservation policy for the Western Shoshones. Because the Basin Shoshones were not under any particular agency, more than one official came up with differing reservation plans for them. J. E. Tourtellotte, superintendent of Indian affairs for Utah Territory, had read the 1863 treaty and concluded that its provisions must be carried out. This involved the creation of more than one large reservation so they could become herders and farmers. He wrote in December 1869: "It would, however, be better to make at once large and permanent reservations for all of the Shoshone Indians."[68] In marked contrast, Henry Douglas, superintendent of Indian affairs for Nevada, who had also read the treaty, envisioned creating only one reservation.[69]

Because of his proximity to the Shoshones in Nevada, Superintendent Douglas took the initiative of placing the Western Shoshones on a reservation. In April 1870 he held a meeting with some Shoshones living near Austin in central Nevada. Douglas wanted them settled on a reservation to become farmers, even though this meant giving up their native way of life. He told them that the whites were land-hungry and would eventually take all the land. Creation of a reservation would preserve a land base for the Shoshones, and the whites would not be able to take it.[70]

Shoshone leader O-haga responded to Douglas's proposal. He informed Douglas that the Shoshones would consider moving to a reservation if it was established in Grass Valley, a few miles north of Austin and the home of O-haga's ancestors. He also made it clear that his group of Shoshones would not move outside of Shoshone country, nor would they consider moving to another place within Shoshone territory: "This is our old home all the time . . . We don't feel like going away too far. Don't know about White Pine County, Humboldt County, or the country away down southeast of here. This is our country. Would like to remain here."[71]

After the meeting with O-haga, Douglas wanted Levi Gheen, the farmer-in-charge of the Shoshones, to find one reservation location suitable for agriculture. But the Indian Office in Washington, D.C., took no action. This episode clearly illustrates the Shoshones' deep attachment to their native valleys—O-haga insisted on remaining in Grass Valley—at the same time that they were willing to accept the new policy of reservations.

The central office of the Indian Bureau took no action on a reservation policy for Western Shoshones until 1873. In that year Secretary of the Interior Charles Delano, in response to an Indian Bureau recommendation, authorized the bureau to place the tribes in Utah and Nevada on reservation land. This was part of the so-called national Indian "peace policy" of confining all tribal people across the country on reservations.[72] The government maintained that the Indians could be better civilized, protected from "unscrupulous" white men, and more effectively controlled if they were placed on only a few reservations. Thus, in the early 1870s the Indian Bureau's goal was to establish only one reservation for the Western Shoshone.

Delano appointed G. W. Ingalls, a U.S. Indian agent-at-large, and John Wesley Powell of the U.S. Topographical Service, who was well known for his expedition on the Colorado River. Edward Smith, commissioner of the Indian Bureau, instructed the two men to "induce" the Nevada Shoshones to leave their homeland and move to the Fort Hall Reservation in southeastern Idaho, or perhaps to the Uintah-Ouray Reservation in eastern Utah. If this strategy failed, the Powell-Ingalls Special Commission was to find a reservation site in Nevada. In this way the bureau turned its back on the treaty of Ruby Valley. In fact, Commissioner Ingalls knew of the government's plan not to abide by the treaty and not to establish large and permanent reservations for the Shoshone in the Basin. He wrote to Smith noting that "we will therefore have to get the consent of the Indians to waive their right as indicated, provided they are removed to Fort Hall or the Uintah."[73]

In late 1873 and early 1874 the Powell-Ingalls Commission held meetings with Shoshone groups around Nevada. Its objective was to buy them off with gifts. For example, in November 1873 the commission met with a large number of Shoshones in Elko and gave them 800 blankets, 200 shirts, 225 pounds of tobacco, and 1,000 pounds of potatoes.[74] This effort to persuade the Shoshones to move to a single reservation failed. They were willing to move only if numerous reservations were established at different locations within Shoshone country. This native attachment to the land prompted the commission to write that "the most important difficulty in the way of collecting these people on reservations, is the fact that each small tribe desires to have a reservation somewhere within the limits of its own territory."[75]

In the end, the Shoshones rejected the commission's consolidation effort. In central Nevada, around the Belmont area in Monitor Valley, Chief Kawich and his followers declined the gifts, stating that "acceptance of the articles would be equivalent to selling their birthright."[76] Kawich interpreted the commission's initiative as a form of bribery, or an attempt to get the Shoshones to sell their land to the Americans.

The Shoshones of east-central Nevada (Duckwater, Currant Creek, and White River) also rejected the idea of moving elsewhere. Apparently, Ingalls tried to persuade them to move to the newly created Moapa River Reservation, located in extreme southern Nevada and designated for the southern Paiutes. In rejecting the federal consolidation plan, the east-central Shoshones stated: "We all want to stay here . . . and not go down on the Muddy [Moapa] to raise Corn . . . be allowed to live in our own dear Mountains and valleys as we have done in times gone."[77]

Thus the Powell-Ingalls Commission was a failure because of Shoshone resistance. In this case the Shoshones successfully rejected national Indian policy, and they remained in their native places in the early and mid-1870s. Perhaps the only success of the commission was its published report, which described the political organization of the Western Shoshones. Powell and Ingalls identified several major band leaders or chiefs, including Temoke of Ruby Valley, Kawich of the Belmont area in central Nevada, Tu-tu-wa of the Reese River Valley region, Captain Sam of the Halleck region, and Mose of Ruby Valley.[78] These leaders, all of whom had subordinates, continued to maintain the band organizations that had come into existence after white contact. Two of them became well-known figures to both Indians and whites: Temoke, who had played the role of peacemaker up to 1863, and Tu-tu-wa, who often mediated differences between Indians and whites.

Unlike the Powell-Ingalls Special Commission, which failed to find even one reservation site for the Western Shoshones, Levi Gheen was successful in his quest. Gheen had served as the local agent to the Shoshones since 1869 and spoke their language. As farmer-in-charge of the Western Shoshones since 1870, he taught the Indians how to farm. At the same time he kept his eyes open for a suitable reservation site and consulted with some of the Western Shoshone leaders. One leader Gheen listened to was Captain Sam, a Tosa wihi (White Knife) Shoshone who often hunted in a place now called Duck Valley, located ninety miles north of Elko, Nevada. Captain Sam regarded this valley as "his country," since it was part of the old White Knife hunting and gathering area. In 1870 he mentioned to Gheen that the valley was rich in natural resources and suitable for agricultural purposes. Perhaps Captain Sam wanted the valley as a reservation since it was located off the main east-west travel route, which followed the Humboldt River. In Duck Valley the Shoshones could live in isolation, removed from much contact with whites. Persuaded by Captain Sam, Gheen asked the Indian Office at different times if he could visit the valley to ascertain its potential as a possible reservation site.

Finally, in March 1877, Gheen was given permission to visit Duck Valley. After his visit, he advised the Indian Office that the valley was a good site and suitable for agricultural purposes. On April 16, 1877, by executive order, the federal government set aside Duck Valley as a reservation for the Western Shoshones.[79] It became the first permanent Western Shoshone reservation. Contrary to popular belief, the Western

Shoshone Reservation (now called the Duck Valley Reservation) was not created to fulfill the provisions of the 1863 treaty. Rather it resulted from the recommendation of Gheen and the leadership of Captain Sam who wanted a reservation for his followers.

Although Gheen knew of the 1863 treaty provisions, he supported the government policy of placing the Shoshones on one reservation. He stated his position clearly in a letter to the commissioner of Indian affairs in 1875: "It would however take time to place *all* the Westerns upon a reservation."[80] Two years later he wrote in the same vein: "It will take several years to congregate *all* the Western Shoshones on a reservation."[81] To Gheen the remoteness of Duck Valley, its potential for agricultural development, and the fact that Captain Sam and the White Knives were willing to move there were more important considerations than the treaty provisions.

When a second reservation was established for the Shoshones of northeastern Nevada in 1877, Gheen played no part in its establishment or administration. On May 10, 1877, the federal government by executive order established the Carlin Farms Reservation to satisfy the agricultural interests of other Tosa wihi Shoshones living in that area. Since 1868 they had labored as farmers for the white residents near Carlin. By the early 1870s they wanted to establish their own farm, recognizing that the Shoshones would never be able to return completely to their native economy of hunting and gathering. Support came from John Palmer, Indian agent for the Northern Paiutes in western Nevada. In 1874 Palmer suggested to the Indian Office that a fertile region twenty-five miles north of Carlin be set aside as a reservation. The Shoshones began to farm in the valley; two years later the government set aside the valley as the Carlin Farms Reservation. Palmer was selected as the local agent to the Indians.[82]

If it was the government's intention to make farmers of the Indians, the Carlin Farms Shoshones provided an excellent example. In 1877 they cultivated 125 acres of land and harvested 1,500 bushels of wheat and 500 bushels of oats and barley. Their domestic herds totaled 150 horses and the same number of cattle. Along with their agricultural pursuits the Indians built barns, corrals, and houses.[83]

Agent Palmer encouraged other Shoshone groups to move to the Carlin Farms Reservation. Thirty-two Indian families lived on the reservation in 1875; two years later there were seventy-five families in all. Government officials urged the Shoshones of Ruby Valley to move there. Captain Buck and his followers did move to Carlin, but Chief Temoke and his supporters refused, still desiring a reservation at Ruby Valley instead. When asked to move to Carlin Farms, Temoke reportedly asserted: "If you move my country I go too. Have my ground here I can't move."[84]

The agricultural ventures of the Tosa wihi Shoshones at Carlin Farms were short-lived. In 1878 the U.S. General Land Office contended that most of the reservation land had been claimed by white settlers before the executive order of May 10, 1877. Those interested in the affairs of the Shoshones were unwilling to accept this conclusion. Palmer stated that he had examined the Nevada land tract records before the executive order was issued. He argued that these records clearly indicated that the area of Carlin Farms had not been claimed by anyone. He pointed out that no one occupied the Carlin Farms valley before the Indians moved there. His statement was supported by A. J. Barnes, Indian agent of Nevada. Barnes said that no one was interested in the Carlin Farms area until the Indians had proved that the valley was an excellent place for agriculture. Both men concluded that the land records had been altered to suit the interests of non-Indian landowners.[85] However, fraud was never proven.

The Indian Office had no choice but to pressure the Shoshones to leave the Carlin Farms Reservation and move to Duck Valley. The Shoshones were reluctant to leave their established homesites. Captain Buck pointed out that he had harvested 110 pounds of barley and wheat, and had a fenced farm and a corral for his stock. In addition, some Carlin Farms Shoshones were reluctant to move to Duck Valley because it was not very far from the area of the Bannock War in southern Idaho. The Indians' reluctance to move was supported by concerned individuals. Agent Palmer urged the Indians not to relocate, as did a Mormon Indian. These efforts were of no avail. By April 1879 the Carlin Farms Shoshones were en route to the Western Shoshone Reservation (Duck Valley).[86] In spite of their reluctance to move, they accepted Duck Valley because it was part of the old Tosa wihi hunting and gathering area.

Although the White Knives of Carlin Farms moved to the Western Shoshone Reservation, the federal government was not successful in inducing most other Western Shoshones to move there. Government agents and officials were well aware of the Shoshones' strong attachment to their home areas. The Shoshones of central Nevada had already made it clear to the federal officials that they would not move to a reservation unless it was located within their territory. Some Shoshones of northeastern Nevada also refused to move to the reservation. A case in point was the Ruby Valley Shoshones under the leadership of Chief Temoke.

In 1878 and 1879 Gheen held two meetings with Temoke and other Indians of northeastern Nevada in an attempt to persuade them to move to Duck Valley. The eighty-year-old leader reported that he was "too old to emigrate." At the same time, he was not opposed to the idea that the Shoshones should move to the reservation. According to Gheen, Temoke "strongly recommended" that Duck Valley should be the future home of the Shoshones and that "every possible means be used to make it attractive to the Indians."[87] However, he and his followers had solid reasons for not moving to Duck Valley. Foremost was their attachment to Ruby Valley, where they had lived more or less permanently since the early 1860s. They hoped that the government would finally set aside the "six miles square" unsurveyed reservation for them. Beginning in 1870 they cultivated small farms within the area of the unsurveyed tract. The valley still had an abundance of natural food resources. In refusing to move to Duck Valley, Temoke told his followers: "I can't go from here [where] I have lots of ducks, pine-nuts, deer. I can't go to Duck Valley."[88] In 1879 the *Elko Weekly Post* reported that the Ruby Valley Shoshones "wish to remain where they are, and not be moved to any distant reservation."[89] Located roughly 130 miles north of Ruby Valley, Duck Valley was generally considered to be a "distant reservation."

Another reason why Temoke and his followers refused to move to Duck Valley was that they were not on the best of terms with the White Knife (Tosa wihi) Shoshones led by Captain Sam, who made up two-thirds of the reservation population. Before 1863 the Temoke Band of Ruby Valley was known as the peace group because of their efforts to end the Indian-white skirmishes. In contrast, the White Knives had wanted to continue fighting up to the early 1860s. After 1863 the two sides, even though both were peaceful, still held animosity toward each other. As a result the Temoke Band had no desire to join the White Knives of Duck Valley.[90] The Shoshones who remained in Ruby Valley also resented the fact that federal agents gave their cattle to the families that left Carlin Farms and moved to Duck Valley. Those who remained in Ruby Valley voiced their disapproval of this action, which they regarded as theft.[91]

In addition to its failure to establish several large reservations for the Western Shoshones, the government also failed to give them the full amount of the agreed treaty compensation. The government had agreed to compensate the Shoshones for permitting non-Indians to explore, settle, and establish improvements on their lands. As stipulated in Article 7 of the 1863 treaty, the government agreed "to pay" the Shoshones "the sum of five thousand dollars in such articles, including cattle for herding or other purposes" on an annual basis "for the term of twenty years [from 1863 to 1883]."[92] Because there were many problems associated with the issuance and disbursement of the treaty goods, the Shoshones never received the full value of their annuities.

One problem in distributing the treaty goods was the location of an appropriate distribution site. The treaty did not specify where the Indians were to receive the goods. Because the treaty was negotiated in Ruby Valley, it was generally assumed that the distribution site would be there. Accordingly, in the 1860s the goods were distributed in Ruby Valley. In the 1870s, however, the goods were distributed at other locations. One distribution site was Elko, Nevada, about fifty miles northeast of Ruby Valley. In 1874 the goods were issued in Battle Mountain, Nevada.[93] Because the Shoshones lived over such a large area, many of them never received any treaty goods.

A second problem was that the negotiators never set a definite annual date for the Shoshones to receive their goods, nor did they designate any person or agency to take charge of the distribution. Because the treaty was negotiated during the first week of October, it was assumed that the treaty goods would be issued to the Indians during that same week in subsequent years. It was also assumed that the employees of the Utah Indian Superintendency would distribute the goods since they were the agency closest to the Shoshones.

Indian Office records indicate that some Shoshones waited in Ruby Valley for their goods during the first week of October 1864. However, the clerks of the Utah Superintendency did not arrive until December. By this time most Indians had left the treaty site and settled down for winter. The clerks located only twenty-five Indians, to whom they distributed goods. The remaining goods were left with Captain George Thurston of Fort Ruby, who later distributed them to a few other Shoshones.[94]

In the years after 1864, when the clerks of the Utah Superintendency failed to meet with a large number of Shoshones, the undistributed goods were left with non-Indian individuals of northeastern Nevada, including the officers of Fort Ruby. These persons were given the authority to distribute the remaining goods. Some of the whites entrusted with this responsibility failed to carry out their task. This prompted Lieutenant W. S. Carpenter of Fort Ruby to make the following comment to F. H. Head, superintendent of Indian affairs for the Utah Territory, in 1867:

> "In the distribution of the Indian goods last year [1866], justice and the rights of the Indians seems to have been sacrificed by leaving the goods in the hands of people who not only neglected to distribute them properly, but used them as their own private property, and even *sold* the same to the rightful owners."[95]

To eliminate this problem, Carpenter suggested that Superintendent Head must "either superintend the issue of all the goods in person, in the presence of all the Indians, or leave them in the hands of responsible disinterested persons of known integrity."[96] Throughout most of the 1870s, Levi Gheen distributed the goods to the Shoshones. From 1877 to 1883 the agents of the Duck Valley reservation issued the goods on the reservation.[97]

Although the Shoshones did receive some useful goods, including cattle, blankets, and clothing, most of the treaty goods proved to be impractical and of little value to the Indians. One item frequently distributed to the Shoshones was flour. This raw ingredient proved to be worthless as the Indians did not have the means or the knowledge to bake bread. The Indians therefore "used" the flour "as white paint for their faces."[98] As Indian Agent J. H. Ingalls remarked in 1875, "I learned that many of the annuity goods were of no use for these Indians, such as fish-hooks [and] fish-lines."[99] Gheen agreed with this statement in 1876 when he noted that "many of the articles heretofore received by them does them but little good."[100]

In no year did the Shoshones receive treaty goods to the full value of $5,000. Much of the money was spent for other purposes. For example, Gheen's salary and travel expenses came from the annuity fund. The payment for transporting the treaty goods from the New York and Chicago warehouses to Nevada also came from the annuity fund, as did the money to pay the salaries of laborers, inspectors, interpreters, blacksmiths, clerks, and physicians who served the Indians. This prompted the editor of the *Elko Independent* to write in January 1873: "We do not know anything about the Indian business, but we do not think that they [the Shoshones] have had their just dues. At this place, there were some 250 Indians in the circle, and the Agent gave them [goods] . . . which competent judges say would not cost to exceed $250 or $300."[101] This opinion was expressed by others as well. Gheen indicated in 1877 that he had "never received that amount [$5,000] for them at any time heretofore."[102] Eventually the Western Shoshones realized that the federal government had cheated them, and they pressed claims against the government (see chapters four through seven).

At the same time that they were busy dealing with the federal government and its agents, the Shoshones continued to observe many of their traditions. They held round dances, songs, and prayers in conjunction with the springtime appearance of native grasses and the fall pine nut harvests. For example, the Reese River Valley Shoshones held round dances in March or April when young yampa root plants emerged. The Shoshones also held communal rabbit drives in the fall. A Reese River Valley rabbit drive lasted five days in October 1877.[103] The Shoshones continued to hunt deer and antelope as well, just as they had done before the coming of the whites.

But Shoshone traditions themselves were changing. The round dances took on a new name in the late 1860s and early 1870s when the whites labeled them fandangos, Spanish for "celebration or dance." The Shoshones eventually accepted this name, and it has been popularly used in the twentieth century. Fewer local round dances (or fandangos) were held, but they were now much larger. This was because the Shoshones were concentrating themselves in particular areas, near white-owned ranches and mining towns. The Shoshones held large annual fandangos at Marshall Canyon north of Austin and at the mining settlement of Belmont in Monitor Valley. Various other Shoshone groups continued to hold fandangos in the fertile valleys where their ancestors had lived, including Duckwater, Reese River, and Ruby Valley. Some fandangos became associated with important American events and holidays. For example, by the 1870s the Shoshones in Austin participated in the annual Fourth of July parade and held a fandango at the same time. The Shoshones around Elko sponsored a fandango in conjunction with the annual Labor Day rodeo. Some Shoshones also held fandangos to convey a message to the whites. In February 1867, during a particularly harsh winter, the Shoshones sponsored a large gathering of 300 persons to request relief from the government. They also held fandangos to iron out differences with tribal neighbors, primarily the Northern Paiutes.[104]

The Shoshones dealt with many new problems in the 1860s and 1870s in addition to their dealings with the government. One of these was diseases, of which smallpox was the most frequent. An epidemic struck the Reese River Valley in 1869, followed by another around Eureka and points farther east in 1872. Because the Shoshones lived in small groups over a large area, the entire population was not stricken ill at once, and for this reason disease did not markedly reduce the Shoshone populations as had happened to other tribes. In the early 1870s Gheen, the local Indian Bureau farm agent for the Shoshones, vaccinated some Shoshones who had come down with smallpox.[105] Besides diseases, some Shoshones were also touched by alcohol. Drinking, which released anger and gave rise to unruly behavior, was a frequent cause of friction between the Indians and whites.

Another new problem was the influx of Northern Paiutes into Shoshone country. In the late 1860s and 1870s Northern Paiutes from western Nevada moved to central Nevada to secure jobs in the mines and ranches in the Reese River Valley and surrounding area. The local Shoshones considered them intruders, and at times ill feeling developed between the two tribes. When the annual Fourth of July celebration took place in Austin, Nevada, in 1869, the two tribes kept apart, camping on opposite sides of town. In July 1878 the Shoshones held a fandango at Marshall Canyon near Austin—for Shoshones only.[106] There was, however, no actual warfare between the two tribes, and in later years they became good neighbors. Proof of this came in the early twentieth century, when the Northern Paiutes invited Shoshones to move to western Nevada.

3

THE WESTERN SHOSHONE
RESERVATION (DUCK VALLEY)
1880—1933

In 1877 the federal government created by presidential executive order the Western Shoshone Reservation (now called the Duck Valley Reservation), along the Nevada-Idaho border. The Indian Bureau wanted all Western Shoshones of the Great Basin to move voluntarily to this reservation. As related in chapter 2, government representatives met with the Shoshones at different places in 1879 to discuss their removal to the reservation. This government effort failed because the Shoshones were too deeply attached to particular places where their ancestors had lived. As a result, only one-third moved to Duck Valley, while the other two-thirds remained at or near their native places.[1]

The Indian Bureau intended to assimilate the Western Shoshones who moved to Duck Valley, by eliminating their native culture and replacing it with yeoman farming and other American ways. Because of their deep-rooted culture, however, the Shoshones were never totally assimilated or Americanized in the late nineteenth and early twentieth centuries. When the government replaced the policy of assimilation with one of "cultural pluralism" in the early 1930s, the Shoshones in Duck Valley still maintained some of their native ways. Although not assimilated, they were acculturated: Many spoke and wrote English, yet retained their native language as well as other native ways.

The Shoshones who finally settled in Duck Valley in 1879 and 1880 came primarily from the former Carlin Farms Reservation. These were for the most part White Knife (Tosa wihi) Shoshones who had traditionally lived in the region north of the Humboldt River in northern Nevada. This group or band of Western Shoshone considered Duck Valley part of their homeland.[2] For this reason they were willing to accept the valley as their new residence.

In the early 1880s, only 300 Nevada Shoshones lived on the Duck

Valley Reservation. This was one reason why the Indian Bureau in early 1884 considered abolishing it and sending the Shoshone residents to the Fort Hall Reservation in southeastern Idaho. Another reason was that the last annuity distribution authorized by the Ruby Valley treaty of 1863 had been issued at Duck Valley in late 1883. Since the twenty-year annuity period had ended, the bureau maintained that the treaty was dead and that the government no longer had any legal obligations to the Nevada Shoshones. Their reservation could therefore be dissolved, and the Duck Valley people could join their Shoshone "brothers" at Fort Hall.[3]

In the end, the government did not abolish the Western Shoshone Reservation. The plan failed largely because of native opposition. At a meeting in March 1884 the Duck Valley Shoshones unanimously rejected removal to Fort Hall. They had several reasons for refusing to move. For some, attachment to Duck Valley, part of White Knife Shoshone territory, was the chief factor. Others opposed removal because they had already experienced the reluctant move from Carlin Farms to Duck Valley in 1879, and had no desire to move again. Still others opposed moving because Fort Hall was adjacent to an area with a large white population.[4] The native leadership openly expressed their opposition to removal. Captain Sam, the principal Shoshone leader, stated: "This is my place . . . Government gave it to me . . . [I was] born here, [my] mother die[d] here . . . I can't go [to] Fort Hall."[5] Sympathetic whites supported the Indians' position; the editor of the *Elko Independent* wrote that "it would certainly be an act of gross injustice and even cruelty, to force them from their native section against their will."[6] In the face of this opposition from the Duck Valley Shoshone, the government dropped the subject after 1884.

In later years the Indian Bureau no longer pressured the large number of nonreservation Western Shoshones of Nevada to move to Duck Valley. Officials hoped, however, that they would gradually move to the reservation, where there would be advantages for them. For example, in 1903 some Shoshones living in White Pine County were stricken with a smallpox epidemic. Calvin Asbury, government agent for Duck Valley, said that it was impossible to take care of these Shoshones since they lived two hundred miles south. He suggested that services could be provided if they moved to Duck Valley. "These Indians," wrote Asbury, "are such as would doubtless have rights on this reservation if they came here but have never lived here and it is doubtful they ever will."[7]

Beginning in 1910 some officials suggested that more off-reservation Western Shoshones might move to the Western Shoshone Reservation if they were given title to individual land allotments. The allotment of reservations stemmed from the Dawes Act of 1887, which authorized the

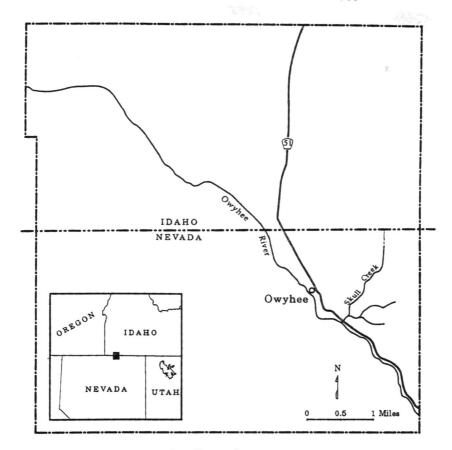

Duck Valley Indian Reservation

subdivision of Indian reservations and the granting of 160-acre allotments to heads of households. The objective was to eliminate the Indians' communal ownership of reservation land and make them into self-sufficient farmers.[8]

In 1910 the 1887 law was amended to give only forty-acre allotments of good land capable of being irrigated. This amendment inspired the Indian Bureau to consider building a dam to preserve runoff on the Owyhee River, upstream from Duck Valley. If this reclamation project were carried out, the reservation residents would be able to harvest two crops of alfalfa instead of one. The reservation would become a flourishing agricultural community, and the off-reservation Nevada Shoshones would surely flock to Duck Valley to join the new economic order. Agent Asbury wrote, "I think it probable that when these scattering Indians hear that allotments are being made a number of them will come here asking for allotments."[9]

But no dam was built on the Owyhee River at this time, and the reservation did not become a flourishing agricultural community. The Indians were granted forty-acre assignments, but these plots were classified as federal trust land, so that the Shoshones were caretakers of their land and not owners.[10] In the end, very few off-reservation Nevada Shoshones moved to Duck Valley in the early years of the century. The Indian Bureau failed in its effort to lure them to the reservation with promises of land and agriculture.

In particular, the Indian Bureau had hoped to persuade the Ruby Valley Shoshones to move to Duck Valley. The Ruby Valley group had insisted that the former "six miles square" unsurveyed reservation be reestablished as a permanent reservation. The Indian Bureau was unwilling to create a second Western Shoshone reservation in the early twentieth century. Instead, it continued to maintain that all Shoshones, including those at Ruby Valley, should move to Duck Valley.[11]

The Indian Bureau's insistence that the Ruby Valley Shoshones move was especially evident from 1912 to 1925. In 1912 C. F. Hauke, a top-level administrator in the central office in Washington, D.C., told them that "any Indian belonging to the Western Shoshone tribe not already enrolled on the Duck Valley Reservation, would have the right to submit application for such enrollment."[12] In 1919 E. B. Merritt, another top-level bureaucrat in the same office, told the Shoshones that "the privilege is still open to these Indians to remove to the Duck Valley Reservation."[13] And in 1925 Charles Engle, irrigation supervisor of the Indian Bureau, told his superiors that "in my opinion these Indians should be removed to the Western Shoshone Reservation according to the terms of the treaty of 1863."[14] In fact the establishment of the Western Shoshone Reservation had nothing to do with the Ruby Valley treaty. As related in chapter 2, it had been created to please Shoshone leader Captain Sam and his followers who wanted to move there. The Ruby Valley Shoshones continued to assert that the "six miles square" unsurveyed reservation was intended to fulfill the treaty since it was recognized as a Shoshone reservation immediately following the treaty negotiations.[15] Government refusal to establish it was unjust. Therefore, they refused to move to Duck Valley.

As late as 1929 the government still hoped that the large number of nonreservation Western Shoshones would "move en masse" to the reservation. In this year Congress finally appropriated $3,500 to consider the possibility of building a reclamation dam on the Owyhee River. If such a project were completed, the Shoshones living in Elko and other places could finally move to the reservation as the government had initially proposed in 1879 and 1880. But still the dam was not built, and no mass removal of Shoshones took place.[16]

Without doubt, the small number of Shoshones at Duck Valley prompted the Indian Bureau to encourage the Northern Paiutes to move there, despite the designation of the reservation for Western Shoshones. The first group of Paiutes, numbering 150, moved to the reservation in 1880 from Paradise Valley, Nevada, a native Paiute valley 150 miles to the west. These Paiutes had opposed moving to the Malheur Reservation in southeastern Oregon, which had been established for the Paiutes in 1873. This group preferred to live farther south than Oregon, even though the Malheur Reservation was still in Paiute territory. They were welcomed to Duck Valley by Shoshone leader Captain Sam, a friend to the Paiutes since he had lived among them before the formation of the Duck Valley Reservation.[17]

At first, there was talk that the Paiutes had no right to live in Duck Valley since it was a reservation for Shoshones. Reservation agent John Mayhugh wrote that Shoshone leader George Washington felt that "this Reservation [is] for the Shoshones and he did not want Paiutes to stay here."[18] However, Mayhugh allowed them to remain. "I am of the opinion," he wrote, "that they could be induced to settle permanently upon the Western S. Res."[19] The Paiutes stayed, and some Paiutes of Oregon were also encouraged to move. Their descendants still live at Duck Valley.

The Nevada Paiutes of Duck Valley were soon joined by the Paddy Cap Band of Northern Paiutes of Oregon. Since 1879 they had been U.S. prisoners of war on the Yakima Reservation in Washington because of their involvement in the Bannock War of 1878. Earlier, the Paddy Caps had lived on the Malheur Reservation. When released from Yakima in 1884, they were homeless since Malheur had already been abolished. The Paddy Caps were given permission to move to either the Pyramid Lake or Walker River reservations, established exclusively for Paiutes. However, the Paiutes considered these places too far south. In June 1884, when the band was ready to leave Washington, the reservation superintendent allowed them to move to Duck Valley, the reservation nearest their homeland in southeastern Oregon.[20]

Government officials saw that the reservation had no room for more Paiutes, especially because some Shoshones did not like living too close to the Paiutes. For this reason, they decided to enlarge the Duck Valley Reservation. By executive order, on May 4, 1886, the federal government added sixty-nine thousand acres to the north side of the reservation for the Paddy Cap Band and other Indians.[21] This addition increased the reservation's size by roughly one-third.

Other Oregon Paiutes moved to the 1886 addition. Most are unknown by name, but one was Willie Dorsey, known as Pa-mo-tao in Paiute, who was born in Jordan Valley, Oregon, in 1860, lived on the Malheur Reservation, was a prisoner at Yakima, and finally settled in Duck Valley in 1885. His wife Nora was born in Weiser, Idaho, in 1861 and had also been a resident of Malheur.[22] From the 1890s on a few other Oregon Paiutes as well as Bannocks from Oregon and Idaho made Duck Valley their permanent home.

Emigrating Paiute families from Nevada continued to settle at Duck Valley. Most came from Paradise Valley, perhaps to join their kin who had lived there since 1880. One family was that of Charlie and Nellie Thacker, who arrived in 1889.[23] Their sons later became leaders in tribal politics.

Intermarriage naturally resulted between the two tribes living at Duck Valley. In 1922 the Indian Bureau reported 331 Shoshones and 234 Paiutes living on the reservation, along with 103 Shoshone-Paiutes. In 1931 there were 274 Shoshones, 210 Paiutes, and 187 Shoshone-Paiutes. This mixing continued as the twentieth century progressed, so that from the 1930s on the reservation people chose to call themselves the Shoshone-Paiute Tribes of the Duck Valley Reservation.[24]

The Western Shoshone Reservation had strong native leadership from its earliest days. The middle-aged captains of the former Carlin Farms Reservation were the natural leaders. Captain Sam, as the one who had initially fought for Duck Valley as a reservation site, was the principal leader. He shared leadership with others, including Captains Charley, George, Buck, and George Washington. These men were the heads of small independent bands that predated reservation life. Each band selected its own location in Duck Valley.[25]

From the beginning, the Indian Bureau insisted that the Shoshone leaders had to submit to federal government rule. John How, superintendent at Duck Valley, created an Indian police force in 1881 to counteract the influence of the captains. How kept the police loyal to him by giving them gifts and special privileges. Unwilling to accept a lowered status, Captain Sam campaigned to remove Superintendent How. He held meetings on and off the reservation and traveled as far south as Cherry Creek and Austin. Eventually, Sam realized that he was battling the entire federal government, of which How was only a minor representative in northeastern Nevada.[26] He therefore accepted Indian Bureau paternalism to some extent in order to preserve a portion of his own authority.

What emerged in the 1880s was a fluid and shaky cooperative relationship between the reservation superintendent and the Shoshone leaders. The Indian Bureau needed the support of native leaders to carry out government policy. At the same time, the leaders preserved their status by cooperating with the government to a certain extent. To reward the leaders for their support, the superintendent continued to give them gifts and privileges. In 1883 John Mayhugh, How's successor, built wood-frame houses for Captains Sam and George, whom he regarded as "head chiefs."[27] The Indian Bureau, however, still regarded itself as the guardian of its Indian wards.

Although subject to government paternalism, the Shoshone leaders were able to overrule some Indian Bureau objectives. Their success in opposing the government's attempt in 1884 to abolish the reservation and move the Shoshones to Fort Hall has already been described. The leaders even persuaded Superintendent Mayhugh to defend their position. Mayhugh wrote to his superiors in Washington stating that "these people are strongly attached to the land" and that they had no desire to move to Idaho.[28]

The Shoshone leaders compromised with some demands of the Indian Bureau. For example, realizing that they could not completely return to their native way of life, the leaders accepted the government's insistence that the Indians should become small-time farmers and cattle ranchers. By 1885 Captains Charley and Buck were branding horses and cattle and also harvesting some hay. Captain George Washington owned fifty cattle and forty-five horses in 1910 and was regarded as a good role model by the federal government.[29]

In the early years of reservation history, the Shoshones held the political power in Duck Valley. When the Paddy Cap Band of Paiutes moved to the 1886 addition, they recognized Paddy Cap as their leader. The two tribes kept apart in following years, but eventually began to cooperate and to share reservation positions. By 1896 the reservation police force consisted of five Shoshones and three Paiutes.[30]

In 1911 the political character of the reservation changed when Shoshone and Paiute leaders came together to create an "Indian council." The council consisted of the old captains—Sam, George Washington, and Paddy Cap—as well as younger leaders. This initiative marked the beginning of an organized reservation-based tribal council. It also allowed the two tribes to unite to challenge Indian Bureau authority. Specifically, they wanted the removal of Superintendent George Haggett. They argued that he was unresponsive to native concerns and requests, including the need for a reservation hospital and land assignments for families.[31] Although unsuccessful in removing Haggett, the council continued to provide a unified native voice.

The Indian council became a formal political entity, and by 1912 it consisted of eight members plus a chair. George Washington, one of the few old captains still alive in the early twentieth century, was elected as the first chair. Most members were younger men who spoke both English and their native language and had attended Indian Bureau schools. Two had even gone to the famed Carlisle Indian School in Pennsylvania. Although it was called the Western Shoshone Council, the council consisted of six Shoshones and three Paiutes—an example of shared political leadership. [32]

Important council developments took place in the years from 1915 to 1920. Council officers were expanded to include a chair, vice-chair, and a tribal secretary. The leadership divided the entire reservation into three electoral districts: Rye Grass Town (later Miller Creek), China Town, and Black Creek (also called Districts One, Two, and Three, respectively). Four council members represented each district on the newly expanded twelve-member council. District One consisted of the Paddy Cap Band, on the Idaho side of the reservation. Districts Two and Three, on the Nevada side, consisted of Shoshones, a few Paiutes, and some Shoshone-Paiutes. Whether or not the leaders recognized it, the council was copying European American models of governance. [33]

In 1919 the council leadership, with assistance from the reservation superintendent, drafted and adopted a tribal constitution, the first in reservation history. This document highlighted the duties of the council officers. It assigned powers to the council at large, allowing the body to adopt new tribal members, to assign forty-acre land tracts to heads of households, and to make rules and regulations regarding reservation affairs. The Shoshones and Paiutes now had an official governing body called the Western Shoshone Council. The council constitution also gave certain powers to the superintendent that permitted him to approve or disapprove of council decisions. The Indian Bureau may have included this provision because the native leadership had demanded the removal of an earlier superintendent the previous year, and their assertiveness was becoming a threat to bureau paternalism. [34]

On three separate occasions, in 1911, 1915, and 1921, the Western Shoshone Council sent delegations to Washington, D.C., to lobby on behalf of the Shoshone and Paiute tribes. The first delegation demanded the removal of the superintendent. The second asked for a new hospital, the construction of a dam, and government help to get rid of an undesirable Christian missionary. [35] The third delegation repeated the request for a dam and a hospital. The delegates also favored the allotment of the reservation, but wanted all the land to go to Indians only. One delegate stated, "The reservation is ours and we do not see why we should open any part of it to the public." [36] The Indian Bureau eventually granted all their requests except for the removal of the local superintendent.

The reservation leadership continued to challenge the authority of the Indian Bureau. Council members in the 1920s disapproved of the government leasing policy, which permitted nearby white cattle owners to graze 7,000 head of cattle on the reservation. They argued that the number of white-owned cattle prevented the Indians from increasing their own herds. Some years later the Indian Bureau finally accepted this argument and ended the grazing of white-owned cattle. Because the raising of cattle had become the major economic enterprise on the reservation, the Western Shoshone Council created the Western Shoshone Stock Association in 1922. This new body, which included some council members, encouraged the raising of cattle and also the production of more hay for cattle feed.[37]

Native leadership became highly visible in 1932 when the U.S. Senate's Subcommittee of the Committee on Indian Affairs visited the Western Shoshone Reservation.[38] The subcommittee had been conducting its own independent investigation of Indian affairs since 1928. During the hearings at the reservation, various leaders expressed the need for improvements on the reservation. For example, Thomas Premo, a fullblood Shoshone, said that a dam was needed as a boost to the local cattle economy: "If we could get a dam big enough to irrigate that land that we now have that is in pasture, and some of which we cut hay from—if we could only get enough water to irrigate all of these twice, I think we would be satisfied . . . As we look at it, everything points to the need of a reservoir, and if we have a reservoir I believe we could become a self-supporting bunch of Indians."[39] Premo was one of several leaders who had attended the Carlisle Indian School in Pennsylvania at the turn of the century. After returning to the reservation, he was elected to the council at different times, from 1911 to 1965, as both chair and council member. His advocacy, along with that of other leaders, finally paid off, for the government finally built a dam in the late 1930s.

In the late nineteenth and early twentieth centuries, the Indian Bureau superintendents assigned to Duck Valley were given the task of eliminating the culture of the Shoshone (and Paiute) people. This effort was part of the government policy of assimilating tribal people across the country. Because the native culture was considered "savage-like" and "heathenistic," the objective was to replace it with the European American culture by making the Indians into working-class individuals and landowners.[40]

On the surface this policy of cultural ethnocide, eliminating the Indians' culture, was largely successful. By 1883 there was only one traditional (that is, plural) marriage among the Indians on the Western Shoshone Reservation. Most reservation residents had already "adopted citizens' dress," or American-style clothes. Although they kept their native names privately, most of the Shoshones used American names publicly, including Mrs. Elegant Price and Mrs. George Washington. By

1904 it was reported that only four men on the reservation still had their traditional long hair.[41]

But the deep-rooted native culture, the result of thousands of years of development, could not be totally eliminated. One practice that persisted into the twentieth century was the isolation of women during menstruation.[42] The superintendent could not forbid this practice since it would cause him embarrassment if he invaded native female privacy.

Nor was the superintendent willing to eliminate native crafts. Some women made and sold baskets for profit. Both men and women produced deerskin (buckskin) work gloves and sold them to the nearby white ranchers. In 1900 alone, they made $2,000 from gloves.[43] The crafts were evidence of the Indians' industrious behavior, which was something the bureau favored, so there was no incentive to eliminate them.

The superintendent could not stamp out the influence of the healers because their cures for physical and mental illnesses were seen as being effective. As late as 1908 Superintendent George Haggett reported that "the Indian doctor [or doctors] has a strong hold on these Indians as yet."[44] However, the native healers, who included both men and women, could not effectively deal with the new diseases introduced after white contact, including tuberculosis and tracoma. As mentioned earlier, in the early twentieth century, both the superintendent and some Shoshones and Paiutes called for a hospital to be built. Finally, in 1917 the government converted the old reservation boarding school—built in 1892 and closed in 1914—into a makeshift hospital staffed with a physician.[45] With a new hospital the traditional healers' influence was markedly weakened but not completely wiped out. To this day some tribal people still use native medicine because it is effective in curing some ailments.

The superintendents also tried to eliminate native social gatherings and replace them with American patriotic holidays, especially the Fourth of July. The Shoshone and Paiutes ended up honoring the Fourth. However, they coopted the celebration by sponsoring the fandango, with its round dancing, singing, and handgames, in conjunction with the Fourth. The fandangos became an important annual event that attracted some Shoshones living elsewhere. The *Elko Free Press* reported in June 1914 that off-reservation Shoshones were traveling toward Duck Valley, about a month before the actual Fourth of July celebration.[46] Pleased that the Indians were at least honoring the Fourth, the superintendents took no drastic measures to end the fandangos, since such an action might have also ended the celebration of the Fourth.

Indian Bureau superintendents tried to eliminate the Indians' reliance upon hunting and gathering, native ways that persisted into the reservation period. The bureau's objective was to transform the Duck Valley people into small-time farmers, a way of life cherished by European

Americans. The government would provide monthly rations until the people were self-sufficient. Most Indians accepted the government plan, not because they favored assimilation, but because their native food sources had been severely reduced. They envisioned farming as a way to supplement their limited reliance on native foods. As early as 1883 some families grew small subsistence gardens of lettuce, cabbage, radishes, onions, and beets.[47]

Unfortunately, the residents of the Western Shoshone Reservation did not enjoy success in their agricultural pursuits. The valley floor lay at an altitude of 5,500 feet, which meant that the summer growing season was short and frosts were unpredictable. Only the hardiest crops survived. Furthermore, the Owyhee River, the primary source of water for irrigation, was almost dry by late June during most years. Without water in this high-dry desert region, the Indians could not effectively irrigate their crops. Thus the total acres cultivated during summer months always remained low: 230 acres in 1884, 320 acres in 1895, 200 acres in 1904, and 110 acres in 1912.[48] The amount of acreage cultivated each year was dependent upon dry or wet years, especially upon spring runoff from the nearby mountains.

By the turn of the century, the Indian Bureau realized that the Shoshones and Paiutes could not survive on small gardens coupled with periodic hunting and gathering. After listening to the tribal leaders, bureau officials decided to introduce cattle ranching. Roughly three-fourths of the reservation was mountainous with some natural spring water and wild hay meadows, a suitable environment for cattle grazing. Superintendent John Mayhugh advised in 1899 that the "attention of these Indians should be turned to the raising of stock."[49] One wonders why the Indian Bureau did not make this decision years earlier. Perhaps it considered cattle raising as a form of "nomadism," something negative and "Indianish" in the eyes of the bureau.

From 1900 the Indian Bureau moved forward with its new cattle program for the Duck Valley people. It channeled federal funds to purchase cattle for those who desired to become ranchers. It initially leased portions of the reservation to white cattle owners living near the reservation and used the proceeds to purchase more cattle. Over the years the herds of the Indians increased: 150 cattle in 1900, 550 in 1905, and 2,591 in 1917. The cattle were a source of food, and were sold at a profit. In 1916 alone, the Shoshones sold 177 heifers and 175 steers for a profit of $16,000.[50] Today, cattle raising has become the principal economic enterprise of several families of the Western Shoshone Reservation.

The Indian Bureau may have hoped that the Duck Valley people would become self-sufficient as ranchers, but this hope remained a dream. The Indian-owned cattle seldom numbered more than 2,000. The tribes could not raise enough alfalfa for winter feed because of the low midsummer level of the Owyhee River. They could grow more forage if a large, permanent dam could be built to preserve the annual spring runoff. The idea of a dam was discussed in 1882, 1888, and 1891, but no serious effort was undertaken until 1915 when the Indian Bureau determined that the best location for a dam was the Wild Horse Site, located thirty miles upriver from the reservation. Unfortunately, a fiscally conservative Congress was unwilling to provide the necessary funds to build the dam.[51] The Wild Horse Dam did not become a reality until 1937. Until then the Shoshone and Paiutes possessed only limited winter feed for the cattle.

Some heads of households realized that they could not become self-sufficient farmers or ranchers and made the decision to leave the reservation temporarily in search of employment. Most ended up working as ranchhands on the white-owned ranches near the reservation. By the 1920s roughly three-fourths of the heads of households were employed as seasonal laborers.[52] But they always returned to their reservation homes for most of the year.

In addition to its attempts to transform the lives of adult Indians, the Indian Bureau also turned its attention to the reservation youth. The federal government pushed for the assimilation of the younger generation through formal schooling. In 1881 the first reservation day school opened. The school offered European American courses, using textbooks such as *The Franklin Primary Arithmetic, Sheldon's Primary,* and *Cornell's First Steps in Geography*. The children also studied the New Testament. The curriculum emphasized the "three Rs." In addition, the children were forbidden to speak their native language or to practice their native ways.[53]

In 1893 the day school was replaced by a boarding school. The Indian Bureau made this change as a more effective means of "civilizing" the Indian children. In other words, the assimilation process was moving too slowly. If the students were placed in a boarding school, and not allowed to go home during weekday evenings, surely they would quickly forget their native language. However, the students continued to speak their native language in private in a rigid boarding school environment that existed well into the twentieth century.[54]

Because of deteriorating physical conditions, the Indian Bureau closed the reservation boarding school in 1915 and replaced it with two reservation day schools. A third day school was established in 1920. In time the bureau realized that its school system was inferior to public schools. In 1931 the three day schools were placed under the jurisdiction of the Nevada public school system.[55] The curriculum of the reservation schools always remained elementary; older students were sent to various large off-reservation boarding schools. But the parents, especially before 1900, opposed having their teenage children sent away from home. The bureau then took control of these students by asserting its authority. By 1910 eight students had attended the Carlisle Indian School in Pennsylvania. Five had gone to the Haskell Institute in Kansas, six to the Grand Junction Indian School in Colorado, three to the Santa Fe School in New Mexico, and fifteen to the Stewart Indian School in Carson City, Nevada.[56]

The government's objective was to move the older students from their home environment as far away as possible with the hope that they would not return and would lose their native identity in the larger society. This plan failed, for most did not assimilate into mainstream America. Nearly all the older students returned to Duck Valley, where they spent the rest of their lives. Some served on the Western Shoshone Council, including Thomas Premo and Fitz Smith, both of whom attended Carlisle, and Willie Wines and Frances Charles, who attended Stewart.[57] The former students never forgot their native culture, including the oral tradition. For example, before his death in 1969, Premo told the story of Captain Buck of Ruby Valley who moved to Duck Valley in 1879:

> So they picked out several people who came this way, to Duck Valley. Maybe there were six of them. Yes, there were six. Three were made delegates, and the other three just went along with them. Captain Buck told what their names were. "They were wise leaders," he said. They came here to look around. This area was called Western Shoshoni Duck Valley. There were many different kinds of food stuffs available here: there were many ducks, many sage hens, lots of deer, and they were not going to run out of firewood. Nor were they going to run out of fish.
>
> Soon afterwards, they came here. They were moved here under Captain Buck's name. This is what they did. They drove their cattle here, which were given to them at Ruby. . . . They also gave some cattle to some of those that did not come from Ruby. Then, when they settled down, their cattle, kept in the care of one man, increased in number.[58]

Premo also reminisced about the time he and some other students were forcibly taken away from their families and sent to Carlisle: "As they were being hauled away on a buggy their mothers ran behind them, crying, as far as the direction of Cold Springs [name of a spring some eight miles from the agency]. They did this because they didn't want them to leave."[59]

Without doubt the government effort to assimilate the Indians had a negative emotional impact on the reservation population. This was one reason why some adults turned to alcohol as a form of escape. As early as 1887, the consumption of alcohol on the reservation was increasing.[60] Because Native Americans could not legally purchase liquor at this time, some Duck Valley residents relied on white bootleggers in the nearby off-reservation border town of Mountain City. By the early twentieth century, drinking was evident at the annual Fourth of July celebrations. The problem of alcohol persists in the late twentieth century.

At different times in the early reservation days, the Shoshones and Paiutes were affected by developments outside the reservation. One of these was the Ghost Dance religion, an attempt to restore the old way of life. Like dozens of other tribes of the Far West, the two tribes of Duck Valley participated in the Ghost Dance religious rites in the late 1880s and early 1890s. The Ghost Dance was started by Northern Paiute prophet Wovoka who lived in Mason Valley, Nevada, some 500 miles southwest of Duck Valley. Wovoka said that the Indians must dance and sing over a period of time. This repeated action would eventually create a massive earthquake that would destroy all white people on the continent. The Indians, on the other hand, would be spared. Furthermore, all deceased Indians, along with the dead game animals, would return to life, and the native ways would be revived. This religious movement was in direct response to the disruption of the native way of life by white encroachment. It was also a response to the pressure the Indians felt from the Indian Bureau's assimilationist policies.[61]

The Shoshones and Paiutes of Duck Valley had already been deeply affected by white encroachment. Naturally, some longed for their native life. Duck Valley therefore became a hotbed for the Ghost Dance in northern Nevada. From August to December 1890, the two tribes sponsored three separate Ghost Dances, each lasting all night for about a week. Dancers at these festivals became exhausted from the religious fervor expressed in dance and song. The Ghost Dances were well attended; the second dance drew at least 1,000 participants, many from Fort Hall and other places.[62]

Reservation superintendent William Plumb blamed the outsiders for influencing the Duck Valley Shoshone and Paiutes; he did not realize that part of the local population itself believed in the religion. Plumb was fearful of the large crowds and requested the bureau to send him ten rifles in case the dancers became unruly. At the Ghost Dances, he asked disorderly outsiders to leave but allowed the friendly ones to remain.[63]

After the Wounded Knee Massacre in South Dakota on December 29, 1890, Agent Plumb restricted all Ghost Dances on the reservation, fearing that a similar outbreak might occur at Duck Valley. But he allowed the Indians to practice their native handgames. When the "Indian Christ" did not come, as promised by Wovoka, the Ghost Dance movement disappeared from the Duck Valley Reservation.[64]

Some Shoshones and Paiutes were also touched by the introduction of the peyote religion, a faith that began among tribes in Mexico. This intertribal religion uses the peyote cactus as a sacrament for healing and cleansing purposes. Peyote was introduced in 1915 to Duck Valley when a native woman had a physical ailment that did not respond to American-style medicine. Instead of turning to the local native healers, she sought out the peyote religion with a practitioner brought from the Fort Hall Reservation in Idaho.[65] Although this new religion was slow to take hold, a few members of the two tribes at Duck Valley chose to follow it. Perhaps some accepted the faith because of its antialcohol message.

The Shoshones and Paiutes also dealt with the issue of involvement in World War I. In February 1918 two Shoshone representatives from Fort Hall came to Duck Valley and asked the local population not to allow their young men to enter the armed forces. Their opposition stemmed from anger toward the whites. They interpreted World War I as an early twentieth-century effort to kill even more Indians by placing young native men at the front line in Europe. Their efforts to gain support, however, were not successful. There was marked opposition from the superintendent. Although some Duck Valley residents sympathized with the antiwar movement, most remained neutral, and some openly supported U.S. involvement. At least one young man, Gus Garity, of the Western Shoshone Reservation eventually served in the armed forces in World War I.[66] He later became actively involved in tribal politics in the 1950s and 1960s.

Shoshones along the Humboldt River, north-central Nevada, ca. 1860. *Special Collections, University of Nevada, Reno Library*.

Jennie (Wilson) Kawich and Bill Kawich, central Nevada, ca. 1905. *Nevada Historical Society*.

Thomas Premo, Shoshone from the Duck Valley Reservation, at Carlisle Indian
School, Pennsylvania, ca. 1905. *Inter-Tribal Council of Nevada, Reno*.

George Yowell, Elko Nevada, ca. 1910. *Nevada State Historical Society, Reno.*

Duck Valley Reservation, date unknown. Back row (center): Alex Gilbert; front row (l–r): unknown, Inez Gilbert, Louella Gilbert, Agnes Gilbert. *Beverly Crum*.

OPPOSITE TOP: Shoshone students in Ely, Nevada, ca. 1920. Back row (3rd and 4th from left): Rosie McQueen, Gladys Johnson; front row (l–r): Majorie (Stanton) Stark, Robin Stanton, unknown, Willie Adams. *Special Collections, University of Nevada, Reno Library*.

OPPOSITE BOTTOM: Shoshones from Death Valley, ca. 1930 (l–r): John Boland, Nellie Thompson, Molly Shoshone, child unknown. *Bancroft Library, Berkeley, Calif*.

Basketmaker, Death Valley, 1931. *Julian Steward Papers, University of Illinois, Champaign-Urbana.*

Jennie Washburn, central Nevada, 1935. *Julian Steward Papers, University of Illinois, Champaign-Urbana.*

Tribe Brings Resolution

Chief Annie Tomy, left; Chief Thomas J. Pabowena, center, and Chief Billy Myers, representatives of the Shoshone Indian tribes, said in Salt Lake City Monday their tribesmen are willing to fight only if the United States is invaded.

Shoshones and Goshutes confer about the growing threat of war. *Salt Lake Tribune, 5 November 1940.*

The Battle Mountain Shoshones invite Senator Patrick McCarran to their fandango, 1947 (l–r): Dan Shovelin, Jim Street, Patrick McCarran, unknown. *Nevada State Historical Society, Reno.*

Young Women from the Duck Valley Reservation, early 1930s (left to right): unknown, Mildred (Premo) Scissons, unknown, Edith (McKee) Shaw, Velma McNeally, and Inez (Gilbert) Leach. *Inter-Tribal Council of Nevada, Reno.*

Harry Dixon, an active Shoshone politician in the 1920s, 1935. *Amy Timbim-boo, Clearfield, Utah*.

Frank Temoke, Sr., 1972, an active Shoshone leader and heredi* chief since the 1950s. *The Northeastern Nevada Museum, Elko, Nevada.*

4

THE NONRESERVATION SHOSHONE
1880–1933

As discussed in chapters 2 and 3, the Indian Bureau's major objective around 1880 was to "concentrate" all the Western Shoshones in Nevada on the Western Shoshone Reservation (Duck Valley) at "as early a date as possible."[1] However, the federal government had failed in its attempts to persuade all the Western Shoshones to move. Deeply attached to their own particular regions, the various groups had no desire to relocate elsewhere. As a result only one-third had moved to Duck Valley by 1880. The rest remained at their native places in the Great Basin.[2] This ratio remained much the same in the early years of the twentieth century.

The federal government punished the nonreservation Western Shoshones by ignoring them, even though they represented the majority of the tribe. This meant that they received little or no federal aid. This policy of neglect was carried out despite the fact that all the Western Shoshones of the Great Basin were in theory under the jurisdiction of the Western Shoshone Agency (Duck Valley) after 1880.

The numerous nonreservation Shoshones therefore eked out a bare living on their own for many years. After 1910, however, the government made belated, meager efforts to help the majority of Basin Shoshones. From 1911 to 1925 the Shoshones were placed under the newly created Reno Agency of the Indian Bureau. When this agency was abolished in 1925, the Shoshones in northeastern Nevada were placed under the already existing Carson Agency. Those living in central and southern Nevada were placed under the Walker River Agency.[3] Regardless of the supervising agency, the Indian Bureau provided only nominal support in the early twentieth century. In fact, nearly all the nonreservation Western Shoshones were classified as "nonwards" and "landless" since they did not live on reservation land with federal trust status.

The nonreservation Western Shoshones did not lose touch with the

Shoshones who lived on the reservation in Duck Valley. Nor did they abandon their distinctive native culture. These Shoshones managed to shape their own history with only limited input from the federal sector. They adapted to the larger white world of the Great Basin, yet at the same time maintained their native identity.

In the late nineteenth and early twentieth centuries, Shoshone culture was best expressed in the the celebrations called fandangos, which featured round dances, songs, handgames, and feasting. These festivals were held in different parts of Shoshone country, including Battle Mountain, Austin, Elko, Smoky Valley, and Ruby Valley. They were led by local leaders, including Captain Bob of Battle Mountain, Joe Gilbert of Austin, Sam Courts of Big Smoky Valley (or Smoky Valley as it is popularly called), and Chief Blackeye of Duckwater. Usually the fandangos attracted large crowds, sometimes as many as 300 to 500 people, for the Shoshones had an active interest in preserving their traditions.[4] At the fandangos, nonreservation Shoshones along with some from Duck Valley gathered to carry out their native traditions and to talk over tribal events and concerns.

The fandango became more than a Shoshone cultural event. The Indians added new elements, including the discussion of modern-day political issues, tribal concerns, and elections. At the Fort Halleck fandango in 1889 the participants talked about the Indian Bureau agents who had served the Indians in Nevada. They concluded that John Mayhugh, former agent for the Western Shoshone Agency, was a competent agent, even though his agency largely overlooked the needs of the nonreservation Shoshones. At the Austin fandango in 1923 the leaders asked for reservation land so that they wouldn't have to pay state taxes. They also held elections at fandangos to choose new leaders. For example, at the Battle Mountain fandango in 1894, they chose Indian Bill to replace Captain Bob who had died earlier that year. In 1922 the Shoshones held a major election at Battle Mountain in which several persons were voted into office. Harry Dixon of Grass Valley was chosen as overall "chief of the Shoshone Indians in Nevada," Jim Leach for Battle Mountain, Dick Beeler as his assistant, Dick Hall for Elko, and Bill Hall for Beowawe. Before white contact the Shoshones did not formally vote for their leaders.[5]

The Shoshones also added new social aspects to the fandangos, including footraces, horse racing, and rodeos. Baseball became perhaps the most important pastime. The Battle Mountain Indian team beat the Battle Mountain white team in 1921. The Duckwater Shoshones played against the Austin Shoshones in 1919. At times, especially after the turn of the century, some fandangos became associated with larger American gatherings. Elko Shoshones held fandangos during Labor Day weekend during the Elko county fair, and the Austin fandangos became part of the

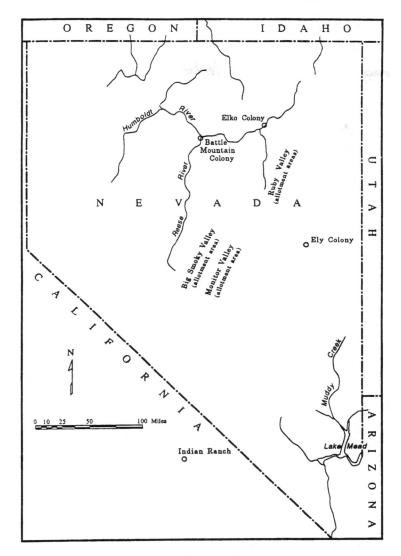

Lands Allocated for Western Shoshone (1910–1931)

Fourth of July celebrations. At other places the fandangos were held in September or October, either before or after the pine nut harvest.[6]

The late Danny Millett of Duckwater reflected upon the gatherings held in Smoky Valley years ago:

Let's talk about the fandango in Smoky Valley . . . Chief run this fandango every year . . . when the people would get through with the haying time. It's around the last of August sometimes. Then this chief let all the people know before or ahead of time about a month or a little bit more too . . . we go up in the mountain in the wagon, pulled with the horses, two horses, and we get some wood, a couple or few times before the people comes. We unload them in the fandango ground where the people going to have the campings and they going to use that wood, because you can't find wood down in the Smoky Valley . . . we see the people coming in the fandango ground in the morning or afternoon or tomorrow. Then you can see them coming on the horses and packing their food on the horses, the blankets, all tied on the horses, and maybe they come on the north, they're coming on the south, or whichever way they come. The chief is standing there, telling them on the road to stop there . . . That fandango for the Indians, long time ago, they tell me that the old timers, they didn't just go for the dances. They make that good for the country. And pine nuts grew good, they said. And sometimes they had pine nuts and just scattered them all over where they were dancing.[7]

As with other tribal groups of the Far West, the Western Shoshones were also influenced by the Ghost Dance religion of the late nineteenth century with its fervent appeal to tradition and its antiwhite message, as described in chapter 3.[8] Because their own tribal way of life had been disrupted by the whites, some Western Shoshone accepted the Ghost Dance and all that it stood for. Beginning in 1890, when the religion was at its zenith, they performed Ghost Dances at different localities in Nevada, including Austin, Marshall Canyon (north of Austin), Deeth, Battle Mountain, Elko, Starr Valley, and Wells. There were several Ghost Dance Shoshone leaders, such as Captain Bob of Battle Mountain and Harry Preacher of Wells.[9] The Shoshones patterned the Ghost Dances after the round dances they had practiced traditionally.

The Ghost Dance religion among the Shoshones had both positive and negative effects. On the negative side it caused hysteria among the whites in Nevada, who were afraid that the Shoshones and other tribes were planning warfare against them. In early November 1890 some settlers of Austin and Ione in central Nevada telegraphed the governor's office, requesting arms and ammunition for protective purposes. The governor granted their request, but the weapons were never used against the Indians. In other parts of Nevada as well, fear caused whites to condemn the Shoshones. The editor of the *Weekly Elko Independent* published the oft-repeated and popular statement that "the only good Indians are dead ones." On more than one occasion the Shoshones informed the whites that they were peaceful and had no intention of making war. On the positive side, the Ghost Dance religion helped revive the traditional round dances in some Shoshone groups that had stopped performing them. For example, the dances had not been performed in Battle Mountain for "over ten years" until revived by the Ghost Dance movement in late 1890.[10]

Because their native hunting and gathering economy had been permanently disrupted, the nonreservation Shoshones continued to search for new means of subsistence. Like families on the reservation, many nonreservation families worked on the scattered and isolated white-owned ranches where the men served as ranchhands and cowboys and the women as housemaids. Some families raised their own small gardens. One Shoshone in Smoky Valley sold his extra produce to the whites in Belmont, Nevada; the whites called him Rutabaga, and his son was Rutabaga Bob. In central Nevada some Shoshones cut and sold wood to the local white people, while others were hired as mailmen, making deliveries in the area of Belmont and Tybo. During the mining boom in the early twentieth century, the Shoshone became a major source of mine labor. It was determined that 60 percent of the employees of the Round Mountain Mining Company in Big Smoky Valley in 1921 were Indian. Still other Shoshones raised cattle and horses for extra income. Regardless of the new economic order, many or most continued to gather and hunt native food, but not as intensively as in the past.[11]

Some off-reservation Shoshone women, like the women on the reservation, made and sold baskets as an added source of income. In precontact times they had made baskets for cooking, storage, and harvesting. These traditional items had geometric designs. By the early twentieth century, Shoshone basketry had begun to change. It was no longer made for utilitarian purposes only; more frequently, baskets were made for sale to white buyers. The women of Inyo County, California (Death Valley, Darwin, and Lone Pine), sold their work to purchase food and medicine. Besides those in Inyo County, California, some women in Nevada also sold their baskets for profit. One of the noted basketmakers of northeastern Nevada was Mary Hall of Beowawe. Her work included traditional geometric designs as well as newly introduced floral designs. Some of her baskets were extremely large, one of them being used as a laundry basket by a white ranch family in the 1920s.[12]

It was tough to make a living in the early years of the twentieth century. Some Shoshones awoke to the fact that they were being used as a cheap source of labor. In 1901 some in the Reese River Valley went on strike and demanded more pay, reduced working hours, and the privilege of eating meals in the bosses' dining room. Undoubtedly, they were influenced by the strikes called by organized white labor at the turn of the century. In 1904 other Shoshones in Eureka County captured and sold wild horses. This caused whites to view these Indians as a threat, since the whites considered the unclaimed horses as their property. In the years after 1910, the U.S. Forest Service required some Indians of central Nevada to pay taxes for grazing their stock on the Toiyabe National Forest, which had been created in 1907. When they could not make the payments, forest officials killed their horses. Even further, in 1909 the state of Nevada passed a law specifying that all Indians had to hunt within designated seasons and only with permits.[13] Thus the off-reservation Shoshones found it difficult to survive after 1900.

A few Shoshones had to stand up to white people to make a living. In September 1905 Johnnie and Minnie Peavine of central Nevada made an agreement with Ed Clifford and other non-Indian mining prospectors. According to its terms the parties involved were to explore for mineral wealth in northern Nye County in the vicinity of Clifford. Because of his knowledge of this part of Shoshone country, Peavine was given a horse, food, and equipment to locate silver deposits. Once lodes were discovered and the wealth extracted, Peavine and his wife were to receive one-fourth of the proceeds. But Clifford and his associates did not pay the Shoshone couple. The Peavines filed suit in the Nye County District Court. After her husband's death, Minnie eventually won a decision in her favor.[14]

A bad economy was one reason why some Shoshone families left their traditional home areas and moved elsewhere. Families in central Nevada moved after the collapse of the mining economy of that region. From 1908 to 1918 the Shoshones of Smoky Valley and adjacent places had benefited from the mining boom. They had worked either as miners or in jobs that resulted from the mining boom, such as wood cutting, selling garden produce, and delivering mail between the small mining settlements of Belmont, Tybo, and Reveille. But with the decline of the mining industry these jobs withered away.[15] To survive, some families moved westward where opportunities were better. By the 1920s nine families of central Nevada, primarily from Smoky Valley, had settled on the Fallon Reservation, and thirteen others on the Walker River Reservation.[16] Both reservations are located in western Nevada and had been created for the Northern Paiutes in the nineteenth century.

Some of the central Nevada Shoshone chose the Walker River Reservation because in 1926 their home area fell under the jurisdiction of Walker River. Superintendent Ray Parrett, fully aware of the bad economic situation in central Nevada, encouraged the Shoshones to move to Walker River. In response James Darrough and Bud Decker, both from Smoky Valley, moved their families and eventually secured twenty-acre allotments on the Paiute reservation. They joined other Shoshone heads of households who were already living there, including Dave (Kawich) Clifford of the Belmont region, Frank and Truman Collins of Duckwater,

Dimmie Jackson of Austin, and John Fisherman and Rutabaga Bob from Smoky Valley.[17]

After a few years the Shoshone families became an integral part of the Paiute communities at Walker River and the Fallon Reservation. In the 1930s Albert Hicks, Sr., was the vice-president of the Fallon Tribal Council, and Bodie Graham was the tribal secretary. Dave Clifford and Horace Greeley were elected to the Walker River Council, also in the 1930s. All these men were Shoshones.[18] Some Shoshones made the two Paiute reservations their permanent homes. By 1960 roughly one-fourth of the Fallon Reservation was Shoshone, and the reservation population today calls itself the Fallon-Paiute-Shoshone Tribe. However, many of the Shoshones returned to central Nevada in the late 1930s and early 1940s after the federal government had purchased new reservation land for them.

There were reasons other than economic factors behind the Shoshone migration from central Nevada. One pull factor was the friendship established between Paiutes and Shoshones working together in the Reese River and Smoky Valley mines up to 1920. When Paiutes returned home, they encouraged some Shoshone friends to come with them. Thus Horace Greeley, a Shoshone, ended up on the Walker River Reservation before the turn of the century, and Albert Hicks, Sr., from Hot Creek in central Nevada, moved to Fallon in 1900.[19]

Another attraction was the Stewart Indian School, established in Carson City in 1890 to educate Indian students. When some Shoshones finished their education there, they remained, securing jobs and often intermarrying with the Paiutes. One of these persons was Bodie Graham of Tonopah who graduated from Stewart in 1901.[20] Graham settled down on the Fallon reservation where he got some land and received tribal membership.

Still another factor was the creation of the Toiyabe National Forest in 1907. Roughly 2.1 million acres of land were set aside as federally owned forest in central Nevada. It included the mountain ranges between the Reese River, Smoky, and Monitor valleys and stretched from Tonopah on south to Austin on the north. The Shoshones had lived in this region for countless generations, first as hunters and gatherers, and later on established homesteads with small subsistence gardens. Once the land became federal forest, the Indians could only graze their stock there by obtaining permits and paying fees, which many could not afford.[21] Thus, the Indians lost another source of income.

Still another factor was the state of Nevada's hunting and fishing laws. In 1909 these laws required all Indians to secure licenses for fishing and hunting. When the Shoshones chose to hunt as their ancestors had done since time immemorial, they were told they had to secure licenses beforehand and that they could only hunt within seasons designated by the whites. These laws restricted a native Shoshone practice or, as the Indians put it, "closed on us."[22]

Besides those of central Nevada, other Shoshones also changed residence in the early years of the twentieth century. At least two Shoshone families left Ruby Valley and moved to the Goshute Reservation, established in 1914 and located along the Nevada-Utah border. Around 1915 Al Steele moved to Goshute after being invited there by his friend John Syme. Around 1920 his son Frank Steele also left Ruby Valley and established residence at Goshute. It appears that Frank wanted to stay in Ruby Valley if the government recognized the existence of the "six miles square" reservation. According to one federal official, Frank Steele "was outspoken in the opinion that a reservation should be provided for them in Ruby Valley and that money was still due them from the government."[23] He was one of the many Shoshones who fully realized that the government had never kept its side of the Ruby Valley treaty bargain.

Eventually, the Steeles became enrolled members of the Goshute Reservation and also became leading political figures. After the Goshutes organized a formal tribal council in 1941, Frank, his two sons Bob and Jimmy, and one daughter Rosa all became council members. Rosa Steele went on to earn a bachelor's degree in teaching from Santa Barbara State Teacher's College (today's University of California at Santa Barbara) in 1940. The Steeles still have a connection to Ruby Valley: Frank Steele's eighty-acre allotment there is now owned by a grandson.[24]

Other Shoshones also moved away from their native areas. Some left the region along the Nevada-California border and moved to the Northern Paiute area of Owens Valley in eastern California. The Shoshones made this decision for at least two reasons. First, in 1912 the Indian Bureau had established the Bishop Sub-Agency as an arm of the larger Carson Indian Agency in Nevada. The Bishop office was intended to serve both Shoshones and Paiutes living in Inyo and Mono counties. When some Shoshones of eastern Inyo County heard about this assistance, they moved westward into Owens Valley to secure some federal support. Second, Owens Valley had become the main travel route and trade center of eastern California, so it offered job opportunities. By 1930, according to an Indian Bureau census roll, the following Shoshone family heads were living in Bishop, Big Pine, and Lone Pine: Frank Bellas, Chappe Bellas, Bob Best, Louis Brown, Willie Brown, Nellie Burkhart, and Georgia Button.[25] The Shoshones intermarried with the Paiutes, and the Indians of Owens Valley now call themselves the Paiute-Shoshone Tribes of Owens Valley.

Most Shoshones remained within their native areas, although some did change locations within the tribal territory up to the early 1930s. Willie and Josie Carson left Ruby Valley and moved to Elko in 1923 after the Indian Bureau built houses for the Shoshones on the newly established 160-acre Elko Colony site. They also wanted their children to attend the new Indian school located near the colony. Some Shoshone families left central Nevada and moved north to Battle Mountain to find jobs on the nearby ranches. Eunice Silva and Hazel Millett, both born at Silver Creek, and Jack Muncey, Dick Beeler, and Hank Tu-tu-wa (Toi-Toi), all of Austin, made Battle Mountain their home after 1910.[26]

Although the nonreservation Western Shoshones did not live on reservation land, and thus were not under constant Indian Bureau supervision, they too were subject to federal government policies. One of these was education for the young people. Older students were sent primarily to two large off-reservation boarding schools: the Stewart Indian School, adjacent to Carson City, Nevada, and the much larger Carlisle Indian School in Pennsylvania. The purpose of these schools was to remove students from their home environments and assimilate them into the dominant society. The Indian Bureau hoped that the native youngsters would lose their cultural and tribal identities.[27]

The assimilation effort was largely a failure. Nearly all the Shoshones sent to the off-reservation schools never did become fully assimilated. Instead, they returned to the Shoshone country of the Great Basin and retained their native identity, although they had been acculturated to some extent by their schooling. Some of the former students even used their education against the federal government. For example, after leaving Carlisle in 1908, James Pabawena returned to Wells where he wrote numerous letters to high officials, including Theodore Roosevelt. He argued that because of the treaty of 1863 the Shoshones were still the owners and occupants of their land. Thus they could hunt without penalty. Pabawena could not understand why Nevada officials arrested the Indians for hunting out of season and without licenses. In his letters he spoke of "this country of ours" and maintained that "I am one of the owners of the American soil."[28]

Bill Gibson of Elko was one Shoshone leader who emerged after the boarding school experience. He attended the Stewart Indian School in the 1890s. After returning to northeastern Nevada, Gibson became an advocate of Western Shoshone treaty rights. On December 15, 1912, Gibson, Pabawena, and other Shoshone leaders held a mass meeting in Elko.[29] It was perhaps the largest gathering since the 1863 treaty and also the first Shoshone claims meeting of the twentieth century. Gibson and his comrades claimed that the provisions of the treaty had not been carried out. Because the government had not yet complied with the treaty, and because the treaty acknowledged the Shoshones as the owners of a treaty territory in the Great Basin, Gibson asserted that the Shoshones had never lost title to their land. Some years after this meeting, he wrote, "My old people has not sold any land to the White people . . . [my people] has not sold land yet."[30] Gibson went on to assert that the Shoshones had the right to hunt inside their treaty territory at "any time." It was Gibson's boarding school education that enabled him to express his views in writing as a Shoshone.

Other Western Shoshone students attended school in their native areas in the Great Basin. In the 1920s two Indian schools were established in northeastern Nevada, one in Elko and the second in Battle Mountain. These public elementary schools, for Shoshone only, were run by the Nevada state public school system with financial assistance from the Indian Bureau. The small two-room schoolhouse in Elko was located near the Indian colony. The one in Battle Mountain was adjacent to the larger all-white elementary school. The schools were built for two main reasons. First, Indian parents preferred having their children educated at home rather than sending them to some distant boarding school. Second, the racist white parents and politicians of Nevada also favored the separate schools because they didn't want their children mingling with the Indians whom they regarded as inferior. This white racism also explains why the Indian children in Ely were placed in a segregated classroom in the Ely public elementary school in the early years of the twentieth century.[31] Thus the whites of Nevada created their own "separate but equal" policy as applied to the Western Shoshones.

Other Shoshone students across the Great Basin attended the regular integrated public schools in their respective locations. In 1918, 114 students were enrolled; their tuition was paid by the Indian Bureau.[32] The enrollment figure was low because some parents simply refused to place their children in the white man's schools. Certainly this was the case with Eunice Silva of Battle Mountain whose parents moved about for this reason. "People say the white people are going to kill the Indian kids," Eunice stated later in her life.[33] Besides the public schools in Nevada, a few Shoshones attended special private schools. Willie Joaquin, Jr., of Battle Mountain attended the Cushing Academy in Massachusetts in the 1920s. He went there at the recommendation of Frank Curran, a former district attorney of Lander County, Nevada, who had attended Cushing some years earlier. Thanks to the education he received there, Joaquin was employed by the Indian Bureau in the 1930s.[34]

Overall, the nonreservation Western Shoshones both disliked and favored the white man's education. They despised it because they recognized the government's agenda—its attempts to change the Indians and rule out native culture. But they also favored education since it enabled Indians to fit into the larger dominant society.

The Shoshones did not always favor the government policies coming out of Washington, D.C. For example, some of them rejected the Indian Citizenship Act of 1924. This act granted U.S. citizenship to those Native Americans who did not have this status before 1924. Most Shoshones became citizens in that year since only a few had owned individual land allotment or had fought in World War I, either of which would have enabled them to become citizens earlier. But when they received word that Congress had applied the law to them and thousands of other Native Americans, their immediate response was rejection. A few of the Shoshones were fearful that their special wardship status would end under citizenship. As long as they were wards of the government, they would continue to receive some Indian Bureau services. Other Shoshones considered themselves as constituting a sovereign nation equal to the United States, so that the United States had no right to make them accept citizenship. These Shoshones referred to the 1863 Ruby Valley treaty, negotiated between two sovereign states. Still others were fearful that they would have to pay taxes, just like white people, which they did after 1924.[35]

To oppose citizenship, several Western Shoshone and Northern Paiute leaders sponsored anticitizenship meetings in northern Nevada from 1924 to 1930. In 1924 alone, they held two meetings in Shoshone country, one in Battle Mountain, and the other in Elko. They held other meetings on the Fort McDermitt (Paiute) Reservation.[36] As a result of these efforts, most Shoshones—at least those in northern Nevada—refused to register to vote in local, state, and national elections. The Shoshones in general did not vote until the 1930s, when Franklin Roosevelt's New Deal brought socioeconomic reforms that the Shoshones favored.

The nonreservation Western Shoshones also became subject to state and federal laws concerning minor and major crimes. This issue came up in January 1883 when W. S. Bryden, sheriff for Nye County, Nevada, asked the Indian Bureau who had jurisdiction over Indian offenses committed off-reservation. The bureau's response was that Indian offenders should be treated like non-Indians and should be tried in local courts. The federal government would not become involved.[37]

The bureau's opinion was incorrect, for the Indian tribes across the country still had jurisdiction over their own crimes in 1883. This legal principle became an issue in Nevada when Spanish Jim, a Shoshone, murdered an Indian woman in Belmont. He was convicted of murder by a white jury in Nye County. This case was appealed to the Nevada supreme court. In the end the charge was dropped on the grounds that Indians by law still had jurisdiction over their own crimes. In 1885 the federal Major Crimes Act gave the American courts control of crimes committed by one Indian against another.[38] Thus, for offenses that occurred after 1885, the Shoshones were sent to the white man's courts.

The nonreservation Shoshones were also affected by federal and state laws concerning liquor. Going back to the early nineteenth century, the federal government had included in its Indian Trade and Intercourse laws that white traders could not sell liquor to the Indians. Government officials had concluded that strong drink was a major cause of trouble between whites and Indians. In 1877, and again in 1885, the state of Nevada supported the federal position by passing state liquor laws providing that whites would be fined or imprisoned if they sold alcohol to the Indians. Some were punished for breaking these laws, and three were confined to the Nevada State Penitentiary in 1905.[39]

Unfortunately, some unscrupulous whites continued to sell liquor since they made huge profits as bootleggers. Some Shoshones were arrested for committing offenses while under the influence. The unlawful selling of liquor became a major concern of some Shoshone leaders at the turn of the century.[40]

In some instances, the nonreservation Shoshones were subject to vigilante justice at the hands of white Nevadans. One incident that took place in early 1911 involved Shoshone Mike and his band, consisting of a wife, three sons, and other followers. Shoshone Mike (also known as Rock Creek Mike, Indian Mike, and Mike Daggett) rejected the notion of settling down on a reservation. Instead, he chose to follow native ways by living off the land. To do so he had to cover a large area of northern Nevada, even outside of Shoshone territory. He often resorted to rustling non-Indian-owned range cattle during the bleak winter months.[41]

In January 1911, one cattle company near the Nevada-California border discovered that some of its stock were missing. A party of four men was sent to investigate. They never returned home and were later found dead. Immediately the whites suspected Shoshone Mike of the murders, although no evidence ever came to light to indicate that he and his followers were guilty. Motivated by a fifteen thousand dollar reward, a posse spent several days tracking Mike and his band. With the help of a Paiute tracker, they finally found the Shoshones in Clover Valley in northeastern Nevada. A battle ensued in which Shoshone Mike and seven others were killed. Only four survived.[42]

Shoshone Mike was victim of a crime that was never proven. Perhaps he was blamed because of his notoriety as an unruly and aggressive individual. According to the Shoshone oral tradition, on occasion he had threatened his own kind. This was one reason why his sister had left the band earlier and moved to the Duck Valley Reservation. After the 1911 incident, some Shoshones distanced themselves from the legacy of Shoshone Mike. The Ruby Valley Shoshones later expressed disapproval of Shoshone Mike.[43]

Another well-known incident in 1918 directly affected the Western Shoshones. This case involved the opposition of the Goshute Reservation

Indians to the draft during World War I. On May 18, 1917, Congress passed the Selective Service Act, which stated that all men between the ages of twenty-one and thirty-one had to register for the draft. Indians were also required to register, unless they could prove noncitizenship status. The superintendents of the various reservations were given the task of registering reservation Indians.[44]

Amos Frank, superintendent of the Goshute Reservation straddling the Nevada-Utah border, became the Goshutes' bitter foe when he tried to make them register. The Indians refused because of the government's failure to honor the Goshute Treaty of 1863. They were also angry because Frank had not dealt with Goshute concerns, including unsolved crimes committed against the Indians. Frank also favored non-Indians, hiring European Americans for reservation jobs before hiring Indians. Therefore the younger Goshutes refused to register, and the elders encouraged them in this course of action.[45]

Federal officials were called in to investigate the Goshute situation; when the Indians remained adamant about their antidraft position, the government took action. On February 22, 1918, three military officers and fifty-one regular troops of Fort Douglas in Salt Lake City entered the Goshute Reservation and arrested seven men: three draft evaders and four older ringleaders who opposed native involvement in the war. Two of them were Western Shoshones from Nevada. Jack Temoke of Ruby Valley was arrested as an evader while visiting friends at Goshute, and Al Steele, who had permanently moved to Goshute from Ruby Valley, was one of the older individuals opposed to the draft. All seven, including the two Shoshones, were released following their arrest, and the charges were dropped. The federal government admitted that those arrested were not U.S. citizens in 1917 and 1918, and therefore they were not subject to the draft.[46]

This World War I drama in the Great Basin did not end with the Indians' release. Once the Goshute affair was publicized in the newspapers, the public overreacted. The whites once again concluded that the Goshutes, as well as the Shoshones in eastern Nevada, were preparing an "uprising" against the white Americans. There was talk that a Goshute had gone to the Shoshones in Ruby Valley, Elko, and even Death Valley, California, to incite Shoshone rebellion. As late as April 1918 there were rumors that German spies were spreading propaganda among the Shoshones.[47] These stories were groundless, a result of domestic wartime hysteria. To convince the whites that Shoshones were friends and not enemies, Muchach Temoke of Ruby Valley stated that the Indians harbored no animosity toward the whites. Although the Shoshones were not U.S. citizens, Temoke said, they would go to war if Germany invaded the United States.[48] By late 1918 the hysteria in the Great Basin had faded away. In the end, two nonreservation Western Shoshones served during World War I: Doc Bird of Wells and Frank Rogers of Round Mountain.

Although the majority of Western Shoshones had remained in their native areas rather than move to the Duck Valley Reservation, the Indian Bureau remained adamant that the nonreservation Shoshones should move to Duck Valley.[49] The bureau opposed the creation of other sizable reservations for the Shoshones in the late nineteenth and early twentieth centuries. But with the establishment of the Reno Agency in 1912, the bureau finally awoke to the fact that the majority of Western Shoshones remained off-reservation. Furthermore, some Shoshones of central Nevada were regarded as squatters by the government for living inside the boundaries of the Toiyabe National Forest, although in fact the formation of this new forest reserve had robbed them of their ancestral land. Other Shoshones living near the national forest could not prove title to their land since they did not have an American-style deed of ownership. To rectify this situation, Calvin Asbury of the Reno Agency had the government set aside fourteen individual allotments in and around the national forest. Six men were given 160-acre allotments outside but near the forest: Sam Courts, Jim Spud, John Fisherman, Tim Hooper, Docke Moore, and Mike Millett. Six others were granted allotments inside the forest boundaries: James Bobb (80 acres), Wagon Johnny (27), Jim Ike (70), Bud Decker (54), Frank Charley (37), and Sambo Smith (29).[50] All these allotments were located in the Reese River, Smoky, and Monitor valleys. Two other Shoshones, Charley Tom and One Arm Bob, were also granted allotments (80 acres and 16 acres, respectively) in central Nevada, located some distance from the Toiyabe Forest.

These fourteen allotments, totalling 1,353 acres, were created under the authority of the Dawes Allotment Act of 1887. This land law and its revisions permitted Indians to secure individual land allotments on so-called public domain land.[51] It must be emphasized that these small allotments in a desert region could not sustain the families living there. This explains why some made the decision to move to Fallon and Walker River in the 1920s, as recounted above.

The Reno Agency also helped eleven Shoshones of Ruby Valley to secure title to small public domain allotments: Muchach Temoke (70 acres), Brownie Mose (80), Frank Jim (40), Frank Steele (80), George Moore (160), Frank Van Fossen (80), Julie Fletcher (80), Little George (160), Burt Moon (160), Friday Bill (160), and Joe Temoke (40). Most of these were located adjacent to or near the Overland Creek, or inside the never surveyed "six miles square" reservation area. Upon the recommendation of the Reno Agency, President William H. Taft established a small, 120-acre reservation by executive order in September 1912.[52] In all, a total of 1,230 acres of land, including the eleven allotments and the small reservation, was set aside in Ruby Valley in the early twentieth century. The government, however, was still unwilling to reestablish the "six miles square" reservation for the Ruby Valley.

The federal government did more than grant small allotments to some Basin Shoshones. In the second decade of the century, it started creating "colonies" for those Nevada tribal people who lived within or adjacent to several towns and cities in Nevada. The "colony" program was "a name apparently unique to Nevada," according to scholar Elmer Rusco. This program was partly a result of the Indian Bureau's new policy of giving attention to those small tribal groups that had been largely ignored for decades.[53] The government hired Lorenzo Creel as a "special supervisor" in 1917 to investigate Nevada's Indians and to determine who should receive federal trust land. Previously, his work had led to the creation of two small reservations for the Shoshone-speaking Goshutes of Utah: the Skull Valley Reservation in 1912 and the larger Goshute Reservation in 1914.[54]

Over a period of months in 1917 Creel visited the nonreservation Indians of Nevada, including several Shoshone groups. He submitted several lengthy reports on his field trips, titling one of them his "Final Report" on so-called "homeless Indians."[55] This title was inaccurate, since as far as Nevada's Indians were concerned they were already living on their native homelands. Creel might more appropriately have called them nonreservation Indians. Nevertheless, his report was convincing proof that the Indian Bureau needed to give more attention to Nevada's neglected native peoples who had no reservation land.

Creel recommended that land be set aside for the nonreservation Shoshones living in Battle Mountain, Elko, and the Duckwater Valley. He did not favor a colony in Ely. The Shoshones in Ely were already living on a small section of land owned by the Ely Townsite Company, located on a hillside south of town. They had to haul water uphill to their dwellings. Creel did mention the possibility of piping water uphill to the settlement, but this would be expensive and would not improve their economic plight. Creel also did not recommend setting aside land for Shoshones living in Eureka, Tonopah, Hot Creek, and the Monitor and Big Smoky valleys, all in central Nevada.[56]

On June 18, 1917, the federal government created by presidential executive order the 680-acre Battle Mountain Colony held in trust for the local Shoshones. Creel expected Battle Mountain and other newly established Nevada colonies to become well-balanced Indian communities with federally run schools, federally built houses with modern conveniences, and community centers. His dream did not become reality for Battle Mountain in the early years. The site was located almost one mile from downtown Battle Mountain, where most of the Indians lived, and no houses were built on the new colony site. In 1919 Indian Bureau officials dug an artesian well for irrigation purposes, but no farming was done. Two years later the American Baptist Home Mission Society tried but failed to establish a mission at the colony, an idea favored by the Indian Bureau. In 1923 the government supplied posts and wire for a fencing project. As before, nothing happened. Without houses to live in at the colony, the Shoshones chose to remain in and near the downtown area where some had jobs. In November 1931 Albert Grorud, an employee of the Senate Committee on Indian Affairs, visited the Shoshones in Battle Mountain and concluded that they needed assistance.[57] In the end no one moved to the colony until the mid-1930s when the government finally built houses.

The second Western Shoshone colony to be established was the 160-acre Elko Colony, set aside by executive order on March 23, 1918. Located on a hill overlooking the city of Elko, this tract had been set aside from 1907 to 1915 for the Shoshones but had reverted to public domain when the Indian Bureau took no interest in its development.[58] Due to Creel's efforts, the site was once again declared federal Indian trust land in 1918. Unlike the situation at Battle Mountain, interested persons helped develop the Elko Colony, including a local physician, Dr. John Worden; James E. Jenkins, the new superintendent of the Reno Agency; and a special committee of the Elko Lions Club. In 1923 the bureau built ten small houses on the colony site, and several Shoshone families moved in. Unfortunately, their homes did not have running water or sewage facilities.[59]

In the early 1930s the Shoshones had to abandon the entire site after the white residents of Elko unjustifiably complained that the sewage of the colony had contaminated part of the city's water supply. The Shoshone occupants moved to a much smaller, thirty-three-acre colony site. This new colony was established by congressional act in 1931 after Congress appropriated funds to purchase it from Dr. Worden. Additional federal funds allowed the government to build thirty houses in 1932.[60]

The ten-acre Ely Colony was the third to be established for the Western Shoshones, even though Creel had not recommended an Indian colony for Ely. It was initiated by Shoshone leader Harry Johnny. In September 1928 Johnny said that the Indians wanted running water piped uphill to the "Indian village"—the same one Creel had referred to in his 1917 report. The Indian Bureau took no action because the land was owned by the Ely Securities Company, and the bureau could not appropriate funds for an Indian water project on privately owned land. To purchase this private land as federal trust land, Senator Tasker Oddie introduced legislation into Congress. His bill became public law in 1930.

With federal funds available, the Ely Colony became a reality on September 28, 1931. The bureau later piped running water to the colony.[61] Because the Indians already had their own houses, no housing project was needed.

Besides the allotments and colonies in Nevada, some acreage was also set aside for a group of Shoshones living in Panamint Valley, California, immediately west of Death Valley. Known as Indian Ranch, the federal government established this 560-acre rancheria (the name given to small Indian reserves in California) by public law on March 3, 1928. Shoshone leader George Hanson and his extended family occupied this land for years, cultivating alfalfa and fruit, and raising goats. In 1923 a flash flood washed out their irrigation system. For a few years the Hansons asked for assistance to restore their irrigation supply. Finally, in 1926, the Indian Bureau responded, but it could do nothing since the Indians didn't own the land according to American law. Congress rectified this situation with the 1928 legislation. By 1930 the water supply had been partially restored on Indian Ranch.[62]

The federal government had set aside a total of 4,026 acres of land for the Basin Shoshones in the early years of the twentieth century. After the establishment of the scattered allotments and colonies, however, the federal government made a distinction between the groups of nonreservation Western Shoshones. Roughly one hundred living on the allotments and colonies were categorized as "wards" of the government and could receive whatever assistance was available from the Indian Bureau. About twelve hundred Shoshones not living on these small tracts were labeled "nonwards" and were not entitled to government aid. As far as the Indian Bureau was concerned, the nonward Shoshones were the responsibility of the state and counties of Nevada. The federal government took this action even though all the Shoshones were considered to be under the jurisdiction of the federal sector. The children of nonwards did receive indirect aid when the government paid their tuition to attend public schools in Nevada.[63]

In this period the nonreservation Western Shoshones did not have one principal leader or any centralized governing body representing all Basin Shoshone groups, reservation and nonreservation, wards and nonwards. Rather, they had regional leaders who dominated particular geographic areas. These leaders dealt with numerous issues and concerns, both Indian and non-Indian. One of these men was Harry Preacher of Wells. On February 27, 1896, some northeastern Nevada Shoshones sponsored a fandango in Elko. They elected Preacher as the "Big Chief of the Shoshones," although his leadership was recognized only by some living in the Wells-Elko area. This was the first time in Western Shoshone history that a native leader was elected by popular vote, even though limited to one area.[64]

Immediately after taking office, Preacher made it clear that he wanted the Shoshones to follow the white man's laws. This included obedience to Nevada's hunting and fishing rules and regulations, which not all Shoshones were willing to accept. He wanted the whites to hire the Indians as laborers, and he wanted the Indians and whites to be good friends living in peace and harmony. Furthermore he wanted the whites to give the Shoshones small plots of land for homesteading.[65] Some whites did hire Shoshones as laborers, as Preacher envisioned, and both groups maintained good relations, although the whites harbored a low opinion of their Indian neighbors.

Over the next several years, Preacher continued to speak out to both Shoshones and whites in northeastern Nevada. In 1900 he made known his frustration with those unscrupulous whites who sold liquor to the Indians and abused Indian women. To reduce if not eliminate these problems, Preacher asked the Nevada state legislature to pass a bill appropriating funds to hire an Indian police force. Indian police officers would be able to arrest those whites who took advantage of the Indians. The Shoshones in turn would pay a tax to help maintain this law enforcement body.[66] Unfortunately, nothing came of Preacher's suggestion.

After the turn of the century Preacher, now an old man, wanted to give up his title as chief. However, at a large gathering held in Elko on December 15, 1912, he was reelected to his post. His influence dissolved soon after, probably because he placed a ban on the Shoshone fandangos out of concern that too much drinking was going on at these gatherings. Unwilling to give up their traditional round dances and handgames, many Shoshones no longer recognized Preacher as a leader. Others had never recognized his leadership because of his stand on Nevada's hunting laws.[67]

For many years the Shoshones of the Reese River Valley area were led by Chief Tu-tu-wa (or Toi-Toi) whose leadership predated the coming of the whites. Despite his advancing age, Tu-tu-wa was still an influential personality in the late nineteenth century. In April 1880 at a large Shoshone meeting in Battle Mountain called by the Indian Bureau, Tu-tu-wa announced his refusal to move to Duck Valley because of his deep attachment to central Nevada, "and the majority . . . took his view of the matter."[68] Thus his leadership was one important factor why some Shoshones refused to move to Duck Valley.

When Tu-tu-wa died of old age in April 1897, his son Tom became the new chief of the Reese River Valley area. This practice of hereditary leadership was perhaps a carryover from indigenous times. Tom Tu-tu-wa's leadership was highly visible after the turn of the century. When the Shoshones held a fandango in Austin in 1905, he addressed the audience, stating that his father had always advocated harmonious relations between the Indians and whites. He also pointed out that his father had allowed the whites to enter and live within Shoshone country. Tom hoped that his own generation of Shoshones would continue to get along with the whites. However, he was concerned about those unscrupulous whites who abused the Indians, stole Indian-owned horses, and sold liquor to the Indians. These activities disrupted good relations between the races. Tu-tu-wa hoped that honest white people would curb the bad behavior of their less scrupulous fellow whites.[69]

For reasons unknown, when Tom Tu-tu-wa died of influenza in Austin in December 1918, he was not replaced by his surviving brother Hank. Instead, the Shoshones of central Nevada sought a replacement. In 1919 some held a fandango in Smoky Valley and chose Joe Gilbert, a noted fandango leader from Austin, as the new chief. For unexplained reasons, Gilbert was replaced in October 1922 when the Shoshones of central and north-central Nevada sponsored another fandango in Battle Mountain. At this gathering Harry Dixon was elected the new chief. He came from Grass Valley, an area about forty miles northeast of Austin. In addition to Dixon, other leaders were chosen to run the affairs of three places where Shoshones lived: Jimmy Leach at Battle Mountain, with Dick Beeler as his assistant, Dick Hall at Elko, and Bill Hall at Beowawe.[70]

Dixon was an active leader in the 1920s. He helped organize an alliance between some Western Shoshones and Northwestern Shoshones from Utah. In 1923 Dixon and two Northwestern Shoshones, Willie Ottogary and George Paharagosam, claimed that Shoshones should not have to pay taxes, including the poll tax, because the tribal members were not U.S. citizens at this time. In the same year these men sponsored a claims meeting in Elko and argued that the United States owed both Western and Northwestern Shoshones compensation for lands not included in the various Shoshone treaties in 1863. They wanted legal representation from noted attorneys, such as Charles Kappler, the compiler of *Kappler's Laws and Treaties*. Dixon served as chair of this Elko claims meeting with James Pabawena of Wells as secretary. One year later Dixon and the others opposed the Indian Citizenship Act of 1924, stressing that if the Indians accepted it, they would lose their rights as well as the bargaining power to secure needed land for the Shoshone people.[71] Unfortunately, they failed on all counts.

To show that his leadership was part of the Tu-tu-wa political legacy, Harry Dixon added "Tootiaina" (an incorrect pronunciation of the name Tu-tu-wa) to his last name. He also considered himself the overall chief of all the Western Shoshones of the Great Basin, basing his claim on the Battle Mountain fandango election of 1922. In reality, Dixon's leadership was recognized only by some Shoshones living in central Nevada and a few others in the northeastern Nevada communities of Battle Mountain and Elko.[72]

Eventually, Harry Dixon-Tootiaina lost his followers. Having made Elko his headquarters, he lost touch with the Shoshones of central Nevada who had looked to the Tu-tu-wa family for leadership over the years. By the mid-1920s Joe Gilbert was again recognized as the Tu-tu-wa chief of the traditional Shoshones of central Nevada. When Gilbert died of old age several years later, he was temporarily replaced by Jim Birchum of Austin in August 1931 when the Shoshones held a fandango at that place. Birchum, an old man, served for only three or four months. In November 1931 the Shoshones of central Nevada elected Alex Gilbert, the son of Joe Gilbert, as the new chief. At this same election, several men were recognized as Tu-tu-wa Band subchiefs of central Nevada: Mike Millett, Dimmy Jackson, Oscar Mike, Willie Butler, Bob Tom, John Sunday, and Richard Birchum.[73] The political organization remained extremely weak, however, since Alex Gilbert had made the Duck Valley Reservation his home and no longer had a strong connection to central Nevada.

Harry Dixon-Tootiaina's egotism, expressed in his claim to be chief of all Western Shoshones, did not appeal to most Shoshone leaders of northeastern Nevada. Those on the Duck Valley Reservation regarded their Western Shoshone Council, formed in 1911, as the official reservation ruling body (see chapter 3). Since Dixon had never resided there, the council rejected his leadership and stated that "so far as Duck Valley is concerned Harry Dixon has nothing to do with us whatsoever."[74] By a vote of seven to one, the Western Shoshone Council of Duck Valley voted against Dixon's self-proclaimed position of overall chief.[75] The Shoshones in Ruby Valley also did not recognize Dixon. In a statement dated August 1929, Chief Muchach Temoke wrote to Milton Badt, an Elko-based attorney who had begun to help the Shoshone push for treaty rights: "I have notice in *Independent* [Elko newspaper] about the matter so we are follows the Treaty of Temoke [Ruby Valley treaty] which we are not following Harry Dixon matter. Now we pulling for you and no other Harry Dixon matter we don't care for. So watch this matter."[76] With almost no followers by 1930, Dixon left Nevada and moved to Utah where he spent most of his time. On occasion he returned to Nevada and voiced his opinions regarding political issues.

Most northeastern Nevada Shoshones not living in Duck Valley recognized the leadership of the well-known Temoke family of Ruby Valley. Like the Tu-tu-wa group, the Temokes also were hereditary leaders in the late nineteenth and early twentieth centuries. Before his death in 1890, Old Temoke, the principal signer of the Ruby Valley treaty, helped persuade most Ruby Valley Shoshones not to move to Duck Valley.

Around 170 Shoshones still lived in Ruby Valley in the early years of the twentieth century.[77]

After Old Temoke's death, his adopted son Joe became the new chief of the Temoke Band of Ruby Valley and of other Shoshones in northeastern Nevada. His leadership was apparent by about 1910 when a land dispute arose. At that time Stanley Wines, a rancher in Ruby Valley, told the Indians to remove themselves from forty acres of land near the Overland Creek, which he had inherited from his father, Ira Wines. The father had secured title to this land under the land laws of Nevada in 1897. However, the older Wines had allowed the Indians to live on the land since he was their friend and hired them as laborers on occasion. The Shoshones had no notion that the Wines family owned this land, where most of the Temoke family and their relations had lived more or less permanently since the 1860s. As the chief, Joe Temoke was one of the first persons to inform the Indian Bureau and the public about the controversy over the forty acres near Overland Creek.[78]

An old man in 1916, Joe Temoke passed the title of chief to a younger family member, Muchach Temoke, the grandson of Old Temoke. For thirty-eight years, Muchach Temoke served as the noted chief of most off-reservation Shoshones in northeastern Nevada. Even before he became chief, Muchach had established a leading role in Shoshone politics, beginning with the Overland Creek land dispute in Ruby Valley. In April 1912 he wrote a letter to the Washington, D.C., office of the Indian Bureau in which he pointed out that at the time of the 1863 treaty of Ruby Valley the area around Overland Creek was recognized as Shoshone land. Furthermore, the Indians had lived at this place permanently since the days of Old Temoke. Therefore, Muchach maintained, Stanley Wines as a late arrival had no right to claim title to the forty acres. Muchach was sure that the government had set aside a reservation in Ruby Valley, but he could not recall its dimensions since Old Temoke's papers were burned, in accordance with tribal custom, when the old chief died in 1890.[79]

Muchach Temoke made a trip to Washington, D.C., in January 1917 to look into the land and treaty affairs of the Western Shoshones. In a statement to Cato Sells, the commissioner of Indian affairs, he pointed out that the 1863 treaty "acknowledged" a large area as belonging to the Shoshones. The government was supposed to create reservations inside this area, which it had not done so far. Muchach made it clear that injustices had been committed against the Ruby Valley Shoshones. Years earlier, the cattle owned by the Shoshones in Ruby Valley had been taken from them and transferred to the Duck Valley Reservation. The Indians saw this move as a ploy to get the Ruby Valley people to move to Duck Valley. In more recent times, the whites in Ruby Valley had claimed the land the Indians considered theirs. Temoke asserted, "They have taken my land, fence, and all away, mostly in alfalfa hay and (red top)." He then said that it was time to establish a reservation in Ruby Valley. If such a reservation were established, many Shoshones who had left the valley over the years might return.[80]

Sells was cool to Muchach's complaints. He countered by arguing that the Ruby Valley treaty had been fulfilled in two ways. First, Duck Valley had been set aside for the Shoshones in accordance with the agreement. Second, the one hundred thousand dollars promised the Shoshones in the treaty had already been spent for their benefit. Sells held that "this office is of the opinion that the Indians have no claim against the Government by reason of said treaty." The commissioner, however, did acknowledge that a "six miles square" reservation had been set aside for the Shoshones in Ruby Valley in 1859, but he noted that it was never formally deeded. He found this information in Charles Royce's *Indian Land Cessions*. Sells was not about to carry out the original intention and suggested instead that the Ruby Valley Shoshones should move to Duck Valley or else secure title to individual plots of land elsewhere in Nevada.[81]

Muchach Temoke was not a leader to yield easily. He was unwilling to accept the decisions of the Indian Bureau. Two years later, in November 1919, he made a second trip to Washington, this time accompanied by Thomas Wahne, a Shoshone from Wells who spoke and wrote English. The two introduced themselves as "chief" and "interpreter" of the "Western Shoshone tribe." As before, Muchach gave a brief history, noting that the Temokes were hereditary leaders and that he was now chief. Old Temoke, the principal treaty signer, had been known for his role as peacemaker. Not only had he negotiated peace between the Shoshones and whites but also he had calmed those Shoshones who hated the whites. For his role as mediator, the government at the time of the treaty had agreed to set aside the "six miles square" reservation. However, the whites took this land at a later date. Without doubt Temoke and Wahne firmly believed that the Shoshone still owned the land despite the fact that whites lived there. They said, "We ask you to tell us, put it down in a letter, when this tract six miles square was deeded to Temoak's band."[82]

As before, the Indian Bureau was not receptive to the Shoshones' plea. Edgar Meritt, the assistant commissioner, reiterated the arguments Sells had advanced two years earlier. He pointed out that Duck Valley had been set aside in accordance with the treaty. He maintained that the Ruby Valley Shoshones could still move there, and he encouraged them to do so. He also stressed that the Indian Bureau would not try to recover the "six miles square" reservation. The only concession he made was to note that the government could submit legislation to purchase more land, along with water rights, in Ruby Valley for the Shoshones.[83]

Muchach Temoke and his supporters gained two small victories. First, in 1920 Stanley Wines gave up title to the forty acres near the Overland Creek. In turn, the Indian Bureau purchased this land from the state of Nevada and gave it to the former Ruby Valley chief, Joe Temoke. Second, in response to Meritt's suggestion, Congress in 1924 appropriated $25,000 to purchase more land in Ruby Valley for the Shoshones.[84] This money wasn't enough to purchase any available ranch land, so it eventually reverted to Congress. The Indians were not successful in their major objective, the restoration of the "six miles square" reservation.

The various Western Shoshone leaders of the Great Basin were largely independent and had their own orbits of influence. Still, several of them did come together on occasion to discuss important issues. For example, on December 15, 1912, many Shoshones gathered in Elko for a three-day political meeting. This "council" gathering was the largest since the signing of the Ruby Valley treaty a half-century earlier. The Shoshones held it to discuss several matters of concern. First, the Ruby Valley land controversy involving Stanley Wines had convinced them that the government would never declare a permanent homeland for them in Ruby Valley. It was time to confront the federal sector, they felt. Second, a younger and much more aggressive generation of Shoshones, including Muchach Temoke, had secured a copy of the Ruby Valley treaty, a document not seen since the death of Old Temoke in 1890. After reading it the Shoshones concluded that the government had never kept its side of the treaty bargain. Unlike their fathers and grandfathers, who had remained peaceful, in accordance with the treaty, the younger Shoshones were now willing to challenge the government. They wanted recognition of a land base and other treaty rights. Third, the Shoshones were encouraged by Delaware tribal attorney Richard C. Adams to openly challenge the federal government. Adams, who practiced law in Washington, D.C., was the founder of the Brotherhood of North American Indians, a group created to pressure the government to fulfill the provisions of nineteenth-century Indian treaties.[85]

Shoshone messengers traveled throughout Shoshone country, drumming up support for the meeting to be held after the pine nut harvest. They held a preliminary meeting in October 1912 in Deeth, near Wells, where the participants discussed Shoshone land and treaty rights not recognized by the whites. Those involved stated clearly that they had no intention of moving to Duck Valley as the Indian Bureau had wanted them to do over the years. Instead they wanted to remain at their present localities. In early November the Shoshones held a fandango near Eureka to give even more publicity to the upcoming December meeting. Apparently, Shoshones from the following places were invited to attend: Austin, Battle Mountain, Beowawe, Calin, Deeth, Duckwater, Eureka, Ruby Valley, Smoky Valley, Starr Valley, and Wells.[86]

On December 15 the Shoshones held their large meeting in Elko. It was attended by several leaders, primarily from northeastern Nevada, including Muchach Temoke, Joe Temoke, Brownie Mose, Bill Gibson, Harry Preacher, and James Pabawena, with Kase Austin as interpreter. Representing the Indian Bureau was Calvin Asbury, superintendent of the newly established Reno Indian Agency. For the most part, the discussion revolved around the Treaty of Ruby Valley. The Ruby Valley Shoshones took the leading role in the discussion. They told Asbury that the treaty "had not been complied with in so far as it contained an agreement to give them a reservation." Although the Duck Valley Reservation had been established for the Shoshones, it was located outside the area claimed by Chief Temoke. Furthermore, Duck Valley had been set aside at the request of Captain Sam and his followers, not Temoke. From their oral tradition the Shoshones knew that the government had intended to establish a permanent reservation for the Shoshones in Ruby Valley in the nineteenth century. The government had never done this. Thus the Ruby Valley Shoshones and others expressed "a desire for an additional reservation in Ruby Valley, Nevada."[87]

The Shoshones also asked about the annual payment of five thousand dollars for twenty years their forefathers had been promised under the treaty. Some of the old folks recalled seeing only small amounts of goods coming from this treaty money. Additionally, the Shoshones pointed out that federal officials had placed cattle in Ruby Valley for the Indians to become herders, in accordance with the treaty. However, the livestock was later taken away and placed on the Western Shoshone Reservation, an action that angered those in Ruby Valley. The Shoshones expressed still other concerns, including the issue of Nevada state laws that restricted Shoshone hunting for subsistence purposes. They also complained about U.S. Forest Service restrictions that prevented them from acquiring wood for cooking and winter fuel.[88]

Although he listened to the Shoshones, Asbury was not in favor of granting all their requests. To him, Duck Valley was the reservation intended for all the Shoshones. Its establishment complied with the treaty, he argued. Asbury encouraged the nonreservation Shoshones to move there and secure land assignments. The likelihood of a new reservation being established in Ruby Valley "was extremely remote" since most land was now in private hands. To purchase the land from white owners would be too expensive. Furthermore, not all Shoshones would move to a new reservation, if established, since they were accustomed to living independently and over a large area. If they chose not to move to Duck Valley, they could file for allotments on public domain. The only encouragement Asbury gave the Shoshones was the news that they were entitled to water in Ruby Valley from the Overland Creek.[89]

At this meeting the Shoshones also revived the informal treaty council that had existed during the treaty negotiations of 1863.[90] Led by the influential chief Temoke, the original council had become inactive after his death in 1890. The Shoshones of the early twentieth century felt that the Temoke family of Ruby Valley should carry on the leadership. Joe Temoke became the first chief of the revived informal treaty council, followed by Muchach Temoke by 1917.

This Shoshone treaty council held occasional meetings in the years after 1912 to discuss unkept treaty promises and also the need for the government to recognize a Shoshone land base through the establishment of more reservations. In the early 1920s the council sponsored fandangos in Ruby Valley promoting the establishment of a reservation there. At this time the council members included Muchach Temoke as chief, Thomas Wahne of Wells as secretary and interpreter, Johnny Thompson of Wells, and Bill Antelope, also of Wells. Bill Gibson of Elko, although a member, attended meetings infrequently, as did others who were less active or involved.[91]

Throughout the 1920s the council members were very much concerned about the rights of the Shoshones. For example, in February 1925 Thomas Wahne as "representative" wrote to Rep. Charles Richards stating that the Shoshones should have the freedom to hunt for subsistence purposes, just as they had done in the "old time." Wahne wrote that "under federal laws, when we . . . made a treaty we was to hunt and kill any kind of game as we want too and also fish."[92]

The entire issue of land and treaty rights received top priority when Shoshone leaders met with federal officials in a public hearing in Elko on September 16, 1932. This hearing was conducted by the U.S. Senate Subcommittee of the Committee on Indian Affairs, which had been conducting an investigation of Indian affairs since 1928. Much of the discussion revolved around the issue of the government's unkept treaty promises. Some Shoshones argued that they still owned the treaty territory because of the Ruby Valley treaty. Harry Stanton, a leader from the Ely Colony, stated: "I have heard . . . that we are on the public domain, but then I don't see why they call that public domain because we lived on that for many years . . . here in Temoak's territory they can't call it that."[93] Having listened to Muchach Temoke, Harry Stanton, Bill Gibson, and others, and not realizing that they were members of an informal treaty council, Senator Elmer Thomas of Oklahoma told the

Shoshones to "appoint a committee or a business council." Thomas continued, "My suggestion is that you follow this procedure and after you have your meeting and have selected your business council, then the council should select someone to represent you." His colleague, Senator Lynn Frazier of North Dakota, then asked Bill Gibson the following question: "Have you Shoshones any business or tribal council now?" Gibson responded by saying, "We haven't anything much like that now."[94] What Gibson meant was that the Shoshones didn't have a formal governing body, although he alluded to the loose-knit or informal treaty council.

Following the suggestion of both Thomas and Frazier, around seventy Shoshones of northeastern Nevada, led by Muchach Temoke and Bill Gibson, organized a large meeting in Elko on October 10, 1932. The first thing they did was to elect eight men to a formal council: Muchach Temoke (Ruby Valley), Jack Temoke (Wells), Bill Gibson (Elko), Jimmy James (Lee), John Couchum (Elko), Jack Muncey (Battle Mountain), Harry Stanton (Ely), and Harry Johnny, also of Ely. Thus, the earlier informal treaty council was enlarged and became the official representative of the northeastern Nevada Shoshones. Jack Temoke was elected chair of this meeting. The council signed a contract with attorney Milton Badt of Elko to serve as legal counsel to press claims against the government for the Shoshones.[95]

Once established, the eight members of the Shoshone treaty council began working on treaty rights. They defined the treaty territory as an area ranging from the Smith Creek Mountains on the west to the area around Ely on the east, and from the Duckwater and Reese River valleys on the south to North Fork on the north (about seventy miles north of Elko). In determining this territory, based on oral tradition and treaty information, the council acted conservatively. It excluded the area south of central Nevada and also the area along the Idaho-Nevada border, although these were places where Shoshones had always lived.[96]

The treaty council, along with other Shoshones at the October 1932 meeting, argued that since 1863 their ancestors had lived up to their side of the treaty. They had remained peaceful, allowed the whites to travel across Shoshone country, and permitted the whites to construct telegraph lines and also to prospect for mineral wealth. The Shoshones were even willing to become cattlemen when the government placed cattle in Ruby Valley for them. But the cattle had been transferred to Duck Valley in 1879.[97]

The treaty council and its supporters argued that the government had not fulfilled its promises to the Shoshone, as outlined in the treaty. No reservation had been established inside Old Temoke's territory. Moreover, the Shoshones had received only a limited amount of treaty goods from the $100,000 their ancestors were entitled to receive over a twenty-year period.[98] The issue of treaty rights was not resolved in the early 1930s, however, and it remains an issue in the early 1990s.

5

THE WESTERN SHOSHONE AND THE NEW DEAL

1933–1941

Like millions of other Americans across the nation, the Western Shoshones of the Great Basin suffered during the hard times of the Great Depression and were touched by the New Deal policies that sought to deal with its effects. By the time newly elected President Franklin D. Roosevelt introduced the New Deal in 1933, numerous banks had closed their doors, countless businesses had gone bankrupt, and millions of people had lost their jobs. To rescue the nation from this economic plight, the Roosevelt administration instituted various socioeconomic and political reforms. It also hired reform-minded individuals to deal with particular sectors of the population. One of these was John Collier, a reformer who had been involved with some Indian tribes since the 1920s. Collier became the commissioner of the Indian Bureau in April 1933; he saw it as his job to make sure that the tribes benefited from New Deal programs.[1]

Some aspects of the New Deal applied to the Native American tribes only. The most important of these was the Indian Reorganization Act (IRA) of 1934. This act of Congress has since been regarded by some scholars as one of the most significant policies affecting the Indian tribes. The IRA had several important elements: it repealed the allotment provision of the 1887 Dawes Act; it gave Indian tribes the right to organize business (tribal) councils and to adopt tribal constitutions and by-laws; it allowed the tribes that adopted charters to borrow from an IRA "revolving fund" for community-based economic development; it provided loans for Indian students seeking higher education; and it gave "preference" to qualified Indians seeking employment in the Indian Bureau.[2]

The 1934 act had other provisions as well, some of which applied to specific tribes. The IRA, however, did not automatically apply to all such entities; each one had to vote affirmatively to become an IRA tribe and to benefit from the act's provisions. Or they could reject it completely, as some did.[3]

One prominent feature of the Indian Bureau under the New Deal was its policy of cultural pluralism—a dramatic change from the older assimilationist policy for the Native Americans. The Indian Bureau now encouraged the tribes to revive or strengthen their native cultures as much as possible. This new policy for Indians was a major feature of Collier's "Indian New Deal" for the native peoples of the United States.

The General New Deal Programs

The biggest beneficiaries of the general New Deal programs were those tribal people already living on reservations. Thus among the Shoshone, those living on the Western Shoshone Reservation (Duck Valley) were the major recipients of New Deal assistance since theirs was the only Shoshone reservation in the Great Basin in the early 1930s. In particular, the Civilian Conservation Corps (CCC) and the Public Works Administration (PWA) had the greatest impact on the Duck Valley residents.[4]

The CCC was a New Deal program intended to conserve the country's natural resources and also to provide job opportunities for the unemployed victims of the Great Depression. Beginning in early 1933 thousands of persons, mostly young men, were paid to carry out conservation-related assignments, including planting trees to reduce soil erosion and building roads, reservoirs, and bridges. The federal government created a separate CCC division for the Native Americans, called the Civilian Conservation Corps, Indian Division (CCC-ID), run by the Indian Bureau. Indian Bureau Commissioner Collier pushed for this arrangement since he maintained that tribal people could best work among themselves as an ethnic labor force.[5]

The basic purpose of the CCC-ID programs on the Duck Valley reservation was to advance the already existing cattle economy. One big project, begun in 1933, was the building of fences. Over a two-year period from 1933 to 1935 Indian crews constructed an eighty-three mile boundary fence around the reservation, to keep the Indians' cattle inside and the white-owned cattle out. They also built fences inside the reservation to reduce soil erosion and to prevent cattle overgrazing. By 1938, 123 miles of interior fences had been completed, dividing the reservation into three major grazing ranges, for early spring and fall, late spring, and summer. Indian crews reseeded the grazing areas between periods of use. Additionally, CCC-ID crews spread poisonous grains to reduce the large population of ground squirrels, which had hindered the growth of

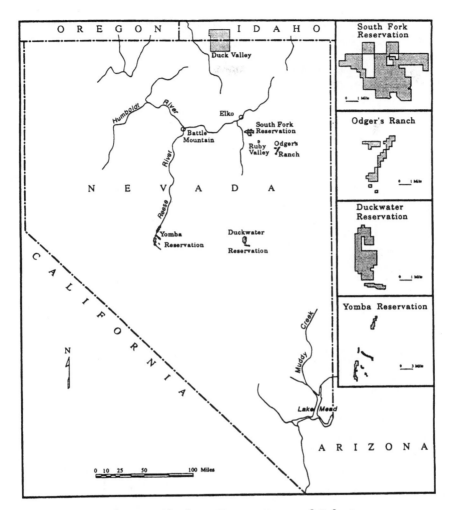

Western Shoshone Reservations and Colonies

range grasses. In the end, all these conservation projects created a healthier reservation environment.[6]

Other CCC-ID projects also revolved around range management, linked directly or indirectly to the reservation cattle economy. For example, Indian crews cleaned various natural spring water holes for cattle use and piped the water to troughs, thereby eliminating the mudholes where cattle had once had to drink. Another project was the construction and improvement of secondary dirt roads to remote areas of the reservation. These all-purpose roads were later used by fence crews making repairs, workers carrying out range management, and families gathering wood for winter and hunting wildlife. Still another project was the construction of reservoirs to conserve water and also reduce soil erosion. The largest and best known was the Sheep Creek Reservoir, completed in 1935. In later years it was stocked with fish and became a popular recreation place.[7]

Overall, the CCC-ID projects, although short-lived, benefited the Shoshones and Paiutes at Duck Valley. Never before in the history of the reservation had so many adults been employed at the same time, including women. In fact, the women were largely responsible for the planting of rye grass for improved rangelands. They were also hired to reduce the rodent and cricket populations. Unfortunately, when Congress reduced expenditures for the CCC programs in the early 1940s, many jobs at Duck Valley ceased to exist. Still, combined with other New Deal projects, the CCC-ID helped improve the cattle economy of the Western Shoshone Reservation.[8]

The Indians of Duck Valley also benefited from the projects initiated under the PWA, which hired thousands of unemployed workers around the country to build needed hospitals, roads, and irrigation and reclamation projects. As with the CCC, some PWA funds were channeled to Indian reservations in the 1930s for such public works projects.[9]

The federal government launched several PWA projects on or near the Western Shoshone Reservation after 1935. The most remarkable was the Wildhorse Dam, completed in June 1937. This sizable concrete arch dam, ninety-two feet high, represented the fulfillment of a dream for the Duck Valley population, especially the cattle owners. Located roughly thirty miles upriver from the reservation's southern boundary, the dam solved the problem of spring runoff. As described earlier, the Owyhee River ran nearly dry by midsummer, so that without a dam the Shoshones and Paiutes could not grow enough alfalfa and wild hay to feed their cattle during winter months. This made it difficult to increase the reservation cattle herds above two thousand head.[10]

The completed Wildhorse Dam, coupled with a new reservation-based diversion dam and a network of new canals, substantially improved the cattle economy. In 1935, the Indians harvested only 997 tons of alfalfa. Thanks to PWA and CCC-ID projects, the harvest increased to 2,003 tons by 1941. Increased agricultural production meant more cattle. By 1941, there were 4,901 head, a dramatic increase.[11]

After the completion of the Wildhorse Dam, the Indian Bureau hoped that each Duck Valley family would own at least fifty to sixty head of cattle. This expectation, however, was not met in the New Deal years. By 1941 only twenty-three families owned more than fifty head, and only fourteen families subsisted entirely on the proceeds from stock raising.

Most families depended on wage labor besides the sale of their cattle. The Indian Bureau also expected 26,000 acres of reservation land to be leveled and irrigated after the completion of the dam. But by 1945, only 7,000 acres were under production. Land-leveling operations were limited in the late 1930s and early 1940s because of reduced funds for the New Deal projects. This lag in land improvement made it impossible for the Duck Valley people to become self-sufficient.[12]

Other PWA projects also affected the Western Shoshone Reservation. One of these was the completion of a hospital in June 1937. This new twenty-bed facility with an operating room greatly reduced the high death rate of the reservation population, and it also relieved many health problems. For example, it was reported that trachoma, a chronic, contagious eye disease, was one of the "major public health problems" in 1938. But by 1940 fewer than two Indians out of one hundred were afflicted with this disease. Other health problems persisted, however, including tuberculosis.

The construction of a large community gymnasium was another visible PWA project on the reservation. Finished in 1938, this facility fulfilled the dreams of various individuals, serving as a center for sports, recreation, and entertainment. It also furthered the acculturation process, since Indian Bureau superintendents did not encourage the Indians to hold native cultural events in the gym. Other PWA projects on the reservation included new houses for agency employees and a new generator plant for agency facilities.[13]

Besides the CCC-ID and the PWA, the Indians of Duck Valley received support from other New Deal agencies. For example, they received 711 drought-relief cattle in 1934 from the Agricultural Adjustment Act (AAA). Some of the elderly received monthly pensions from the Social Security Administration. Unfortunately, social security required that its recipients be poor, even destitute, to obtain welfare aid. The old folks at Duck Valley therefore had to give up their meager holdings, such as cattle, to obtain social security benefits. This caused a decline in the number of cattle owners on the reservation from 160 in 1935 to 81 by 1961.[14]

The nonreservation Western Shoshones were more numerous but less fortunate than those living at Duck Valley. The Indian Bureau made no effort to create special New Deal projects for them, not even for those living on the small colonies at Battle Mountain, Elko, and Ely. The bureau probably felt that it would be impractical to set up special CCC-ID projects for handfuls of Shoshones living over a large area. However, Alida Bowler, superintendent of the Carson Indian Agency, the jurisdiction responsible for the northeastern Nevada nonreservation Shoshones, did her best to see that the Shoshones received some benefits from New Deal programs intended for the general population. Unfortunately, the white administrators in Nevada discriminated against the Indians, and they received little if any assistance.[15]

An example of racial discrimination was the Nevada Emergency Relief Administration (NERA), a state-run New Deal agency that received funds directly from the larger Federal Emergency Relief Administration (FERA) in Washington, D.C. FERA was established in 1933 to provide different forms of relief assistance to the unemployed. FERA funds, however, were channeled to the state-run agencies that possessed discretionary power at the local level. In Nevada, the principal beneficiaries of NERA were the white people, while the native tribes received only limited assistance. Only two Shoshone women in Ely were hired as NERA domestic household employees. Only two Shoshones in Eureka County had their medical expenses paid for by NERA. A few other Shoshones elsewhere received surplus commodities and clothing under NERA. In 1936 only 13 of the 163 Shoshones living in Lander County received support.[16] Limited assistance prompted Superintendent Bowler to assert that NERA officials discriminated "against Indians merely because they are Indians."[17] According to Bowler, the Battle Mountain Shoshones, in particular, were denied relief because the Lander County officials concluded that public support would make them dependent and "lazy."[18] Thus, the officials kept most benefits for white Nevadans and channeled very little if anything to the native population.

The nonreservation Shoshones were somewhat better off under two other New Deal agencies, the PWA and the Works Progress Administration (WPA). These were run by the federal government itself, although the state administered the programs at the local level. In 1936 alone, 10 percent of the annual income earned by the Shoshones in northern Nye County came from PWA and WPA combined. The Shoshones in Ruby Valley earned nearly 12 percent of their income from PWA and WPA. Thus, some Shoshone groups received a fair amount of assistance. But others received little if anything, again because of discrimination at the local level. Referring to the Battle Mountain Shoshones and others in Lander County, Superintendent Bowler wrote, "We found that in the whole region not a single Indian is eligible for relief under the W.P.A."[19]

Hoping for better treatment under New Deal programs, some nonreservation Shoshones made the decision to move onto reservations. At least one Battle Mountain man moved his family permanently to the Duck Valley reservation after being hired as a worker on the PWA Wildhorse Dam in the mid-1930s. Another Shoshone migrated to the Warm Springs Reservation in Oregon to secure a CCC-ID job.

A few Shoshones received support from the Indian Bureau's own New Deal assistance program, the Rehabilitation Division. But the only beneficiaries of this program were the residents of the three colonies and the

Shoshones living in Death Valley, California. The Indian Bureau built a laundromat and twelve ordinary houses in a semicircle in the Battle Mountain Colony. This was the first substantial federal support the Battle Mountain group had ever received. The Ely Colony Shoshones received two new houses, a laundromat, and a sewage system, plus the refurbishing of the existing houses. The Elko Colony acquired one new house and a water system. Two houses were built on the Indian trust allotments in Ruby Valley. The bureau built nine adobe houses and one laundromat at the Indian village in Death Valley, California. However, the majority of Shoshones who did not live on colony land or in Death Valley received nothing under the Indian Bureau Rehabilitation Division.[20]

Information provided by some of the New Deal agencies made the federal government aware that most Western Shoshones in the Great Basin had never lived on reservation land and had been largely ignored by the federal government over the years. One of these agencies was the Civil Works Administration (CWA), which channeled funds to the Indian Bureau to conduct extensive socioeconomic surveys among the tribal populations. Superintendent Ray Parrett of the Walker River Agency used his CWA resources to draft a report stating that the nonreservation Shoshones under his jurisdiction had "never been provided with a reservation for their needs, therefore they should be given suitable tracts of land on which they could live and obtain a future livelihood."[21] Parrett was referring to the Shoshones of central and southern Nevada who were under his jurisdiction from 1925 to 1935. Beginning in October 1935, these and all nonreservation Shoshones fell under the jurisdiction of the Carson Agency.

The National Resources Board (NRB), another New Deal agency, also focused upon the nonreservation Western Shoshones. It too channeled funds to the Indian Bureau to conduct studies of tribal populations. Once again, Parrett drafted a report suggesting that reservation land be provided for the Shoshones under his jurisdiction. The Carson Agency, headed by Bowler, drafted a similar report on the Shoshones under its jurisdiction in northeastern Nevada. Like Parrett, Bowler stressed the need for reservation land for the large numbers of Shoshones who had never moved to Duck Valley.[22] These reports paved the way for the eventual creation of more reservations for the Western Shoshones in the late 1930s and early 1940s.

The Indian Reorganization Act of 1934: The Land Provision

The Western Shoshones of the Great Basin were also affected by the Indian Reorganization Act of 1934. The IRA provision that had the

greatest impact on the nonreservation Western Shoshones was the purchase of land to create new reservations. The person who dealt with this
aspect of the IRA was Alida Bowler, the Carson Indian Agency superintendent. When she was hired in September 1934 Bowler became the
first woman to hold the position of superintendent of an agency under
the Indian Bureau.[23]

Bowler had been a friend of Collier since the early 1920s and also was
a member of the American Indian Defense Association, the reform-
minded group established in 1923 by Collier and his friends. Although
she had been involved in the so-called Indian reform movement for
several years, Bowler was unfamiliar with Nevada's Indian tribes when
she took office. However, she staunchly supported Collier's reform policies and asserted that "all of these scattered Indians need to come within
the provisions of the Indian Reorganization Act."[24] These "scattered
Indians" included 1,264 nonreservation Western Shoshones of northeastern Nevada who fell under the jurisdiction of the Carson Agency.

To familiarize herself with the history of the tribes under her jurisdiction, Bowler studied Indian Bureau documents. She quickly learned of
the 1863 Treaty of Ruby Valley and its recognition of a sizable tribal
territory. Further, she learned that the descendants of the nineteenth-
century Shoshones had recently pressed claims against the government
for unkept promises in the 1863 treaty. Bowler also familiarized herself
with some of the early principal leaders of northeastern Nevada Shoshone
in the nineteenth century, such as Old Temoke.[25]

Bowler learned that the nonreservation Western Shoshones were not
centralized but lived scattered over a large area. This troubled her
because she envisioned the Native American tribes as living in close-knit
communal societies.[26] Seemingly, the Basin Shoshones lacked this characteristic because of their dispersed population.

To create a sense of community for the nonreservation Western Shoshones, Bowler devised a plan. She suggested one large "subsistence
homestead," or reservation, to be created within the 1863 treaty territory.[27] The objective was to find good quality land so the new occupants
could become agriculturists. But in espousing this plan, Bowler was
following the Indian Bureau's unsuccessful nineteenth-century policy of
concentrating the Basin Shoshones on one reservation. She was not aware
that this course of action had already failed long ago when the majority of
Shoshones refused to leave their native places and move to Duck Valley
in 1879 and 1880 (see chapter 2).

To search for a suitable reservation location, Bowler traveled to northeastern Nevada in late 1934 and early 1935. She immediately wrote off
the Shoshone colonies at Battle Mountain, Elko, and Ely, appropriately
calling them unfit for future economic development, suitable only for

living purposes. She found out that some Shoshones in Elko wanted a reservation near Elko in northern Nevada. The leader of this movement was Bill Gibson who had been pushing for a "twenty mile square" reservation since 1929. He erroneously claimed that the government had promised the Shoshones a reservation in the South Fork Valley in 1863. Furthermore, Gibson and some others claimed Old Temoke had given up his hunting territory for the reservation that was supposed to have been set aside there.[28] This information was incorrect, for the treaty of 1863 did not specify exact locations of reservations, although it did point out that they were to be located within the treaty territory. Chief Temoke never did barter away his land for a reservation.

South Fork Valley, located some thirty miles south of Elko, was a place with fertile soil and available water in the form of runoff from the nearby mountains. Bowler saw it as an appropriate location for a reservation for the nonreservation Western Shoshone. She received support from some of the native leaders who also favored "one large reservation."[29]

Superintendent Bowler soon learned that not all nonreservation Shoshones favored South Fork Valley as a future home. Deeply attached to their own native valleys within the larger Shoshone territory, different groups objected to the plan of one centrally located reservation. One vocal opponent was Chief Muchach Temoke of Ruby Valley, the grandson of Old Temoke. As discussed earlier, Temoke and others wanted the restoration of the "six miles square" unsurveyed reservation, which had been established in 1859, "reoccupied" in 1863, but not preserved by the Indian Bureau as a Shoshone reservation. By the late nineteenth century, the white ranchers had claimed much of the land. Nevertheless, Temoke and others continued to claim that this was an injustice. As late as the 1930s, they still requested that the "six miles square" reservation of Ruby Valley be restored.[30] They had no desire to move to South Fork or any other location.

Another group of Western Shoshones that did not favor the South Fork site were those temporarily living on the Walker River Reservation in west-central Nevada. These Shoshones had originally spent most of their lives in their native valleys of central Nevada, including the Reese River and Smoky valleys. As noted in chapter 4, they had moved to the Walker River Reservation in the 1920s for various reasons. One factor in their decision was the collapse of the once flourishing mining economy of central Nevada; another was federal government restrictions upon native hunting and grazing activities. Moving to Walker River was a matter of survival. After hearing about the IRA land provision, the Shoshones in Walker River desired to return to their native places in central Nevada.[31]

Those at Walker River therefore created the Nye County Shoshone Committee, which asked the Indian Bureau to create a reservation in the

Reese River Valley in Nye County that would be suitable for cattle grazing. Up to this time the areas of central and southern Nevada had come under the jurisdiction of the Walker River Agency. Only when the region was placed under the Carson Agency in 1935 did Superintendent Bowler learn of the Shoshone drive for a reservation in Reese River. These Shoshones also were determined not to move elsewhere. Bowler had to face the fact that not all Shoshones would move to South Fork if one big reservation were established there. She now scrapped her original plan and worked for a second IRA reservation to be located in Reese River.[32]

Bowler's hope that the nonreservation Shoshones of central and southern Nevada would move to a newly created central reservation in the Reese River Valley also dissolved. After learning about the Reese River project, other Shoshones of the region rejected any future consolidation. Danny Millett of Smoky Valley, east of the Reese River Valley, wrote to Bowler and stated this position. Thus, Shoshones of Smoky Valley, the Duckwater Valley in east-central Nevada, and the Fish Lake Valley in southern Nevada all wanted separate reservations in their own native territories. Now Bowler began to push for more reservation sites. After seeing the favorable conditions in the Duckwater Valley, she urged the creation of a third IRA reservation there. Although she was not optimistic about the success of her plan, the superintendent kept in mind other possible locations.[33]

Bowler's first goal was the creation of a reservation in the South Fork Valley. From the start she did not support the Shoshones' wish for a "twenty mile square" reservation. Perhaps she knew the government would not appropriate enough money for the acquisition of such a large reservation. Or perhaps she realized that not all white ranchers of the area were willing to sell their land to the government. However, Bowler did favor purchasing as many white-owned ranches as possible. The initial objective was to acquire nineteen ranches consisting of 24,000 acres. Unfortunately, because of limited funds under the IRA land program, the federal government purchased only four ranches totaling 11,071 acres from 1938 to 1943. This land was called the South Fork Indian Reservation in 1941. Nineteen Shoshone families moved to the new land base in 1939, followed by five others in 1943. Most came from the nearby Elko Colony, while six came from Battle Mountain and three from Ruby Valley. These families wanted to call their home the Sohopin Reservation (Cottonwood Tree Reservation), since Sohopin is the native name of the South Fork Valley. However, that name was not chosen. In later years, more land was added to the reservation, which now consists of 13,638 acres.[34]

Superintendent Bowler was never optimistic about establishing reservation land for the Shoshones living in Ruby Valley. She probably knew that the Indian Bureau could not recover the "six miles square" reservation that had once existed in the nineteenth century. Additionally, Bowler disliked the quality of the area in and around the Indian allotments established some twenty years earlier. However, the Indian Bureau knew that Chief Muchach Temoke and others were "wholly unwilling to live anywhere but here [Ruby Valley], the home of their ancestors."[35] The Carson Agency was therefore forced to seek land for them in Ruby Valley. Bowler's first objective was to purchase land near the allotments, but only one white rancher was willing to sell his land, and his price was too high. The best that Bowler and her staff could do was to purchase Odger's Ranch, consisting of 1,984 acres located roughly twenty-five miles from the allotment nucleus. The bureau purchased Odger's Ranch in October 1939.[36] The Temoke family, however, refused to move there because it wanted the restoration of the "six miles square" reservation. Odger's Ranch is now classified as part of the South Fork Reservation, bringing the total acreage to 15,036.

The Indian Bureau also established a new IRA reservation in the Reese River Valley. In July and November 1937, under Bowler's administration the Carson Agency acquired two white-owned ranches: the Bowler (no relation to the superintendent) and the Doyle in Nye County. As before, limited funds in the IRA land program allowed for the purchase of only these two ranches initially. They were renamed the Upper and Lower Districts in 1938 and became the Yomba Reservation. The word *yomba* (yampa) means "wild carrot," a native root eaten by the Shoshones and found in abundance in the Reese River Valley. Because of the small size of the new reservation—3,721 acres—only sixteen Shoshone families could move there in 1938. Four of them came from the Walker River Reservation and were members of the Nye County Shoshone Committee. The other families already lived in and around Reese River. All the families were chosen by the committee in conjunction with Superintendent Bowler. In the early 1940s more families moved there when the Indian Bureau purchased two more white-owned ranches, the Dieringer in 1940 and the Worthington in 1941. In all, the Yomba Reservation now consists of 4,681 acres.[37]

To celebrate the creation of their new reservation homeland, the Shoshones at Yomba sponsored a large fandango in August 1937. It featured handgames, round dances, horse races, and a barbecue. Without doubt, some Shoshones celebrated this event because they were overjoyed about returning to their homeland of central Nevada after having lived on the Walker River Reservation for over a decade. Although the Indian Bureau now encouraged the Shoshones to revive their native traditions, those who moved to Yomba had no need to bring back the fandango, because they had never given it up. Since the Shoshones of central Nevada had never been under strict government supervision before 1933, they were not subject to the Indian Bureau's assimilationist policies in the late nineteenth and early twentieth centuries. Annual fandangos were held on the Yomba Reservation in the late 1930s and into the 1940s.[38]

The Indian Bureau established still another IRA reservation for the nonreservation Western Shoshones in Duckwater. Both whites and Indians wanted a reservation there. In 1934 James Jenkins, a former Indian Bureau employee who heard about the IRA, suggested the Duckwater Valley as a good location. By 1937 several families from Smoky Valley had come to realize that the Indian Bureau had ruled out their native valley as a reservation site. They therefore joined forces with Shoshones of Duckwater and other places to work for the establishment of a reservation in the Duckwater Valley. Specifically, they wanted nine white-owned ranches. The Indian Bureau could not take immediate action because of a shortage of funds. Finally, in 1940, it was able to purchase two ranches, the Florio Home Ranch and the Florio Bank Ranch, for a total of 3,240 acres. These became the Duckwater Reservation. Only twenty families could move to the new site: six from Smoky Valley, two from Tonopah, one from Wells, and the rest from in and around Duckwater. Other families also moved there in 1943 when the Indian Bureau purchased the Munson Ranch. In all, the Duckwater Reservation now consists of 3,642 acres.[39]

Although the federal government was mainly concerned with the Shoshones who had never lived on reservation land up to the 1930s, the Indian Bureau did take an interest in the land needs of those living at Duck Valley. In 1938 it purchased 160 acres of white-owned land, located inside the reservation boundaries. The rancher who owned this homestead had lived there before the arrival of the Paddy Cap Band of northern Paiutes. The Indian Bureau also tried to purchase the heavily wooded area lying south of the reservation as well as six white-owned ranches located southeast of the reservation along the Owyhee River.[40] But the white owners were unwilling to part with their valuable land. Therefore the Indian Bureau was able to add only 160 acres to Duck Valley.

In the end, the following land base was set aside for Western Shoshones under the Indian Reorganization Act of 1934: the South Fork Reservation, the Yomba Reservation, the Duckwater Reservation, Odger's Ranch, and the 160-acre allotment inside the Duck Valley Reservation. These totaled 24,000 acres of new reservation land. Although this figure may seem rather low, it is significant when compared to the pre-IRA period. Before the passage of the 1934 act, the government had set aside only 4,026 acres of land for the nonreservation Shoshones who had rejected moving to Duck Valley up to the early 1930s. The pre-1934 land base consisted of the Ruby Valley allotments (1,230 acres), the central Nevada allotments (1,353 acres), the Battle Mountain Colony (680 acres), the Elko Colony (193 acres, consisting of 160 and 33 at two separate places), the Ely Colony (10 acres), and Indian Ranch in Panamint Valley, California (560 acres).

Even more significant, during the implementation of the IRA the Indian Bureau finally rejected its earlier position that all the Shoshones of the Great Basin should move to Duck Valley. Instead, it accepted the Shoshones' cultural trait of deep attachment to the land and took the initiative in creating reservations in some native Shoshone valleys. Superintendent Bowler must be given credit for having scrapped her earlier plan of one centrally located reservation. Out of her deep respect for Shoshone culture, she ended up rejecting the idea of consolidation and concentration in favor of the Shoshones' request for more than one reservation in their native valleys. In this case the Shoshones actually determined the course of action the Indian Bureau initiated with respect to their future in the 1930s and 1940s.

Unfortunately, not enough reservation land was set aside for the Western Shoshones in the New Deal period. The Indian Bureau had difficulty securing funds from Congress for its IRA land purchase program. This explains why the Shoshone reservations were not created until the late 1930s and early 1940s, and also why only limited numbers of white-owned ranches were purchased in the South Fork, Reese River, and Duckwater valleys. Limited reservation land permitted only 120 of the 847 nonreservation Shoshones of northeastern Nevada to move to the 13,000 acre South Fork Reservation. Odger's Ranch could accommodate only five families. The Yomba and Duckwater reservations had room for only 231 of the 349 Shoshones who lived in central and southern Nevada. Thus, many Shoshones remained nonreservation and nonwards; their nonreservation status prevented them from qualifying for different forms of federal assistance.

Some Shoshones remained dissatisfied even after the creation of the IRA reservations. After all, Muchach Temoke and others wanted the restoration of the "six miles square" in Ruby Valley, while what they actually got was the small, 1,984 acre Odger's Ranch, located some distance from the Temoke homestead area. Bill Gibson and others of Elko wanted a "twenty mile square" reservation. What they actually received was the 13,000 acre South Fork Reservation. Before moving to Duckwater, the Smoky Valley Shoshones had wanted a reservation in their own native valley. But the Indian Bureau ruled out the valley for various reasons, such as its alkaline soil, which rendered it unsuitable for agriculture or cattle grazing. Moreover, the white-owned ranches in Smoky Valley were too far apart, which would prevent the creation of a centralized reservation community if a reservation was located there. The Indian Bureau considered establishing reservations for the Shoshones in Beatty and the Fish Lake Valley of southern Nevada, but did not do so because of limited funds.[41]

The federal government policy of setting aside national park land and federal public domain land made some Shoshones unhappy. In 1933 the government designated nearly all of Death Valley, California, as the Death Valley National Monument, placing it under the jurisdiction of the National Park Service. The federal sector took no notice of the fact that this area was still the native home of the Timbisha Shoshones. By 1936 Superintendent Bowler had learned that the Timbisha Shoshones might be evicted. Her office therefore worked out a deal with the National Park Service allowing the Shoshones to live in a forty acre "Indian Village" near Furnace Creek, the park's headquarters. The Indian Bureau also provided the Park Service with five thousand dollars to build adobe houses in the new village. The Shoshones who lived there were not fully satisfied with this arrangement. In 1938 and again in 1942 they requested a permanent reservation in Death Valley.[42] But the Park Service, even to this day, remains adamantly opposed to establishment of an Indian reservation within park boundaries.

Other Shoshones were troubled by the passage of the Taylor Grazing Act of 1934. This act created the Bureau of Land Management (BLM), which became the official manager of most of the federal public domain land in Nevada. Some Shoshones who firmly believed in the provisions of the 1863 Treaty of Ruby Valley asserted that they still owned their land, based on treaty rights. They stressed that the 1863 treaty did not take away Shoshone land but acknowledged the Indians as the owners of a vast domain in Nevada. They were upset that much of their aboriginal territory was now classified as BLM land. To oppose the government land policy and insist that the treaty must be honored, twelve Shoshone leaders, including Albert Stanton of Ely and Billy Meyers of Wells, held a meeting in Wells, Nevada, in July 1939. Part of their written statement read as follows: "We the Western Shoshone tribe are in Possession all the Land, fish, fowl, the water rights, the games, the forests, are all for the red man."[43] They stated that the newly declared BLM land and other federally claimed property was actually Shoshone country because of treaty rights. The subject of Shoshone land title later became a national issue, especially after 1960.

Some Shoshones were troubled by the land provision of the Indian Reorganization Act itself. They maintained that the Shoshones already owned the land under the treaty, so that reservations would actually restrict their treaty land. Muchach Temoke stated this argument in December 1938: "No other way take up a land but according under this authority such treaty. No purchase land said land but according by the law said treaty."[44] For this reason Temoke and his followers ended up rejecting the IRA in the late 1930s. As already indicated, they wanted the restoration of the "six miles square" reservation promised them in 1863.

IRA Political Reorganization on the Duck Valley Reservation

The first group of Western Shoshones to act upon the Indian Reorganization Act's political provision were those on the Western Shoshone Reservation (Duck Valley). After holding several meetings in 1934, some Shoshone and Paiute leaders ended up favoring the IRA. They concluded that the 1934 law could give their existing twelve-member tribal council more power since the objective of the IRA was local tribal "self-government." As already mentioned, the Duck Valley tribes had had a council since 1911 and had already drafted two tribal constitutions, one in 1919 and the second in 1933. Additionally, the leadership believed that by voting in favor of the IRA, tribal members would be able to secure IRA revolving credit funds to purchase more cattle. The Shoshones also listened as Indian Bureau officials argued in favor of the act. One of these officials was George LaVatta, a Shoshone enrolled in the Fort Hall Reservation. LaVatta met with the Duck Valley leadership in 1934 and told them that "Indians should have a voice in their own affairs."[45] Without doubt, because LaVatta was himself a fellow Shoshone, some leaders took his position seriously.

As mentioned earlier, the IRA did not automatically apply to Native American people across the country. Individual tribes had to vote either in favor of or against the act. In October 1934, 191 Duck Valley residents voted affirmatively, while 12 voted against (54 members were absent because of seasonal labor and did not vote). On the surface it appeared that the two tribes overwhelmingly endorsed the IRA, but in reality only 203 of 373 eligible voters had voted, while 116 others on the reservation stayed away from the polls. The 1933 constitution had ruled out those whom the Indian Bureau labeled as nonprogressive (those who opposed the earlier Indian Bureau assimilationist policies discussed in chapters 3 and 4), and this, more than any other factor, may explain why the 116 did not vote. The solicitor's office of the Department of the Interior, however, ruled that all eligible nonvotes were considered as votes in favor of the act. The Indian Bureau therefore reasoned that 361 of the 373 eligible voters had voted in favor of the IRA. In a later election held in March 1936, 183 voters approved a new tribal constitution entitled "Constitution and By-Laws of the Shoshone-Paiute Tribes." In August 1936, 145 voted to accept a tribal charter.[46] Thus by late 1936 the Shoshones and Paiutes of Duck Valley became an organized IRA tribe.

The new council established in 1936 made many changes. Gone was the old twelve-member council that had existed since 1911. The leaders and Indian Bureau officials involved in the reorganization process from 1934 to 1936 felt that a "smaller number [council] would be more practicable for their needs." The new IRA council therefore consisted of seven members. Another change was in the council's name. Instead of Western Shoshone Tribal Council, the leadership preferred a new name, Shoshone-Paiute Business Council, because the council membership had always included Paiutes and Shoshone-Paiutes as well as Shoshones. The reservation's three electoral districts, which had existed for two decades, were eliminated, and beginning in 1936 tribal council members were elected at large by popular vote. The reorganizers took this action in an attempt to unify the reservation community rather than maintain three separate divisions.[47] Recall that the Collier administration wanted the tribes to develop close-knit communal societies.

Like the old council, the new Shoshone-Paiute Business Council included Shoshones, Paiutes, and Shoshone-Paiutes. The first elected chair was Thomas Premo (1936–1939), a Shoshone, a former student at Carlisle, and a member of the old council since 1912. The second chair was Harry Thacker (1939–1942), a Paiute who had attended the Stewart Indian School. The third was George Brady (1942–1945), another Shoshone. The new seven-member councils in the New Deal period consisted primarily of the middle-aged leaders who had served on the former twelve-member council. They were considered progressive by the Indian Bureau since they spoke English as well as their native languages. The leaders elected to the council were mostly on good terms with one another. This is reflected in the name they chose, the Shoshone-Paiute Tribes of the Duck Valley Reservation; the original name Western Shoshone Reservation went out of use in the 1930s.[48]

The Shoshone-Paiute Business Council possessed much more power than its predecessor, thanks to the 1936 IRA tribal constitution. The constitution gave the council the right to "manage all economic affairs and enterprises of the tribes." It could levy taxes on both tribal members and non-Indians who wanted to establish businesses on the reservation. It could now hire legal counsel or attorneys. It permitted tribal members to start business cooperatives and associations. The council also controlled law and order on the reservation.[49] None of these functions had existed under the old twelve-man council. Of course, increased authority was a major reason why the reservation leadership chose to go under the IRA.

Besides carrying out functions of the old council—such as assigning forty-acre tracts and enrolling new tribal members—the IRA council used its power in many ways. The council's major initiatives in the 1930s and 1940s dealt with the cattle economy. It chartered the cattle association that had been formed in 1922. It issued IRA revolving loans to the association to purchase Hereford bulls to increase the reservation cattle herds. The association was authorized to assume ownership of all bulls on the reservation and also to manage cattle grazing on the reservation. The council also issued IRA loans to individual tribal members to purchase cattle. In 1941 alone, IRA loan funds helped the Indians purchase 108 cows. Because the reservation community wanted more cattle, the council no longer permitted the grazing of white-owned cattle within the reservation boundaries, a practice that had gone on for nearly four decades. The council granted the use of reservation land for certain specific purposes, such as an experimental farm for which eighty acres were set aside. Decades later, in the 1970s, the council allowed a group of tribal members to form a cooperative, which in turn created a communal farm of 650 acres.[50] From an economic standpoint, the Shoshone-Paiute Business Council was an active force in the late 1930s and early 1940s, and in later years.

Although the Shoshone-Paiute Business Council earned good marks in the economic domain, it was visibly weak in other areas. Although it sanctioned the annual Fourth of July fandangos, which had existed since the late nineteenth century, the council took no other measures to elevate native awareness or appreciation of Shoshone and Paiute culture. No round dances or other native traditions took place in the new community gymnasium. Instead, this facility was used for sports and for American-style traditions, including a Christmas Eve gift exchange. In 1939 the council considered outlawing the practice of the peyote religion on the reservation. But through the urging of Indian Bureau Commissioner John Collier, peyote use persisted. Some tribal members today still practice the peyote religion.[51]

The IRA gave the Shoshone-Paiute Business Council a feeling of power in the years following 1936. Generally speaking, the council cooperated with the local Indian Bureau superintendents. But when the leadership felt that bureau officials were being unfair to the Indians or not doing their job properly, the council asserted itself. For example, in 1951 the council requested the removal of Superintendent Bert Courtright who was abusing his position.[52]

In spite of its increased powers, the Shoshone-Paiute Business Council remained under the paternal control of the federal government. The phraseology of the 1936 tribal constitution made it clear that the powers of the council were "subject to any limitation imposed by the Constitution or Statutes of the United States." In addition, the secretary of the interior had the authority to veto or overturn any council ordinance he considered undesirable. If the Duck Valley tribes wanted to amend their new IRA constitution, the changes had to be reviewed by the interior secretary.

Any decision made by the council relating to the disposition of property had to be reviewed by the Indian Bureau.[53] The Indian Bureau also had the authority to approve or reject any legal transaction of the council. Thus the Shoshone-Paiute Business Council had the power of self-government, but only under the control of the federal government.

One objective of the Shoshone-Paiute Business Council was to "establish a more perfect tribal organization," but this dream did not become a reality for all the residents of Duck Valley. In fact, some sectors of the reservation population were largely excluded from the political process by certain tribal politicians who became the dominant force on the tribal council. There came a point when some Shoshones felt that they had lost political control of a reservation that had been set aside for them. Feeling that they no longer possessed a power base, these Shoshones in 1984 considered political cession by forming a "separate Band" and joining ranks with the larger Shoshone population living farther south in Nevada. In 1987 a few leaders created the Western Shoshone Business Council with the name Tosa wihi (White Knife) written on its official letterhead.[54]

Another group largely excluded from the political process was the Paddy Cap Band of Northern Paiutes. Up to the early 1930s, it was represented on the old Western Shoshone Council since the band constituted one of the reservation's three electoral districts. However, the Paddy Caps were labeled nonprogressive and barred from politics as a result of the earlier 1933 constitution, which specified that only progressive individuals could serve on the council. In theory they were still part of the twelve-member council but lacked a voice in the early 1930s. Thus, when the ruling tribal politicians decided to dissolve the old council along with the three electoral districts, the Paddy Cap Paiutes were not present to fight for the existence of the old order. In an era of at-large voting the assertive Paiute-Shoshones were able to take control of the smaller, seven-member IRA council. Like the identifiable Shoshones, the Paddy Caps lost their political power—something they have complained about for the past four decades. As late as 1975 the Paiutes favored the re-creation of electoral districts.[55] This change, however, has not come about, and members of the tribal council continue to be elected by at-large voting.

The Shoshone-Paiute Business Council did not encourage the election of women, although women were allowed to vote in tribal elections. In this respect the council was a continuation of the nineteenth-century order, when Indian Bureau men dealt with Indian men. In the fifty-one-year history of the Duck Valley council, only two women, both Shoshones, have been elected to office. Laura Townsend, the daughter of long-time tribal politician Thomas Premo, was elected as chair in the mid-1970s. More recently, in the late 1980s, Winona Charles was voted in as a regular council member.[56]

In the end, the principal beneficiaries of the Shoshone-Paiute Business Council were the Paiute-Shoshone politicians who ended up controlling the council, especially in the years after World War II. These men and their families placed more emphasis on their Paiute side rather than their Shoshone heritage. Thus, when the federal government settled the Northern Paiute claims case in the late 1970s, the Paiute-Shoshones accepted payment as Northern Paiutes.

The Formation of the Te-Moak Bands of Western Shoshone Indians

While the reorganization process of the Shoshones and Paiutes of the Duck Valley Reservation moved relatively smoothly in the 1930s, the same was not true for the larger numbers of Western Shoshones who lived elsewhere in the Great Basin. A case in point is the Te-Moak Bands of Western Shoshone Indians, one of the three IRA organizations created for and by the Shoshones who had never moved to Duck Valley.

The Indian Bureau official involved in the formation of the Te-Moak Bands organization was Superintendent Bowler of the Carson Agency. She firmly believed that the 1,264 nonreservation Shoshones of northeastern Nevada, under her jurisdiction, needed to come under the provisions of the IRA. She maintained that the IRA was a positive force since it could provide land and loan funds, as well as tribal organization for those tribes who voted to accept the 1934 act, as described above.[57]

Bowler recognized that her mission would be a difficult one. The IRA, after all, was designed for tribes already living on reservation land. The Western Shoshones under her jurisdiction had never lived on reservations, except for the few at the small colonies of Battle Mountain, Elko, and Ely and the tiny allotments in Ruby Valley. Also, the Shoshone population of northeastern Nevada was widely dispersed. This population distribution, so characteristic of the Basin tribes, would make it difficult for the Shoshones to function under a centralized political entity, something that Bowler envisioned for them under the IRA. So far, they had no formal governing body similar to the Western Shoshone Tribal Council that had existed at Duck Valley since 1911. On the other hand, they did have the informal treaty council that had signed the contract with Elko attorney Milton Badt. Under it Badt was granted the authority to pursue claims against the federal government for unkept treaty promises stemming from the nineteenth century (see chapter 4).[58]

Firmly committed to the Indian Bureau's new policy of cultural pluralism, Bowler wanted the Shoshones to establish an IRA government that was native in character. Having examined Indian Bureau documents, she concluded that the Shoshones of the nineteenth century were "for the most part, members of a tribe commonly known as 'Old Chief

Temoak's [Temoke] People'."[59] Bowler gathered correctly that the Shoshones had possessed a loose-knit federated council of independent band
organizations. This council looked to Old Temoke as the overall chief
because of his charismatic leadership. As noted, Temoke was the principal
signer of the 1863 Ruby Valley treaty, which acknowledged that the
Shoshones possessed millions of acres of land in Nevada. Although the
council had become lax over the years, the Shoshones still maintained
some political unity, best exemplified by the establishment of the treaty
council of 1932. Bowler concluded that this body would provide the
foundation for a future IRA council.

Because the Shoshones were spread over such a large area, Bowler did
not have the time or resources to meet everyone in 1934 and 1935. One
of those whom she did not meet was Muchach Temoke, the grandson of
Old Temoke, whose home in Ruby Valley was far off the main travel route.
She did meet the colony Shoshones, who turned out to be the only ones
who voted on the IRA. The colony groups held three separate elections
in June 1935. Of the fourteen eligible voters of the Battle Mountain
Colony, nine voted in favor of the IRA, while the other five did not vote.
Of the forty who were eligible in Elko, thirty-four voted in favor and six
abstained. The Ely Colony Shoshones voted eight in favor, six against,
and twenty-one abstained.[60] In all, only fifty-seven nonreservation Shoshones, of a total population of 1,264 individuals, voted in favor of the
act. The results of the voting showed that the majority of potential adult
Shoshones voters were not involved in this decision, including those
families living in Ruby Valley, Beowawe, Carlin, Starr Valley, Deeth,
Wells, and on the isolated ranches of northeastern Nevada where a large
number were employed. However, the fifty-seven favorable votes were all
that Bowler needed for IRA acceptance.

Why did the colony Shoshones vote the way they did? The Battle
Mountain group favored the act because of an endorsement by Lottie
Boulden, a Shoshone born and raised in Battle Mountain who was a
student at the University of Nevada at Reno in the 1930s. Boulden came
home in 1935 as a summer social worker for the Carson Agency. She
enthusiastically campaigned for the provisions of the IRA the day before
the election. The Elko Colony Shoshones voted for the act after learning
about the IRA land provision. Of course, Bill Gibson and other leaders
favored the establishment of a reservation in the South Fork Valley,
something that was later realized under the IRA.[61] They too voted in the
affirmative.

At the Ely Colony, on the other hand, only eight Ely Colony Shoshones voted in favor, while twenty-one abstained, thereby rejecting the
IRA. Their decision was the result of anti-IRA sentiment that had been
building in northeastern Nevada in 1934 and 1935. The movement was

led by Albert Stanton of Ely, Thomas Pabawena of Wells, and Harry Dixon Tootiaina who had moved to Utah a few years earlier, but who periodically returned to Nevada to voice his concerns. These Shoshones viewed the 1863 Ruby Valley treaty as the supreme law, and they argued that the government was trying to supplant it with the 1934 act. They maintained that the act would thwart the Indians' effort to press claims against the government for unkept treaty promises, even though the IRA itself stated the contrary. Some held that the government needed to fulfill the treaty obligations before the Shoshones would consider the act. They felt that Bowler was pressuring them into accepting the IRA, and therefore wrote: "And this Nevada Indians' Superintendent [Bowler] she leaves law enforcement on Indians here: we don't satisfaction that: this is self-government [IRA], hurt everybody feeling now."[62] Not until the 1960s did the Ely group finally decide to come under an IRA form of government.

Fully aware of the rising opposition, Bowler worked hard to persuade some Shoshone leaders to support the IRA. She gained the backing of Bill Gibson of Elko and for a time secured the support of Muchach Temoke of Ruby Valley.[63] It was probably Temoke's support that encouraged Bowler to move forward, since he was one of the most influential leaders. Temoke, however, always remained suspicious of the act; he was one of those who held that the Ruby Valley treaty was the only law under which the Shoshones must operate.

Bowler met with a large number of Western Shoshones in Elko in May 1936 and encouraged them to go under the IRA. There is no evidence to suggest that they wanted to form a council with a modern constitution, by-laws, and charter. However, some members of the 1932 treaty council realized that a larger number of organized Indians meant a stronger political base. As a unified body, the Shoshones might effectively press the 1863 treaty claims against the government. With this major objective in mind, various Shoshone leaders, including most of those from the treaty council, agreed to organize a federated council with elected representatives coming from the colonies and other groups of nonreservation Shoshones located throughout northeastern Nevada.[64]

In mid-May 1936, six members of the treaty council (two had already rejected the IRA) sat down with Superintendent Bowler and Field Agent George LaVatta and worked out a draft of a constitution. The Shoshone participants, with Indian Bureau backing, agreed to call their new IRA organization the Te-Moak Bands of Western Shoshone Indians. They adopted this name in recognition of Old Temoke (the spelling *Te-Moak* was used in the treaty). The political jurisdiction of the Te-Moak Bands would correspond roughly to the area considered as the treaty territory. Each group of between fifty and one hundred Shoshones living inside this area would organize their own local community council. The local councils in turn would each send a representative to the proposed federated Te-Moak Bands council. Thus the groups at Austin, Battle Mountain, Beowawe, Elko, Ely, and Ruby Valley would each have an elected representative. Any new Shoshone reservation community created under the IRA would also have an elected representative. The federated council would elect its own officers, including a "tribal chief" and a "tribal sub-chief." The participating Shoshone leaders and Indian Bureau officials hoped that the formation of a Te-Moak Bands council would reestablish the native form of government that had existed in the 1860s.[65]

Several months later, in October 1936, the political process of the Te-Moak Bands received a major blow when its draft constitution was rejected by the central office of the Indian Bureau in Washington, D.C. William Zimmerman, Jr., assistant commissioner under Collier, wrote that the nonreservation and colony Shoshones of northeastern Nevada were nothing more than "scattered groups of Western Shoshone" Indians, constituting neither a tribe nor organized bands. Their identity as a tribe, he stated, had dissolved after the majority had moved to Duck Valley in the nineteenth century.[66] But Zimmerman was dead wrong. As a Washington bureaucrat who had never spent time in Nevada, he failed to realize that only a small minority of Shoshones had moved to Duck Valley, while the majority remained off-reservation in the Great Basin. Furthermore, the majority who had never moved to Duck Valley still considered themselves a tribe. When Muchach Temoke and Thomas Wahne had traveled to the nation's capital in 1919, they had introduced themselves as "members of the Western Shoshone tribe."[67] Zimmerman failed to recognize the Shoshones as a tribe because they didn't live on reservations and were widely dispersed. His image of a tribe was a large group that lived in one locality, preferably on a reservation, as emphasized in the IRA itself. He lacked any understanding of the Great Basin Shoshones' social organization and political structure. The only concession he made was that perhaps the colony Shoshones, living on trust land, might first organize as the Te-Moak Bands and then adopt the other groups at a later date.

Another blow to the Te-Moak Bands organization was the fact that not all Western Shoshones wanted to be involved. Specifically, the Shoshones living around Austin, in central Nevada, did not wish to be included. These Shoshones had never recognized the leadership of Old Temoke in the nineteenth century. Their ancestors had recognized other leaders, including Kawich and Tu-tu-wa. The followers of Tu-tu-wa believed in hereditary leadership and had had their own band organization as late as the early 1930s. As noted in chapter 4, they selected Alex Gilbert as the new Tu-tu-wa chief for the central Nevada region in 1931. This group had no interest in the Te-Moak Bands organization efforts. Thus the Indian Bureau eliminated Austin from the draft constitution.[68]

Not until late 1937 did the Indian Bureau finally authorize the Te-Moak Bands to organize. Following Zimmerman's earlier suggestion, only the Elko Colony Shoshones could organize at first; they would then have to adopt the other groups. This course of action alienated some of the leaders. The treaty council, which now called itself the Te-Moak Bands of Western Shoshone Council, could not become the official governing body. At this time, Muchach Temoke, one leading member, lost interest and withdrew from the Te-Moak organization efforts, even though the organizers continued to use his family's name.[69] Without doubt, Temoke was extremely disappointed, since he probably expected to become the chief of the Te-Moak Bands to perpetuate the hereditary leadership his family had held in the nineteenth century. His self-removal weakened the treaty council even further.

In response to the directive from Washington, the Elko Colony Shoshones voted on their constitution and by-laws in May 1938. Of the sixty eligible voters, forty-seven voted to accept. Overall, these Elko voters had a favorable attitude toward the IRA. Many of them would soon be moving to the new South Fork Reservation near Elko, which had been created under the IRA. Some months later, in October, the first Te-Moak Bands council election took place. All five council members voted into office came from Elko: Jimmy James, Harry Tom, Charles Malotte, Sr., Dick Richards, and Ralph Healey. In December the colony by thirty-seven votes approved the tribal charter. Thus, by late 1938 the new Te-Moak Bands organization, toward which Bowler had worked since 1934, became a reality. However, the new organization lacked representation from the larger numbers of Shoshones who lived in northeastern Nevada. The treaty council ceased to exist after the formation of the Te-Moak Bands.[70]

For much of its early history, the Te-Moak Bands organization was not a federated council. Nor was it representative of all the Western Shoshones of northeastern Nevada. Thus, when the Te-Moak Bands held its second election in 1940 to adopt other groups, the Shoshones at Beowawe, Ely, Ruby Valley, and Wells chose not to participate. The Battle Mountain Colony sent one representative in 1940, but after 1941, it ceased to be involved. The Elko representatives moved to the newly established South Fork Reservation in the early 1940s. Those Shoshones who remained in Elko dropped out. From 1942 to 1966 the Te-Moak Bands council actually represented only the South Fork Reservation, since South Fork was the only location participating.[71]

The Te-Moak Bands council, however, was an active organization in its early years, focusing its attention primarily on South Fork. In conjunction with the Indian Bureau, it selected the nineteen families of Battle Mountain and Elko who moved to the South Fork Reservation. It also selected the two or three families who later moved to Odger's Ranch, since this small reserve was part of the Te-Moak Bands jurisdiction. The council also secured IRA loans and issued them to the families who settled in South Fork. It created and chartered a livestock association for the South Fork Reservation.[72]

In recent years, the Te-Moak Bands organization has become a federated governing body representing most Shoshones in northeastern Nevada. This development came about when a younger generation of Shoshones decided to make the organization operate as it was originally intended (see chapter 7). Currently the Te-Moak Bands organization includes Battle Mountain, Elko, Odger's Ranch, the South Fork Reservation, and the Wells Colony.[73] To this day, however, some older Shoshones still keep their distance from the organization. For example, Frank Temoke, Sr., has never served on the council even though in 1953 he replaced his father as the hereditary chief of Ruby Valley and also for those who recognize his leadership.[74]

The Formation of the Yomba and Duckwater Shoshone Tribes

Superintendent Bowler also wanted the nonreservation Western Shoshones of central Nevada to be part of the Te-Moak Bands organization. This was part of her effort to create a single tribal political organization for the widely dispersed groups of Shoshones. However, she quickly discovered that not all Shoshones wanted to come under one large political body, a notion that was foreign to them. Modifying her original plans, Bowler hoped that Shoshones native to central Nevada might form their own federated council. She suggested that they might form the Kawich Bands in recognition of Chief Kawich who was the leader of many nineteenth-century Shoshones living in central and southwestern Nevada.[75] This name would match that of the Te-Moak Bands to the north. But the idea collapsed when the Shoshones of central Nevada wanted to live on separate reservations, forming separate political organizations.

The first group of central Nevada Shoshones to organize politically under the IRA were those who moved to the Yomba Reservation in the Reese River Valley in 1938. They called their governing body the Yomba Tribal Council. The council actually had its beginnings four years earlier, in 1934, when several central Nevada Shoshone families were still living on the Walker River Reservation in western Nevada. As already mentioned, they had been living among the Paiutes for a decade after leaving their native homes. More than anything else, they desired to return to central Nevada, to the area called Nye County.

In mid-1934 Indian Bureau officials discussed the provisions of the IRA with the Indian residents of Walker River. Immediately, the Shoshone families became excited over two provisions: the one to create new reservations for those Indians who did not have their own homes, and the one to provide revolving loans for tribes to establish tribal enterprises. These Shoshones saw the IRA as a way to return to their native places in central Nevada, possibly to live on a new reservation where they might qualify for IRA loans to purchase cattle.[76]

In response to the IRA, the Shoshones at Walker River organized the Nye County Shoshone Committee. The members consisted of Dave (Kawich) Clifford, Alice (Kawich) Hooper, Bud Decker, James Darrough, and Willie Bobb, all Shoshones native to the valleys of central Nevada.[77] Clifford and Hooper were the grandchildren of the influential Chief Kawich (also Cowitz or Cowitch) who lived close to Belmont, Nevada, in the mid-nineteenth century. Because of his deep attachment to the land, Kawich had rejected the Powell-Ingalls suggestion of 1874 that his followers should leave their homeland and move elsewhere. When Old Kawich died some years later, he was replaced by his son Bill Kawich, the father of Clifford and Hooper. Thus the brother and sister were perpetuating a native leadership line. Their major objective was to secure a reservation in their homeland.

This committee was responsible for the formation of the Yomba Reservation in 1937, in the Reese River Valley of central Nevada. Superintendent Bowler and the committee selected sixteen families to move to the new reservation. As a reward for their effort, the families of four committee members were among the sixteen: Alice Hooper, Bud Decker, James Darrough, and Willie Bobb. Dave Clifford moved to Yomba for one year and then returned to Walker River because his wife had land there. The twelve other families were already living in central Nevada, in the Reese River Valley and the nearby Smoky Valley.[78]

After settling on the Yomba Reservation, the Nye County Shoshone Committee decided to drop its original name. First, it was inappropriate for a committee that did not represent all the Shoshones living in Nye County. Additionally, several of the Shoshone families of the region expressed little if any interest in moving to the Reese River Valley. Instead, they preferred new reservation land elsewhere. Those who moved to Yomba wanted a council name to correspond with the name of their reservation. In the spring of 1938, the committee was renamed the Yomba Tribal Business Committee.[79] For some reason the Shoshones at Yomba chose not to name their organization the Kawich Bands, as Bowler had suggested earlier. Perhaps this was because the ancestors of some

Yomba families had not recognized the leadership of Kawich in the nineteenth century. Rather, they had followed Chief Tu-tu-wa, who was a native of the Reese River Valley.

Unlike other tribal groups, the Shoshones at Yomba never did vote to accept or reject the IRA. The deadline to vote on the 1934 act was June 18, 1936. The Shoshones could not vote since at that time they were still living at Walker River and were not considered Paiutes. On the other hand, the Indian Bureau did allow them to organize under the 1934 act since the families were living on an IRA reservation by 1938 and also wanted IRA loans to purchase cattle. It appears that the Yomba Shoshones had no desire to have an IRA constitution with by-laws and a corporate charter. But since IRA organization was a prerequisite to secure loans, they voted thirty to zero in favor of their "Constitution and By-Laws of the Yomba Shoshone Tribe of the Yomba Reservation" in December 1939.[80] At the same time, they voted to approve a corporate charter.

In contrast to those involved in the formation of the Te-Moak Bands, the Shoshones who settled on the Yomba Reservation did not wrestle over the issue of treaty rights. Most ancestors of the Shoshones of central Nevada had not participated in the 1863 Ruby Valley treaty. In fact, the members of the earlier Nye County Shoshone Committee had called themselves the "unsigned Indians," meaning that their ancestors were not involved in the 1863 treaty.[81]

Not until 1940 did the Yomba Shoshones of Reese River hold their first IRA tribal election. The following men were elected to the first Yomba Tribal Council: James Bobb as chair, Bud Decker, Willie Williams, Willie Bobb, Wixon Charley, and Harry Frank. For the first time in their history, a group of Shoshones of central Nevada now had a formal, American-style tribal council with a constitution and by-laws. This was also the first time they had had direct dealings with the Indian Bureau. Their status as nonwards was officially ended. The Indian Bureau's neglect of them, ever since their ancestors had chosen not to move to Duck Valley, ended at last under the Indian New Deal.[82]

Like other tribes that voted in favor of an IRA governing apparatus, the Yomba Tribal Council was granted various powers, including the authority to hire attorneys, to purchase and manage property, and to choose its own officers. But at the same time, council decisions were subject to the scrutiny of the Indian Bureau. The Yomba Shoshones had a new power base, but their self-government was limited. Nevertheless, they were able to secure reservation land and loans under the IRA. In 1940 the Yomba council borrowed twenty-four thousand dollars to purchase cattle. Their herds numbered only 300 in 1938 but totaled 1,554 by 1944.[83]

The last group of Western Shoshones to organize under the IRA were those Shoshones who settled on the Duckwater Reservation in 1940. Like those at Yomba, they had formed a governing committee before their reservation was established. This political organization was founded in May 1937 when Superintendent Bowler met with some central Nevadan Shoshones who wanted a reservation in the Duckwater Valley. They either did not want to move to the newly established Yomba reservation or had already been told that it was too small for more residents. Aware that the Indian Bureau had already recommended against a reservation in Smoky Valley, and perhaps other places as well, the Shoshones favored Duckwater for two reasons. One was that a local, indebted white rancher wanted to sell his ranch to the Indians. Additionally, the valley had available water and good grazing land for a future cattle business.[84]

Fully supporting their intentions, Superintendent Bowler encouraged the Shoshones to create a committee and to write letters to Congress urging it to provide funds for the establishment of a reservation. Bowler made this suggestion because the appropriation for the IRA land program had been largely depleted, and more funds were needed to establish more reservations. In response to her suggestion, the Shoshones formed the Committee of Southern Shoshone Indians, consisting of nine members: Chief Blackeye of Duckwater, Tom Adams of Sharp, Richard Birchum of Austin, Willie Smith and Raymond Graham of Round Mountain, Mike Millett of Smoky Valley, Henry Sam and Wagon Johnnie of Tonopah, and Brownie Sam of Smoky Valley.[85] This committee was the precursor of today's Duckwater Tribal Council. Its major objective in the late 1930s was the formation of a reservation in Duckwater.

Over a three-year period from 1937 to 1940 the committee wrote numerous letters to key individuals, including President Franklin D. Roosevelt and Senators James Scrugham and Key Pittman of Nevada, asking for necessary congressional funds for the IRA land program. Their mission was successful. The Indian Bureau purchased two white-owned ranches and established the Duckwater Reservation in 1940.[86] In 1943 the government purchased a third ranch, and the entire reservation land base now totals 3,642 acres.

In conjunction with Don Foster, the Carson Agency superintendent who replaced Bowler, the Committee of Southern Shoshone Indians selected the twenty-one families who moved to Duckwater in 1940. Eight families came from Smoky Valley; ten others came from Cherry Creek, Warm Springs, White River, Little Fish Lake, Sharp, Eden Creek, Wells, and Tonopah. The three remaining families already lived in Duckwater.[87]

Like the Shoshones at Yomba, those who settled at Duckwater were unable to vote on the IRA. Yet they too needed to operate under an IRA form of government to secure government loans for cattle. Indian Bureau field agent George LaVatta assisted them in drafting the "Constitution and By-Laws of the Duckwater Shoshone Tribe of the Duckwater Reservation." In November 1940 the eligible voters voted thirty-six to zero to adopt the document. They also adopted a tribal charter, and the Duckwater Tribal Council officially came into existence. The tribe held its first IRA election in January 1941. The following persons were elected: Wagon Johnnie as chair, Raymond Graham as vice-chair, Brownie Sam, Johnnie George, and Johnnie Charles.[88] Three of these men had served on the earlier committee.

It must be emphasized that the Indian Bureau determined the form of the constitutions and by-laws and tribal charters that came into existence under the IRA. The Indian Bureau created its Organization Division in 1935 to assist the tribes in reorganizing under the 1934 act. The division used a "model constitution" (Circular Book No. 113984) as a guide to help the tribes to draft their IRA documents.[89] This explains why the Indian documents to some extent resemble the U.S. Constitution. The preamble to the Duck Valley constitution includes the phrase "to establish a more perfect" reservation government, and it also includes a Bill of Rights with certain basic constitutional guarantees. All IRA governing documents were sent to the bureau's Organization Division for revision and approval. Overall, the native people themselves had only limited input.

Because the Indian Bureau played the leading role in drafting the constitutions and by-laws and charters, the Shoshone leaders across Nevada often had difficulty understanding their IRA governing documents. In 1936 when Thomas Premo, the first Shoshone chair of the new IRA council on the Duck Valley Reservation, traveled to Washington, D.C., as one of two delegates, one of his concerns was the need to thoroughly understand the jargon-ridden tribal charter, loaded with legal terminology.[90] In 1941 at a large Indian conference in Carson City, Brownie Sam, one of the founders of the Duckwater Tribal Council, stated that "most of the Indians do not understand all yet but the council is learning all the time."[91] At the same conference, Willie Woods of South Fork noted that "we have been trying to study [our] constitution and take responsibility."[92] To this day some individuals are still trying to make sense out of the IRA tribal constitutions and by-laws and charters, documents that only an attorney or a college-educated businessperson can fully understand.

Not all Western Shoshones organized politically under the IRA, especially those living in southern Nevada and southeastern California. George Hanson and his extended family of the Indian Ranch in Panamint Valley, California, voted eight to zero in favor of the IRA in June 1935. Yet they never did organize under the 1934 act, nor did they create a formal tribal council. Most likely the Indian Bureau was busy assisting other Great Basin groups and simply overlooked this small Shoshone band.[93] In contrast, the nearby Shoshones of Death Valley, California, did establish a three-member tribal council in December 1937, consisting of Hank Patterson as chair, Tom Wilson as vice-chair, and Fred Thompson as secretary. Superintendent Bowler encouraged them to form this council, which could work with the Indian Bureau.[94] The Death Valley Shoshones, however, could not organize as an IRA group because they did not live on federal trust land set aside as an Indian reservation.

In the end, the IRA had created three new political subdivisions within the larger Western Shoshone population of the Great Basin: the Te-Moak Bands of Western Shoshone Indians, the Yomba Shoshone Tribe of the Yomba Reservation, and the Duckwater Shoshone Tribe of the Duckwater Reservation. Of course, these entities had never existed before the 1930s. These new divisions created new identities and pushed into the background the older pre-IRA identities. Such was the case with the Tu-tu-wa Band organization, which still existed in the early 1930s. When the Duckwater and Yomba reservations were created, many members of the old Tu-tu-wa Band, living mostly in the Smoky and Reese River valleys, moved to these IRA reservations. Although the Tu-tu-wa identity became secondary, it has not been completely forgotten, and some Shoshones can still trace their ancestry back to this group. In December 1947, a few Shoshones wrote to the *Reno Gazette* calling themselves members of the "Too-toa-ina [Tu-tu-wa] band."[95]

Although most Shoshones accepted the new political subdivisions, others did not. Some still maintain that the IRA governments fractured the Shoshone people into separate groups who no longer saw themselves as unified. Edward McDade from the South Fork Reservation pointed out this situation in 1965: "I want to remain a Shoshone and be recognized as a member of one Shoshone Nation, not as a member of a Shoshone sub-tribe."[96] Saggie Williams of Battle Mountain expressed a nearly identical view in 1980: "The people were no longer of one mind. The Indian Reorganization Act destroyed the unity of the people . . . Before the IRA, the people were the voice."[97] Nevertheless, the IRA governments remain intact today.

Other Aspects of the New Deal

The Western Shoshone people were affected by educational changes that took place during the New Deal. First, the state-run segregated Indian schools in Battle Mountain and Elko, created in 1923 for white racist motives, were eliminated. These Indian schools were always inferior educationally to white schools. Therefore, at the request of the Indian Bureau, especially Superintendent Bowler, the Elko Indian school was abolished in 1935 and the one in Battle Mountain in 1936. The Indian students attending local integrated schools had their tuition paid for under the Johnson-O'Malley Act (JOM) of 1934, which provided for the expenses of Indian students in public schools. The students on the Duck Valley Reservation attended the newly established Swayne Public School, established on the reservation in 1931; their tuition was also provided by JOM.[98]

At the same time the Indian Bureau created its own new elementary schools for Indian children living in isolated places that lacked educational opportunities. The Reese River Day School was established on the new Yomba Reservation in 1939, followed by the Duckwater Day School in 1941.[99] These schools received no JOM support since they were under the jurisdiction of the Indian Bureau.

The Indian Bureau also took an interest in the higher education of native students. Three Western Shoshone students attended college in the 1930s. One of these was Lottie Boulden of Battle Mountain, mentioned earlier. She secured an Indian Bureau educational loan, enabling her to earn a bachelor's degree in economics from the University of Nevada at Reno in 1937.[100] Before the 1930s the federal government had been only nominally interested in the postsecondary education of Native Americans.

Some aspects of Indian education remained unchanged. For example, many Indian students continued to be sent to the large off-reservation boarding schools, including the Stewart Indian School and the Sherman Institute in Riverside, California. This old policy remained in effect for students living in areas that lacked a high school. The Duck Valley Reservation did not offer reservation-based secondary education until the mid-1940s.

The issue of treaty claims continued to be a major concern of the Western Shoshones in the 1930s. As noted in chapter 4, the Shoshone leaders of northeastern Nevada negotiated a contract with Elko attorney Milton Badt in 1932, allowing him to serve as their legal counsel. They sought to press claims against the federal government for unkept promises stemming from the 1863 Ruby Valley treaty. The 1932 contract, however, was considered invalid due to improper procedure. In 1935 and 1936, new contracts were signed, officially paving the way for Badt to proceed toward a final settlement.[101]

Badt's task was a difficult one. To file claims in the U.S. Court of Claims, a tribe first had to secure a special jurisdictional act from Congress. Badt persuaded the Nevada congressional delegation to introduce congressional bills on behalf of the Western Shoshones. From 1934 to 1944, Nevada congressmen introduced nine separate bills into Congress.[102] All failed. If only one had passed, it would have allowed the Shoshones to sue in the Court of Claims.

The jurisdictional bills implied that the Shoshones could not recover their treaty territory. As far as Badt and other public officials were concerned, Shoshone land had been permanently lost, but the tribe should be compensated for this loss. If the Shoshones won their suit, they would be awarded money. The treaty territory would be surveyed and valued at $1.25 per acre. The money would not be distributed in per capita payments. Instead, it would be used to purchase more land for the Shoshones and to build houses on the land.[103]

The Western Shoshones in general were not aware of the contents of the jurisdictional bills. If some of the leaders had understood them, they would have rejected them. Some Shoshones still claimed title to their treaty territory and therefore did not want money. Aware that the jurisdictional bills had failed and wanting a quick settlement, Muchach Temoke complained in 1938, "What the law makers waiting for . . . You government enforce your own laws, but not investigate our Court of Claims . . . I am not received my rights."[104] Temoke maintained that the treaty claims needed to be settled before the Shoshones would consider the IRA. No settlement was reached in the 1930s and 1940s.

One outcome of the New Deal was the growth of scholarly interest in the Native American tribes. This development resulted from the rise of anthropology as a field of study in the 1920s and 1930s and also from the Indian Bureau's interest in revitalizing native cultures. The Indian Bureau created its Applied Anthropology Unit (AAU) for this purpose in the mid-1930s.[105]

Julian Steward, who held a Ph.D. degree in anthropology from the University of California at Berkeley, was one scholar who studied the Western Shoshone. In 1935 and 1936 he conducted six months of field research among the Shoshone and other tribes of the Great Basin. Steward identified Shoshones living in separate localities, from Death Valley, California, to northern Nevada. Here was solid evidence that the Shoshones continued to occupy the native places of their ancestors.[106]

Steward's fieldwork resulted in several publications, including two substantial studies: *Basin-Plateau Aboriginal Sociopolitical Groups* (1938) and *Culture Element Distributions: XIII, Nevada Shoshone* (1940). In these as well as other works, Steward argued that the Basin tribes, including the Shoshones, were "simple hunters and gatherers," with a simple social organization based on the family. Their life-style was determined by the desert region, which had limited natural resources.[107]

In early 1936 the Indian Bureau called upon Steward to advise how the Shoshones and other Basin tribes might best adapt to its new policy of cultural revival. Commissioner Collier wanted to revive native ways and intertwine them with modern life. Steward was selected because of his earlier research and also because of his employment in the Bureau of American Ethnology, an agency that agreed to assist the Indian Bureau.[108]

In December 1936 Steward submitted his report to the Indian Bureau, entitled "Report on Shoshonean Tribes (Utah, Idaho, Nevada, Eastern California)." His study proved to be no help. He maintained that the Basin Shoshone had not possessed band organizations in native times, nor did band organizations currently exist. He completely misread their rich cultural heritage, concentrating only on the material aspects. Steward therefore opposed the Indian Bureau's effort to organize the Shoshone politically as the Te-Moak Bands. He wrote, "Do not complicate and endanger them with a tribal council, do not baffle them with a constitution and charter, do not make them wards of the government." Steward's solution was to allow Shoshones to assimilate slowly into mainstream America.[109] He opposed the government plan to purchase larger, centralized reservations for the Shoshones. If the Indian Bureau wanted to buy land, he maintained, it should acquire small parcels for independent families. His report was rejected by the Indian Bureau.

Another scholar who studied the Western Shoshones in the mid-1930s was Jack S. Harris, a graduate student in anthropology from Columbia University, New York. Unlike Steward, Harris focused his attention on only one group of Shoshones, the White Knife of the Duck Valley Reservation. His study "The White Knife Shoshoni of Nevada" (1940) dealt with precontact culture, and also with cultural change in the postcontact period. Harris argued that the White Knives had been acculturated because they now lived in the modern world and enjoyed American luxuries, including the automobile. On the other hand, they still preserved aspects of their native culture, including the handgames and round dances held during the annual Fourth of July celebrations. His study was an early example of the emergence of acculturation studies in the 1930s, a watershed in cultural anthropology.[110]

The Indian Bureau objective to revitalize native culture was largely unnecessary, for the Shoshones already possessed a native culture, including art. The women still wove baskets, and their skills did not have to be relearned. The Carson Agency of the Indian Bureau created the Wai-Pai-Shoshone Craftsmen, Inc., in 1938 to help artisans produce and market their work. It made some profits in the late 1930s and early 1940s. But this program faded out of existence by the mid-1940s when a new Indian Bureau administration no longer had an interest in encouraging native art. Regardless of the policy change, some basketmakers found their own markets. Among these were the Shoshone women of Darwin, California, who continued to sell their baskets to white buyers in nearby Lone Pine, California.[111]

Nor did the Shoshones need encouragement regarding native religious practices. For example, the Sun Dance religion was introduced into Nevada from the Bannock Creek district of the Fort Hall Reservation in

Idaho in the early twentieth century. Some Shoshone held the dances at three northeastern Nevada locations: Elko, Ely, and Wells. The dances were intended to heal the sick and continued to be held in the 1930s. In July 1937 alone, two Sun Dances were held at two different places, near Ely and Wells. The Indian Bureau did not encourage the Shoshones to practice this religion; instead, the Shoshones themselves took the initiative to sponsor the Sun Dance ceremonies. [112]

A few Shoshones practiced the peyote religion in the 1930s. Like the Sun Dance, peyote was brought into the Great Basin in the early twentieth century. Its originator was Sam Lone Bear, a Lakota from the Pine Ridge Reservation in South Dakota. By 1939 some Shoshones who had settled on the Fallon Reservation in western Nevada had accepted the peyote faith. One of these was Jim Street who had earlier lived on the Goshute Reservation along the Utah-Nevada state line. The religion involves the use of the peyote cactus plant, which grows in northern Mexico and certain areas of the southwestern United States. Those who take peyote as a religious sacrament stress that their religion emphasizes hard work and abstinence from alcohol. Although Commissioner Collier encouraged the peyote religion, his freedom of religion policy was not needed, for the Nevada Indians practiced the religion anyway, regardless of new Indian Bureau policy. [113]

Lastly, the Indian Bureau did not have to encourage the Shoshones to practice their native fandangos. In the 1930s fandangos continued to be held at different places, both on- and off-reservation. But fandango locations became fewer. After the formation of the Yomba and Duckwater reservations, fandangos were no longer held at the older traditional sites in the Reese River and Smoky valleys. Instead, the fandangos were held on the newly formed IRA reservations. The Yomba Reservation became a center of annual fandango activities in the late 1930s and 1940s. [114]

6

FROM THE NEW DEAL
TO TERMINATION
1941–1960

The decade of the 1940s brought two major changes that dramatically affected all the native peoples of the United States. The first was U.S. involvement in World War II (1941–1945). After Japan attacked and destroyed much of the American naval fleet in Pearl Harbor on December 7, 1941, the United States immediately declared war against Japan, siding with the Allies (England, France, etc.) against the Axis (Germany, Japan, etc.). The nation began to channel its resources into domestic wartime production and overseas military operations. One consequence was that most New Deal programs, including the Civilian Conservation Corps and Public Works Administration, were eliminated in 1942. In the end, the New Deal was a victim of U.S. involvement in World War II.[1]

The second major development was a new federal Indian policy called "termination" (1945–1960). It was a multifaceted and sometimes contradictory policy reflecting an age of conservatism, conformity, and prosperity. Government officials spoke of "freeing" and "emancipating" the Indians, or simply assimilating them into mainstream America. Congress reduced and, in some instances, eliminated funds for various Indian programs under the Bureau of Indian Affairs (BIA, the new name for the old Indian Bureau). It also provided some new funds to help the tribes become self-sustaining before "cutting them loose." Congress eliminated a few older statutory laws applying to Indians only. The policymakers sought to abolish some Indian reservations and encouraged the Indians to relocate in urban areas and join ranks with white Americans. The BIA made plans to transfer its functions to other federal agencies, various state governments, and the Indians themselves. Government officials expected the natives to become more independent and responsible in handling their own affairs. In short, the federal government wanted to "get out of the Indian business" by dissolving its long-standing guardian-ship over the Indian tribes.[2]

Like many other tribal groups across the country, the Western Shoshones were "targeted" for termination beginning in 1945. The Basin Shoshones, however, did not simply accept the government's postwar Indian policy. Rather, they reacted to the changes by accepting some elements of termination and rejecting others. The Shoshones were not always unanimous in their opinions, and often took sides over the various facets of the new policy. In general the Shoshones did not welcome termination. They frequently expressed opposition and seldom showed acceptance. Because of the Shoshones' opposition, the federal government made no effort to force termination upon them. For this reason, most aspects of termination had only a minimal impact on the Shoshones.

Although the United States did not enter World War II until December 1941, its policymakers had anticipated U.S. participation well before the bombing of Pearl Harbor. Accordingly, on September 20, 1940, Congress passed the Selective Service Act, the first peace-time draft in the nation's history. Since all Native Americans were classified as U.S. citizens, the result of a 1924 congressional act, eligible Indians were required to register for the draft. Reservation superintendents had the task of registering those who lived on reservations, while Indians living off-reservation were required to report to county offices for registration.[3]

The Western Shoshone population soon heard about the peace-time draft law. The older leaders were disturbed that the nation demanded that young Indian men register for the military service. Some maintained that young Shoshones should not have to go to war because of the 1863 Ruby Valley treaty, which had provided for peace and friendship. A few leaders interpreted this peace treaty as a permanent agreement. There-fore, they believed, the young men should not have to register for military service.[4]

During the first week of October 1940, some Western Shoshone leaders, led by Muchach Temoke, Willie Harney, and Johnny Johnson, held a meeting in Ruby Valley and drafted a resolution regarding America's impending participation in World War II. Having no direct interest in the war, these Shoshone leaders wanted the United States to stay out of Europe. But if the country was invaded, the Shoshones would willingly join ranks with the general population to fight the enemy. It must be emphasized, however, that they did not exactly want to defend white Americans—they were much more concerned about protecting "native land, America," or Newe Sokopia (Indian land).[5] These Shoshones were telling the young men that registering for the draft was not important, unless the United States was invaded.

On October 24, 1940, a larger number of Western Shoshones, along with Northwestern Shoshones from Utah and Goshutes from the Goshute Reservation, held a meeting in Wells, Nevada. This gathering included Albert Stanton from Ely, Annie Tommy from Goshute, George Paharagosam from Washakie, Utah, and Jim Charley, Billy Myers, Charlie Brigham, and Thomas Pabawena, all from Wells. These individuals took the resolution drafted by Muchach Temoke and others three weeks earlier and expanded upon it. Specifically, they included portions of the Ruby Valley and Box Elder treaties made by the United States with the Western and Northwestern Shoshones in 1863. Their message was that since peace treaties had been made with both tribes seventy-seven years earlier, the Shoshones should not have to fight in a U.S. war. Additionally, they maintained—incorrectly—that the government had promised Indian veterans both land and money for fighting in World War I. Because the veterans had never been paid these benefits, the Indians of 1940 should not have to register for the draft.[6]

After the Wells meeting, three Shoshone delegates traveled to Salt Lake City to publicize their resolution. There they met with officials from the *Salt Lake Tribune,* the Utah governor's office, and Fort Douglas, a military base in Salt Lake. The officials sent the resolution to the Indian Bureau. In response the bureau worked hard to oppose the antidraft resolution and to defuse Shoshone opposition. It labeled the leaders involved as a "small" or "minority" group with little or no influence over the larger Western Shoshone population.[7]

In the end, dozens of young Western Shoshones registered for the draft beginning in late 1940. They had several motives for registering, including their desire to be adventuresome and the need to make money. Many, perhaps most, were registered by Indian Bureau superintendents: 43 registered on the Duck Valley Reservation, 9 on the South Fork Reservation, 11 from the Battle Mountain Colony, 6 from the Ely Colony, 7 from the Elko Colony, 7 from the Duckwater Reservation, 3 from the Yomba Reservation, and 5 from the Fallon Reservation. Others not living on reservations or in colonies registered at local county draft offices. In this category, 7 registered from Death Valley, California, and 11 from Austin, Nevada.[8] Nearly all these young men were later drafted and served in the armed services during World War II.

Not all Native Americans waited to be drafted; some took the initiative and enlisted in the various branches of the armed forces. For example, in 1942 twenty-three members of the Stewart Indian School football team enlisted in the military service, some before they had received their high school diplomas. At least three were Western Shoshones: John Billie, Earl Crum, and Bobby Birchum.[9] World War II was the most popular war in

American history, and the Indians were not immune to the fervor of popular patriotic feeling. This explains why some tribal members enlisted in the armed forces instead of waiting to be drafted.

While fighting overseas, many Western Shoshone troops wrote home to family members to describe the war and their experiences. Richard Birchum of Austin wrote from Belgium in 1945 to highlight the large-scale fighting in Europe near the war's end. Telling of one particular battle, Birchum wrote, "I never thought I would come out alive."[10]

U.S. involvement in World War II also affected Indian life at home. Indian reservations across the country did not escape wartime patriotism and hysteria. On the Duck Valley Reservation, the Shoshones and Paiutes shifted their attention from the New Deal to the war situation. When the reservation community produced its first tribal newsletter in 1940, called the *Duck Valley News,* one of the feature articles focused on German aggression in Europe. After the bombing of Pearl Harbor, the tribal council held a special meeting to discuss "the war conditions and what the Indians can do to help win the war, and to prepare for anything that might arise here on the reservation." The council made several recommendations: the people must preserve enough food to feed themselves, the tribes could help finance America's war by buying "Defense Bonds and Stamps," the Indians must be prepared for unexpected air raids by foreign invaders, suspicious persons must be reported to the appropriate authorities, and guards should be placed around the Wild Horse Dam for security. Some of these recommendations were carried out in part, and such measures continued to be discussed in later meetings.[11]

Indian Bureau support for all the Western Shoshone communities was substantially reduced during the war years. One employee of the Carson Agency told the Shoshones on the Yomba Reservation "that it was hard . . . to dig a well as there were no more funds."[12] The Yomba group was told to support the war effort by growing "Victory Gardens" and supporting the nation's "Farm Defense Program." These suggestions were impractical, given that the Shoshones lived in a desert region. The Indians at Yomba asked that the government purchase two more white-owned ranches to be added to the reservation. But because of wartime budget limitations, the Indian Bureau did not enlarge the reservation.[13]

After the war ended in August 1945, some Shoshone casualties were honored posthumously for having given their lives in the service of the United States. Francis Muncey of Battle Mountain was one of these. While a junior in high school at age nineteen, he enlisted in the armed forces in February 1944 and was killed in action in February 1945. Muncey was awarded the Silver Star after his death. The town of Battle Mountain named its local American Legion post the Francis Muncey Post No. 15 in honor of Muncey.[14] On the Duck Valley Reservation, the

Shoshones and Paiutes created their own American Legion post and named it the Jack Hanks Post No. 48, in recognition of Andrew Jack and Clarence Hanks who were also killed in action.

In July 1946, roughly a year after World War II had ended, some Shoshones sponsored a Sun Dance near Wells. As noted previously, these religious dances had been held occasionally since the 1920s. The two singers at this time were Thomas Pabawena of Wells and Bert Bullcreek of Goshute. The four dancers were Shoshone women: Mary Stanton of Ely, Mary Hall and her daughter Eva Piffero of Beowawe, and Pheban Shontnezt from Idaho. These dancers conducted the Sun Dance ceremony for three days inside a structure of aspen trees. Traditionally, the ceremony was intended for healing. But in 1946 it had an added dimension: to honor the living veterans who had returned from wartime service.[15]

Once the war was over, the nation could once again turn its attention to domestic policies and programs. For the Indians, the most obvious consequence was the federal government's new termination policy. Termination had more than one component, including the Indian Claims Commission (ICC) Act of 1946. This act allowed the tribes to sue the government for past injustices. They could file several classes of claims, including claims arising from unkept treaty promises and also claims arising from the illegal seizure of land without compensation. The act created a three-member commission to "hear and determine" Indian cases filed. If the tribes won their suit they would be awarded a money settlement subject to "offsets" for services the government had rendered to the Indians over the years. No land, however, would be returned to tribes if they won their suit. The ICC allowed the tribes to bring their claims before the commission by "any member of an Indian tribe, band, or other identifiable group of Indians as representative of all its members." If the tribes had a tribal governing body recognized by the federal government, this organization was chosen as the representative entity. Of course, the tribes had the right to hire attorneys of their "own selection."[16] The ICC became tied in with the government's postwar termination program because Indian claims "coincided with the congressional drive to terminate federal responsibility for the Indians" and it became "a necessary preliminary step toward termination."[17] Unlike the Indian Reorganization Act (IRA) of 1934, the ICC was not something the tribes were to vote for or against. Here was a clear case of government paternalism.

The ICC proved to be a mixed blessing for the Western Shoshones. It was difficult for any tribe to sue the federal government before 1946. Going back to 1863 all Indians were barred from pressing claims in the U.S. Court of Claims unless they first secured a special jurisdictional act from Congress.[18] The Western Shoshones had been pressing their claims for years. Beginning in 1934 various bills were submitted to Congress to secure a Western Shoshone jurisdictional act, but without success.[19] The ICC made it easy for the Great Basin Shoshones to file suit after 1946. However, both before and after the passage of the ICC act, a large number of Shoshones, called "traditionals," wanted the federal government to acknowledge the Indians' ownership of tribal land in Nevada in accordance with the Ruby Valley treaty of 1863.[20] As already mentioned, this treaty specified that the Shoshones "claimed and occupied"—that is, owned—at least one-fourth of the land in eastern Nevada.[21] The traditionals argued that this land still belonged to the Indians, and therefore they refused any compensation. These Shoshones soon realized that the 1946 act provided no mechanism for the acknowledgment of a tribal land base. For this reason they considered the ICC as another federal attempt to replace the 1863 treaty or to abrogate treaty rights.

Although the ICC was opposed by the traditionals, it was favored by those Shoshones who desired federal money for reservation-based economic development. These Shoshones welcomed any new government policy if it meant more money for immediate use to purchase practical goods, including cattle, farm equipment, and more land. Like the earlier Indian Reorganization Act of 1934, the ICC polarized the Western Shoshone people; its legacy is still visible today.

It was not the Western Shoshones who took the initiative concerning their claims immediately following the passage of the ICC. Rather it was non-Indian claims attorney Ernest L. Wilkinson of Utah who took the first step or action. With his main law offices in Washington, D.C., Wilkinson was no stranger to Indian claims. He was one of the architects of the ICC and pushed for its passage through Congress. Before 1946 he had served as claims attorney for some far western tribes, including the Northern Utes and Northwestern Shoshones, both of Utah.[22] In 1940 Wilkinson became connected with the Western Shoshone claims case by negotiating a contract with attorney Milton Badt of Elko, Nevada, who had served as the Western Shoshone claims attorney since 1932.[23] In 1945 Badt became district judge of the Fourth Judicial District in Nevada; he turned his Shoshone case over to his Elko law partner, Orville Wilson.[24] Within a year after the passage of the ICC, Wilkinson and Wilson became the official claims attorneys, recognized by those Shoshones who wanted the money settlement. Of the two attorneys, Wilkinson was the more aggressive, for Indian claims cases were his bread and butter. He became the principal legal counsel for several tribes, including the Western Shoshones. As far as Wilkinson was concerned, the Western Shoshones had lost title to their land and were therefore entitled to a money settlement. He expressed his viewpoint a few days after the passage of the ICC: "If we prosecute the Western Shoshone case, we should do it on the theory of loss of immemorial possession."[25]

The BIA also took an active role in the Shoshone claims case. E. J. Diehl, superintendent of the Western Shoshone Agency in Nevada, had informed some of the Shoshones about the ICC as early as September 1946.[26] Diehl read the act carefully and concluded that the Western Shoshones must organize in order to file their claims before the Indian Claims Commission. He knew that the Shoshones lived over a large area in the Great Basin and were organized under small political subgroups. This could present a problem in deciding who would represent the entire tribe before the commission.

On his own, in October 1946, Superintendent Diehl encouraged some of the Shoshones to organize a three-member claims committee under the Te-Moak Bands of Western Shoshone Indians.[27] This governing body, with a council and a constitution and charter, had come into existence in 1938 under the Indian Reorganization Act of 1934 (see chapter 5). It was intended to become a large federated body, representing all the northeastern Nevada Western Shoshone communities located in the area roughly conterminous with the territory designated in the Ruby Valley treaty of 1863.[28] Up to 1966, however, the Te-Moak Bands council represented only the residents of the South Fork Reservation, one of the Nevada reservations established under the IRA and situated some thirty miles south of Elko.[29] Many Shoshones not living at South Fork had felt that the government was trying to replace the Ruby Valley treaty with the IRA. For this reason they had rejected the IRA, as well as membership in the Te-Moak Bands. Unfamiliar with Shoshone history, Diehl assumed that the Te-Moak Bands organization had become a federated body and therefore represented a sizable number of Western Shoshones. It seemed the logical choice to represent all the Great Basin Shoshones. The three-member claims committee turned out to be ineffective. Diehl could not work with it on a regular basis as his office was located some 130 miles north of South Fork, on the Duck Valley Reservation, on the border of Nevada and Idaho.

Diehl then encouraged the Shoshones of the Duck Valley Reservation to organize a claims committee.[30] Unlike the Te-Moak Bands committee, the Duck Valley committee proved to be effective. First, its members worked toward a money settlement. They thought in terms of economic development and recognized the value of securing funds to purchase cattle and farm equipment. Second, these leaders had learned to cooperate with the government during the Indian New Deal period (1933–1945) when reservation Indians had benefited from various economic reform programs. Third, the committee members had some political expertise, since they had been instrumental in the formation of their respective IRA tribal councils.[31] Fourth, the committee worked with Diehl on a regular basis, so the superintendent naturally had some influence over them. Fifth, its members as well as other Shoshones had become indebted under the IRA's revolving credit loan program. By securing claims money, they reasoned, they could soon free themselves of debt. For all these reasons, the committee encouraged the BIA to sponsor a general claims meeting with the larger Shoshone population to discuss the issue.

As a result, the Western Shoshone held a general claims meeting in Elko on February 10, 1947. Approximately fifty Shoshones of northeastern Nevada attended the meeting. This turned out to be the first of numerous post-World War II claims meetings held over the following years, even into the 1990s. The Te-Moak Bands of Western Shoshone Indians sponsored the meeting with the endorsement of Superintendent Diehl and the Duck Valley claims committee. Diehl dominated the meeting. He informed the Indians that their 1936 contract with Badt as claims attorney, which included Wilkinson in 1940, had expired, so that they needed to negotiate a new one. Such a contract was necessary because the Shoshones needed legal assistance to sue the government through the ICC for unkept promises under the Ruby Valley treaty. Although he never mentioned their names, Diehl favored Wilkinson and Wilson. Diehl stated that the Te-Moak Bands organization should represent the larger Western Shoshone Tribe as it was "most fairly representative." Furthermore, the Te-Moak Bands jurisdiction area coincided roughly with the treaty territory. The federal government already recognized the Te-Moak Bands due to its status as an IRA government. Diehl used maps to back up his points. Former claims attorney Badt was also present and, of course, favored his law partner Wilson as well as Wilkinson as attorneys. Some native leaders from Duck Valley and South Fork supported the statements made by Diehl. Not surprisingly, the Te-Moak Bands council passed a resolution favoring the hiring of Wilkinson and Wilson as attorneys for the Western Shoshone people.[32] This meeting set the stage for future developments, for the Te-Moak Bands eventually became the representative of the larger Western Shoshone Tribe, and Wilkinson and Wilson were hired as the claims attorneys.

The February 10 meeting was not free of controversy. Richard Birchum of Austin, one of the members of the Te-Moak Bands claims committee, which had been organized in October 1946, was replaced by Sam Johnny of Elko. Birchum stepped aside because he opposed the hiring of Wilkinson and Wilson. He joined forces with those Shoshones who sought to hire other attorneys in an effort to have the Western Shoshone treaty territory recognized. This issue was discussed at the Elko meeting, and the participants favoring the ICC tried to write off the opposing side by labeling them as a "dissatisfied small group."[33] In fact, the Indians fighting for land represented a larger and more vocal force.

Opposition had been growing before the Elko meeting and continued to increase afterwards. In mid-January 1947 the traditional leaders came together to oppose those who favored the money settlement. The leaders included Muchach Temoke and his followers of Ruby Valley, and Albert Stanton, Billy Myers, and the Pabawena brothers (James, Thomas, and David), all of the Ely/Wells area. Specifically, they wanted to hire their own attorneys to fight for land entitlement. They also did not want the Duck Valley Shoshones to participate, arguing that the Duck Valley Reservation was located outside the so-called treaty territory.[34] In early March Muchach Temoke, George McQueen from Ely, and Jacob Browning, a Northern Shoshone spokesman from the Fort Hall Reservation in Idaho, traveled to Washington, D.C., and unsuccessfully tried to convince Wilkinson that he should represent their position. The delegation held that the "New Dealers"—those Shoshones operating under the Indian Reorganization Act of 1934—should not participate in any claims settlement.[35] They argued that the "self-government" Indians had sold out the 1863 treaty by accepting the IRA of 1934. In late March the traditionals came together in Battle Mountain, Nevada, and temporarily took the name Te-Moak Tribe (as opposed to the Te-Moak Bands). The Te-Moak Tribe asserted that it would not participate with the Indians seeking a money settlement, nor would it accept the contract with Wilkinson and Wilson. Instead, the group chose to fight for land. The following statement summarizes their position: "The Te-Moak Tribe is objecting to the program for the reason that they feel the claim, if paid, will be a money settlement whereas they wish to have land provided for them, pursuant to the terms of the treaty of 1863."[36]

It became apparent to all involved that the February 10 meeting in Elko was not representative of all the Western Shoshone people of the Great Basin. In late February Wilkinson specified that a larger number of Shoshones, in addition to the Te-Moak Bands and the Duck Valley Shoshones, needed to endorse a contract. He had in mind the support of other IRA Shoshone councils, including those of the Yomba and Duckwater reservations. Wilkinson wrote to Wilson, "I think it vital, therefore, that you have a General Council called of all the Western Bands of Shoshones."[37] Wilson also questioned the Elko meeting, stating that he was "not clear as to whether or not the meeting in Elko could be called a general council."[38] Whether or not the two attorneys knew it, only a minority of Shoshones lived at Duck Valley, while the Te-Moak Bands organization represented roughly 100 Shoshones from the South Fork Reservation.

In an effort to inform more Shoshones of the ICC, the Te-Moak Bands sponsored a second claims meeting, this time in Wells, Nevada, on March 29, 1947. Although the meeting was actually called at the request of the Northwestern Shoshones of Utah, it was attended by a larger number of Indians coming from the following places: Goshutes and Northwestern Shoshones from Utah, and Western Shoshones from Duck Valley, Odger's Ranch, South Fork, and Wells. Unlike the earlier Elko meeting, this one was dominated by the Indians themselves. They elected officers and chose Thomas Premo of Duck Valley as chair. Premo believed that all the Shoshones should operate under one banner. He explained that the Indians needed to hire attorneys. The Te-Moak Bands organization, he believed, was the identifiable representative, since it was already recognized by the federal government. He tried to convince some of those present that the IRA had nothing to do with the claims issue. In the end, Premo invited all the Shoshones to attend yet another meeting to be held in Elko.[39]

To prepare for the next Elko meeting, the Duck Valley claims committee, the Te-Moak Bands leadership of South Fork, and Superintendent Diehl visited various Shoshone communities in the spring of 1947. Finally, in early May Diehl sent official notices out to thirty-four different places, including Death Valley, California, informing the Great Basin Shoshone population to send official delegates to Elko on June 1, 1947.[40]

On June 1, 1947, over one hundred Shoshones gathered in Elko in one of the largest gatherings since the signing of the 1863 treaty. Representatives came from the following places: Austin, Battle Mountain, Beowawe, Duck Valley, Duckwater, Elko, Odger's Ranch, Reno, South Fork, Wells, and Yomba.[41] For the first time in their history, the larger number of Shoshones of central and southern Nevada were brought into the claims picture. The ancestors of most of these Indians had not participated in the treaty of Ruby Valley, and some called themselves the "unsigned Indians" as late as the 1930s.[42]

Unlike the previous meetings, this gathering featured a great deal of discussion. Superintendent Diehl opened the meeting and announced that he was pleased with the large turnout. Reinforcing his earlier statements, he made the following points: The Shoshones needed to hire attorneys to help them press claims against the government owing to the unkept promises under the Ruby Valley treaty; they would win a money settlement if successful in their suit; and the Te-Moak Bands of Western Shoshone Indians should be the identifiable representative as the "largest group." It was apparent that not everyone fully understood the claims situation under the ICC. Dewey Dann, a Shoshone from Beowawe, Nevada, asked, "What kind of a thing is the 'claims' that you are talking about—sounds like a gold mine to me—is that what it is?" An unidentified person said, "A lot of us don't understand these things you fellows are talking about, we are still in the dark." Attorney Orville Wilson explained, "Well, the lands have been taken away from you and you will never get it back. So the only other thing you can do now is to sue the government and get money for the lands you lost." This was the first time the ICC situation had been explained at a large meeting.[43]

The second Elko meeting resulted in passage of a resolution and allowed the Te-Moak Bands to make an agreement with Wilkinson and Wilson. In addition, the Duck Valley claims committee was to serve as the independent adviser of the Te-Moak Bands and also to sign the necessary paperwork.[44] Soon after the meeting, on August 16, the Te-Moak Bands and attorneys Wilkinson and Wilson signed an official contract.[45] The Elko meeting of early June was therefore a victory for the BIA, the claims attorneys, and those Shoshones pushing for a money settlement.

Most of the traditionals boycotted the June meeting. They were later joined by some who had attended the meeting and learned that there was no question of a land settlement. Clearly, the June meeting enlarged and solidified the traditionalist opposition. On June 12 Muchach Temoke and Oren George, a Northern Paiute sympathizer and spokesman, traveled to Washington, D.C. This was the fourth time in his life, and the second time that year, that Temoke had visited the nation's capital, each time to fight for treaty rights and land entitlement. Muchach made these trips because he was recognized as the hereditary chief, a position first held by his grandfather, Old Temoke, the principal signer of the Ruby Valley treaty. While in Washington Temoke made it clear that his followers rejected the June 1 meeting. To accept the money would mean the loss of the land in Ruby Valley. Also, the Western Shoshone "treaty rights will be jeopardized," Temoke argued. Temoke recognized Charles Malotte, Sr., only as the head of Te-Moak Bands, and not as the hereditary chief. Again, Temoke did not want the Duck Valley Shoshones to participate in the claims case, since he believed that only the Ruby Valley Shoshones were entitled to treaty rights.[46]

On August 27 twenty-seven leaders, including Muchach Temoke, signed a contract with Elko attorney George Wright. Although the contract was ambiguous and did not specify what would be recovered, it was an indication that the traditionals had rejected the Te-Moak Bands' contract with Wilkinson and Wilson. It also showed that several Shoshone leaders chose to fight for land. The following persons, who had organized their own claims committee, signed the contract: Dewey Dann of Beowawe as chair, John Temoke of Ruby Valley, James Jackson of Cherry Creek, Sam Long of Ruby Valley, Charlotte Jim of Ruby Valley, and Alice Jackson of Cherry Creek. It was endorsed by the following traditional leaders who were descendants of the signers of the Ruby Valley treaty:

Muchach Temoke, Sam Holly, George Mose, Albert Stanton, Frank Temoke, Sr., Richard Birchum, James Pabawena, Johnny Long, Ida Blossom, Johnny Johnson, Harry Johnny, and Doc Blossom.[47]

By late 1947 the solidarity of the traditionals began to weaken. First, their claims attorney Wright backed away from his clients, saying, "It is my opinion that the land will not be returned to the Indians, but that damages [money] will be rewarded."[48] Second, some of the Shoshones were unwilling to recognize Muchach Temoke as the overall leader of the opposition. A few Battle Mountain Shoshones called themselves the Too-Toaina Tribe, implying that their ancestors had looked up to Chief Tu-tu-wa of the Reese River Valley in the nineteenth century and not to Old Temoke.[49] Some of the Wells Shoshones reverted to their earlier suspicion of Muchach because his family name was given to the Te-Moak Bands organization. These Shoshones held that "Temoak is not our chief he got his own band and Temoak band joined the self-government in the year 1934."[50] The Wells group failed to realize that Muchach Temoke had also rejected the Indian Reorganization Act and therefore did not recognize the Te-Moak Bands organization, even though it used his family name.

Regardless of their differences, the traditionals stood firm on two things: rejection of any money settlement favored by Wilkinson and Wilson and the Te-Moak Bands organization, and the intention of fighting for the recognition of treaty land ownership. They stuck to their convictions in the years following the 1947 contract. In February 1951 Muchach Temoke wrote that "these Indians . . . are Self Government Indians of South Fork Reservation of Lee, Nevada. Their Chiefs . . . have been filing contract with their attorney Orville R. Wilson of Elko, Nevada. What they want to do is sell this boundary line under my name Temoak. Me and the people do not associate with the Indians at Lee, Nevada."[51] Temoke said that he would not go along with those who wanted to sell the land. In December of the same year some of the traditionals held a meeting in Battle Mountain and laid out several important points:

> We want all land within the said boundary [1863 treaty territory] . . .
> We would like full control as to whatever the white man can cut down . . .
> We don't like the white man to cut down cedar trees unless it is brought
> from the Indians . . . No white man allowed to hunt unless by permission
> from Indians. All wild games belong to Indians . . . The self govt. people
> has taken control of the treaty rights of Indians and we do not like it. We
> don't want any interference with the self government. They (self-govern-
> ment) have made contract with Attorney Wilkerson [sic] & Wilson of Elko,
> Nevada which they had no right without the permission of treaty Indians.[52]

In November 1953 David Pabawena of Wells asserted that "any of wild game is belonging to Shoshone Nation of Indians inside of their country claimed, and any of the wild game is their property."[53] Pabawena and other traditionals were saying that the Western Shoshones still owned their land and had rights and privileges to use the land for survival.

The claims attorneys did not allow any opposition to deter them. On May 31, 1950, Wilkinson convened a large claims meeting in Salt Lake City with representatives from all the major Shoshone groups in Nevada, Idaho, and Utah. His purpose was to persuade the Western, Northwestern, and Northern Shoshones to file "one common claim on behalf of the [entire] Shoshone Nation" of the Intermountain West. As usual the Duck Valley claims committee approved of this, and its members moved and seconded a motion to carry out Wilkinson's request. When the votes were tallied, the Western Shoshone councils under the Indian Reorganization Act—the Te-Moak Bands organization (two members), all three members of the Duck Valley committee, four members of the Yomba Tribal Council, three members of the Duckwater Tribal Council, and one independent Shoshone—favored the resolution. Although seven Western Shoshone traditionals attended this meeting, they did not bother to vote, an expression of their opposition to Wilkinson and those Indians who supported him. Instead, the traditionals were represented by their own attorneys: B. C. Call of Brigham City, Utah, represented those from the Ely-Wells area, and Grand Aadneson of Idaho represented Chief Muchach Temoke, Oren George, and James Street of Nevada.[54]

This Salt Lake meeting gave Wilkinson the green light he needed. He submitted the entire Shoshone Nation claims before the Indian Claims Commission on August 10, 1951, and the case became known as Docket 326. A year later the Department of Justice rejected the suit, most likely because Wilkinson could not provide evidence that the Shoshone groups had held title to their land in aboriginal time. His firm, which became Wilkinson, Cragun, and Barker in 1953, therefore hired anthropologist Omer C. Stewart of the University of Colorado to conduct extensive research.[55] In August and September 1957 Stewart presented his findings before the ICC hearings in Denver and Washington, D.C. He provided evidence "that the Shoshone Nation exclusively used, possessed and occupied the area" of the Far Intermountain West.[56] His findings later made it possible for the Shoshones to proceed in their claims against the government. As for Wilkinson, he withdrew from the Shoshone cases in 1951 after becoming president of Brigham Young University. His work on the Western Shoshone case was taken over by his Washington, D.C., partner Robert Barker.[57]

The Wilkinson/Wilson contract of 1947 expired in April 1958. The BIA sponsored a claims meeting on July 31, 1959, to sign a new contract. Of those who attended, forty-five voted in favor of renewal while nineteen voted against it. The Te-Moak Bands tribal council again signed the contract. As had been done before, an elected, independent claims committee of three also signed: Arthur Manning of Duck Valley as chair, Frank Temoke, Jr., of Elko, and Clarence Blossom of Battle Mountain. Various persons gave talks, including new BIA superintendent Burton Ladd, former claims attorney Milton Badt, and attorney Barker. Barker provided updated information but confirmed the earlier position that only money would be awarded to the Indians if they won their suit. Controversy arose when John Pope, a non-Shoshone, sought to have himself elected as chair of the meeting. Pope and his followers sought to oppose the signing of the new contract and to reject any money settlement. After three separate votes, the floor voted down Pope's leadership move, although the last tally was close: thirty-two for him and thirty-five against him.[58] Again, this was an indication that the Western Shoshones were still split over the issue of money versus land.

Again, there was opposition after the meeting when on September 23, 1959, Chief Frank Temoke, Sr., of Ruby Valley wrote to Rep. Wayne Aspinall, complaining about the August 21 meeting. Among his list of complaints he said that the BIA and the claims attorneys were trying to "cram down our throats" the money settlement. Temoke wanted the federal government to recognize Western Shoshone treaty rights instead.[59] Temoke was speaking out because he was now the hereditary chief of the Temoke Band of Ruby Valley Shoshones. He had succeeded his father in 1953 after Muchach had become too old to effectively fight for treaty rights. Frank Temoke united the traditional Shoshones in the 1950s by forming an organization called the "Western Shoshone Nation, with a Traditional Council," and the group fought for the recognition of the treaty territory. Temoke thus brought back into existence the pre-IRA "traditional council" (or treaty council), although it no longer had the larger representation that it had before the late 1930s.[60]

In examining the Western Shoshone claims issue, several key questions arise. First, did the Shoshones have the freedom to select attorneys of their own choice? The answer is no; the attorneys made the decision themselves along with the BIA. Their decision was simply ratified by some Indians. Admittedly, only the Shoshones favoring the money settlement accepted Wilkinson and Wilson, while the traditionals remained opposed. Second, if the Shoshones had been allowed to vote to accept or reject the ICC, what would have been their decision? It is difficult if not impossible to say. The Shoshones were apparently about equally divided over the issue of land versus money. Most of the traditionals boycotted the claims meeting and did not vote on matters directly connected to the claims issue, as an expression of their opposition to the ICC. It is clear that the ICC favored those Indians who went along with the federal government, for the 1946 law catered to those Indians operating under the Indian Reorganization Act and ruled out those who had never recognized the 1934 law. In the end, the ICC was tied in with another component of termination, for the idea was to put money into the pockets of the Indians and then set them free in the future.

Soon after passage of the ICC, the BIA conceived another important component of termination, called the Long Range Program (LRP). The LRP was formally established in a May 1948 memorandum sent to the regional BIA offices and local reservation agencies.[61] The program was a response to an announcement from Congress that funds would eventually be reduced and then eliminated for Indian programs. The Indians would be released from federal supervision and would have to find their "rightful place" in the larger society. The BIA, in turn, had to design a new program to make the Indians self-sufficient and independent. The government would provide funds to carry out this plan, so that the Indians could secure more land, cattle, farm equipment, and better education for tribal members. Sometime in the future, after the Indians had developed strong, viable economies, the BIA would withdraw funding and relinquish supervision over them—in essence, termination.[62] Of course, this process would take years, and it would necessarily depend on Indian participation.

The first group of Western Shoshones to hear about the LRP were those living on the Duck Valley Reservation. Superintendent Diehl informed them of it in 1948. The program was attractive to various leaders, including Thomas Premo, chair of the local business council, because it could boost the reservation cattle economy, which had grown since the days of the New Deal programs. At the same time they were skeptical because the program also meant "eventual release . . . from governmental control." The local council, which also included the Northern Paiutes living in Duck Valley, held a meeting in December 1948 and decided not to make any quick decision but to discuss long-range planning at a general meeting that would include a larger number of Western Shoshones.[63]

One individual who was anxious to discuss the LRP was Shoshone leader Joe Gibson, who had moved from Elko to Duck Valley. In April 1949 Gibson approached the Duck Valley council, asking permission to sponsor and organize a larger Western Shoshone meeting to discuss the new program. Gibson recognized that it was an "emancipation program," which meant the end of federal support in the future.[64] He also understood that in the short run it could help the Shoshones, just as the Indian New Deal programs had. Gibson approached the Duck Valley people because he knew that some of their leaders were willing to discuss new ideas. Furthermore, he already had connections with the local leadership, as a member of the three-man claims committee, organized in early 1947.

Gibson organized and hosted a general Western Shoshone meeting in Elko on May 2, 1949. This was intended to be the first of a series of long-range planning meetings in which the Shoshone people would hold discussions and design tribal economic plans. Although it was not well attended, there were leaders from Duck Valley, the Te-Moak Bands organization from South Fork, and the Shoshone-speaking Goshutes of the Goshute Reservation, located along the Utah-Nevada border. The new BIA superintendent, Bert Courtright, opened the meeting. He informed the audience of the intent of the LRP: that "on some near distant date the government would release the Indians from wardship, or turn the Indians over to the control of the states." Courtright encouraged the Indians to return home and conduct further talks at the local level. Once this had been done, the Shoshones could hold a second large meeting and work out a comprehensive plan for the entire tribe. He tried to convince the audience that the pending claims had no connection to long-range planning. But Courtright contradicted himself by stating that "the Indians should include in their programs some mention of what they intended to do with any judgement [claims] money won."[65] On this point he made a direct connection between the Western Shoshone claims case and the LRP. In other words, if the Shoshones won their claims money, they could use it to carry out their plans.

The remainder of the May 2 meeting was given over to the Indians who wished to express an opinion about the LRP. It became apparent at this early date that the Shoshones had already begun to split into two groups on this issue. Joe Gibson was one who favored the LRP and indicated that the Indians needed money for houses, cattle, and education. Opposition came primarily from those who had also opposed the Wilkinson/Wilson contract of 1947. Alice Jackson of Cherry Creek stated that the "long-range program sounds all right, but it might come out all wrong." In the end she opposed it. Her husband, Jim Jackson, questioned the value of the LRP, stating that "maybe this long-range program will stand on or against our treaty." This first LRP meeting reached no final conclusion. The audience, despite their opposing viewpoints, did agree on one thing: that the Western Shoshone people needed more land and money to improve their socioeconomic status.[66]

The Western Shoshones' second general meeting on the LRP was held June 22, 1949, also in Elko and again sponsored by Gibson. This meeting was similar to the first one. Most of the audience came from the various northeastern Nevada Indian communities. As before, Superintendent

Courtright pointed out that the LRP was "to make the control of government disappear so that the government will not supervise at all." He restated his earlier position that if the Shoshones won their claims settlement they could use the award money to carry out their long-range programs.[67] By this time the audience was polarized into pro- and anti-LRP groups. Those who favored long-range planning came from the IRA tribal councils (primarily Duck Valley and South Fork) and had also favored the Wilkinson/Wilson contract of 1947. The anti-LRP group were for the most part the same ones who opposed the ICC and the IRA. These Shoshones chose to operate under the Treaty of Ruby Valley and therefore rejected any new government policy.

The polarization of opinion at the Elko meeting was evident when the audience voted in a three-person LRP committee consisting of Alice Jackson as chair, Thomas Premo, and Charles Malotte, Sr. Using her leadership status, Jackson campaigned against the LRP.[68] She read statements by other Shoshones who also opposed the LRP, including one by Chief Muchach Temoke, which read: "We strongly object to favor the Long Range Program . . . We recognize and believe in our treaty, we do not want land under the Long Range Program, we want land under our Treaty . . . we don't want the white people to enforce the State law on us."[69] The Yomba Shoshones of the Yomba Reservation in central Nevada also opposed the program, and Alice Jackson read their statement: "We do not believe it is possible for us to bind our children to give up our present way of life under any program, long range or otherwise."[70] The anti-LRP group had definitely taken control of the meeting. In response, the smaller pro-LRP group broke away and formed its own separate LRP committee consisting of persons from Duck Valley and South Fork. They sought to secure more supporters by inviting more central and southern Nevada Shoshones to the next LRP meeting.[71]

On September 1, 1949, the Western Shoshones held their third and final general LRP meeting. To impress and persuade the Indians the BIA brought in two high officials. Colonel E. Morgan Pryce, area director of the BIA's newly established Portland Area Office, argued that "we are here only to help you help yourself. In time you folks will learn to help yourselves." His subordinate George P. LaVatta, a Shoshone from the Fort Hall Reservation who had assisted some of the Western Shoshones to organize under the IRA a decade earlier, stated that "the government is going to turn us loose when we are ready." He argued that there was no connection between the land and treaty claims and the issue of long-range planning. LaVatta then asked the Shoshones what they wanted. Various Shoshone leaders stated that they wanted land, education, livestock, and so forth.[72] Unlike the second meeting, this third gathering was peaceful, perhaps because the Shoshones realized that they all wanted the same thing from the government. Their basic disagreements concerned the claims issue and the acceptance or rejection of changing government policies. Joe Gibson, and for that matter the BIA, did not bother to organize any further general LRP meetings. It was obvious that a majority of Western Shoshones would not go along with the BIA's Long Range Program. In short, they largely rejected this aspect of termination.

When the BIA could not secure consensus, it tried to work out separate plans with some of the Shoshone groups. One was the Battle Mountain Colony. The BIA gave attention to this colony after Senator Patrick McCarran of Nevada visited it in early 1948. In February he wrote a letter to the BIA, stating that the colony conditions were deplorable and that improvements were needed. McCarran was referring to the twelve Indian houses, none which had electricity or modern facilities. In response to the senator's visit and letter, Superintendent Courtright also visited the colony and wrote a report that called for the installation of a new water pump and more land for the colony residents.[73] In mid-1949 Colonel Pryce of Portland came to Battle Mountain and, having investigated the situation, also recommended improvements, including electrical power and foundations for the houses.[74] McCarran's initial request became tied to the LRP. In late 1949 a bill that used the words "withdrawal of federal services and supervision" was introduced into Congress. It called for government assistance for the Battle Mountain Colony, including money for more land and livestock, among other things.[75] Supposedly, once the Battle Mountain group became self-sufficient, the BIA would terminate its relations with them. But the bill never passed Congress, and was not even considered at the committee level. The fiscally conservative representatives, even though they favored termination, were not willing to provide the funds to make the Battle Mountain Indians self-sufficient. Here was an inconsistency indeed in the federal government's termination policy. Perhaps the national legislators hoped that future claims money would serve the purpose.

The BIA then turned its attention to the Elko Indian Colony. In April 1950 Superintendent Courtright, along with other BIA officials, recommended that Congress appropriate $20,000 to improve the colony. Specifically, the twenty-eight Indian houses, some built in the 1930s, would be connected to the water and sewage systems of the city of Elko.[76] Again, Congress failed to consider this request. The BIA then lost interest in the Elko Colony. In a rather strange twist of events from 1951 to 1957, the white residents of Elko became the champions of improvements for the Elko Indians. The white Elko residents were concerned not so much with the plight of the Indians as with their own health and welfare. By the 1950s the city of Elko had grown so that it adjoined the Indian colony.

The whites knew that the colony had no sewage system and that the families used outdoor toilets. The Elko residents were informed in 1954 that an Indian youngster had died of typhoid fever. Immediately they linked this death to unsanitary living conditions, although this argument could not be substantiated.[77] In March 1957 John Gammick, Elko's water and sanitation supervisor, traveled to Washington, D.C., and convinced the Nevada congressional delegation to provide funds to connect the colony to the city utilities.[78] As a result, Senator Walter Baring, with support from Rep. Alan Bible, submitted legislation to Congress. Two federal agencies, the BIA and the Public Health Service, supported the legislation.[79] Congress duly appropriated $40,000 in August 1957 to improve the Elko Colony.[80] By 1958 the entire colony was connected to the city's water and sewage systems. The twenty-eight Indian houses now had flush toilets and indoor sinks.[81]

Besides the Elko Indian Colony, the only other Shoshone community to benefit from the LRP was that at Duck Valley. Although this group favored the program, it also firmly believed that the Indians' relations with the government should not be terminated immediately. In September 1949, and again in December 1954, the Duck Valley group discussed long-range planning. Because their community was based on a cattle-raising economy, the tribal business council favored "land leveling, reservoirs for irrigation," and "farm pasture and crop lands."[82] The BIA provided $176,168 in early 1958 for the leveling of 1,200 acres of land for agricultural purposes.[83] By the 1960s the Shoshones and Paiutes at Duck Valley were producing larger crops of alfalfa, which enabled them to increase their cattle herds.

Still another aspect of termination was the federal government's efforts to gather data about the tribes to determine their readiness for termination. The first such effort came in February 1947 when acting BIA commissioner William Zimmerman appeared at a congressional hearing. The representatives asked Zimmerman how the BIA might be able to reduce its expenditures in preparation for federal termination of tribal groups. Using BIA information Zimmerman divided the tribes into three groups: those who could be terminated immediately, those who could be terminated within ten years, and those who would remain under the BIA until prepared for withdrawal sometime in the distant future. Zimmerman based his conclusions on four criteria: the tribe's degree of acculturation, its available resources, its willingness to accept withdrawal, and the willingness of the state governments to take over BIA functions. Zimmerman placed the Western Shoshones in the third group, those who would remain under the BIA for some considerable time.[84] This report led to the long-range planning discussions among the Shoshones in 1949, in which the BIA tried to work out a comprehensive plan to make the

Western Shoshones self-sustaining before terminating them in the distant future.

A 1953 report (House Report 2053), also based on BIA information, later followed Zimmerman's report. Its purpose was "to determine" tribal "qualifications for management of their own affairs without further supervision of the Federal Government."[85] Unlike Zimmerman's brief report, this one had much more data concerning the Western Shoshone. It included historical and statistical information, a list of published and unpublished reports concerning the Shoshone groups, and also a breakdown of tribal funds and assets. Some of the information in this 1953 report was extracted from two earlier reports, the *Ten Year Program for the Carson Agency, 1944* and the *Ten Year Program for the Western Shoshone Jurisdiction, Nevada and Idaho, 1944.*[86] These two wartime reports were an attempt to prepare socioeconomic plans for the Great Basin Shoshones after the war. Unfortunately, they were used instead to provide background information for termination. The 1953 report was informational and provided no recommendations regarding termination.

Congress released a second report (House Report 2680) as a follow-up to the 1953 report, again focusing on federal withdrawal. This report, which most likely the Shoshone people did not see when it was published, inaccurately concluded that all the Western Shoshone groups in Nevada were ready to be withdrawn from federal supervision. It specified that the Shoshones, along with several other tribes, were "qualified to handle their own affairs immediately." This fabricated conclusion was based on the number of Shoshone families declared to be "competent" to run their own affairs without federal assistance. Here was the report's breakdown:

	"Competent"	"Marginal"	"Incompetent"
Battle Mountain	15	10	4
Duck Valley	120	75	53
Duckwater	11	6	4
Elko	30	10	9
Ely	23	15	10
Ruby Valley	10	4	3
South Fork	20	4	5
Yomba	14	4	2

Because the report determined that many Shoshones were "competent," it concluded that the federal government could terminate relations with all tribal members, even those who were not prepared.[87] This report encouraged Congress to initiate legislation regarding Western Shoshone termination.

As it turned out, the culmination of congressional interest in termination was House Concurrent Resolution (HCR) 108 of 1953, which made no mention of the Western Shoshones. Once Congress had secured information about the Indian tribes, its members introduced legislation to terminate federal relations with the tribes. One of the earliest bills, preceding HCR 108, was S 2726, introduced in 1949 by Senator George Malone of Nevada. Like other politicians of the Far West, Malone was no friend of the Indians and sought to end the historic ward/guardian relationship. His bill sought "to abolish the function of the Bureau of Indian Affairs . . . to remove the guardianship over Indians and trusteeship over Indian land" and most important to repeal the Indian Reorganization Act of 1934. With the elimination of the IRA the tribes would no longer have tribal governments and thus could no longer secure federal loans for education and economic development. In essence, any kind of interaction between the Indians and the government would cease, and the Indians as individuals would be regarded as being like any other American citizen.[88]

Malone's bill never became law, but it was taken seriously by some of the tribal leaders of the Te-Moak Bands council of the South Fork Reservation. In January and February 1950 the Te-Moak Bands council, in two separate meetings, discussed the bill and decided to support it, under the condition that Congress would appropriate $70,000 for the South Fork Reservation for a "long range program." Under this plan the Indians would be able to purchase more land, cattle, and farm equipment. In addition, the council authorized Joe Gibson, who had left Duck Valley and returned to Elko, to study the bill and make suggestions concerning the termination policy.[89]

Two years later Gibson finally completed his written report. By this time S 2726 had already died in Congress, but it was still alive in principle. Gibson made it clear that he was in favor of termination. He wanted the Indians to experience American-style democracy and to become full-fledged citizens who would be treated like everyone else. He encouraged the Shoshones to prepare for the future without federal support. Once federal assistance was no longer forthcoming, Gibson argued, the Indians would turn to the private sector for socioeconomic development. The Indians could organize local "advisory boards" to take the place of the BIA. These governing bodies would run tribal affairs, secure loan money, sell tribal livestock, and purchase more tribal land. Obviously, Gibson was in favor of the Shoshones remaining in Indian communities and not dispersing as individuals, unless certain members were unwilling to fit in. In his report Gibson made both valid and invalid points. He was right in pointing out that termination was dangerous if carried out too quickly. But he was wrong in stating that "many tribal groups" favored termination. He also wrongly stated that "the Indians had made no progress whatever under the present paternalism of the federal government." He failed to point out that some of the Shoshones had become successful cattlemen under the Indian Reorganization Act. Gibson's report, however, was at least one person's attempt to make sense out of the government's new policy for Indians. He must be credited for practicing Indian assertiveness even though his plan was not endorsed by the vast majority of Shoshone people.[90]

Finally, in August 1953 Congress secured an Indian termination initiative with HCR 108. The resolution dealt with three areas. First, it specified that all Indians were to be "subject to the same laws" and "entitled to the same privileges" as any other American citizen. It also stated that the wardship status of Indians would cease to exist. Second, tribes in particular states "should be freed from federal supervision" as quickly as possible, and BIA agencies in other states would be "abolished" in the near future. Third, the Department of the Interior would study the status of other tribes in preparation for large-scale withdrawal of federal support. Although it mentioned the names of several tribes, it did not mention the Nevada tribes, including the Western Shoshone.[91]

In response to HCR 108 various representatives began introducing bills into Congress in January 1954 to terminate federal relations with specific tribal groups. Rep. Clifton Young of Nevada, also a terminationist, introduced HR 7552. The bill's purpose was "to provide for the termination of federal supervision over the property of certain tribes, bands, and colonies of Indians in the State of Nevada." In addition to several small tribal groups, the government singled out two Shoshone groups for termination: those living on the land allotments in Ruby Valley and the Battle Mountain Colony. There was no explanation of why these two groups were earmarked for termination, but it seems likely that Young selected the poorest, weakest, and smallest groups—those regarded as unable to oppose the government's termination efforts. The Nevada colonies, including Battle Mountain, were also singled out because they were located adjacent to or within towns, and occupied land that the whites wanted for municipal development. HR 7552 specified that the tribal groups designated for termination were to draw up a tribal enrollment list. Once this was done, the Indians would have two years to decide what to do with the tribal trust property held by the government. The bill specified some options. The Indians could form a corporation to take the place of the BIA, and this body would manage the property. Or the tribe could choose certain trustees to serve as managers. Or the Indians could simply distribute all the property, including land, and cease to exist as a tribal or group entity.[92]

The BIA now had to convince the Western Shoshones of Battle

Mountain and Ruby Valley to accept HR 7552. On February 4, 1954, Wesley Bobo, a BIA official, met with ten Battle Mountain Shoshones. Apparently Bobo told the gathering that another group of Shoshones, those living at South Fork under the Te-Moak Bands council, favored the bill. Clearly, he hoped to convince the Battle Mountain group to follow suit. But the discussion at Battle Mountain was brief; the Indian leaders wished to discuss the bill among themselves without the presence of a federal official.[93] When they had talked it over, four of them—Clarence and Renee Blossom, George Dixon, and Saggie Williams—sent a letter to the Bureau flatly rejecting HR 7552. They stated:

> The Indians, Western Band of Shoshone Nation or Tribe of Indians, wish to do away with the bill H.R. 7552 . . . The Indians here at the Battle Mountain colony has been completely neglected by the various Indian superintendents for many years. The tribe here feels that they have been mistreated for time immemorial so therefore, we, the said Western Band of Shoshone Indians, wish to continue as ward Indians. The entire group are following their ancestors' treaty rights and wish to do so in the future . . . Also, we have no intention whatsoever to be included along with the Lee Reservation [South Fork] group, as we are not under the long-range program but making our living as bare subsidence, which can be accurately described only as rural slums.[94]

It must have come as a surprise to federal officials that a small group of Indians, regarded as politically weak, had challenged the federal government. The Battle Mountain leaders correctly pointed out that the colony had been largely neglected by the BIA.[95] As before, the leaders made it clear that they firmly believed in the 1863 Ruby Valley treaty, viewing it as the supreme law, which could not be replaced or subordinated by any other law, including the pending HR 7552.

As far as the Te-Moak Bands council was concerned, some of its members did favor HR 7552. In fact, on February 26, 1954, the council passed a resolution that read: "Resolved, That the Te-Moak Tribal Council has no objections, and hereby grants permission for the people living in the Elko colony, or any other group, or individual within the Te-Moak Bands to withdraw from the jurisdiction and supervision of the Te-Moak Tribal Council and come under the provisions as stipulated in H.R. 7552; thereby, receiving benefits through patented fee titles to land, homes, and sales of surplus land."[96]

The Te-Moak council considered that it had jurisdiction over the Elko Colony because the Te-Moak Bands constitution of 1938 included Elko.[97] BIA officials, of course, had pressured the council into including the Elko Colony in the resolution, at the request of the city officials of Elko who wanted the colony terminated under HR 7552 even though it was not included in the bill.[98]

Not all the leaders of the Te-Moak Bands of the South Fork Reservation agreed with or supported HR 7552 and its application to the Western Shoshone groups. On March 26, 1954, some Nevada Indians concerned about termination held a meeting with the Nevada Legislative Committee. These leaders unanimously opposed termination. Willie Woods, a South Fork leader, stressed that the Shoshones would not consider termination until the government had fulfilled the provisions of the Ruby Valley treaty.[99] It was becoming obvious at this point that Shoshone opposition to HR 7552 was widespread, even though only two groups were earmarked for termination under the bill. Not surprisingly, on April 14, 1954, the Shoshone leaders at Wells, Nevada, led by Albert Stanton, opposed termination and specified that "we do require to remain under federal wardship for the time being."[100]

Regardless of the rising Nevada Indian opposition, Congress held hearings regarding HR 7552 in Reno on April 16, 1954. There was some talk about the Elko Colony, mainly because Elko's city manager testified in favor of the termination of the colony.[101] But since Elko was not included in the bill, the subject was dropped. The Battle Mountain Colony opposition was highly visible even though most of the leaders did not bother to attend. Jim Street was the spokesman for the leaders: "They didn't want this bill . . . They want me to speak for this treaty rights . . . because this other bill has been coming out in the legislature, this long-range program and all that. They didn't want that."[102] Street argued that the Shoshones chose to remain under the Ruby Valley treaty and that this treaty must be acknowledged by the federal government. Furthermore, the Indians were entitled to benefits under this treaty, but little if anything had been forthcoming. Ed Lauritzen, commissioner of Lander County, Nevada, where Battle Mountain is located, also pointed out that the Battle Mountain Shoshones opposed termination.[103] A third witness, Clara Woodson, a Shoshone from Elko who was born and raised in Battle Mountain, also confirmed the Battle Mountain opposition, stating that "they think when the bill is passed they will be taken off the reservations and colonies."[104] Of course, the Indians' suspicions were correct, because the purpose of termination was to dissolve the Indian land base.

The Ruby Valley Shoshones, led by Chief Frank Temoke, Sr., also opposed the bill. Temoke secured the support of Elko attorney Leo Puccinelli who stated at the hearings that his clients "unalterably opposed at this time . . . H.R. 7552 mainly because they feel that they have nothing to live on now."[105] Without doubt Puccinelli was referring to the small Indian land base in Ruby Valley, which consisted of a few scattered allotments amounting to roughly 1,200 acres. Temoke and his followers, Puccinelli pointed out, were pushing for restoration of the "six miles square" reservation that was supposed to have been set aside immediately following the signing of the 1863 treaty.[106] But the BIA had never surveyed this reservation, and white ranchers in Ruby Valley eventually took over the land. At the time of the 1954 hearings Temoke was asserting his newly acquired leadership status by working to organize the Western Shoshone Nation "traditional council," with representatives from some of the northeastern Nevada communities. Because of HR 7552 Temoke and his supporters, along with Puccinelli, had turned their attention to opposing the new termination legislation.

After the April 16, 1954, hearing the Nevada Indians continued to oppose HR 7552. For example, in November 1954 the Shoshone-Paiute Business Council of Duck Valley opposed termination, stating "this Tribe is opposed to any legislation removing federal control over this Reservation."[107] The Duck Valley leaders were under the impression that if HR 7552 was passed, it would set off a chain reaction leading to the termination of other reservations in Nevada. In opposing termination in 1954, the Duck Valley people had made a dramatic shift. Some five years earlier they had been advocates of termination and in favor of the LRP. But by the mid-1950s they had come to realize that termination also included the abolition of Indian reservations. The Duck Valley Indians were not about to allow their reservation to be dissolved, especially because it was owned communally and was one of a few reservations that had never been fragmented by the Dawes Allotment Act of 1887.

Because of the widespread opposition to HR 7552, Congress never considered the bill. The Indians had made it clear that they were in no economic position to be released from federal supervision. In the case of the Battle Mountain Colony, the twelve Indian houses did not have electricity, sewage, or running water. Also, the Shoshones made it clear that the government had an obligation to carry out the provisions of the Ruby Valley treaty and to acknowledge treaty rights. There was no sense trying to force a new policy upon the Indians without first honoring the 1863 treaty. Rep. Young's bill therefore died, and the Western Shoshone—unlike other tribes, such as the Menominee of Wisconsin—were spared the "disastrous effects" of termination.

Congress was still not ready to end its termination war against the Indians. In 1955 Senator Malone introduced a new bill, S 401, which was almost identical to his earlier bill in 1949. Again, the Shoshones voiced their opposition. On June 7, 1955, the Shoshone-Paiute Business Council passed a resolution that read: "BE IT RESOLVED by the Business Council of the Shoshone-Paiute Tribes that they hereby go on record as opposing the adoption of S. 401."[108] One year later Rep. Young introduced HR

3239 "to provide for the termination . . . of certain colonies of Indians in the State of Nevada."[109] Only the colonies, including Elko, were singled out, most likely at the request of the white communities whose leaders desired Indian land. As before, the BIA and Interior Department favored this bill, incorrectly noting that the "members of these colonies have in general attained sufficient skill and ability to manage their own affairs."[110]

Fortunately for the Western Shoshone, these bills went nowhere. In the late 1950s the federal government began backing away from its overall termination plan for the American Indians. The shifting tide was evident in September 1958 when Interior Secretary Fred Seaton made a speech in Flagstaff, Arizona: "No Indian tribe or group should end its relationship with the Federal Government unless such tribe has clearly demonstrated first, that it understands the plan under which such a program would go forward, and second, that the tribe or group affected concurs and supports the plan proposed."[111] Even the state of Nevada backed away from termination. In 1960 the two houses of the Nevada legislature passed a joint resolution that read: "Resolved by the Assembly and Senate of the State of Nevada, jointly, that each member of Nevada's Congressional delegation is hereby memorialized to take such positive action as he may deem necessary to prevent a termination of the federal trust of Indian lands in Nevada."[112]

The Shoshone reservations and colonies in Nevada escaped the dissolution that would have come with termination, but the Shoshones at Indian Ranch in Panamint Valley, California, were less fortunate. This 560 acre reserve had been the home of George Hanson and his extended family for many years. However, all family members moved away after George's death in 1945. After a few years the eight adult heirs to the land agreed to lease Indian Ranch to a non-Indian, and by the mid-1950s they even considered selling it.[113]

When the Hanson family heard about the federal government plan to terminate rancherias in California, they initially favored the proposal since it would be a way to sell Indian Ranch at a profit. The ranch was therefore included in HR 7833 (1957), which sought to terminate dozens of small Indian rancherias in California. But the Hansons turned around and quickly rejected termination after they realized that the ranch, home of their ancestors, would be lost forever. Unfortunately, Congress did not withdraw Indian Ranch from the impending legislation. When the bill became Public Law (PL) 85–671 (1958), the ranch was one of forty rancherias earmarked for dissolution in California. Although the Hansons continued to oppose termination after 1958, their ranch was finally terminated in 1963: daughter Isabel Hanson, grandson Dugan Hanson, and granddaughter Addie Hanson Santos each received one-third.[114]

The policy of termination had still other aspects. One was PL 280, passed by Congress in August 1953. This law allowed five states to assume civil and criminal jurisdiction over the Indian reservations located within state boundaries. This action was taken to reduce or eliminate jurisdictional disputes. It was also part of the federal government's drive to turn Indian affairs over to the states.[115]

Although PL 280 did not include the state of Nevada, one of its provisions specified that states not named in the law could use legislative power to assume jurisdiction. Furthermore, these states did not have to secure approval of or hold discussions with the Indians. As a result, in 1955 Nevada passed a law that gave the state the power to "assume jurisdiction over public offenses committed by or against Indians in the area of Indian country in Nevada, as well as jurisdiction over civil cases of actions between Indians."[116] Additionally, this law gave the individual counties the option to accept or reject jurisdiction. All of Nevada's counties accepted, and the Indian colonies and reservations, except for Duck Valley, fell under Nevada rule. Duck Valley was exempted because the Shoshones and Paiutes wanted to remain under federal jurisdiction.[117] The vast majority of Shoshones were unaware of PL 280 and the 1955 Nevada jurisdiction law. Some years afterward Oscar Johnny, a Shoshone leader from Elko, reflected upon this development: "Most Indians living on Indian Reservations and Colonies have been placed under State and County Law. This action is on the part of the State of Nevada. Was taken without the consent of the Indian people."[118]

It is safe to conclude that if the Western Shoshones had known of PL 280, they would have rejected it. In fact, they did reject it some twenty years later, in the mid-1970s, when Nevada gave the tribes the option to remain under state law or return to federal jurisdiction. All the reservations and colonies, except for the Ely Colony of Shoshones, voted in favor of retrocession. By 1975 nearly all the Nevada Indians were once again under federal jurisdiction.[119] In February 1988 the Ely Shoshones joined ranks.[120]

The BIA established a program called Operation Relocation in 1952, with the intention of encouraging or inducing the Indians to leave their reservations and move to urban areas. It was hoped that they would eventually assimilate into mainstream America.[121] For reasons not entirely clear, the government did not pressure the Nevada Shoshones into leaving their reservations in the 1950s. Perhaps the BIA was aware of Shoshone opposition to the various components of termination and understood that any attempt to encourage their relocation would be rejected as well. Nevertheless, in February 1956 federal officials tried but failed to encourage the Duck Valley Indians to accept the new policy. One BIA official told them about the positive aspects of the program, such as paid transportation, clothing, and a bright future for the young people in

America's cities.[122] But the Duck Valley residents refused to listen. The BIA apparently did not approach other Shoshone communities in the 1950s.

Still another component of termination applied to the Great Basin Shoshones was agricultural extension. In July 1955 the BIA made a contract with the Agricultural Extension Service of the University of Nevada, in which the university was given full charge of the agricultural programs on ten Nevada Indian reservations, including the Shoshone reservations of Duck Valley, Duckwater, South Fork, and Yomba. Under the new arrangement, extension agents were assigned to help the Indians with crop and livestock improvement, among other activities, in an attempt to make the Indians more self-sustaining. Also, it was an attempt to "mainstream" the Indians into the larger Nevada population. As the director of the program stated, it "will cause the Indians to be more quickly assimilated into the overall extension programs" in the state.[123] As it had done with some of the other termination activities, the federal government made this administrative change without consent or approval of the Indians. Except for the Indians at Duck Valley, it appears that the tribes were unaware of the change. As for the Duck Valley residents, they opposed this aspect of termination, stating that the Indians would receive less attention under the state of Nevada.[124] In the end, this change actually benefited Nevada's Indians, for the Agricultural Extension Service of the University of Nevada provided more technical assistance and advice than the BIA had done. By the late 1950s the University of Nevada was serving several tribes and making slow but steady progress.

Two schools for the Shoshones were also victims of termination: the Reese River Day School on the Yomba Reservation and the Duckwater Day School, established by the Indian Bureau in 1939 and 1941 respectively. The bureau turned the Yomba school over to the state of Nevada in 1944, followed by the Duckwater school in 1949. However, the federal government remained involved since it provided Johnson-O'Malley Act funds for operational expenses, even though the schools were run by the Nevada public school system.[125]

If the overall termination drive sought to assimilate Indian people, this effort failed. The Shoshones continued to practice their native culture to varying degrees in the 1940s and 1950s. In 1947 the Shoshones on the Yomba Reservation held a large fandango that was said to be a "big success."[126] However, the Yomba fandangos were held less and less often. The Battle Mountain Colony, the stronghold for fandangos in the postwar period, sponsored annual fandangos in 1948 and 1949. At the 1948 gathering, the Shoshones invited Senator Patrick McCarran as a speaker and made him an honorary chief. The Shoshones bestowed this status with the hope that he would favor their interests—specifically with reference to the need for more land—but McCarran ended up favoring termination in the 1950s. For unknown reasons the Battle Mountain Colony did not hold fandangos for the next nine years until 1958, when the Shoshones revived the annual event. It remained in existence in the 1960s and 1970s. Fandangos continued to feature handgames, round dances, the big barbecue, and political speeches.[127]

Clearly, the Western Shoshone people in general did not favor the overall termination policy, and they expressed their opposition whenever the opportunity arose. In September 1959 Chief Frank Temoke stated, "We furthermore ask for congressional investigation of the handling of Indian Affairs in general and that present policies for termination and resultant of tribal lands be stopped at once."[128] Several months later, in March 1960, he went on to say: "We ask you as our representatives to introduce legislation designed to *stop all termination of Indian tribes and lands.*"[129] Other Shoshone leaders also expressed their opposition to termination. Clarence Blossom of Battle Mountain asserted in March 1960 that "in fact they [federal officials] are more interested in termination and disposal of Indian lands."[130] Of course, Blossom and others firmly believed that the federal government had a responsibility to protect the interests of the Shoshones, including the Indians' title to their land. When the BIA initiated termination, the Shoshones opposed its objectives.

Despite their philosophical differences and heterogenous viewpoints, the Western Shoshone people chose to remain a tribal entity in the age of termination. The Shoshones thought in terms of "tribal survival" in a period when the government wanted them to forget tribalness and, instead, to think and act as American individuals. The Shoshones opposed this plan. For example, when the Duck Valley group realized that its communally owned reservation could be abolished under HCR 108, they repeatedly opposed this resolution. And when Chief Frank Temoke realized that the overall termination policy did not favor the interests of the Shoshones, he attempted to get the Western Shoshone Nation organization to fight for treaty rights as well as for Shoshone ownership of the aboriginal homeland in the Great Basin. One can conclude that the Shoshone people were principal "actors" at the "front" of their own "historical stage" in the period of termination, an era in which the government sought to assimilate the Indians into the larger dominant society.[131]

7

RECENT WESTERN SHOSHONE
HISTORY
1960–1990

In the post-1960 era all the Western Shoshone communities were touched to varying degrees by the socioeconomic reforms under President John Kennedy's "New Frontier" (1961–1963), followed by President Lyndon Johnson's "Great Society" (1964–1968), and then the BIA "self-determination" initiatives of the 1970s and 1980s.[1] The New Frontier and Great Society were antipoverty programs that provided assistance to economically depressed communities, including Indian reservations. These antipoverty programs also encouraged the Indians to run their own affairs and build their own communities with federal support. The BIA's self-determination program followed this same pattern and also encouraged the tribes to take charge of their own destinies. Together these reforms shifted federal government policy away from efforts to assimilate Indians into mainstream America. The new programs allowed the tribes to rebuild their own communities and remain as culturally distinct people. The reforms brought about changes in the Western Shoshone communities, yet the Indians managed to retain their distinctly Native American culture.

For the Shoshones, the biggest change of the post-1960 period was having to deal with other federal agencies in addition to the BIA. Up to the 1950s the BIA had been the principal agency that dealt with all tribes, including the Shoshones. But the proliferation of socioeconomic reforms caused other agencies to become involved both directly and indirectly. The Shoshones accepted the assistance offered by these programs; they were economically disadvantaged and knew they could benefit from the reforms. At the same time, because of their long history of assertiveness, some Shoshones rejected particular federal initiatives.

The "Great Father's" Indian Programs

One of the most striking reforms, which quite literally changed the face of Western Shoshone country, was housing. Part of the New Frontier program, the housing reform began in 1963 when the Department of Housing and Urban Development (HUD), in connection with the BIA, created a new program called the Mutual Help Homeowners Program.[2] This program allowed the federal government to purchase building supplies; with supervision from building contractors, the Indians helped in building their own new houses. To purchase their new dwellings, which included carpeted floors and electrical appliances, the Indian residents paid a low monthly fee to the federal government. Once the cost was paid off, they owned their homes outright.

The first Shoshone community to benefit from the new housing program was the Duck Valley Indian Reservation. Under federal housing laws the Indians were required to organize a local housing authority to oversee the completion of the project.[3] In 1963 the Duck Valley Indians organized the Duck Valley Housing Authority, which requested thirty houses.[4] Only fifteen were granted. Over a two-year period fifteen families helped build their own houses. In July 1966 the reservation community dedicated this first group of houses, each of which had three bedrooms, a living room, kitchen, laundry room, bathroom, and a large storage room. Not to forget native culture, the community included some native dancing as part of the housing dedication program.[5]

Over the next two decades the federal government helped the Indians build numerous other new houses in Duck Valley. In the early 1980s alone, seventy-six houses were built. A striking feature of the new project was "cluster housing" or the creation of new Indian neighborhoods. One of these was in Owyhee, the agency headquarters; the other, farther north, became labeled New Town.[6] When one enters Duck Valley from the south, the Self-Help Mutual Houses are readily identifiable as part of the reservation community.

The Duck Valley Housing Program had positive and negative effects on the Shoshones. This was the first time since the 1930s that the federal government had provided new living quarters for tribal people. Furthermore, the Indian residents now enjoyed modern living with electricity and running water. But the new houses did create some problems. Traditionally, the Shoshones, like their Paiute neighbors, had relished a sense of space and openness. The cluster housing made the residents feel as if they had lost this tribal world view. This was a clear case of an Anglo-American concept—the close-knit neighborhood—that did not conform to the Great Basin Indians' traditional outlook. The new houses also created more leisure time, especially for the young people. No longer were they required to go outside to cut wood or haul water during winter months. This additional leisure time may have contributed to a sense of upheaval among the younger generation in the late 1960s and early 1970s.[7] Additionally, the Indian residents were required to pay monthly

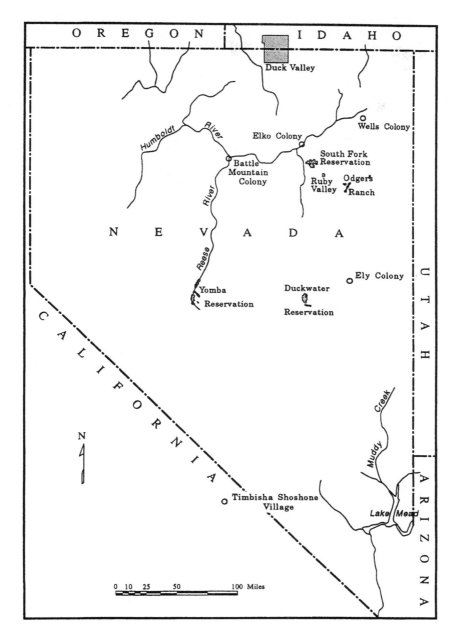

Present Land Base of the Western Shoshone

fees based on income. In some instances families were so poor that they could not make the necessary payments. As a result, some lost their homes. These problems were by no means unique to Duck Valley.

The development of new houses for the other Western Shoshone communities came much more slowly, probably because the government discriminated in favor of large reservation communities, such as Duck Valley. The much smaller Elko Colony is a case in point. By late 1963 its community leaders saw that the thirty-four acre colony site was run-down. Influenced in part by the spirit of self-help projects of the early 1960s, the colony residents decided to undertake a massive cleanup and rehabilitation program. With support primarily from the BIA, the Shoshones hauled away debris, graveled their roads, and repaired and painted the old colony houses, most of which had been built in the 1930s under the New Deal rehabilitation program.[8] However, no new houses were built in the Elko Colony until 1970, when thirty Mutual Help HUD houses were completed.[9] Many of the families planted lawns and built fences around their new dwellings. Additionally, the older gravel roads were paved, and the streets were given names. Thus part of the Elko Colony had a completely new look by the 1970s, as a result of the federal government's housing program.

Like the Shoshones and Paiutes of Duck Valley, the Elko Colony Shoshones operated under a housing authority; theirs was called the Te-Moak Western Shoshone Housing Authority, organized in August 1966.[10] The Elko Colony and the South Fork Reservation were the original members, and they were later joined by the Battle Mountain and Wells colonies. In 1977 the Te-Moak housing authority oversaw the completion of twenty-six Mutual Self-Help houses at the Elko Colony and seven on the South Fork Reservation.[11] In the early 1980s the authority undertook the building of 188 one-story units: 58 were built on the original, 160-acre Elko Colony site, located north of Interstate 80; 8 were built on the South Fork Reservation; 27 were built in the Battle Mountain Colony, on the site south of I-80; and 25 were built in the Wells Colony.[12] In these places, as in Duck Valley, the new houses changed the face of the community.

The Wells Colony situation was different. In the mid-1970s the Shoshone families living there wanted HUD houses, but they had no land base on which to build. At a March 1976 meeting held with BIA officials and the Wells city council, the Shoshones requested a permanent site for homes.[13] Their request was granted in 1977 when Congress passed Public Law (PL) 95–133, which granted eighty acres of trust land to the Wells Shoshones. The group then chose to affiliate with the Te-Moak Bands of Western Shoshone Indians.[14] The twenty-five HUD houses built at Wells in 1981 were part of the Te-Moak housing authority.

The Shoshones of the Ely Colony also became aware of the new federal housing program in the mid-1960s. They organized the Ely Tribal Housing Authority in August 1966.[15] But they quickly realized that only two acres of their ten-acre colony site were suitable for the construction of new houses. The tribal council, which created the housing authority, took two actions. First, it passed a resolution in April 1969 asking the government for "more land for mutual help houses."[16] Finally, in November 1977, Congress passed PL 95–191, which set aside ninety acres of former BLM land as more tribal land for the Ely Shoshones. In the mid-1980s many of the tribal members moved into thirty-eight new HUD houses on the new site located along the Pioche Highway in extreme east Ely.[17] Second, in 1973 the council signed a contract to lease ten acres of land from the city of Ely for fifty-five years. In 1976, seventeen new HUD houses were built on this site, located in the northeastern part of Ely.[18]

The Duckwater and Yomba reservations in central Nevada, because of their extreme isolation and other problems, were unable to participate in the housing movement in its early years. For example, for the first forty years of its existence the Duckwater Reservation did not have electricity. This meant that the Shoshones could not even consider new federally sponsored housing, since the HUD units were dependent on electrical power. But in 1971 the Duckwater Reservation finally received electricity.[19] The community then began to change rapidly: Nine houses were built in 1973, followed by twelve more in 1979, and twenty in 1986.[20] Residents celebrated the completion of some of the new houses in 1973 by sponsoring a traditional round dance.[21]

The struggle to secure a housing project on the Yomba Reservation took much longer. Beginning in 1965 the council continuously asked for new houses. As late as 1974 the requests were rejected because the reservation did not yet have electricity and the tribe had not created a housing authority.[22] Finally, electrical power was brought in, and the reservation created its own housing authority. Still, not until August 1981 did the Yomba Shoshones move into twenty-two new HUD houses. This was their first housing project since the late 1940s and early 1950s when they built the older cinder-block houses.[23]

The Western Shoshone people also benefited from the BIA Housing Improvement Program (HIP) established in 1965.[24] The Battle Mountain Colony received $60,000 in HIP funds in 1972 to renovate fifteen older houses purchased a year earlier from the Getchell Mines Company located near Winnemucca, Nevada. The tribe bought these houses at a price of $1,150 per unit with funds from the Nevada State Highway Department. The state agency appropriated the money because Interstate-80 crossed the colony site. Before the Getchell houses were purchased the BIA agreed to provide HIP funds for home improvement.

However, once the purchases were made the Indian Bureau failed to carry out its promise.[25] The Battle Mountain leadership insisted, and the Bureau finally channeled HIP monies for rehabilitation purposes.[26]

Other Shoshone communities also secured HIP resources. In 1968 Duck Valley repaired the twenty rehabilitation houses built in the 1930s.[27] Duckwater used HIP monies in 1972 to repair four older houses, and South Fork initiated a home improvement program in 1971.[28] HIP still existed in the late 1980s, and several Shoshone families have used its resources to make necessary repairs on the newer HUD houses.

Over 200 new HUD houses were built in Shoshone country. Unfortunately, some of the houses are of inferior quality. They were built too quickly and too many at a time. Many are prefabricated structures because the building contractors wanted to cut construction costs. Nevertheless, the Shoshone people of the Great Basin are better off with their new dwellings. Before they were built the people lived in old substandard structures, many of which had been built in the 1930s under the New Deal. Before HUD came to Shoshone country the old houses of the Elko Colony were described as "deplorable."[29] The Battle Mountain leaders wrote of their houses in 1969: "The living quarters here at the colony is a disgrace to live in, it is unsanitary."[30] Today the Shoshone people no longer make such statements. The housing program also helped increase the land base of the Shoshones by 170 acres.

Another post-1960 program that touched the lives of some Western Shoshones was the Manpower Development Training Act (MDTA) of 1962. It too was part of the Kennedy administration's effort to combat poverty across the country. The act sought to retrain and reeducate persons who had become unemployed as a result of automation of manufacturing functions. Training programs were initiated under MDTA, and the participants received on-the-job training to prepare for new roles in society.[31]

It appears that only three Western Shoshone communities benefited from MDTA because the program required the use of existing facilities for instruction and on-the-job training. The government created one manpower program on the Duck Valley Reservation in 1964. Using the large utility shop of the Owyhee High School, the Department of Labor's MDTA program introduced two courses. One involved over twenty men who took evening classes to study farm maintenance and mechanics. The second was range management, in which the same adult students studied methods of preserving their cattle-grazing areas.[32] Like so many other federal programs, these two lasted only three or four years. Some years later, in 1972, the government introduced a new MDTA program at Duck Valley in which nine men and two women were taught leatherwork and secured on-the-job training making horse collars, chaps, saddle pockets, bridles, and saddles.[33] Two of the students ended up becoming successful leathercrafters. In 1975 the federal government introduced a third MDTA training program in which the participants were taught silver and turquoise jewelry-making.[34] This program was a failure, however, for the students could not find markets for their crafts. Unlike southwestern tribes, the people of the Great Basin did not have a tradition of making or wearing turquoise jewelry, and the Duck Valley craftspeople could not compete against those already firmly established in the Southwest.

The Elko Colony and the South Fork Reservation were also touched by MDTA. In late 1967 and early 1968 several individuals took classes in farm mechanics, shop management, welding, gas engines, and cattle and crop management at the Elko High School shop facilities.[35] Like the Duck Valley classes, the Elko program was short-lived. In 1971 some Elko/South Fork adults received more MDTA on-the-job training to become carpenters. When this program ended the trainees had skills but did not have the transportation to take advantage of some job opportunities located outside the immediate area.[36] MDTA, although based on good intentions, was largely a failure among the Western Shoshones. Furthermore, MDTA never did reach the Shoshone colonies and reservations of Battle Mountain, Duckwater, Ely, Yomba, and Wells.

Another federal program that affected the Western Shoshone was the Economic Development Administration (EDA) of 1965. EDA was an extension of the earlier Area Redevelopment Administration (ARA), in existence from 1961 to 1965. Kennedy established ARA after witnessing the grinding poverty of the coal-mining region of the Appalachian Mountains. ARA sought to restore the depressed economy by providing federal loans and grants to create new jobs for the unemployed and also to encourage the establishment of new industries. The idea was to "move jobs in, not people out."[37] Unfortunately, ARA made administrative blunders and was heavily criticized. When the agency was abolished in 1965, it was quickly replaced by EDA with the same purpose in mind.[38]

Before it was abolished, the ARA, which had created a special Indian office, encouraged the tribes across the country to draft long-range goals for tribal economic development. With the technical support of the BIA the Nevada groups (including the Battle Mountain, Elko, and Ely colonies and the Duck Valley, Duckwater, South Fork, and Yomba reservations) drafted "ten-year development program" goals in 1966. These economic plans called for the rehabilitation and rebuilding of the Great Basin Indian communities with federal dollars. For example, the Western Shoshone reports recommended remodeling old Indian houses at two colonies (Battle Mountain and Ely) and on three reservations (Duckwater, South Fork, Yomba) and building new houses at the Elko Colony and South Fork Reservation. They also requested the construction of new community centers on all the Shoshone reservations and colonies, except for Ely, probably because of its small size and unsuitable terrain. For those Shoshone communities involved in agricultural and cattle enterprises, the reports called for repair and building of fences and the improvement of irrigation networks. They also asked that the roads at the Elko Colony and South Fork Reservation be paved and that a paved road be constructed to the Yomba Reservation. The reports recommended the initiation of special projects in some Shoshone communities. This included the drafting of a tribal constitution for the Ely Colony and the revision of the Te-Moak Bands constitution to include members other than South Fork residents. For the Duck Valley and Duckwater reservations, they called for the development of recreation and tourism (by stocking fish) and also human resource development (the introduction of kindergarten classes for tribal youth). All the Western Shoshone reports acknowledged the bleak economic situation of Shoshone country in the mid-1960s. Unemployment was at roughly 50 percent. One factor was the reliance on intermittent seasonal labor. The overall objective was to reduce if not eliminate unemployment by 1975 (a ten-year goal) by rebuilding the reservations and colonies with Indian labor.[39]

These Western Shoshone reports, the result of the push for economic reform under Kennedy and Johnson, appeared to be unrealistic in the mid-1960s. However, many or most of their recommendations were actually carried out later. What was not initiated by the BIA or HUD or some other federal agency was accomplished with financial support from the EDA. In the 1970s and early 1980s EDA built sizable community centers or multipurpose tribal buildings in all the Shoshone communities.[40] The Shoshones used these facilities for different purposes, including recreation, medical care, council meetings, and office space for tribal business. They were badly needed because the Shoshone reservations and colonies had had small and inadequate facilities or no tribal centers at all. EDA backing also brought into existence other community facilities. In 1978 the Elko Colony dedicated its new Tribal Senior Citizens Center, the new Tribal Administration Building, and the Shoshone Skyline Complex, consisting of an office building used by the BIA, a public health facility, and a fire station.[41] The Ely Colony established a day care center in 1983, combining EDA and HUD resources.[42]

Some Western Shoshone enterprises also began with EDA support in the 1970s and early 1980s. For example, in 1971 the Elko Colony established the El-Shonie Corporation, headed by tribal leader Davis Gonzales. During its initial year, twenty tribal members were employed with support from EDA and the MDTA of 1962. The El-Shonie workers tied fishing flies and later assembled electrical power unit cables under contract with the Micro Electric Company, a Phoenix-based firm.[43]

Unfortunately, as a result of competition from both national and international businesses, El-Shonie eventually folded.

In 1982 the Duck Valley Reservation dedicated its new tribal farm, which consisted of "four 160-acre irrigated circles of barley" for a total of 640 acres with rotating sprinkler systems. Tribal members, including Nick Archuleta who had earned his bachelor's degree in agriculture from California State University, Chico, managed the farm.[44] For various reasons the farm did not prosper, but it too symbolized the new spirit of tribal economic development with support from EDA.

Another antipoverty program of the 1960s was the Office of Economic Opportunity (OEO), established in 1964 by the Economic Opportunity Act. OEO followed the same rationale as other programs. It sought to eliminate "the paradox of poverty in the midst of plenty" by providing opportunities to poor communities.[45] Title I created the Job Corps, which offered work-training and work-study for the jobless. Title II was an all-encompassing provision. It provided for the creation of Community Action Programs (CAP), which would administer the antipoverty programs in local communities. It introduced preschool tutoring and remedial and adult education programs, as well as other kinds of services, including health exams, programs for the elderly, day-care centers, and programs for teenagers. Title III offered loans for the development of small cooperative farms. Title IV provided small business loans. Title V provided more on-the-job training for poor communities. And Title VI created Volunteers in Service to America (VISTA), which gave college-educated persons the opportunity to serve poor communities.[46] The federal sector assigned different agencies to carry out certain OEO programs: The Department of Labor administered the Neighborhood Youth Corps program for teenage employment; the Department of Health, Education, and Welfare (HEW) managed most educational programs; and OEO itself ran Job Corps, VISTA, and CAP.[47]

Unlike other antipoverty programs of the 1960s, OEO had far-reaching consequences. Its programs were implemented on nearly all the Western Shoshone reservations and colonies. One of the more successful was the Neighborhood Youth Corps (NYC). The Duck Valley Reservation introduced its NYC program in 1966 and 1967. The teenagers carried out numerous work details. They helped build the tribal corrals and assisted in the rehabilitation of the Sheep Creek Reservoir (a popular place for both Indian and non-Indian sports enthusiasts). Others did general clean-up work in and around the reservation agency. Still others worked in the agency facilities, including the hospital and the BIA offices.[48] NYC was also highly visible in the Elko Colony. In December 1966 eight teens worked in the colony doing various jobs. Additionally, one served as a teacher's aide in the local high school, the U.S. Forest Service employed two, one served as a clerk-typist in the Elko Employment Office, and one worked in the Elko Selective Service Office.[49] Elko teens were still employed under NYC in 1972, with one working in the Elko Public Library and another two serving as custodians in the Elko Junior High School.[50] On the South Fork Reservation young persons helped tear down the old tribal barn and painted various dwellings on the reservation in the late 1960s and 1970s.[51] By 1974 twenty-three teenagers in Elko and South Fork were still employed by NYC.[52] Farther south the Duckwater teens painted the small reservation post office and cleaned cattle guards in 1967 and 1968.[53] Four NYC workers of the Ely Colony participated in the construction of HUD houses in 1972 and 1973.[54] NYC also existed on the Battle Mountain Colony and the Yomba Reservation in the late 1960s and early 1970s.

Before the appropriation was eliminated by Congress in the mid-1970s, dozens of Western Shoshone youth benefited from NYC. Shoshone leaders approved of the program. Not only did it provide Indian teenagers the opportunity to earn money, but it also taught them the value of work and the meaning of money.[55] NYC also had some problems. Because the program was implemented so quickly, little supervision existed in the initial stages. Hence the program was described as "out of control" on the Duck Valley Reservation in the mid-1960s. Furthermore, NYC "came and then it left fast."[56] Like so many other reform programs, NYC had only a brief existence.

Directly linked to NYC was the formation of a Shoshone youth club on the Elko Colony in 1966.[57] The young people, many of whom worked under NYC, formed the organization in the spirit of NYC and the OEO. Although slow to get going, the Elko Indian Youth Club became an active body by the early 1970s. It cosponsored the First Annual Indian Youth Convention of Nevada in August 1972. The club invited guest speakers to Elko to give motivational talks and encourage the young people to pursue higher education.[58] Members of the Elko club also attended a larger regional youth conference on the Utah State University campus in April 1973. Here they heard Indian speakers from around the country and also listened to the nationally known Indian musical group, X-IT.[59] In November 1972 the club formed a chapter of the National Indian Youth Council (NIYC), a national organization founded several years earlier to address the concerns of the younger generation of Native Americans.[60] Influenced by the NIYC as well as the Red Power movement of the late 1960s and early 1970s, the Elko Youth Club called for the elimination of the stereotypic and derogatory mascot/emblem of the Elko High School. The club was victorious in late 1973, when the high school replaced its comical Indian head emblem with a more dignified version.[61] As these examples show, the activist spirit of NYC and the OEO went beyond job opportunities. The young people also started youth clubs in the Battle Mountain and Ely colonies in the 1970s and 1980s.

Upward Bound was still another OEO program that was adopted by the Western Shoshones. The program sought to encourage low income students to continue education beyond high school and also to help them adjust to the larger society. As part of the program, high school sophomores and juniors lived on college campuses for two months during the summer, receiving basic academic instruction, tutoring, and counseling. They were able to study native cultures and take part in recreational activities.[62]

Several Western Shoshone students participated in the Upward Bound program sponsored by the University of Nevada at Reno in the late 1960s and early 1970s.[63] This program was one factor in increasing the number of Shoshone students attending colleges and universities. In 1965 only three Duck Valley students were enrolled in college; by 1988 the number had increased to forty.[64] Several Upward Bound participants went on to earn degrees, including Leah Brady of the Elko Colony who earned a B.A. degree in special education from the University of Nevada at Reno in 1977.[65] Clearly, Upward Bound was an important program for the younger generation of Western Shoshone people.

Another facet of OEO was Head Start, a preschool program intended to give youngsters a head start in life by beginning education at an earlier age. Head Start was not a widespread program among the Western Shoshone, for it required the use of already existing facilities. As a result only the Duck Valley Reservation and the Elko Colony (which included youngsters from South Fork) initially developed Head Start programs. Using two local churches and other facilities, the Duck Valley Reservation inaugurated its program in 1966 with thirty-six youngsters.[66] White public school teachers ran it, although the program hired local natives as teachers' aides. In the same year the Elko Colony set up its program with fifteen preschoolers who were taught in local public school facilities.[67] In the end, Head Start turned out to be a valuable program, for it gradually increased the enrollment of Indian students at the elementary and secondary levels. For example, in 1969, the senior class at Owyhee High School of Duck Valley numbered only twelve; twenty years later, the enrollment stood at twenty-six. This 100 percent increase was attributed to several factors, including the impact of Head Start. When OEO funds dried up in the early 1970s, Duck Valley turned to other sources to keep the program alive. The reservation now has a new Head Start building.

VISTA volunteers under OEO came to at least four Western Shoshone communities—Duck Valley, Duckwater, Elko Colony, and South Fork. They made a lasting impact on these communities. On the Duck Valley Reservation the volunteers tutored students at the reservation-based public school. This was perhaps the first time in the history of the community when many students had received individual attention in the educational system. Volunteers also conducted a demographic survey and published the findings in booklet form. The survey turned out to be a valuable reference for federal and state agencies working with the tribe.[68] In the Elko Colony one volunteer, Roger Downing, produced a movie about the history and tribal government of the colony. Titled *Western Shoshone Documentary*, it was shown to the Elko community in May 1978 during the dedication ceremony of EDA and HUD structures.[69] VISTA workers also tutored Indian students in junior and senior high school at both Elko and South Fork.[70] In the Ely Colony the volunteers helped the tribe draft a constitution and bylaws and also assisted them in securing a ninety-acre addition in 1977.[71] On the Duckwater Reservation volunteers served as teachers when the tribe opened its own tribally operated school in 1973.[72] The VISTA volunteers, many of whom were college-educated, provided valuable support to the Shoshone people in Nevada.

Other OEO programs also came to the Western Shoshone people in the second half of the 1960s and early 1970s. One was the Work Incentive Program (also called Operation Mainstream, or simply Mainstream), which was an adult version of NYC. In many instances adults and teens worked together in the program. Work Incentive was not implemented in all Shoshone communities, but it did provide temporary employment for individuals from Duck Valley, Elko, and South Fork.[73] Besides this work program, some of the Shoshone communities used OEO funds to create child day-care and senior citizens centers. These programs for the young and old still exist but are now funded by other sources.

The Inter-Tribal Council of Nevada (ITC-N) served as the parent organization of all the Indian-based OEO programs in Nevada. The Indians themselves founded ITC-N in 1964 to improve the socioeconomic status of the Nevada tribes.[74] When the Economic Opportunity Act became law in 1965, its administrative child, OEO, allocated funds to ITC-N. ITC-N in turn trained and hired OEO personnel who worked at a local reservation or colony. More often than not these local administrators were enrolled tribal members who served in a variety of positions, such as alcoholism counselors and talent search directors for the youth. Because of ITC-N's overall authority, the Nevada tribes had not developed the type of strong Community Action Programs that existed elsewhere in the nation. ITC-N's power base, with headquarters in Reno, also caused problems for tribes that did not live in the immediate vicinity. In the early years there was talk that ITC-N favored those living in western Nevada. Thus the tribes living in remote areas, including some

Shoshones in northeastern Nevada, had to fight for their share of OEO resources. [75]

By the early 1970s Congress no longer authorized funds for the numerous OEO-sponsored programs established across the nation. Thus OEO came to an end after an existence of only seven years. In that short time the program made many valuable contributions to Western Shoshone life: It created short-term employment opportunities and provided specialized training for the adults; it provided services to teenagers; it encouraged higher education; it introduced preschooling; it gave white volunteers the opportunity to work with the Indian tribes; and it created specialized programs, some of which still exist.

But OEO also had disadvantages. For one thing, the job opportunities were not permanent. For another, most adults who received specialized training never secured jobs in those fields. There were complaints of nepotism, charges that certain individuals or families secured available job opportunities for themselves and excluded others. Further, the OEO programs were never evenly spread over Western Shoshone country. And of course OEO did not eradicate poverty and unemployment among the Shoshones. The unemployment rate stood at 43 percent for the Yomba Reservation in 1977, at 50 percent for the Elko Colony in 1978, and at the extremely high level of 76 percent in Ely in 1986. [76] Clearly, OEO failed to alleviate poverty among the Shoshones.

When OEO funds dried up in the early 1970s, the Western Shoshones were able to benefit from other federal agency funds for short-term employment opportunities. The Comprehensive Employment and Training Act (CETA) of 1973 was one such program. The act turned the federally funded manpower training programs over to local governments in the states. [77] Many Shoshones secured short-term manual labor jobs under CETA in the 1970s and 1980s. This was the case in all the Shoshone communities, except perhaps for Battle Mountain and Wells. But CETA was more than manual labor, for it also gave some of the Shoshones the opportunity to develop their own programs. For example, the Duckwater Reservation used CETA funds to create a summer youth program and also to enlarge tribal office space. [78] The Elko Colony developed a silversmith project in 1975 in its new EDA-funded Arts and Crafts building. [79] But like the earlier Duck Valley Reservation experience, the Elko enterprise failed, and for the same reasons. On the Duck Valley Reservation three high school students used CETA to develop a tribal newsletter, *Duck Valley News*, beginning in 1980. [80] CETA was basically an extension of the work programs inaugurated under OEO, but it provided more room for creativity. Like OEO and other federally funded programs, CETA was also short-lived.

The Western Shoshone people benefited from federal "revenue sharing" beginning in 1972 when Congress gave rebates to states from income tax revenues. The states in turn channeled these funds to local governments for discretionary use.[81] Indian tribal governments in Nevada, including the Western Shoshones, benefited from revenue sharing and used it for different purposes: Battle Mountain reimbursed tribal council leaders for attending meetings, Elko funded its senior citizens program, Ely planted trees around the colony, and South Fork established an emergency fund.[82] Duckwater gave an accurate breakdown of how its revenue-sharing funds were used annually: of the $2,476 received from July 1977 to June 1978, $203 was used for local law enforcement, $771 for recreation, $618 for economic development, and $824 for housing and construction.[83]

At this same time the BIA also channeled funds to tribes, making it possible for them to create Indian Action Teams (IAT) in the 1970s. Basically IAT served the same function as CETA and OEO with an emphasis on employment opportunities. On the Yomba Reservation IAT workers fixed fences and renovated two surplus buildings that the tribe had purchased from the Nevada Test Site in the mid-1970s.[84] These two facilities now serve as tribal offices. IAT provided special training as well. For example, some individuals from South Fork took classes in carpentry, masonry, blueprint reading, and welding in the mid-1970s. The ITC-N allocated IAT monies to the tribes.[85]

Clearly, the 1970s was an active decade for Native Americans. Congress in this period passed several pieces of legislation to benefit Native Americans, including the Indian Education Act of 1972. The act grew out of the Kennedy Report of 1969, which had declared that Indian education in America was a "national tragedy." The report emphasized that native students were receiving a substandard education. It recommended that the BIA end its paternalism and allow tribes the freedom to run their own programs with federal support. Hence, the report called for "self-determination," a term that became popular in the 1970s. The Indian Education Act of 1972 was one effort to carry out this new approach.[86] It permitted tribes to create "innovative" programs that emphasized "cultural enrichment" and used "new approaches."[87]

One Western Shoshone community, the Duckwater Reservation, was deeply affected by the Indian Education Act. In 1973, in the spirit of self-determination, the Duckwater Shoshones decided to establish their own tribally run school. The Shoshones were angry at being told that Indian students were not as intelligent or capable as whites.[88] Deeply offended by this racist thinking the Indians withdrew their children from the local Nye County public school system. The leaders quickly proceeded to organize a school board, consisting of seven members, and with the support of sympathetic whites, including a VISTA volunteer, they drafted proposals to secure federal funds for a tribally run school. They secured funds under Title IV of the 1972 act and established the school in November 1973.[89]

The Duckwater Shoshone Elementary School, which held classes in the local Mormon church, enrolled eighteen Shoshones and three whites in its opening year. The first class of four students graduated in 1975.[90] The school was an excellent example of cultural enrichment. Not only did the students receive daily instruction in the Shoshone language, they also learned tribal stories, handgames, bear dances, and tribal history from native elders, including Danny Millett.[91] Stimulated by this new educational experience, students of high school age produced a brief tribal history in 1986.[92]

The Indian Self-Determination and Education Act of 1975, intended to reduce government paternalism over the tribes, has also affected the Western Shoshones. Under the act the BIA began turning over its functions and responsibilities to the tribes. Like other tribes, the Shoshones in the 1970s and 1980s took over former BIA functions, including enrollment, finance, social services, and health care. The self-determination act has caused the local Indian groups to compete against one another for limited money resources. Also the act assumes that the local tribal groups possess administrative and financial expertise, when this is not always the case. Some Shoshones are skeptical of the act, which they view as a slow form of government termination since the BIA intends to phase itself out altogether. Still, the Shoshones now live with the new self-determination policy, which they call "638 funding," after Public Law (PL) 93–638.[93]

Cultural Resurgence

The Western Shoshone people experienced a cultural awakening in the post-1960 period, in which a larger number of Shoshones once again began to emphasize their native tradition and culture.

This cultural resurgence is in part a legacy of the nationwide Red Power movement of the late 1960s and early 1970s. Inspired in part by the American civil rights movement and Third World movements, native tribes were no longer willing to accept white racism and ethnocentrism. Nor were they willing to accept the whites' argument that Indian culture and traditions were "heathenistic" and not worth saving. In rejecting mainstream American values, at least to some extent, native people began to develop pride in their own cultures, placing emphasis upon native heritage and tradition. This new attitude of the 1960s made an impact on many tribal people who sought to revitalize tribal traditions in which they had not engaged extensively or openly in years.[94]

A renewed emphasis on tribal tradition and religion was nurtured in an age of liberalism and gradual white acceptance of cultural pluralism. In the 1960s Americans were beginning to accept that America is not a complete "melting pot." Rather, the nation is characterized by diversity. With this new awareness, Congress passed laws to encourage ethnic identity and pluralism, such as the Ethnic Heritage Studies Act of 1972 and the Bilingual Education Act of 1968.[95]

Some post-1960 federal laws applied directly to the Native Americans. One of these was the so-called Indian Civil Rights Act of 1968. Although controversial among the Indian populations, the act did give tribal people on reservations certain basic freedoms, including religious freedom.[96] Ten years later Congress passed the American Indian Religious Freedom Act, which further allowed tribal people to possess sacred objects and to practice religious ceremonies. It also sought to protect native religious ceremonial sites.[97]

As Americans began to accept cultural pluralism, many Shoshones began to feel comfortable practicing native customs. In the period from the 1960s to the 1980s, some Shoshone communities revived their annual fandangos, which had fallen out of use in the 1950s.[98] The revivals tended to be sporadic, however. In the mid-1960s Frank Temoke, Sr., and his supporters under the Western Shoshone Nation of Indians, which included Glenn Holley of Battle Mountain and Oscar Johnny of Elko, sponsored fandangos in Ruby Valley.[99] In September 1976 the Elko Colony held a fandango in conjunction with the Elko County Fair and Livestock Show—the first time in years that a fandango had been held in Elko.[100]

Various Shoshone groups also undertook the teaching of the Shoshone language in the 1970s and 1980s. On the Duck Valley Reservation in the summer of 1971, two non-Indian linguists from the University of Utah and Beverly Crum, a Shoshone and a fluent native speaker, taught the first formal language class. They placed emphasis upon both the spoken and written word, although Shoshone was originally an oral, not a written, language, and it has never been fully written down.[101] In 1974 the Elko Colony held a Shoshone language class.[102] Both of these programs, however, were short-lived because of lack of funding; the position of instructor was not a full-time job. In 1976 the Te-Moak Tribal Council revived the teaching of the language and offered it to three communities: Elko, Wells, and South Fork.[103] The most ambitious program was undertaken by the Duckwater Shoshones. In 1981 the Duckwater community created the first bilingual education program in Nevada. The program started with a bilingual conference attended by scholars and educators, including Tohono O'odam linguist Ofelia Zepeda.[104] Duckwater now teaches the Shoshone language, both spoken and written, every day in its tribally operated school.

Another Western Shoshone effort to preserve tradition was the production of a tribal history. In the mid-1970s the Shoshones, along with other tribes in Nevada, cooperated with the ITC-N and the American West Center of the University of Utah to conduct research into tribal histories. By 1976 four separate tribal history books, including one entitled *Newe: A Western Shoshone History*, had been published by the ITC-N.[105]

The Shoshone history *Newe* discussed the native way of life before white contact and covered in detail the history of Shoshone-white relations in the nineteenth century. It concluded with a section on reservation life at all the Shoshone reservations and colonies in the late nineteenth and twentieth centuries. Although a good portion of the study was based on documents found in the National Archives, the authors also relied heavily upon oral interviews with tribal elders. Hence the native voice speaks clearly in *Newe*. This Shoshone history attempted to go beyond information and tribal knowledge, for it also sought to eliminate white stereotypes and misconceptions about the Shoshone people. Thus the history spoke positively about the native people, praising their "well-planned" way of life. The Newe did not waste time, they were not "aimless" nomads, they "take care not to upset the delicate balance of their environment," they "were not materialistic," and they "had a deep respect for all things."[106]

Some of the individual Great Basin reservation communities also published their own local tribal histories. In July 1977 Cheri Robertson, local historian for the Fallon-Paiute-Shoshone Tribes of the Fallon Reservation, produced a booklet entitled *After the Drying Up of the Water*, funded by Title IV of the Indian Education Act of 1972. Her narrative about the Paiute-Shoshones of Fallon dealt with the native way of life before the coming of the whites. Robertson gave a brief sketch of tribal history after white contact and a somewhat longer treatment of the contemporary scene. Photographs greatly enhanced her study. Perhaps the most important aspect of her work was the oral interviews she conducted with tribal elders, including Shoshones Willie and Iola Byers and Pug and Juanita Ike.[107] Although this fact goes unmentioned by Robertson, approximately one-quarter of the Fallon reservation population is Shoshone. In the early years of the twentieth century, several Shoshone families of central Nevada moved to Fallon. Over the years they became integrated into the Fallon Indian community. By 1936 two Shoshones were members of the Fallon Tribal Business Council: Albert Hicks, Sr., was vice-president, and Bodie Graham was secretary.[108]

The second reservation community to produce a tribal history was the

Duck Valley Reservation. In 1983 Whitney McKinney, a Shoshone and tribal historian, produced the *History of the Shoshone-Paiutes of the Duck Valley Indian Reservation*. Like the other tribal histories, Mc-Kinney's work stressed that the Great Basin people possessed a "rich cultural heritage" that included an oral tradition. Most of McKinney's study focused upon Indian-white relations, especially in the nineteenth century. He discussed the all-important Ruby Valley treaty of 1863, the formation of the Duck Valley Reservation in 1877, how some Shoshones were taken by military force to Duck Valley in the late nineteenth century, and also the federal government's unsuccessful efforts to induce the Shoshones to leave Duck Valley in 1884 and move to the Fort Hall Reservation in southern Idaho. However, McKinney gave only limited attention to the twentieth century. He did discuss the Shoshone Mike massacre of 1911 and also wrote of the Duck Valley Indians' drive to pressure the government to build a dam to preserve water runoff for irrigation purposes, a dream that was fulfilled in 1937 with the construction of the Wildhorse Dam. He paid less attention to the Northern Paiutes of Duck Valley, but did describe Captain Paddy settling in Duck Valley in the mid-1880s and the enlargement of the reservation in 1886 to accommodate the Paddy Cap Band.[109]

Most recently, the Duckwater Shoshones of the Duckwater Reservation in east-central Nevada have produced their own local tribal history. Entitled *Duckwater Shoshone History* and published in 1986, the booklet was the work of several young people associated with the Duckwater Shoshone Elementary School Curriculum Development Team. The study proceeds both chronologically and by subject, beginning with a creation story, a discussion of Shoshone life before white contact, and the events leading up to the formation of the reservation in 1940. It gives sufficient coverage to reservation life, including the working of the tribal council, the introduction of formal education in the early 1940s, the creation of a tribally run school in 1973, the emergence of a cattle economy, the development of federally sponsored housing, and the preservation of culture, best expressed in the fandango. To facilitate classroom use of the text, each subsection is followed by a list of questions to be answered by the reader. Even more important, the booklet is bilingual, Shoshone and English.[110]

Besides these history books, at least two Shoshone communities initiated local tribal history projects. In 1976 the Elko Colony established its Elko History Project Museum, housed in the senior citizens center. Tribal artisans displayed their beadwork, glove making, and other crafts. Larry Piffero, tribal historian, played a key role in setting up the museum exhibit.[111] In 1979 the Duck Valley Shoshones and Paiutes also developed a history project that included its history book, a photographic display of

Duck Valley, and a documented history and photographic presentation of Wildhorse Dam.[112]

The Western Shoshones have also marked their place in the nation's history by honoring tribal members who died fighting for the United States. At least forty-three young Shoshones fought in the Vietnam War. Three of them were killed in action: Lloyd Jackson of Austin, Jay A. Munsey of Battle Mountain, and Wilfred Sam of Elko. Over the years the various Shoshone communities have honored their veterans of foreign wars, including Vietnam veterans. For example, in November 1990 the Elko Colony Women's Association and the Elko Band Council sponsored a Native American Veteran's Day ceremony to honor both living and deceased Shoshone veterans. Those honored included Felix Ike, a veteran of the Vietnam War who served as chair of the Te-Moak Bands organization in the 1980s.[113]

Western Shoshone traditionalism in recent years has also been expressed in the fine arts. One embodiment of the artistic dimension of Shoshone life is graphic artist Jack Malotte, a member of the South Fork Shoshone group. From 1971 to 1974 he attended the California College of Arts and Crafts in Oakland. After receiving his bachelor's degree Malotte returned to Nevada where he became a creative and productive artist. His themes deal with the Great Basin environment. Malotte has been commissioned to depict Basin themes for various Nevada native groups, including the Western Shoshone Sacred Lands Association, and his work has been widely published in various sources, including the *Native Nevadan*. Besides his work in Nevada, Malotte also has exhibited nationally and competed in national contests, winning awards such as the Tanner's All Indian Invitational Art Exhibition in Phoenix.[114]

The Shoshones, along with other tribes in the Great Basin, sponsored large, intertribal religious and spiritual gatherings in the 1980s. The initial one took place on the Duck Valley Reservation in 1982. Many individuals and organized groups in Nevada attended this first annual Great Basin Indian Spiritual Conference, including Corbin Harney (Shoshone spiritual elder), Carrie Dann (Shoshone spokesperson from Beowawe), and the Native Nevadans for Political Education and Action (a native-based organization markedly opposed to the proposed MX missile). Traditional leaders from outside Nevada also attended, including Phillip Deere (Muskogee) and Fred Coyote (Wailaki from the Round Valley Reservation in California).[115]

Although the primary purpose of the five-day conference was to "discuss and learn about the traditional world views and way of life of the Great Basin tribes," it went far beyond this objective. The organizers also conducted special workshops on hide tanning, basket weaving, and other native arts. Many of the participants discussed politics. Some were critical of the tribal councils created by the Indian Reorganization Act, which they felt had become rubber stamps for BIA decisions. Since 1984 the Great Basin spiritual conferences have been held in the Little Current Creek Canyon, east of the Duckwater Reservation in east-central Nevada.[116]

In addition to the Great Basin annual conference, the Duckwater Shoshones also began sponsoring an annual gathering in the 1980s. The first Duckwater Festival took place on the Duckwater Reservation in 1984. It included native handgames, dances, feasting, and footraces and games for native youth. The gathering ended with a barbecue for all the participants.[117] In 1985 the Duckwater festival included several Western Shoshone speakers who talked about Shoshone culture, history, and values. One was Raymond Yowell, a long-time political figure among the Shoshone. Placing emphasis on traditionalism, he stressed that the land is sacred and should not be abused by people. Furthermore, the people must take care of the land and live in unity with it. Because the land is Newe Sokopia, Yowell emphasized, it "is not for sale."[118]

In the late 1980s the Western Shoshone National Council (WSNC), established in 1984, also hosted annual gatherings. Held in central Nevada, near Austin, the WSNC events combined cultural, political, and spiritual activities.[119] Perhaps the biggest concern of the WSNC gatherings was the issue of Western Shoshone claims.

The most recent large gatherings have taken place in Ruby Valley, the home of the 1863 treaty. In October 1988 the Western Shoshone Elders Council, founded in April of that year and led by traditional chief Frank Temoke, Sr., sponsored the first annual Ruby Valley Treaty Days. The objective of the three-day festival, which included native dancing, music, storytelling, and political speeches, was to recognize the importance of the one and only legally ratified treaty negotiated between the United States and the Shoshone people. At this first gathering Chief Temoke announced that his youngest son Gordon would become the next hereditary chief. At both the 1988 and 1989 gatherings, filmmakers filmed part of the proceedings. In 1988 Joel Freedman, a New York movie producer, completed his sequel to an earlier movie on the Shoshones entitled *Broken Treaty at Battle Mountain*. In 1989 two German filmmakers filmed portions of the Treaty Days.[120]

The Shoshones sponsored these large gatherings for more than cultural reasons. They were also a way to share political concerns, such as opposition to the proposed MX missile, the "sagebrush rebellion" of the late 1970s and 1980s, and to publicize the pending Shoshone land claims case.

The Political Dimension

The Western Shoshone people have been politically active in the post-1960 period, especially the Te-Moak Bands organization, created under the Indian Reorganization Act of 1934. As previously mentioned, the Te-Moak council in the early years of its existence did not become a federated and representative governing body of all the northeastern Nevada Shoshones as it was originally intended. In 1962 the Te-Moak council, all members from South Fork, passed an ordinance by a vote of four to zero in favor of withdrawing the South Fork Reservation from the Te-Moak Bands organization.[121] The BIA did not respond to this ordinance. In 1965 the council again expressed its desire to sever ties with the Te-Moak organization and form an independent governing body.[122] Again the BIA did not respond. Without doubt the BIA knew that if South Fork successfully withdrew, then the Te-Moak Bands organization would cease to exist (see chapter 5).

Beginning in the mid-1960s a younger generation of Shoshones, who thought in terms of political unification and new ideas, realized that the Te-Moak Bands organization could become a federated governing body of the northeastern Nevada Shoshone communities. In 1966 the Elko Colony elected William Jack Woods and Frank Temoke, Jr., as the Elko representatives to the council.[123] This election was a major turning point in the history of the Te-Moak Bands council.

Some of the other northeastern Nevada Shoshones have also joined the council in the post-1960 period. In 1974 the Battle Mountain Colony elected Leslie Blossom and Glenn Holley to the council.[124] The Battle Mountain group had not participated in years, although it had elected one representative in 1940. Battle Mountain chose to rejoin in 1974 because it wanted to benefit from the revenue-sharing funds that had been channeled to the Te-Moak Bands organization. In 1977 the Wells Colony joined the Te-Moak Bands council, and it sent elected representatives to the council in the 1980s.[125] The Wells group, which had never been part of the organization, chose to join in the late 1970s in an effort to be part of a larger political entity.

To this day not all the northeastern Nevada Shoshone communities have joined the Te-Moak Bands of Western Shoshone Indians. Because of their distance from the Te-Moak organization headquarters in Elko, or perhaps for other reasons, the Ely Shoshones chose to form their own autonomous political body. They voted in favor of a new constitution in February 1966. This governing document, drafted by the BIA and much more inclusive than the first Ely constitution of 1959, is patterned after other Indian Reorganization Act tribal constitutions. It states that the territory of the Ely Colony is the ten-acre colony site and any additional land acquired in the future. The governing body, called the Ely Colony Council, consists of five members elected every two years. These elected members choose their own officers: a chair, vice-chair, and a secretary-treasurer. The council has the power to "employ legal counsel" and "to create and regulate subordinate organizations." The Ely constitution includes several clauses that define tribal membership, directs the course of action for tribal elections, and also includes initiative, referendum, and recall clauses.[126] Today, the Ely Colony is politically autonomous, even though the BIA originally wanted it to be part of the Te-Moak Bands organization.

The Te-Moak Bands council would have been even larger if the Shoshones of Duck Valley had decided to join the organization. In 1984 the Duck Valley group considered this action because it had lost its political power base to the Northern Paiutes. To regain a sense of strength, the Shoshones thought about political merger with the Te-Moaks since some of their ancestors had originally come from the Te-Moak area. But in the end the Duck Valley Shoshones rejected this proposal. They decided to "save Duck Valley for all Western Shoshones" since the portion of the reservation covered in the 1877 executive order was actually set aside for the Shoshones in the first place.[127] Thus, as mentioned in chapter 5, they formed the Western Shoshone Business Council, separate from the older Shoshone-Paiute Business Council. However, the Shoshones still have some elected members on the older IRA body.

The Shoshones living in Death Valley, California, were affected politically by a new BIA program called federal acknowledgment, set up in September 1978. It was the culmination of years of struggle on the part of numerous so-called unrecognized native groups that had not received support or services from the federal government—in short, who had been overlooked and ignored by the BIA. The Task Force on Urban and Rural Non-Reservation Indians of the American Indian Policy Review Commission highlighted this situation in its published report of 1976. In response, Congress initiated legislation in 1977 and 1978 to recognize those tribes that had not fallen under the jurisdiction of the BIA. This legislation was not necessary, for the BIA carried out an administrative directive creating the Federal Acknowledgement Program in 1978.[128]

For a native group to become recognized or acknowledged as a tribe under the Federal Acknowledgement Program, they had to meet seven criteria spelled out by the acknowledgment directive of 1978: (1) the group had to prove that they were "Indian" both in the past and in the present; (2) they had to live in a specific geographic place or area; (3) they had to possess political hegemony over their members; (4) they had to possess a "governing document"; (5) they had to provide a membership roll; (6) persons listed on this roll could not be enrolled in any other tribal group; and (7) the group had to be untouched by the BIA's earlier termination program of the 1950s. Meeting these criteria required evidence based on written record. The group had to petition for acknowledgment. This meant that groups had to seek the services of scholars who could help conduct ethnohistorical research.[129]

The Shoshone group of Death Valley, actively seeking political reorganization in the late 1970s, quickly learned about the BIA's new Federal Acknowledgment Program. The group petitioned for participation in April 1979. John Herron, a cultural anthropologist for the National Park Service, produced an ethnohistorical report proving that the Death Valley Shoshones fulfilled all seven criteria. The Death Valley group had always been recognized as an "Indian" entity—a statement based not only on native oral history but also on recognition from whites. As early as 1849 white pioneers identified natives living in the Death Valley area. The whites called these native people "Panamint" Shoshones before the turn of the century. They were recognized as "Indian" in the early twentieth century by officials of the short-lived BIA office located in Bishop, California. The Death Valley group also proved that they occupied a specific area in and around Death Valley, including nearby places, such as the Panamint and Saline valleys. The group provided solid evidence of their political history. They had had traditional leaders both before and after white contact. In 1937 the Shoshones living in Furnace Creek, adjacent to the National Monument headquarters, had formed a formal tribal council consisting of three elected leaders. One of their objectives was to strive for the establishment of a reservation within the monument boundaries. Although this council faded away after a few years, the group continued to have leaders, including Pauline Esteves who was an important spokesperson from the 1960s onward. The Death Valley group also had a governing document, drafted in January 1978 and entitled "Articles of Association of the Death Valley Band." The group also provided a list of 199 tribal members who lived either in Death Valley or in the surrounding area. This tribal count was based on census rolls taken in 1933 and 1936. These persons were not listed under any other tribal entity. And except for seven persons listed as heirs to the Indian Ranch rancheria in Panamint Valley, all others had never been subject to the BIA's earlier termination policy.[130]

It was no surprise that the Death Valley Shoshones received full acknowledgment by the BIA in November 1982 and also were recognized as a tribe by the assistant secretary of the interior in January 1983. The group now calls itself the Timbisha Band of Shoshone Indians.[131] The native name derives from the Shoshone word Tempisa which is the name for Furnace Creek, the tribe's official headquarters.[132] Now recognized as a tribe, the Timbisha Band continues to demand a reservation land base in Death Valley.

The strongest political move made by the Western Shoshone in the years since 1960 was the formation of a centralized political entity. In January 1984 the Shoshone leadership came together and established the Western Shoshone National Council (WSNC).[133] The idea of a unified group had been around for a long time. In fact, there had been earlier efforts to create a body that went beyond the local tribal councils created under the Indian Reorganization Act. The first attempt was in September 1963 when several leaders from western and central Nevada formed the Unaffiliated Western Shoshone, Inc.[134] Its purpose was to deal exclusively with the issue of Shoshone claims—to push for a quick money settlement as advanced by the Indian Claims Commission. However the organization received little support and did not survive. In May 1964 other Shoshones of central and eastern Nevada formed the Western Shoshone Tribe.[135] It also pushed for a quick money settlement and received minimal backing. This body was also short-lived.

The third and most successful effort was made by Chief Frank Temoke, Sr., of Ruby Valley and those who supported him. In April 1965 Temoke and many other Shoshones of northeastern Nevada held an important meeting in Elko. They stated that those fighting for the recognition of land, and who also opposed the Indian Claims Commission, were politically weak because the Shoshone people were divided into "subgroups," or tribal governing bodies created under the Indian Reorganization Act. It would be better, Temoke and others argued, if the Shoshones organized one political unit to serve as the voice for all the Western Shoshone people. Edward McDade of South Fork expressed the sentiment of those at the Elko meeting: "I want to remain a Shoshone and be recognized as a member of one Shoshone Nation, not as a member of a Shoshone sub-tribe."[136]

The result of the meeting was the reestablishment of the Western Shoshone Nation. Chief Frank Temoke, Sr., led the organization with Oscar Johnny of Elko as subchief. The organizaion actually had been created earlier, in 1953, when Temoke became the new hereditary chief. The organization remained small, however, until after 1960, when a larger number of Shoshones rejected the Indian Claims Commission's argument of 1962 specifying that the Shoshone had lost title to their land as a result of "gradual encroachment."[137]

By the late 1960s the Western Shoshone Nation had a well-established "traditional council" with eleven representatives coming from Elko, Battle Mountain, South Fork, and Duck Valley. But there were no representatives from the IRA tribal councils. In fact, the traditional council opposed the IRA councils, which had endorsed the decisions of the Indian Claims Commission.[138] Without representation from the IRA tribal councils, the traditional council did not represent all the Western Shoshone people of the Great Basin. Those whom it did represent were the traditionalists opposed to any money settlement from the government.

For various reasons the traditional council became less and less active in the early 1970s. However, its work was carried on by other newly formed political bodies organized in the 1970s. The most noted was the Western Shoshone Sacred Lands Association (WSSLA), created in 1974 and led by Glenn Holley of the Battle Mountain Colony. Holley was one of the members of the earlier traditional council.[139] The WSSLA still exists today and has representation on the WSNC.

The WSNC was the culmination of the Western Shoshones' efforts to form a centralized political entity. The main factor finally uniting the Shoshone groups politically was the Ninth Circuit Court of Appeals decision of May 1983, *United States v. Mary and Carrie Dann,* popularly known as the *Dann* decision. This important court decision ruled that the Shoshones had not lost title to their aboriginal territory as decided earlier by the Indian Claims Commission.[140] Elated by this victory the Shoshone groups held numerous meetings, resulting in the formation of the Western Shoshone National Council in 1984.

The membership of the WSNC is made up of most Western Shoshone groups of the Great Basin. This includes the IRA tribal councils of Duckwater, Yomba, and the Te-Moak Bands. The smaller governing bodies of the Te-Moak Bands (Elko, Battle Mountain, South Fork, and Wells) each have separate representation. The WSNC also includes those Shoshones who share reservations with the Northern Paiutes, including those at Duck Valley and Fallon. It also includes Shoshone groups whose membership goes beyond one particular Shoshone colony or reservation. Therefore the WSSLA (1974), the Timbisha Shoshones of Death Valley, and the more recent Great Basin Western Shoshone Descendants (1979), with members primarily from the Reno area, also have representatives on the WSNC. The national council also includes extended family and special interest groups, such as the Dann Band of Crescent Valley and the Western Shoshone Traditional Cattlemen's Association of the South Fork Reservation.[141] For the monthly WSNC meetings to be legitimate, a quorum of five members must be present at all meetings.

The WSNC elects officers, including a chief, subchief, and secretary. Jerry Millett served from 1984 to late 1988 as the first chief. Before taking office he served as chair of the Duckwater Shoshone Tribe. His leadership made the Duckwater Reservation a leading force among the Shoshone people.[142] Since 1988 the WSNC has been led by Raymond Yowell of South Fork. Yowell had been involved in the Shoshone land claims case since 1965 and also served as executive director of the Inter-Tribal Council in the late 1960s and early 1970s.[143] Both Millett and Yowell have done much to keep alive the Shoshone land struggle.

Although the tribal headquarters of the Duckwater Reservation serves as the office of the WSNC, the monthly meetings are held in Austin, Nevada. The participants chose Austin because it is the most central location for the Western Shoshone people. On occasion the meetings are held elsewhere. In March 1984 the national council gathered in Reno to meet with officials from the Phoenix Area Office of the BIA. Other meetings have been held at Duck Valley, Battle Mountain, and the Duckwater Reservation. During the spring of 1985 the council held a series of meetings throughout Western Shoshone country to keep the population informed about recent developments in the Shoshone claims case.[144]

The WSNC has sent representatives and delegations to different places. In November 1984 the WSNC sent Shoshone elders to Washington, D.C., to hear oral testimony presented before the Supreme Court. Delegates have gone to Geneva, Switzerland, to participate in conventions focusing on the concerns of indigenous "Fourth World" peoples.[145]

The WSNC has been involved in other activities as well. One important activity is fund-raising. The council produced Western Shoshone Nation T-shirts, worn by many people today. The proceeds from fund-raising activities are used to help pay the salary of attorneys representing the Shoshones, including Thomas Luebben of Albuquerque. The council also produced a newsletter whose first issue was released in May 1986. This paper provides current information about the Shoshone claims issue. The council also supports those tribal councils—Duckwater, Yomba, and South Fork—that have chosen not to pay grazing fees for Indian cattle on BLM land. The Shoshones argue that the BLM land is actually Shoshone land, so that Indian cattle owners should not have to pay taxes. The WSNC has created committees to deal with particular Shoshone issues and concerns.[146]

One of the most active WSNC committees is the Environmental Protection Committee, which seeks to protect and preserve the aboriginal land base of the Western Shoshone. The committee has actively opposed the expansion of the Nevada nuclear test site, located sixty-five miles northwest of Las Vegas and partly in Shoshone territory. The Shoshones and non-Indian environmentalists have ardently opposed the dumping of nuclear waste at Yucca Mountain. The environmental committee, headed by William Rosse, a leader of the Yomba Reservation, has protested at the Nevada test site area. The Shoshones along with their non-Indian friends have also been arrested at the site for acting on their convictions.[147]

An outstanding feature of the WSNC is its power to regulate the hunting and fishing of the members of the Western Shoshone Nation. The council assigned this responsibility to the Western Shoshone Wildlife and Plant Resource Commission, established in 1988. In 1986 the Shoshones brought suit against the Nevada Department of Wildlife, arguing that the state had no right to impose its hunting and fishing laws upon the Shoshone people. Of course, the Indians argued that they still owned their aboriginal land and that their rights were guaranteed under the Ruby Valley treaty. Before the suit was brought to trial, an agreement was worked out between the WSNC and the Department of Wildlife. In January 1988 the state granted the council the power to regulate Shoshone hunting and fishing in the area considered to be native tribal country. The state could not enforce its own laws on this land base. However, some exceptions were made. The hunting of bighorn sheep and mountain goats remained under state jurisdiction. The Shoshones could take only one elk each year for ceremonial purposes. The hunting of bobcats and sage hens was permitted only within the seasons determined by the state of Nevada. The WSNC created a resource commission in 1988 to regulate and control Shoshone hunting and fishing. The commission issued identification cards and ruled that Shoshone hunters could not hunt for sport or use game animals for commercial purposes. Tribal members who violated the rules were subject to penalty.[148]

The WSNC has dealt with a host of other issues. One is the boundary of the Western Shoshone territory. Since 1984 the national council has expressed dissatisfaction with the Shoshone land base boundary determined by the Indian Claims Commission. The ICC map was the work of anthropologist Omer C. Stewart of the University of Colorado. Without consulting the Shoshones, he drafted his map based on a few available government documents.[149] Unfortunately, Stewart's delineation of Shoshone territory was much smaller than what was recognized by the Shoshones themselves. The WSNC therefore drafted a new map in 1986, showing a much larger aboriginal land base of the Shoshone people. Unlike the ICC map, which identified northern Nevada as the northernmost boundary, the WSNC map placed the northern boundary at the Snake River in southern Idaho on the grounds that the Treaty of Ruby Valley had referred to the "Shoshone River Valley," which is today's Snake River. The larger area claimed by the WSNC extended into southeastern California.[150]

The biggest concern of the WSNC is the issue of land claims. Since its formation in 1984 the council has been deeply involved in the entire claims process—the main reason why it was established in the first place. The council takes the position that the Western Shoshone Nation still owns most of its aboriginal land base in the Great Basin.[151]

Western Shoshone Claims

The most controversial issue confronting the Western Shoshone today is that of land claims. As described in chapter 6, Congress created the Indian Claims Commission in 1946 to allow the tribes to file suit against the federal government for past injustices. If a tribe won its suit in the claims commission, it was awarded a monetary compensation; no land would be returned to any tribe. Many tribes wanted the return of land, but they had no recourse under the 1946 law. Numerous Western Shoshones have insisted that the title to their land, as acknowledged by the 1863 Treaty of Ruby Valley, should be recognized by the government. But the federal government has refused to concede and insists that the Shoshones must accept money for the so-called loss of aboriginal territory. The battle between the Shoshones and the federal government intensified after the ICC made an all-important decision in 1962. In that year the ICC ruled that by the "gradual encroachment" of white settlers and other European Americans, the Western Shoshones were deprived of their lands. Lacking any actual "date of taking," the ICC, in conjunction with the claims attorneys and the Justice Department, stipulated July 1, 1872, as the "date of valuation" for the purpose of determining compensation for a "taking."[152] This ruling assumed that thousands of white Americans had moved into the Great Basin and had literally taken over the homelands of the Shoshones. The ICC made this ruling without any input from the Shoshones themselves, another example of governmental paternalism.

The ICC decisions of 1962 set the stage for years of continuous battle between the Shoshones and the government. In the first couple of years the government and Shoshones sponsored several claims meetings. These meetings made the battleground abundantly clear. In March 1963 in Elko, the Wilkinson, Cragun, and Barker law firm, which had been representing the Shoshones since 1947, sponsored the first claims meeting. Many of the 300 Shoshones who showed up were unfamiliar with the claims proceedings. One observer wrote that they "were there to listen and to learn more." But the Shoshones quickly learned that attorney Robert Barker was cooperating with the federal government. They began challenging their legal counsel and asked some serious questions: "Who determined the boundary for the claim?" "Was there any possibility of getting the land back?" "Can the Indians help to make the appraisal?"[153] The attorneys answered most of these questions in the negative. After the claims attorneys had endorsed the 1962 ICC decision, increasing numbers of Shoshones turned against the Wilkinson, Cragun, and Barker law firm, the BIA, and the ICC. One of these persons, Carrie Dann of Beowawe, made it clear that "she and her followers would not settle for the sale of any of the land but that they wanted the deed to the land."[154] Some Shoshones, including Clancy Blossom of Battle Mountain, who had earlier endorsed Barker, now switched sides and gave support to those wanting the land returned.

On the other hand, many Shoshones chose to cooperate with the claims attorneys. After many years of dependency and federal paternalism, these persons felt that they had no voice in their own affairs. Their sense of powerlessness, as well as economic need, led them to be willing to accept a money settlement. Thus the claims process drove the Shoshones into two camps: those wanting title to the land and those wanting a monetary settlement. This "land versus money" polarity had actually begun earlier, in the late 1940s, intensifying by the 1960s.

In late 1963 some nonreservation Shoshones from the Reno area and other parts of western Nevada created a short-lived organization called the Unaffiliated Western Shoshone, Inc. Its objective was to unify the Shoshones through an "organized control group" or "federation" and to demand a quick monetary settlement.[155] This organization quickly collapsed because it received little support.

Opponents to the Unaffiliated Western Shoshone, Inc., responded quickly. Edward McDade from South Fork, advocated seeking land title rather than money. In February 1964 he stated his position: "You will find out that you are actually selling your Indian rights . . . Under this treaty [of Ruby Valley of 1863] . . . there isn't any mention of selling our lands. The land will always take care of you . . . For myself, no one will ever buy my Indian rights. They are sacred."[156]

The Shoshones fighting for land title countered the opposition by sponsoring their own mass claims meeting in Elko in April 1965. The purpose was to discuss the impending Western Shoshone claims and Shoshone political unification. On the issue of claims the participants, led by Chief Frank Temoke, Sr., rejected any future monetary settlement. They chose to fight for the sacred land. Temoke gave an eloquent speech in which he stated in part, "This earth is our Mother and it is not for sale, I have spoken."[157] On the issue of unification, Temoke and others maintained that the Shoshones were politically weak because they were divided into "subgroups," including the IRA councils at Duckwater, Yomba, and South Fork. It would be better, they asserted, if the Shoshones would organize into one political entity that could serve as the voice for all the Western Shoshone people.[158]

Western Shoshone opposition to the claims process grew in strength from this April 1965 meeting. It also marked the expansion of the "traditional council" of the Western Shoshone Nation, a political body of the northeastern Nevada Shoshones whose ancestors had signed the Ruby Valley treaty. This informal council, under the hereditary leadership of the Temoke family since the 1860s, had almost died out over the years. But it took on new life in the 1960s with the traditionalists' rejection of the claims process.[159]

Shoshone opposition was evident when attorney Barker called a meeting in July 1965. He wanted the Shoshones to vote in favor of a BIA loan that would be used to hire expert appraisers to determine the value of the 24 million acres supposedly lost. Once this was done, it would be possible to determine how much the Shoshones should be paid. The editor of the *Native Nevadan* wrote that "nearly half" of the Shoshones "walked-out" of the meeting.[160] No vote could be taken on Barker's request.

To prevent a stalemate, attorney Barker chose to work with those Shoshones who were willing to cooperate with him. He persuaded some leaders to call four separate meetings with two objectives in mind: to get them to vote in favor of the needed BIA loan application and also to get them to elect two Shoshone leaders from each of the meetings who would then serve on a newly created Western Shoshone claims committee.[161] This body, once established, would work with the Wilkinson, Cragun, and Barker law firm and endorse all ICC decisions.

In late September and early October 1965 the four meetings were held with the following results: 86 voted in favor of the loan and 4 voted against at the Austin meeting; 38 voted for and 3 against in Ely; 70 for and 6 against on the Duck Valley Reservation; and 25 for and 4 against in Elko. In all, 219 voted in the affirmative, while 17 opposed. Attorney Barker and the BIA considered these results to be a strong affirmative voice for the loan, and also a justification for the newly created claims committee with the following membership: Emmett Rosse and LeRoy Brady from the Austin meeting, William McQueen and Raymond Graham from Ely, Arthur Manning and Willis Premo from Duck Valley, and William Jack Woods and Raymond Yowell from Elko.[162] This claims committee functioned until 1980.

On the surface, it appeared that Barker had received the endorsement of the Western Shoshone populace. But appearances were deceptive. For example, of the ninety people who attended the Elko meeting, sixty walked out in protest. Furthermore, most who voted at the Duck Valley election were actually enrolled as Northern Paiute, not Shoshone, and were therefore not qualified to vote.[163]

Once the $145,000 loan money was appropriated for appraisals, the law firm quickly subcontracted experts to appraise the land in question. The cutoff point of 1872 served to determine the value of lost Shoshone land. As a result, the commission determined that the Shoshones were entitled to $26 million for the loss of 24 million acres of aboriginal territory.[164] It must be emphasized that the Shoshones themselves played no part in these conclusions.

The BIA called a claims meeting at Elko in August 1973, seeking to persuade the Shoshones to accept the government's argument that the Shoshones had lost the land and that their only recourse was to accept the $26 million when the case reached a conclusion. Steve Feraca of the Tribal Operations Division of the central office in Washington, D.C., represented the BIA. He spoke at some length and said in part: "The Western Shoshone Treaty of 1863 does not give the Shoshones any land, it takes away land . . . according to the treaty you lost everything."[165] Obviously, Feraca did not bother to study the treaty because Article V states that the Shoshones "claimed and occupied" a large land base in the Great Basin area.[166] However, his mission was to persuade the Shoshones to go along with the BIA, the ICC, and Barker and his law firm. During the meeting Feraca had the support of the Western Shoshone Claims Committee as well as part of the audience.[167] But he failed to convince the traditionalists: those fighting for land walked out of the meeting.

An interesting development of the 1973 Elko meeting was the presence of New York filmmaker Joel Freedman. Freedman included a portion of the meeting in his film, *Broken Treaty at Battle Mountain,* released to the public in 1975. This movie was significant because it focused upon the traditional Shoshone world view of the earth as sacred. Thus the traditionalists opposed the BLM's policy of "chaining," or uprooting the natural Great Basin vegetation, including pinyon trees, to make room for new forage grasses for cattle. As mentioned in chapter 1, the pinyon nuts were a food staple of the Shoshones before white contact, and the chaining of pinyon trees has taken place on the same lands the Indians regard as their native territory.[168]

While the movie was being filmed in the early 1970s, the claims battle intensified. In 1974 the BLM brought charges against Shoshone sisters Mary and Carrie Dann of Beowawe, charging them with illegally grazing their cattle on BLM land. Immediately, the sisters countered that they were actually grazing cattle on native Shoshone land claimed by the government.[169] The Danns were part of the traditional Shoshone force who had already rejected the ICC position. They themselves brought suit against the government in May 1974.

Their case became known as *United States v. Mary and Carrie Dann,* or simply the *Dann* case. Within two years, Judge Bruce Thompson of the federal district court in Reno ruled against the sisters, upholding the ICC ruling that the Shoshones had lost title to their land. The case was sent to the Ninth Circuit Court of Appeals in San Francisco. In April 1978, the circuit court opposed both the district court and the ICC and stated that the title was still an open question. It therefore requested the district court to make a definite decision concerning the issue of title.[170] The *Dann* case remained unresolved in the 1970s and was not decided until the 1980s.

The Danns' claim to land title was defended by the newly established Western Shoshone Sacred Lands Association (originally the Western Shoshone Education and Legal Defense Association), founded in 1974. Glenn Holley of Battle Mountain led WSSLA with full support from grass-roots Shoshone leaders, including the Danns and Chief Frank Temoke, Sr., of Ruby Valley. Holley made it very clear in the 1970s that the traditional Shoshones would not accept money for land. He succinctly stated: "Our Mother Earth is sacred and is not for sale."[171] In November 1974 WSSLA asked that the entire claims proceedings be halted, but the ICC rejected the request. WSSLA then appealed to the U.S. Court of Claims. But this tribunal also ruled against Shoshone interests in favor of the ICC decisions. WSSLA finally turned to the U.S. Supreme Court, but the nation's highest court refused even to hear the case.[172] Despite these setbacks, WSSLA remained extremely active during the 1970s, working along with the Dann sisters who were also part of the organization.

WSSLA wasn't the only organized Shoshone body to oppose the claims process. In November 1976 the Te-Moak Bands Council dramatically shifted its position. The council had been cooperating with the Wilkinson, Cragun, and Barker law firm, which it had hired in 1947, and had also been serving as the representative of the Western Shoshone identifiable group before the ICC. By a vote of three to two it fired the law firm and asked that the entire claims process be halted. It chose to challenge federal paternalism. Chair Leslie Blossom said, "We had No Choice between taking money or trying to get land back. Mr. Barker made the choice for us and told the commission that we had no title and our treaty was no good."[173] Like the Danns and WSSLA, the council also has chosen to reject the money award and now claims full title to the land. The council requested that the Supreme Court hear the case, but again it refused.[174]

A dramatic event during this period was Shoshone leader Raymond Yowell's break with the Wilkinson, Cragun, and Barker law firm, the Western Shoshone Claims Committee, and also those Shoshone wanting a money settlement. Yowell had served on the claims committee since its inception in 1965. But in September 1977 he switched sides and joined ranks with those fighting for the land. His change of mind was significant because of his leadership status among the Shoshone. Yowell had served on the Te-Moak Bands Council and also as president of the Inter-Tribal Council of Nevada. He became fed up with the paternalistic attitude and actions of attorney Barker. Yowell stressed that the claims committee was nothing more than a "rubber stamp" for the law firm. He concluded that Barker and the other claims attorneys were only interested in making money. Further, Yowell accused the firm of encouraging factionalism among the Shoshones: "For over twenty years, Mr. Barker has been the cause of much fighting between ourselves and has done nothing to preserve or enforce our rights except try to give up our rights for money so he can get his ten percent."[175]

Despite widespread Shoshone opposition by the late 1970s, the federal government was not deterred from its objective of settling the Shoshone claims case. When the ICC was disbanded in 1978 the Western Shoshone case was transferred to the U.S. Court of Claims. On December 6, 1979, the clerk of this court authorized the establishment of a special account for the $26 million for the Shoshones.[176] Perhaps the government hoped that this action would end the Western Shoshone claims case forever.

The case was not settled, and the 1980s proved to be a continuation of already existing conditions. In fact, the new decade started off with an explosion when a mass claims meeting was held in Elko in July 1980. The purpose of the meeting, called by the BIA, was to have the Shoshones decide how the $26 million should be distributed. Of the 400 persons who attended, 85 testified for three minutes each. But instead of favoring a money distribution, the vast majority rejected the money and wanted the land. Here are two representative statements: Sylvia Dick of Elko stressed that "the land is not for sale"; and Nevada Penoli of Wells, a member of the claims committee established in 1965, abandoned the Barker camp and asserted, "We just want the land."[177] Because of widespread verbal opposition, no conclusion was reached concerning the monetary distribution. Some Shoshones, however, wanted per-capita payments based on one-quarter or more blood. But they were definitely in the minority. Clearly, Barker's claims committee had fallen apart.

The Elko meeting was perhaps the peak of Shoshone opposition to the monetary claims settlement. Opposition to a monetary settlement had grown substantially over the past two decades, for several reasons. First, many Shoshones had come to realize that there were too many contradictions concerning the claims case. For example, in April 1980 Judge Bruce Thompson of the federal district court ruled in the *Dann* case that the Shoshones had lost title to their land in December 1979, not in July 1872 by "gradual encroachment." Judge Thompson held that the action of the Court of Claims clerk in certifying the transfer of the $26 million to a special account for the Shoshone constituted the Shoshone loss of land.[178] Thus, the federal goverment had invented two separate dates when the Shoshones had supposedly lost title to their traditional homeland.

Second, some Shoshones finally felt secure challenging the federal government in a new era that encouraged freedom of expression. In the

1970s the BIA inaugurated the Indian policy called self-determination, intended to encourage the tribes to run their own affairs with less federal paternalism.[179] This meant speaking for themselves as well as running their own programs. In this new atmosphere of freedom, some Shoshones, who earlier had felt powerless, now had a sense of power and chose to voice their own position, regardless of the BIA.

A third factor was the proposed MX missile system of 1979.[180] If implemented, the MX missile sites would have engulfed a good portion of aboriginal Shoshone territory. The traditionalists maintained that this area was sacred Shoshone country. Most threatened were the Duckwater and Yomba reservations, both located near the proposed missile sites. If a few elected leaders of these two reservations had favored the monetary settlement in the early 1970s, they now changed their minds and joined forces with WSSLA and other Shoshones fighting for the land.[181]

Fourth, other Shoshones were threatened by the so-called sagebrush rebellion of the late 1970s and early 1980s. This land acquisition movement was led by non-Indian cattlemen who wanted much more land. These business leaders did not like how much of the Great Basin region was controlled by the federal government. They therefore pushed hard for legislation that would transfer federally owned land to state ownership. Once this was accomplished, the land would then be opened up to private interests.[182] The ranchers wanted the same areas the Shoshones regarded as their native homelands; naturally, the Indians strongly opposed the so-called rebellion.

In this atmosphere of heavy opposition many Shoshones rejected the April 1980 district court decision stating that the Shoshones had lost their land in 1979. The *Dann* case was appealed, and in May 1983 the circuit court ruled in favor of the Danns, stating that they had never lost title to their land, either in 1872 or in 1979.[183] This important victory encouraged the Shoshone leaders to form the Western Shoshone National Council.

The Shoshones fighting for land were elated by the 1983 victory, but they felt different about the February 1985 Supreme Court decision regarding the *Dann* case. The Supreme Court overturned the circuit court decision of May 1983, ruling that the Shoshones had lost title to their land when the $26 million was placed in the special account in December 1979. The only positive aspect of the 1985 decision was the Supreme Court's ruling that the Shoshones could press claims for so-called "individual aboriginal rights" at the lower court level.[184]

Following the 1985 Supreme Court decision Judge Thompson of the district court in Reno ruled in August 1986 that the Danns possessed the right to graze their livestock on lands lying within aboriginal Shoshone territory. Thus they had "individual aboriginal rights."[185] On the surface, it appeared that the Danns had won a victory in 1986. But in reality the court maintained that the Shoshones could only use the land, they didn't have title to it.

Although increasing numbers of Shoshones wanted title to the land, there have always been some who preferred a quick monetary settlement. In March 1988 these individuals secured the support of Salt Lake City attorney John Paul Kennedy. Using his influence Kennedy had Rep. Barbara Vucanovich of Nevada submit legislation to Congress. Officially called The Western Shoshone Claims Distribution Act, this house bill (H.R. 3384) was introduced into Congress in late 1989, but it died when the 101st Congress ended. Vucanovich reintroduced nearly identical legislation (H.R. 3897) in 1992, but it had not been voted on by September of 1993.[186]

On the other hand, those fighting for land have been equally persistent. Surely this is the case with the newly established Western Shoshone Elders Council, established in April 1988 to encourage the teaching of Shoshone culture and knowledge to the younger generation. But the Elders Council took on an added responsibility of opposing both Kennedy and Vucanovich. In March 1989 the council sponsored a mass claims meeting in Elko to oppose them. Many people spoke, and Glenn Holley asserted that "we need to unify as one group and fight these monsters."[187]

Those fighting for land have also rejected the most recent decision concerning the *Dann* case. In January 1989 the Ninth Circuit Court of Appeals abandoned its earlier position and stated that the Shoshones did lose title to their land in 1872. After hearing this most recent ruling, Carrie Dann argued: "As far as I'm concerned, this date they've set in the 1870s is fiction."[188]

The decade of the 1980s ended on a high note for those fighting for land. In 1989 the movie *To Protect Mother Earth* was released to the public. It was a fitting sequel to *Broken Treaty at Battle Mountain* and again produced by Joel Freedman and narrated by actor Robert Redford.[189] The movie expressed the deeply held conviction of those who were determined to keep fighting for their aboriginal territory, the land in which their ancestors have lived since time immemorial.

EPILOGUE

Many Western Shoshone experiences are similar to those of other tribes, especially with respect to federal Indian policy. Like numerous other tribes, the Shoshones were subjected to the reservation, and to the assimilationist and other policies of the nineteenth and twentieth centuries. At the same time, however, each tribe has had unique experiences, making it impossible to talk about a typical or standard tribal history. For example, many tribes were deeply affected by the Dawes Act of 1887, resulting in the loss of millions of acres of land and the fragmentation of most reservations. The Western Shoshones, however, lost no land. The one Shoshone reservation of the allotment period (1887–1934), Duck Valley, was never allotted for the following reasons: it did not have sufficient water for irrigation before the completion of the Wild Horse Dam in the 1930s; it was considered to be unproductive by land-hungry whites since it was located in the dry Basin region; and it was isolated in the far reaches of the Basin area. In the end, the Shoshones actually gained land under the Dawes Act when the federal government set aside 2,463 acres of public domain allotments for some Shoshones in the early years of the twentieth century. At about the same time the Shoshones secured an additional 1,563 acres of land in the form of three colonies, one rancheria, and one small reservation.

For the most part the Western Shoshones no longer live like their ancestors of the precontact days. Their modern way of life is the result of European American influence. Today, they live in American-style houses, wear American clothing, hold elections periodically, and operate under tribal governments sanctioned by the federal government. The Shoshones have accepted the need to adapt in order to survive in the larger society. For this reason the younger generation has accepted formal education, including higher education. A few persons have earned advanced degrees as of 1990, including one M.D., one Ph.D., and one law degree.

If white Americans and their policies have had an impact on the Shoshones over the last 140 years, the Shoshones themselves have also influenced the whites. This influence has been primarily linguistic: for example, the use of Shoshone words in place-names. In examining a map of the Great Basin, one can identify many Shoshone place-names. Kawich Range, Kawich Valley, Kawich Canyon, and Kawich Peak, all located in south-central Nevada, were named after a Shoshone leader of the nineteenth century. The Toiyabe Range of central Nevada and the Toiyabe National Forest, located in different parts of the Basin, are derived from the Shoshone word *toyapin,* which means "mountain." The southern Nevada town of Tonopah takes its name from the Shoshone word for "greasewood spring." The name Shoshone itself—although its origin is unknown—is also a popular place name and label. There are settlements named Shoshone in south-central Idaho and southeastern California, as well as the Shoshone Mountains in central Nevada. And for a number of years the Shoshone Coca-Cola Bottling Company existed in Reno.[1]

At least one white organization in Nevada used Shoshone words or names in the late nineteenth and early twentieth centuries. This was the Elko-based chapter of the Improved Order of Red Men. In 1873 the chapter gave itself the name Shoshone Tribe No. 5 in recognition of the Shoshones of northeastern Nevada. This name was eventually eliminated and was replaced in 1917 by the Tosawee Tribe No. 1, named after the Tosa wihi (White Knife) Shoshones of northeastern Nevada. The Improved Order of Red Men had a long history of using Indian names to emphasize nativism, or America's unique identity separate from Europe. But despite its name, the Improved Order never consisted of the Native Americans themselves. Instead, it was a white American organization created in 1813 to promote patriotism.[2] The Elko chapter, even though it used Shoshone names, never encouraged Indian participation or membership. Nationwide, the organization continues to perpetuate stereotypes and misconceptions of Native Americans through its use of generic "Indian" dress and rituals. Most Indian people are offended by this portrayal.

Another type of Shoshone influence on white culture can be seen in the adoption by whites of the native method of hunting rabbits. As mentioned in chapter 1, the Shoshones and other Basin tribes conducted communal rabbit drives because it was difficult for a single hunter to kill the speedy animals. By the early twentieth century, white Nevadans were also conducting communal rabbit drives. They were concerned about the rabbits destroying gardens, haystacks, and orchards. Rabbit drives proved to be the most effective way to reduce the animal population. The whites also hunted for sport. One Nevada newspaper, the *Ely Record,* reported in 1928 that "for several years the people of Lund, Preston and White River communities [east-central Nevada] have staged a Christmas rabbit hunt." One major difference between Indian and white hunting was its goal: the Indians had always used rabbits for food and blankets, while the whites hunted to reduce the animal population and for sport.

The Shoshones also helped build modern Nevada with their labor. In the second half of the nineteenth century, the scattered white-owned ranches needed laborers in order to survive. They turned to the Shoshones and other tribes. Many of Nevada's first cowboys and ranchhands were Native Americans. As quoted in chapter 2, the *Reese River Reveille* in 1873 reported that "many ranchers have had the same Indians working for them for years." The Shoshones continued to be a valuable work force after the turn of the century. As noted in chapter 4, the Shoshones represented roughly 60 percent of the work force of the Round Mountain Mining Company in 1921. Without doubt, Indian labor was a significant part of Nevada's historical development.

The Western Shoshone people have made their presence known over the years. Just as important, they maintain their culture in the closing years of the twentieth century. They continue to practice native ways, including speaking their own language, although their native life-style is no longer like that of their ancestors. Further, they remain an active force in the Great Basin region. As a case in point, the Western Shoshones continue to sponsor important, visible gatherings in their ancestral area, including the Ruby Valley Treaty Days.

NOTES

Preface

[1]Patricia Limerick, *The Legacy of Conquest* (New York: W. W. Norton, 1987), pp. 21–22, 35, 179.

[2]Todd Benson, "The Consequences of Reservation Life: Native Californians on the Round Valley Reservation, 1871–1884," *Pacific Historical Review* 40:2 (May 1991):221–28.

[3]Robert Berkhofer, Jr., "Cultural Pluralism versus Ethnocentrism in the New Indian History," in *The American Indian and the Problem of History,* ed. Calvin Martin (New York: Oxford University Press, 1988), p. 127.

[4]*Newe: A Western Shoshone History* (Reno: Inter-Tribal Council of Nevada, 1976).

[5]My use of the phrase "grass roots" comes from Colin G. Calloway, *New Directions in American Indian History* (Norman: University of Oklahoma Press, 1988), p. 127.

[6]Peter Iverson, "Indian Tribal Histories," in *Scholars and the Indian Experience,* ed. W. R. Swagerly (Bloomington: Indiana University Press, 1984), p. 205.

[7]Calloway, *New Directions in American Indian History,* p. 127.

[8]For a critical assessment of the frontier thesis, see David A. Nichols's article, "Civilization over Savage: Frederick Jackson Turner and the Indian," *South Dakota History* 2:4 (Fall 1972):386–88.

[9]Veronica E. Velarde Tiller, *The Jicarilla Apache Tribe: A History, 1846–1970* (Lincoln: University of Nebraska Press), p. vii.

Chapter 1: The Native Way of Life

[1]*Newe: A Western Shoshone History,* p. 3.

[2]Rosie Pabawena (Shoshone), interview with Beverly Crum (Shoshone), Wells, Nevada, 29 August 1979; Johnny Dick (Shoshone), "Origin Myth"; Julie Panguish (Shoshone), "Origin Myth," 1939, collected by Alden Hayes; Julian Steward, *Some Western Shoshone Myths,* Anthropological Papers 31, Bureau of American Ethnology, Bulletin 136 (Washington, D.C.: Government Printing Office, 1943), p. 264. This story has different versions, depending on region and storyteller.

[3]Kimball T. Harper, "Historical Environments," in *Handbook of North American Indians, Vol. 11: Great Basin,* ed. Warren L. D'Azevedo (Washington, D.C.: Government Printing Office/Smithsonian Institution, 1986), pp. 51–63.

[4]David Hurst Thomas, Lorann S.A. Pendleton, and Stephen C. Cappannari, "Western Shoshone," in *Handbook of North American Indians, Vol. 11: Great Basin,* pp. 280–83.

[5]*Newe: A Western Shoshone History,* p. 13; oral interview with a Shoshone elder who wished to be anonymous.

[6]Julian H. Steward, *Culture Element Distributions: XIII, Nevada Shoshone,* Anthropological Records 4 (Berkeley: University of California Press, 1941), pp. 254–55.

[7]Beverly Crum, "The Menu Needs to Be Changed," unpublished research paper, 7 May 1976, University of Utah, p. 5; Beverly Crum and Wick R. Miller, *How to Read and Write Shoshoni: A Book of Spelling Lessons, Readings, and Glossary for Shoshone Speakers* (Salt Lake City, 1987).

[8]*Newe: A Western Shoshone History,* p. 5.

[9]Richard O. Clemmer, "The Piñon-Pine: Old Ally or New Pest? Western Shoshone Indians vs. the Bureau of Land Management in Nevada," *Environmental Review* 9 (1985):132–36.

[10]Ibid.; Ronald M. Lanner, *The Piñon-Pine: A Natural and Cultural History* (Reno: University of Nevada Press, 1981), pp. 74–81, 101.

[11]*Newe: A Western Shoshone History,* p. 13; see also Crum, "The Menu Needs to Be Changed," p. 8.

[12]"Imaa Hupia" (The Early Morning Song), translated and transcribed by Beverly Crum.

[13]June Tom (Shoshone), "Indian Legend," *Many Smokes* 3:2 (Spring 1968):4–5. Similar accounts include that of Lottie Boulden (Shoshone), "Battle Mountain Girl Wins in Essay Contest," *Battle Mountain Scout (Scout),* 3 July 1931, pp. 1, 3; and that of Chester Arthur (Shoshone), "Theft of Pine Nuts," 1939.

[14]*Newe: A Western Shoshone History,* p. 10; Steward, *Culture Element Distributions,* p. 222; Julian H. Steward, *Basin-Plateau Aboriginal Sociopolitical Groups,* Bureau of American Ethnology, Bulletin 120 (Washington, D.C.: Government Printing Office, 1938), pp. 74, 82, 106, 112, 119, 122.

[15]*Newe: A Western Shoshone History,* pp. 9–10; Steward, *Culture Element Distributions,* pp. 218–20; Steward, *Basin-Plateau Aboriginal Sociopolitical Groups,* pp. 34–36, 122.

[16]"Antelope Song," translated and transcribed by Beverly Crum.

[17]Crum, "The Menu Needs to be Changed," p. 11.

[18]Jack S. Harris, "The White Knife Shoshoni of Nevada," in *Acculturation in Seven American Indian Tribes,* ed. Ralph Linton (New York: D. Appleton-Century, 1940), p. 44; *Newe: A Western Shoshone History,* p. 7.

[19]*Newe: A Western Shoshone History,* pp. 5, 13; Steward, *Culture Element Distributions,* p. 265.

[20]Steward, *Basin-Plateau Aboriginal Sociopolitical Groups,* pp. 95–64; Harris, "The White Knife Shoshoni of Nevada," pp. 43, 46, 53–55.

[21]"Cradleboards Offer Comfort, Protection for Newborns," *The Native Nevadan (NN),* November 1984, pp. 14–15.

[22]*Newe: A Western Shoshone History,* pp. 3–13.

[23]Ibid., pp. 6–8, 13.

[24]Told by Lucy Hull (Shoshone), July 1972.

[25]Percy Train, James R. Henrichs, and W. Andrew Archer, *Medicinal Uses of*

Plants by Indian Tribes of Nevada, Contributions Towards a Flora of Nevada no. 33 (Reno: Bureau of Plant Industry, 1 December 1941), p. 12.

[26]Told by Lucy Hull, July 1972.

[27]Beverly Crum, "Newe Hupia: Shoshone Poetry Songs," *Journal of California and Great Basin Anthropology, Papers in Linguistics* 2 (1980):3–23.

[28]Ibid.

[29]Sung by a Shoshone elder who wishes to be anonymous.

[30]"Uppi Katete" (There in a Distant Place), translated and transcribed by Beverly Crum.

[31]Ake Kultkrantz, "Mythology and Religious Concepts," in *Handbook of North American Indians, Vol. 11: Great Basin,* pp. 632–39; Catherine S. Fowler, "Subsistence," in *Handbook of North American Indians, Vol. 11: Great Basin,* pp. 96–97.

[32]Charlie Wrinkle and George Gregory, "How Man Came to Have Five Fingers," Book Two, collected by Mark Kerr, 1936, Eastern California Museum, Independence, California. This same story is found in Charles Irwin's *Shoshone Indians of Inyo County, California: The Kerr Manuscript* (Socorro, N.M.: Ballena Press/Eastern California Museum Cooperative Publication, 1980), p. 64.

[33]Annie Bealer (Shoshone), "Coyote and Sagehen," 1939, unpublished story.

[34]Hubert Howe Bancroft, *The Native Races, Vol. 1: Wild Tribes* (San Francisco: A. L. Bancroft, 1883), pp. 440–41.

[35]Richard N. Current, T. Harry Williams, and Frank Freidel, *American History: A Survey,* 5th ed. (New York: Alfred A. Knopf, 1979), p. 223; Michael C. Meyer and William L. Sherman, *The Course of Mexican History* (New York: Oxford University Press, 1979), pp. 285–312.

[36]Charles Gibson, *Spain in America* (New York: Harper Colophon Books, 1966), pp. 1–24, 182–204.

[37]Ray Allen Billington, *The Far Western Frontier, 1830–1860* (New York: Harper Torchbooks, 1962), pp. 41–68; Arrell Morgan Gibson, *The West in the Life of the Nation* (Lexington, Mass.: D. C. Heath, 1976), pp. 243–62.

[38]*Newe: A Western Shoshone History,* p. 14; Susan R. Sharrock, "A History of the Indians of Nevada from First White Contact to the Reservation Period: Extracted from Eye-Witness Accounts," unpublished paper, 1 June 1967, pp. 3–4, S. Lyman Tyler Papers, Special Collections, University of Utah, Salt Lake City.

[39]Quoted in Sharrock, "A History of the Indians of Nevada," p. 4.

[40]James J. Rawls, *Indians of California: The Changing Image* (Norman: University of Oklahoma Press, 1984), p. 49.

[41]Gibson, *The West in the Life of the Nation,* p. 257.

[42]*Newe: A Western Shoshone History,* pp. 14–17.

[43]Ibid.

[44]Sharrock, "A History of the Indians of Nevada," pp. 4–5, summary section.

[45]*Newe: A Western Shoshone History,* pp. 17–19.

[46]Gibson, *The West in the Life of the Nation,* pp. 341–45.

[47]Ibid.; *Newe: A Western Shoshone History,* p. 20; Sharrock, "A History of the Indians of Nevada," pp. 8–9.

Chapter 2: Warfare and Adjustment:
The Western Shoshone and the Americans, 1848–1880

[1]*Newe: A Western Shoshone History,* p. 23.

[2]Ibid., p. 24; Walton Bean and James J. Rawls, *California: An Interpretive*

History, 5th ed. (New York: McGraw-Hill, 1988), pp. 82–89, 93; Gibson, *The West in the Life of the Nation,* pp. 363–65.

[3]Jacob Holeman to Luke Lea, 28 June 1852, Utah Superintendency, Letters Received (LR), Indian Affairs, Record Group (RG) 75, National Archives (NA).

[4]Garland Hurt to Brigham Young, 27 August 1855, LR, RG 75, NA; Hurt to Young, 30 September 1855, in *Annual Reports of the Commissioner of Indian Affairs,* 1855 (hereafter referred to as *ARCIA,* with designated year), p. 198.

[5]*Newe: A Western Shoshone History,* p. 25; Harris, "The White Knife Shoshoni of Nevada," pp. 72–75; see also *ARCIA,* 1850–62.

[6]Jacob Forney to C. E. Mix, 23 September 1858, Utah Superintendency, Office of Indian Affairs (OIA), LR, RG 75, NA.

[7]Richard O. Clemmer, "Seed-Eaters and Chert-Carriers: The Economic Basis for Continuity and Historic Western Shoshone Identities," unpublished paper, University of Denver, October 1990; Omer C. Stewart, "Temoke Band of Shoshone and the Oasis Concept," *Nevada Historical Society Quarterly* 23 (Winter 1980):246–61.

[8]Harris, "The White Knife Shoshoni of Nevada," pp. 74–79; *ARCIA,* 1856, p. 228; For a detailed study of the Shoshone-white wars, see Brigham D. Madsen, *The Shoshoni Frontier and the Bear River Massacre* (Salt Lake City: University of Utah Press, 1985).

[9]Floyd A. O'Neil and Stanford Layton, "Of Pride and Politics: Brigham Young as Indian Superintendent," *Utah Historical Quarterly* 46 (Summer 1978):236–50; Howard A. Christy, "Open Hand and Mailed Fist: Mormon-Indian Relations in Utah, 1847–52," *Utah Historical Quarterly* 46 (Summer 1978):216–35; Lawrence G. Coates, "Brigham Young and Mormon Indian Policies: The Formative Period, 1836–1859," *Brigham Young University Studies* 18 (Spring 1978):428–52.

[10]See the references cited in note 9 above; also Francis Paul Prucha, *The Great Father: The United States Government and the American Indians,* 2 vols. (Lincoln: University of Nebraska Press, 1984), 1:209–10.

[11]Jacob Holeman to Luke Lea, 28 July 1852, Utah, LR, RG 75, NA; Holeman to Brigham Young, 25 September 1852, *ARCIA,* 1852, pp. 151–53.

[12]Ibid.; Holeman to Young, 30 September 1853, *ARCIA,* 1853.

[13]*Newe: A Western Shoshone History,* pp. 26–30.

[14]Garland Hurt to Manypenny, 14 July 1855, Utah, LR, RG 75, NA.

[15]Treaty of 1855, 7 August 1855, Utah, LR, RG 75, NA.

[16]*Newe: A Western Shoshone History,* p. 35.

[17]Ibid., pp. 31, 34.

[18]Hurt to Young, 27 August 1855, Utah, LR, RG 75, NA; Holeman to Lea, 28 June 1852, *ARCIA,* 1852; Hurt to Manypenny, 30 September 1855, *ARCIA,* 1855.

[19]Hurt to Young, September 1856, *ARCIA,* 1856, pp. 227–30; Holeman to Young, 30 September 1853, *ARCIA,* 1853.

[20]Forney to James W. Denver, 15 February 1859, Utah, LR (Microfilm [M] 234, Reel [R] 899), RG 75, NA; Forney to C. E. Mix, 23 September 1858, Utah, LR (M 234, R 898), RG 75, NA; Forney to Dole, 19 April 1861, Utah, LR (M 234, R 900), RG 75, NA.

[21]Forney to Dole, 19 April 1861, Utah, LR (M 234, R 900), RG 75, NA; William Rogers to Commissioner of Indian Affairs (CIA), December 15, 1860, Utah (M 234, R 900), RG 75, NA; Hurt to Young, September 1856, *ARCIA,* 1856, p. 230.

[22]Rogers to Davies, 18 December 1860, Utah, LR (M 234, R 900), RG 75, NA; William Rogers statement, 15 December 1860, Utah, LR (M 234, R 900), RG 75, NA; Rogers to McDongal, 17 March 1862, Utah, LR (M 234, R 901), RG 75, NA.

[23]Davies to CIA, 20 January 1861, Utah, LR (M 234, R 900), RG 75, NA.

[24]James Nye to William Seward, 21 December 1861, U.S. Congress, Senate, Ex. Doc. No. 36, Serial 1122, p. 4; Ashley Dawley statement, 1917, Reno Agency Records, RG 75, Federal Archives and Records Center (FARC), San Bruno, California (SB); Warren Wasson to Nye, 28 January 1862, Nevada, LR (M 234, R 538), RG 75, NA. Over the years the name Temoke has been spelled in different ways. This is pointed out by anthropologist Omer C. Stewart, who writes that the "spellings include Tim-oak, Tumok, Tomoke, Te-Moak, Tumoak, Timook, and others." Like Stewart, I use the spelling *Temoke* because it is accepted and used by the Shoshone family of Nevada. See Stewart, "Temoak Band of Shoshone and the Oasis Concept," p. 250.

[25]Nye to Seward, 21 December 1861; Nye to Dole, 3 February 1862, Nevada, LR (M 234, R 538), RG 75, NA. Capt. Henry Mellen to Col. R. C. Drum, 22 December 1862; Brig. Gen. G. Wright to Brig. Gen. L. Thomas, 30 March 1863; and P. A. Gallagher to Lieut. Wade Ustick, 2 April 1863; all in *The War of the Rebellion*, vol. L, pt. 2, Doc. No. 59, Serial 3584 (Washington, D.C.: Government Printing Office [GPO], 1897), pp. 258–59, 369–70, 379.

[26]Ibid.; Madsen, *The Shoshoni Frontier*, pp. 143, 167–69.

[27]U.S. Department of War, *The War of the Rebellion*, vol. L, pt. 2, pp. 143–44.

[28]Beverly Crum, "Basin Area Neweneen (Shoshonis)," unpublished research paper, Salt Lake City, 1975.

[29]Thomas Premo's (Shoshone) story of "Captain Buck," translated by his daughter Beverly Crum, in Crum and Miller, *How to Read and Write Shoshoni*, pp. 60–64.

[30]Martha H. Bowers and Hans Muessig, *History of Central Nevada: An Overview of the Battle Mountain District*, Cultural Resource Series 4 (Reno: Nevada State Office of the Bureau of Land Management, 1982), p. 19.

[31]Warren Wasson to James W. Nye, 28 January 1862, Nevada Superintendency (NS), OIA, LR, 1862, RG 75, NA; *Newe: A Western Shoshone History*, p. 48.

[32]Warren Wasson to James W. Nye, 28 January 1862; James Duane Doty to James Nye, 28 June 1862, Tasker Oddie Papers, Nevada Historical Society, Reno; Chief Too-Toaina statement to James Nye, 28 June 1862, Western Shoshone Agency Records (WSA), Box 336, RG 75, FARC-SB; interview with Irene Adamson, 24 August 1993, Battle Mountain, Nevada.

[33]W. H. Hutchinson, *California: The Golden Shore by the Sundown Sea*, rev. ed. (Belmont, Calif. : Star Publishing, 1984), pp. 213–14.

[34]Report of the Utah Superintendency, 1 October 1861, *ARCIA*, 1861, p. 135; Dole to Doty, 22 July 1862, OIA, Utah, LR, RG 75, NA.

[35]"Treaty between the United States of America and the Western Bands of Shoshone Indians," 1 October 1863, 18 Stat. 689–92.

[36]Ibid.

[37]"Indian Treaty," *Reese River Reveille (RRR)*, 21 October 1863, p. 2.

[38]Tommy Wahne to Charles Richards, 16 February 1925, Central Classified Files (CCF), 13460-25-Reno-115, RG 75, NA; "Shoshoni Indians Insist that Treaty of 1863 Was Violated by the United States Government; Trial May Decide," *Elko Free Press (Free Press)*, 4 April 1928, p. 1; "Indian Treaty Case Is Set," *Elko Independent (Independent)*, 7 February 1928, p. 1.

[39]Doty to Dole, 10 November 1863, OIA, Utah, LR (M 234, R 901), RG 75, NA.

[40]Ibid.

[41]Milton Badt to A. A. Grorud, 3 December 1932, and Alida Bowler to Badt, 10 February 1936, Sen. 83, A-F9, RG 46, NA. See also claims file: 51838–32–Western Shoshone (WS)-174.1, RG 75, NA.

[42]Col. J. B. Moore, letter, 11 November 1863, Records of Fort Ruby, Old Military Records, RG 398, NA; T. T. Dwight to CIA, 27 July 1867, OIA, Nevada, LR, RG 75, NA; Harris, "The White Knife Shoshoni of Nevada," p. 79.

[43]Nye to J. P. Usher, 20 September 1864, OIA, Nevada, LR (M 234, R 538), RG 75, NA; Franklin Campbell to H. G. Parker, 22 August 1866, *ARCIA*, 1866; *Returns from U.S. Military Posts, 1800–1916* (M 617, R 439), Fort Halleck (June 1867–December 1875); J. F. Ray, letter, February 1874, OIA, Nevada, LR, RG 75, NA; Gheen to Smith, 30 November 1875, OIA, Nevada, LR (M 234, R 541), RG 75, NA.

[44]Gheen to Smith, 17 October 1876, OIA, Nevada, LR (M 234, R 542), RG 75, NA; Gheen to Smith, 18 October 1876, OIA, Nevada, LR (M 234, R 542), RG 75, NA.

[45]Steven Crum, "The 'White Pine War' of 1875: A Case of White Hysteria," *Utah Historical Quarterly* 59 (Summer 1991):286–99.

[46]Ibid.

[47]Ibid.

[48]Ibid.

[49]Ibid.

[50]Hank Corless, *The Weiser Indians: Shoshoni Peacemakers* (Salt Lake City: University of Utah, 1990), pp. 87–113; Brigham D. Madsen, *The Northern Shoshoni* (Caldwell, Idaho: Caxton Printers, 1980), pp. 83–89.

[51]"Indians Buying Ammunition," *RRR*, 17 June 1878, p. 3; "The Indian Troubles," *Elko Weekly Post*, 22 June 1878, p. 2.

[52]"The Shoshones Speak," *Belmont Courier*, 29 June 1878, p. 3.

[53]"The Good Shoshones," *RRR*, 1 July 1878, p. 3; Gheen to E. A. Hayt, 18 July 1878, OIA, Nevada, LR (M 234, R 543, Frame [F] 361–80), RG 75, NA.

[54]Bowers and Muessig, *History of Central Nevada: An Overview of the Battle Mountain District*; Steven R. James, *Prehistory, Ethnohistory, and History of Eastern Nevada: A Cultural Resources Summary of the Elko and Ely Districts*, Cultural Resource Series 3 (Reno: Nevada State Office of the Bureau of Land Management, 1981); *Western Shoshone Identifiable Group, Represented by the Te-Moak Bands of Western Shoshone Indians, Nevada, Plaintiff v. The United States of America*, Docket No. 326–16, pp. 24, 26, 31.

[55]Bowers and Muessig, *History of Central Nevada*, pp. 16–97; James, *Prehistory, Ethnohistory, and History of Eastern Nevada*, pp. 214–265.

[56]Lanner, *The Piñon Pine: A Natural and Cultural History*, pp. 116–30.

[57]"Currants," *RRR*, 27 August 1864, p. 3; "The Nut Pine," *RRR*, 10 November 1865, p. 1; "An Indian," *Independent*, 3 May 1873, p. 3.

[58]"A Trip Southeast," *RRR*, 7 June 1867, p. 1; Gheen to CIA, 15 March 1873, Nevada, LR (M 234, R 540, F 932–34), RG 75, NA; Gheen to CIA, 3 October 1874, Nevada, LR (M 234, R 541, F 212–14), RG 75, NA; Gheen to Smith, 20 August 1875, Nevada, LR (M 234, R 541, F 778–79), RG 75, NA; "Indian Farmers," *RRR*, 30 August 1877, p. 3.

[59]"Labor," *RRR*, 27 August 1873, p. 3.

[60]"Indian Hats," *RRR*, 7 June 1865, p. 1; "Clean Street," *RRR*, 20 August 1873, p. 3; Gheen to H. J. Morrow, OIA, Nevada, LR, RG 75, NA.

[61]Nye to Dole, 3 February 1862, OIA, Nevada, LR (M 234, R 538), RG 75, NA.

[62]18 Stat. 689–92.

[63]Steven Crum, "The Ruby Valley Indian Reservation of Northeastern Nevada: 'Six Miles Square'," *Nevada Historical Society Quarterly* 30 (Spring 1987):4–5.

[64]Ibid., p. 5.

[65]Ibid.

[66]Ibid.

[67]Ibid., p. 6.

[68]Tourtellotte to Parker, 3 December 1869, OIA, Utah, LR, RG 75, NA.

[69]Douglas to Parker, 26 May 1870, OIA, Nevada, LR, RG 75, NA.

[70]Meeting with the Shoshones, 12 May 1870, OIA, Nevada, LR (M 234, R 539), RG 75, NA.

[71]Ibid.

[72]Francis Paul Prucha, *American Indian Policy in Crisis: Christian Reformers and the Indian, 1865–1900* (Norman: University of Oklahoma Press, 1976), pp. 106, 108.

[73]CIA to G. W. Ingalls, 22 April 1873, OIA, Nevada, LR, RG 75, NA; Ingalls to Smith, 14 May 1873, OIA, Nevada, LR (M 234, R 540), RG 75, NA.

[74]"Western Shoshone," *Independent,* 15 November 1873, p. 3.

[75]Powell and Ingalls to CIA, 18 June 1873, in *Anthropology of the Numa,* ed. Don D. and Catherine S. Fowler (Washington, D.C.: Smithsonian Institution Press, 1971), p. 99.

[76]"Unsuccessful," *RRR,* 8 January 1874, p. 3.

[77]"Tom Parda, on behalf of all the Indians on Duck Water, Current Creek, and White River," 16 November 1873, WSA, RG 75, FARC-SB.

[78]"Report of J. W. Powell and G. W. Ingalls," 18 December 1873, U.S. Congress, House, Exec. Docs., 43rd Cong., 1st sess., Serial 1601, p. 420.

[79]Gheen to Smith, 30 November 1875, OIA, Nevada, LR (M 234, R 541), RG 75, NA; *Executive Orders Relating to Indian Reservations, May 14, 1855 to July 1, 1912* (Washington, D.C.: GPO, 1912), p. 110.

[80]Gheen to Smith, 30 November 1875, OIA, Nevada, LR, RG 75, NA.

[81]Gheen to CIA, 24 August 1877, ARCIA, 1877, p. 153.

[82]*Executive Orders Relating to Indian Reservations,* p. 109; John Palmer to Bateman, 24 December 1874, OIA, Nevada, LR (M 234, R 541), RG 75, NA; A. J. Barnes to CIA, 22 August 1876, ARCIA, 1876, p. 115.

[83]ARCIA, 1877, pp. 312–13; news item, *Reno Evening Gazette,* 17 March 1879.

[84]Lorenzo Creek to L. A. Dorrington, 30 June 1917, p. 20, Reno Agency, RG 75, NA-PS; "An Interview with Members of the Temoak Band of Homeless Indians," 17 January 1927, CCF, 56890–13-WS-211, RG 75, NA.

[85]Williams to Hayt, 3 May 1878; Barnes to Hayt, 15 October 1878; Barnes to Hayt, 14 January 1879; Palmer to Barnes, 15 September 1878; Hayes to Barnes, 18 September 1878; all in OIA, Nevada, LR (M 234, R 543), RG 75, NA.

[86]Statements by Carlin Farms captains, 24 March 1879; How to Hayt, 21 March 1879; news item, *Reno Evening Gazette,* 17 March 1879; news item, *Daily Elko Independent,* 20 March 1879; How to Hayt, 8 April 1879; all in OIA, Nevada, LR (M 234, R 544), RG 75, NA.

[87]Gheen to CIA, 14 September 1878, ARCIA, 1878, pp. 104–5.

[88]Te-moak Band interview, 17 January 1927, CCF, 56890–13-WS-211, RG 75, NA.

[89]"Indians, Ranching," *Elko Weekly Post,* 26 April 1879, p. 3.

[90]Harris, "The White Knife Shoshoni of Nevada," p. 88; Ashley Dawley statement, 1917; Te-Moak Band interview, 17 January 1927.

[91]Te-Moak Band interview, 17 January 1927; Creel to Dorrington, 30 June 1917, p. 20.

[92]18 Stat. 689–92.

[93]Lockhart to Dole, 9 January 1865, OIA, Nevada, LR, RG 75, NA; Ingalls to Smith, 20 October 1874, OIA, Nevada, LR (M 234, R 541), RG 75, NA; Gheen to Smith, 2 June 1877, OIA, Nevada, LR (M 234, R 542), RG 75, NA; Gheen to Hayt, 30 May 1878, OIA, Nevada, LR (M 234, R 543), RG 75, NA.

[94]Thurston to Lewis, 21 December 1864, Fort Ruby records, RG 398, NA; Thurston to Irish, 29 December 1864, and Thurston to Lewis, 31 December 1864, RG 398, NA; Dole to Irish, 26 December 1864, OIA, Utah, LR (M 234, R 538), RG 75, NA.

[95]Carpenter to Head, 8 November 1867, Fort Ruby records, RG 398, NA.

[96]Ibid.

[97]Gheen to Hayt, 30 May 1878, OIA, Nevada, LR (M 234, R 543), RG 75, NA.

[98]Harris, "The White Knife Shoshoni of Nevada," p. 80.

[99]Ingalls to Smith, 20 January 1875, OIA, Nevada, LR (M 234, R 541), RG 75, NA.

[100]Gheen to Hayt, 30 May 1876, OIA, Nevada, LR (M 234, R 543), RG 75, NA.

[101]"Indian Affairs," *Independent,* 18 January 1873, p. 3.

[102]Gheen to Smith, 13 March 1877, OIA, Nevada, LR (M 234, R 542), RG 75, NA.

[103]"Peace Concluded," *RRR,* 28 August 1871, p. 2; "Indian Fandango," *RRR,* 17 March 1873, p. 1; "A Rabbit Drive," *RRR,* 17 October 1877, p. 3.

[104]"Indian Powwow," *RRR,* 21 March 1942, p. 1; "Celebration of the Fourth," *RRR,* 6 July 1868, p. 1; "Indian Fandango," *RRR,* 5 July 1870, p. 2; "From the Country," *RRR,* 2 April 1878, p. 3.

[105]Parker to Taylor, 8 May 1869, OIA, Nevada, LR (M 234, R 538), RG 75, NA; Gheen to Morrow, 22 July 1874, OIA, Nevada, LR (M 234, R 541), RG 75, NA; Gheen to Smith, 31 July 1876, OIA, Nevada, LR (M 234, R 542), RG 75, NA.

[106]"The Indians and the Fourth," *RRR,* 3 July 1869, p. 3; "The Fourth of July Celebration," *RRR,* 10 July 1869, p. 1; "Peace Concluded," *RRR,* 28 August 1871, p. 2; "Shoshone Fandango," *RRR,* 7 June 1878, p. 3.

Chapter 3: The Western Shoshone Reservation (Duck Valley), 1880–1933

[1]John How to R. E. Trowbridge, 24 May 1880, LR, Nevada, RG 75, NA; "Indian Talk," *Battle Mountain Messenger,* 17 April 1880, p. 3.

[2]Harris, "The White Knife Shoshoni of Nevada," pp. 39–118.

[3]"The Duck Valley Indians," *Independent,* 9 March 1884, p. 3; "The Duck Valley Reservation," *Independent,* 6 April 1884, p. 1.

[4]Special Agent Report, 3 March 1884, LR, 1884–4654, RG 75, NA.

[5]Ibid.

[6]"Proposition to Remove the Duck Valley Indians," *Independent,* 24 February 1884, p. 1.

[7]Calvin Asbury to CIA, 24 February 1904, Western Shoshone (WS), Box 384, RG 75, FARC-SB.

[8]George Haggett to CIA, 9 March 1909, WS, Box 385, RG 75, FARC-SB; Francis Paul Prucha, *The Great Father,* abridged ed. (Lincoln: University of Nebraska Press, 1986), pp. 224–28.

[9]C. H. Asbury to CIA, 2 April 1914, WS, Box 325, RG 75, FARC-SB.

[10]Haggett to CIA, 24 February 1913, WS, Box 368, RG 75, FARC-SB; C. H. Hauke to Haggett, 7 April 1913, WS, Box 325, RG 75, FARC-SB.

[11]Crum, "The Ruby Valley Indian Reservation," pp. 1–18.

[12]Hauke to Muchuch Timoke, 28 September 1912, CCF, 70328–12-GS-313, RG 75, NA.

[13]E. B. Merritt to Tommy Wahne/Muchuch Temoke, 1 December 1919, CCF, 9355–17-WS-313, Pt. 1, RG 75, NA.

[14]Charles Engle, "Report on Water Supply and Irrigation Conditions among Ruby Valley Indians," 31 October 1925, p. 10, CCF, 9355–17-WS-313, Pt. 1, RG 75, NA.

[15]Crum, "The Ruby Valley Indian Reservation," pp. 1–18.

[16]"Elko Indians May All Move," *Independent*, 9 March 1929, p. 1.

[17]How to Trowbridge, 1 May 1880, Nevada (M 234, R 545, F 217–19), RG 75, NA.

[18]John Mayhugh to Hiram Price, 18 September 1882, p. 2, LR, 1882–17727, RG 75, NA.

[19]Mayhugh to Price, 13 July 1882, p. 4, WS, Box 372, RG 75, FARC-SB.

[20]Mayhugh to J. D. C. Atkins, 8 August 1885, LR, 1882–11126, RG 75, NA.

[21]*Executive Orders Relating to Indian Reservations*, p. 110.

[22]Benson Gibson, *Survivors of the Bannock War* (privately printed, 1990), pp. 29–30, 32.

[23]"Death Takes Prominent Paiute," *NN*, 4 February 1977, pp. 3, 14.

[24]*ARCIA*, 1922, p. 33; *ARCIA*, 1931, p. 49.

[25]*ARCIA*, 1883, p. 112; *ARCIA*, 1884, p. 130.

[26]*ARCIA*, 1881, p. 132–34.

[27]*ARCIA*, 1883, p. 112.

[28]Mayhugh to CIA, 8 September 1884, *ARCIA*, 1884.

[29]*ARCIA*, 1885, pp. 148–49; Report of Joe H. Norris, 30 July 1910, WS, RG 75, NA.

[30]*ARCIA*, 1896, p. 571.

[31]"Statement of Delegation of Indians from Western Shoshone Agency, Nevada," 21 February 1911, CCF, 38148–11-WS-056, RG 75, FARC-SB.

[32]Council statement, 23 January 1912, WS, Box 323, RG 75, FARC-SB; Council statement, 11 November 1913, WS, Box 325, RG 75, FARC-SB.

[33]Council Book, Indian Council, 1 April 1922–16 March 1935, in possession of a tribal member at Duck Valley.

[34]Tribal Constitution, 17 March 1919, CCF, 9794-C-36-WS-057, RG 75, NA; Dorrington to CIA, 27 August 1918, CCF, 78855-WS-154, RG 75, NA.

[35]"Statement of Delegation," 21 February 1911, CCF, 38148–11-WS-056, RG 75, FARC-SB; E. B. Meritt to Fitz Smith and Thomas Premo, 18 February 1915, Reno Agency, Box 289, RG 75, FARC-SB.

[36]Hearings before E. B. Meritt, 18 January 1921, p. 2, CCF, 4755–22-WS-056, RG 75, NA.

[37]McNeilly to CIA, 26 August 1930, CCF, 45970–30-WS-054, RG 75, NA; Melis, "Working Plan Report of the Grazing Resources and Activities of the Western Shoshone Indian Reservation," p. 26, CCF, 69545–30-WS-301, RG 75, NA; Much and Melis to CIA, 13 May 1932, pp. 2, 3, CCF, 296490–31-WS-301, RG 75, NA; Constitution and By-Laws of the Western Shoshone Stock Association, 21 March 1922, WS, Box 364, FARC-SB.

[38]Anthony Godfrey, "Congressional-Indian Politics: Senate Survey of Conditions among the Indians of the United States," Ph.D. diss., University of Utah, 1985.

[39]U.S. Congress, Senate, *Survey of Conditions of the Indians in the United States*, hearings before a Subcommittee of the Committee on Indian Affairs, 72nd Cong., 1st sess., 1934, pt. 28, pp. 15008–9.

[40]Prucha, *The Great Father,* abridged ed., pp. 198–241.

[41]*ARCIA,* 1883, pp. 114–15.

[42]*ARCIA,* 1885, p. 148.

[43]*ARCIA,* 1902, p. 249; *ARCIA,* 1900, p. 284.

[44]Haggett to CIA, 6 May 1908, WS, Box 385, RG75, FARC-SB.

[45]"Statement of Delegation of Indians from Western Shoshone Agency, Nevada," 21 February 1911, WS, RG 75, NA; Merritt to Smith and Premo, 18 February 1915, WS, RG 75, FARC-SB; White to CIA, 5 November 1917, p. 2, WS, RG 75, NA.

[46]*ARCIA,* 1893, p. 214; "Indians Leaving for Duck Valley," *Free Press,* 3 June 1914, p. 1.

[47]*ARCIA,* 1883, pp. 112–15.

[48]*ARCIA,* 1884, pp. 312–13; *ARCIA,* 1895, pp. 586–87; *ARCIA,* 1904, pp. 622–23; *ARCIA,* 1912, p. 235.

[49]*ARCIA,* 1899, p. 241.

[50]*ARCIA,* 1900, p. 284; *ARCIA,* 1901, pp. 278–79; *ARCIA,* 1905, p. 259; "Cattle Sold at Western Shoshone Agency from July 1, 1916 to December 31, 1916," WS, RG 75, FARC-SB.

[51]Halbert T. Johnson, "Report of Investigation of the Western Shoshone (Duck Valley) Indian Irrigation Project," 1916, pp. 27–28, Oddie Papers, Nevada Historical Society, Reno.

[52]Perry to CIA, 16 October 1926, p. 2, WS, RG 75, NA.

[53]*ARCIA,* 1882, p. 122.

[54]*ARCIA,* 1893, p. 214.

[55]*ARCIA,* 1915, p. 159; *ARCIA,* 1920, p. 151; *ARCIA,* 1931, p. 59.

[56]Haggett to CIA, 18 May 1910, WS, Box 385, RG 75, FARC-SB.

[57]Ibid.

[58]Told by Tom Premo, 1968, Owyhee, Nevada, published in Crum and Miller, *How to Read and Write Shoshoni.*

[59]Beverly Crum interview with Mildred Scissions (daughters of Thomas Premo), Owyhee, Nevada, 23 January 1992.

[60]Thomas Hayson to John Scott, 16 August 1877, LR, 1877–22888, RG 75, NA; William Hargrove to Post Master, 6 January 1896, WS, Box 374, RG 75, FARC-SB; Haggett to William Johnson, 16 June 1908, WS, Box 388, RG 75, FARC-SB.

[61]Arrell Morgan Gibson, *The American Indian: Prehistory to the Present* (Lexington, Mass.: D. C. Heath, 1980), pp. 477–78.

[62]Plumb to CIA, 8 November 1890, WS, Box 372, RG 75, FARC-SB; Plumb to CIA, 6 December 1890, WS, Box 372, RG 75, FARC-SB.

[63]Plumb to CIA, 6 December 1890, WS, Box 372, RG 75, FARC-SB.

[64]Plumb to CIA, 10 January 1891, WS, Box 372, RG 75, FARC-SB.

[65]Thomas Premo, Raymond Thacker, and Louis Dave to CIA, 6 March 1939, Collier Papers, Peyote file, RG 75, NA.

[66]H. D. Lawshe to CIA, 18 February 1918, CCF, 16341–18-WS-175, RG 75, NA; B. F. Roth to CIA, 29 July 1924, WS, Box 367A, RG 75, FARC-SB.

Chapter 4: The Nonreservation Shoshone, 1880–1933

[1]John How to Trowbridge, 24 May 1880, LR, Nevada, RG 75, NA.

[2]*ARCIA,* 1879, p. 111; Jenkins to CIA, 1 May 1922, Reno Agency, RG 75, FARC-SB.

³Frederic Snyder to E. E. McNeilly, 1 February 1926, Nevada, RG 75, FARC-SB; G. A. Trotter to CIA, 12 February 1926, Nevada, RG 75, FARC-SB.

⁴"Indian Fandango at Hot Springs," *Manhattan Post*, 26 August 1911, p. 1; "Indian 'Fandango' Will Be Held Here," *Free Press*, 16 August 1926, p. 1; "The Indian Fandango," *Central Nevadan*, 17 October 1895, p. 3.

⁵"Indian Powwow," *Free Press*, 15 June 1889, p. 3; "The Fandango," *Central Nevadan*, 12 April 1894, p. 3; "Shoshone Indians Elect New Chief," *Scout*, 7 October 1922, p. 1.

⁶"Indians Well Satisfied with Their Celebration," *Scout*, 15 October 1921, p. 1; "Indians Have Big Time at Duckwater," *Free Press*, 22 September 1919, p. 1; "Indians Enjoy Barbeque and Old Time Fandango," *Free Press*, 4 September 1913, p. 1; "Indians Will Hold a Big Fandango," *RRR*, 18 June 1921, p. 1; "Indians Have Big Time at Duckwater," *Free Press*, 22 September 1919, p. 1.

⁷Maribeth Hamby interview with Danny Millett, 29 February 1988, Duckwater, Nev.

⁸On the Ghost Dance religion, see the following: Robert M. Utley, *The Indian Frontier of the American West, 1846–1890* (Albuquerque: University of New Mexico Press, 1984), pp. 251–52; Gibson, *The American Indian: Prehistory to the Present*, pp. 477–78.

⁹"Good Place for Ghost Dances," *White Pine News*, 24 January 1891, p. 3; "Harry the Preacher," *Weekly Elko Independent*, 1 February 1891, p. 4; "Only Peaceable Motives," *RRR*, 20 March 1891, p. 3; "A Fandango Next Friday," *Central Nevadan*, 26 March 1891, p. 3.

¹⁰"Indian Scare," *RRR*, 7 November 1890, p. 3; "Indian Uprising in Nye County," *White Pine News*, 15 November 1890, p. 3; "Visiting Indian," *Weekly Elko Independent*, 11 January 1891, p. 3; "Harry the Preacher," *Weekly Elko Independent*, 1 February 1891, p. 4; "A Fandango Next Friday," *Central Nevadan*, 26 March 1891, p. 3; "What Is a Fandango?" *Central Nevadan*, 20 November 1890, p. 3.

¹¹Steven Crum interview with Marie (Bob) Allison, 5 September 1991, Fallon, Nev.; Creel to Dorrington, 8 July 1921, Box 288, Reno Agency, RG 75, FARC-SB; Dave K. Clifford to Key Pittman, 18 February 1935, Box 73, Key Pittman Papers, Library of Congress (LC); Creel to H. G. Wilson, 24 January 1922, Lorenzo Creel Papers, University of Nevada at Reno.

¹²Eva Slater, "Panamint Shoshone Basketry, 1920–1940," *American Indian Art Magazine* (Winter 1985):58–63, 75; Bruce Bernstein, "Panamint-Shoshone Basketry, 1890–1950," *American Indian Basketry* 5 (n.d.):5–12; Beth Sennett-Walker, "The Panamint Basketry of Scotty's Castle," *American Indian Basketry* 5 (n.d.):13–17; Edna Patterson, "Mary Hall: Western Shoshone Basketmaker," *Northeastern Nevada Historical Society Quarterly* 85:4 (Fall 1985):108.

¹³"Unemployed Indians," *RRR*, 24 July 1901, p. 3; "Diamond Valley Indian Rodeo," *Free Press*, 16 April 1904, p. 3; James X. Darrough to Key Pittman, 2 April 1917, Pittman Papers, Box 65, LC; *Statutes of the State of Nevada, 1909* (Carson City, Nevada: State Printing Office, 1909), pp. 38–40.

¹⁴*Johnny Peavine vs. Ed Clifford, Jr., et al.*, filed 4 June 1906, Nye County Recorder's Office, Tonopah; "Indian Rights," *Central Nevadan*, 10 May 1906, p. 1; "Indian Finds Ore on Reservation," undated newspaper clipping, Clipping files, Nevada Historical Society, Reno.

¹⁵Clifford to Pittman, 18 February 1935, Pittman Papers, Box 73, LC; Bowers and Muessig, *History of Central Nevada: An Overview of the Battle Mountain District*, p. 37.

[16]Dave Kawich Clifford to Key Pittman, 18 February 1935, Pittman Papers, Box 73, LC; Reese River Project Plan, 13 July 1936, p. 1, Bureau of Indian Affairs (BIA), Phoenix Area Office (PAO), RG 75, FARC-Laguna Niguel (LN).

[17]Ray Parrett to CIA, 29 October 1928, CCF, 6370–26-Walker River-053, RG 75, NA; Indian Census Roll, 1 April 1930 (M 595, R 632), F-152–179.

[18]"Resolutions to Congress," 3 February 1936, CCF, 6212–36-Carson-066, RG 75, NA; "Social and Economic Information for the Walker River Paiute Tribe," 1937, CCF, 19791–36-Carson-259, RG 75, NA.

[19]Lorenzo Creek to L. A. Dorrington, 8 July 1921, Box 288, Reno Agency, FARC-SB, RG 75; "A. P. Hicks, Shoshone, Dies at 85," *NN*, 24 January 1975, p. 11; S. W. Pugh to J. M. Graham, 14 June 1910, Walker River Agency Records, FARC-SB.

[20]Daniel F. Littlefield, Jr., and James W. Parins, eds., *American Indian and Alaska Native Newspapers and Periodicals, 1829–1924* (Westport, Conn.: Greenwood Press, 1984), p. 159.

[21]"Indian Prosperity," *Independent*, 7 September 1900, p. 2; Clifford to Pittman, 18 February 1935, Pittman Papers, Box 73, LC; Harold K. Steen, *The U.S. Forest Service: A History* (Seattle: University of Washington Press, 1976), pp. 84, 99.

[22]*Statutes of the State of Nevada, 1909*, pp.38–40; Clifford to Pittman, 18 February 1935, Pittman Papers, Box 73, LC.

[23]Lorenzo Creel to L. A. Dorrington, 24 October 1917, Reno Agency, Box 290, FARC-SB.

[24]Goshute Tribal Minutes, 28 October 1941, 15 November 1945, BIA, Eastern Nevada Agency (ENA); Ruby Valley Allotment Information, Edna Patterson Papers, Northeastern Nevada Museum, Elko.

[25]Interview with Pauline Esteves, 24 August 1989, Death Valley, Calif.; Indian Census Roll, Walker River Agency, 1 April 1930 (M 595, R 632), FF 7–18.

[26]"Hazel Millett Named April's Senior of the Month," *Battle Mountain Bugle*, 16 April 1986, p. 5; "Eunice Silva Remembers," *Battle Mountain Bugle*, 22 August 1979, p. 10.

[27]Margaret Connell Szasz, *Education and the American Indian*, 2nd ed. (Albuquerque: University of New Mexico Press, 1977), pp. 8–15.

[28]James Pabawena, unpublished letters, 1908–15, CCF, 24195–08-GS-313.1, RG 75, NA.

[29]"Indians to Elect a New Chief," *Free Press*, 27 November 1912, p. 1.

[30]Bill Gibson to John Collier, 30 December 1936, BIA, ENA.

[31]"Indian School to Open Monday," *Free Press*, 17 October 1923, p. 1; Otis J. Morgans to CIA, 15 August 1936, WSA, RG 75, FARC-SB; "Elko May Secure U.S. Indian School in the Near Future," *Free Press*, 21 October 1913, p. 1; "Wants Separate School for Indian Children," *Free Press*, 3 June 1915, p. 1.

[32]E. B. Meritt to James Royce, 24 May 1918, CCF, 29475–18-Carson-803, RG 75, NA.

[33]"Eunice Silva Remembers," *Battle Mountain Bugle*, 22 August 1979, p. 10.

[34]"Indian Youth Visits President on Way to Massachusetts," *Scout*, 2 December 1922, p. 1.

[35]"Indians Will Not Lose Annuities," *The Humboldt Star*, 5 September 1924, p. 1; "Letter Gives Indians' Reasons for Refusal to Cast Ballots," *The Humboldt Star*, 20 October 1924, p. 3; "Piutes, Shoshones Issue Non-Voting Ultimatum," *The Humboldt Star*, 13 October 1927, pp. 1, 4.

[36]See citations in note 35 above; "Indians Say Going to 'Fight' for Rights; To Not Vote, Decree Says," *The Humboldt Star*, 4 October 1928, pp. 1, 4.

[37]W. S. Bryden to Secretary of Interior, 25 January 1883, LR, 1883–2269, RG 75, NA; Bryden to E. L. Stevens, 30 April 1883, LR, 1883–8373, RG 75, NA; E. S. Stevens to W. S. Bryden, 12 May 1883, LS, RG 75, NA.

[38]*Reports of Cases Determined in the Supreme Court of the State of Nevada, 1883, 1884,* vol. 18 (San Francisco: Bancroft-Whitney, 1891), pp. 182–209.

[39]*Statutes of the State of Nevada* (1877), pp. 133–34; (1885), pp. 41–42; "Nevada Convicts," *Independent,* 12 May 1905, p. 2.

[40]"Selling Whiskey to Indians," *Free Press,* 23 February 1883, p. 3; "Indian Kills Indian," *Nevada State Herald,* 27 June 1902, p. 5; "Indian Chief Places Ban on Fandango and Issues Edict Forbidding Gathering," *Free Press,* 19 September 1913, p. 1.

[41]*Newe: A Western Shoshone History,* pp. 71–72; McKinney, *A History of the Shoshone-Paiutes of the Duck Valley Indian Reservation,* pp. 103–5.

[42]See citations in note 41 above.

[43]See citations in note 41 above; "An Interview with Members of the Te-moak Band of Homeless Indians," 17 January 1927, CCF, 56890-13-WS-211, RG 75, NA.

[44]Richard N. Ellis, " 'Indians at Ibapah in Revolt': Goshutes, the Draft and the Indian Bureau, 1917–1919," *Nevada Historical Society Quarterly* 19 (Fall 1976):163–70; David L. Wood, "Gosiute-Shoshone Draft Resistance, 1917–18," *Utah Historical Quarterly* 49 (Spring 1981):173–88.

[45]See citations in note 44 above.

[46]See citations in note 44 above.

[47]Homer Mooney to William Woodburn, 2 April 1918, Uintah-Ouray, RG 75, FARC-Denver; A. R. Frank to U.S. Attorney, 28 February 1918, Dorrington Papers, Box 4, RG 75, FARC-SB.

[48]"Chief of Ruby Indians Makes a Statement," *Nevada State Herald,* 19 April 1918, p. 5.

[49]Crum, "The Ruby Valley Indian Reservation," pp. 9–11.

[50]Records of the Realty Division, Western Nevada Agency, BIA, Carson City; C. H. Asbury to CIA, 8 May 1914, CCF, 41230-14-General Services-313.1, RG 75, NA.

[51]Prucha, *The Great Father,* abridged ed., pp. 224–28.

[52]Crum, "The Ruby Valley Indian Reservation," pp. 7–8.

[53]Elmer R. Rusco, "Purchasing Lands for Nevada Indian Colonies, 1916–1917," *Nevada Historical Society Quarterly* 32 (Spring 1989):1, 3, 17–19.

[54]Steven J. Crum, "The Skull Valley Band of the Goshute Tribe—Deeply Attached to Their Native Homeland," *Utah Historical Quarterly* 55 (Summer 1987):259–60, 262.

[55]Lorenzo Creel, "Final Report, Relief, Homeless Indians, Nevada," 30 June 1917, CCF, 41726-09-Carson-150, Pt. 1A, pp. 8, 22–23, NA.

[56]Ibid., pp. 23–25.

[57]*Newe: A Western Shoshone History,* p. 84. James Jenkins to CIA, 10 November 1922, p. 2, and Jenkins to CIA, 20 September 1923, p. 2, both in Carson Agency Records, RG 75, FARC-SB; Agreement, 18 June 1919, CCF, 41726-09-Carson-150, Pt. 6; J. Winfield Scott to L. J. Lonergan, 30 July 1921, CCF, 78336-21-Reno-816.2, RG 75, NA; Jenkins to CIA, 12 October 1923, Carson, RG 75, FARC-SB; "Federal Indian Agent Quizzes Conditions in B.M. Vicinity," *Scout,* 20 November 1931, p. 1.

[58]*Newe: A Western Shoshone History,* p. 85; C. F. Hauke to CIA, 24 October 1917, Reno, Box 290, RG 75, FARC-SB.

[59]*Newe: A Western Shoshone History,* p. 85.

[60]Elko County Lions Club to B. G. McBride, 28 September 1923, Reno, Box 287, RG 75, FARC-SB; memorandum by Leonard Ware, 7 October 1958, Nevada, RG 75, Washington National Records Center (WNRC), Suitland, Maryland; *Newe: A Western Shoshone History,* p. 86.

[61]Harry Johnny to Tasker Oddie, 5 September 1928, CCF, 45329–28-Carson-341, RG 75, NA; "Oddie Bill to Aid Ely Indians Goes to House," *Ely Record,* 16 May 1930, p. 1; memorandum by Leonard Ware, 22 May 1958, Nevada, RG 75, WNRC; *Newe: A Western Shoshone History,* pp. 88–89.

[62]Ray R. Parrett to H. V. Clotts, 20 June 1926, CCF, 42055–26-Walker River-341, RG 75, NA; E. B. Meritt to Ray Parrett, 3 May 1928, CCF, 42055–26-Walker River-341, RG 75, NA; F. G. Boyles to Ray Parrett, 3 February 1930, File 308, Box 14, Tribal Records, Sacramento Area Office, RG 75, FARC-SB.

[63]Ginn to Secretary of Interior, 3 August 1925, and Merritt to Oddie, 13 August 1925, both in Oddie Papers, Nevada Historical Society, Reno.

[64]"A Shoshone Proclamation," *Independent,* 23 February 1896, p. 2; "Chief Harry's Proclamation," *Independent,* 15 March 1896, p. 4.

[65]See citations in note 64 above.

[66]"Harry Preacher's New Scheme," *Nevada State Herald,* 30 November 1900, p. 1.

[67]"Indians to Elect a New Chief," *Free Press,* 27 November 1912, p. 1; "Indian Chief Places Ban on Fandango and Issues Edict Forbidding Gathering," *Free Press,* 19 September 1913, p. 1; Fort Hall Superintendent to Charles Burke, 12 May 1925, p. 12, CCF, 15577–23-Fort Hall-054, RG 75, NA.

[68]"Indian Talk," *Battle Mountain Messenger,* 17 April 1880, p. 3.

[69]"Death of the Shoshone Chief," *RRR,* 21 April 1897, p. 3; "A Card from Chief Toi Toi," *Goldfield Weekly News,* 27 October 1905, p. 2.

[70]"Last Rites over Shoshone Chief," *RRR,* 28 December 1918, p. 1; "Shoshone Fandango," *RRR,* 12 July 1919, p. 2; "Shoshone Indians Elect New Chief," *Scout,* 7 October 1922, p. 1.

[71]Willie Ottogary, George Paharagosam, and Harry Dixon to Whom Concerned, 6 July 1923, CCF, 56426–23-WS-302, RG 75, NA; Resolution, 17 September 1923, CCF, 158–25-WS-174.1, RG 75, NA; Ottogary, Paharagosam, and Dixon to Whom Concerned, 23 September 1924, CCF, 78095–24-Reno-300, RG 75, NA.

[72]Harry J. Dixon to Sen. Tasker Oddie, 12 February 1925, 14 February 1927, and James E. Jenkins to CIA, 12 November 1924, both in Oddie Papers, Nevada Historical Society, Reno.

[73]"Fandango Finish: Bronco Jim New Shoshone Chief," *RRR,* 22 August 1931, p. 1; "Gilbert Declared Hereditary Chief of Shoshone Tribe," *RRR,* 5 December 1931, p. 1.

[74]"Not under a Chief," *Independent,* 27 August 1929, p. 2.

[75]Tribal Minutes, in *Council Book, Indian Council,* 1929 (in possession of a tribal member on the Duck Valley Indian Reservation).

[76]Quoted in Edna Patterson, Louise A. Ulph, and Victor Goodwin, *Nevada's Northeast Frontier* (Sparks, Nev.: Western Printing and Publishing, 1969), p. 44.

[77]"An Interview with Members of the Te-moak Band of Homeless Indians," 17 January 1927, CCF, 56890–13-WS-211, RG 75, NA.

[78]Grant Patterson to C. H. Asbury, 15 July 1914, Box 290, Reno Agency, FARC-SB; Joseph Jensen to General Land Office (GLO), 1 October 1915, CCF, 125909–15–313-GS, RG 75, NA.

[79]Mutacko Timoch, letter, 15 April 1912, CCF, 40126–12-WS-313, RG 75, NA.
[80]Muchuch Timoke to CIA, 27 January 1917, CCF, 9355–17-WS-313, pt. 1, RG 75, NA.
[81]Cato Sells to Muchuch Timoche, 31 January 1917, CCF, 9355–17–313-WS, pt. 1, RG 75, NA.
[82]Muchach Temoke and Tommy Wahne to CIA, 25 November 1919, CCF, 9355–17-WS-313, pt. 1, RG 75, NA.
[83]E. B. Meritt to Tommy Wahne and Muchuch Temoak, 1 December 1919, CCF, 9355–17-WS-313, pt. 1, RG 75, NA.
[84]Crum, "The Ruby Valley Indian Reservation," p. 11.
[85]Kase Austin, letter, 18 October 1912, Box 278, Reno Indian Agency Records, RG 75, FARC-SB; Bill Gibson, letter, 4 November 1929, CCF, 9355–17-WS-313, Pt. 2; "Indians to Elect a New Chief," *Free Press*, 27 November 1912, p. 1.
[86]Kase Austin, letters, 18 October 1912, 9 November 1912, Box 278, Reno Agency, RG 75, FARC-SB.
[87]Calvin Asbury to CIA, 26 December 1912, Box 278, Reno Agency, RG 75, FARC-SB.
[88]Ibid.
[89]Ibid.; statement by Brownie Mose, 23 September 1929, and statement by Kase Austin, 8 October 1929, CCF, 9355–17-WS-313, pt. 2, RG 75, NA.
[90]*Newe Sogobia: The Western Shoshone People and the Lands* (Battle Mountain, Nev.: Western Shoshone Sacred Lands Association, 1982), p. 13. Apparently, years ago, this council was called the Council of Western Shoshones.
[91]Tommy Wahne to Key Pittman, 14 May 1921, 11 July 1921, 26 July 1921, Box 105, Pittman Papers, LC; Bill Gibson, letter, 4 November 1929, CCF, 9355–17-WS-313, Pt. 2, RG 75, NA.
[92]Tommy Wahne to Charles Richards, 16 February 1925, CCF, 13460–25-Reno-115, RG 75, NA.
[93]"Survey of Conditions of the Indians in the United States," hearings before a Subcommittee of the Committee on Indian Affairs, U.S. Senate, 72nd Cong., 1st sess., Pt. 28 (Nevada), p. 14834.
[94]Ibid., pp. 14811–12.
[95]Ibid., pp. 14847–54.
[96]Ibid.
[97]Ibid.
[98]Ibid.

Chapter 5: The Western Shoshone and the New Deal, 1933–1941

[1]For general information relating to the Great Depression and the initiation of the New Deal, refer to the following: John D. Hicks, *Republican Ascendancy, 1921–1933* (New York: Harper and Row, 1960); William E. Leuchtenburg, *Franklin D. Roosevelt and the New Deal, 1932–1940* (New York: Harper and Row, 1963); and Arthur M. Schlesinger, Jr., *The Coming of the New Deal* (Boston: Houghton Mifflin, 1958). See also Kenneth R. Philp, *John Collier's Crusade for Indian Reform, 1920–1954* (Tucson: University of Arizona Press, 1977), pp. 120–34. For a discussion of how the New Deal affected the Western Shoshones, see the following: Richard O. Clemmer, "Hopis, Western Shoshones, and Southern Utes: Three Different Responses to the Indian Reorganization Act of 1934," *American Indian Culture and Research Journal* 10:2 (1986):15–40; Steven Crum, "The Western Shoshone of Nevada and the Indian New Deal," Ph.D. diss., University

of Utah, 1983; Elmer R. Rusco, "The Organization of the Te-Moak Bands of Western Shoshone," *Nevada Historical Society Quarterly* 25 (Fall 1982):175–96.

[2]Act of 18 June 1934, 48 Stat. 984–88.

[3]Philp, *John Collier's Crusade*, pp. 143–59; Lawrence C. Kelly, "The Indian Reorganization Act: The Dream and the Reality," *Pacific Historical Review* 46 (August 1975):291–312; Michael T. Smith, "The Wheeler-Howard Act of 1934: The Indian New Deal," *Journal of the West* 10 (July 1971):524–34.

[4]Parman, "The Indian and the Civilian Conservation Corps," *Pacific Historical Review* 40 (1971):42. Except for the Indian Reorganization Act, the Civilian Conservation Corps, Indian Division (CCC-ID), has received more scholarly attention than other aspects of the Indian New Deal. Readers should be aware of the following tribal case studies: Calvin W. Gower, "The CCC Indian Division: Aid for Depressed Americans, 1933–1942," *Minnesota History* 43 (1972):3–13; Roger Bromert, "The Sioux and the Indian-CCC," *South Dakota History* 8 (Fall 1978):340–56.

[5]Parman, "The Indian and the Civilian Conservation Corps," pp. 39–56; Bromert, "The Sioux and the Indian-CCC," pp. 340–56.

[6]Melis to CIA, 29 July 1934, CCC-ID, 20985–33-WS-344, Pt. 1, RG 75, NA; N. F. Caywood to CIA, 13 May 1935, CCC-ID, 20985–33-WS-344, Pt. 1, RG 75, NA; A. C. Cooley to CIA, 23 January 1940, p. 3, Rehabilitation Division, 76105-P-2, RG 75, NA; "CCC-ID Work Program," Fiscal Year 1941, 27 May 1942, BIA, PAO, RG 74, FARC-LN.

[7]"CCC-ID Work Program," BIA, PAO, RG 75, FARC-LN.

[8]McNeilly to CIA, 22 May 1928, p. 2, WSA, RG 75, FARC-SB; McNeilly to CIA, 2 August 1933, CCC-ID, 20985–33-WS-344, Pt. 1, RG 75, NA; Melis to CIA, 29 July 1934, p. 1, CCC-ID, 20985–33-WS-344, Pt. 1, RG 75, NA; Technical Cooperation-Bureau of Indian Affairs (TC-BIA), "Basic Plan for Long Time Grazing Program," July 1937, p. 28, CCF, 6685–39-WS-031, RG 75, NA.

[9]Schlesinger, *Coming of the New Deal*, pp. 282–88.

[10]Public Works Administration (PWA), Progress Report, 13 June 1936, Federal Project (FP) 205, BIA, PAO, RG 75, FARC-LN; G .B. Keesee, "Report on Construction of Wild Horse Dam," 14 August 1937, BIA, PAO, RG 75, FARC-LN.

[11]Paul F. Henderson to F. M. Clinton, 13 December 1949, CCF, 2402–48-WS-341.8, RG 75, NA; Annual Extension Report, Narrative Section, 1941, Table 1, CCF, 211–42-WS-031, RG 75, NA.

[12]"Information for J. E. White," 1941, pp. 1, 5, BIA, PAO, RG 75, FARC-LN; Henderson to Clinton, 13 December 1949, CCF, 2402–48-WS-341.8, RG 75, NA.

[13]"Report of the Inspection," FP 375, 4 August 1936, PWA, RG 75, NA; McNeilly to CIA, 2 September 1936, FP 375, PWA, RG 75, NA; Worley to CIA, 14 June 1937, p. 2, WS, RG 75, FARC-SB; Snavely to CIA, 17 November 1938, p. 4, WS, RG 75, FARC-SB; McNeilly to Paul L. Fickinger, 5 March 1936, FP 537, PWA, RG 75, NA; On the site visit by O. H. Murray, see 28 October 1937, FP 537, PWA, RG 75, NA.

[14]Schlesinger, *Coming of the New Deal*, pp. 40–54; C. Roger Lambert, "The Drought Cattle Purchase, 1934–1935: Problems and Complaints," *Agricultural History* 45 (April 1971):85; "Extension Program," Western Shoshone Reservation, 25 April 1938, p. 3, CCF, 1348–38-WS-031, RG 75, NA; "Cattle Counted at Western Shoshone Agency, 1917," WS, RG 75, FARC-SB; "Western Shoshone-Paiute Livestock Association Cattle Count—February 1961," 20 March 1961, BIA, PAO, RG 75, FARC-LN.

[15]Bowler to CIA, 3 August 1935, p. 4, CCF, 42774–35-Carson-720, RG 75, NA. For an excellent discussion of Bowler's activities, see Rusco, "The Organization of the Te-Moak Bands of Western Shoshone," pp. 175–96.

[16]Leuchtenburg, *Roosevelt and the New Deal*, p. 120; Nevada Emergency Relief Administration (NERA), "Review of Work Relief Activities in Nevada," 1 April 1934–1 July 1935, unpublished report, Nevada Historical Society Archives, Reno; Harry L. Hopkins to State Emergency Relief Administrators, 17 July 1933, Indian Records, 1–270, RG 48, NA; Gertrude F. Hosmer to CIA, 4 October 1934, p. 4, CCF, 64564–34-Carson-032, RG 75, NA; Lucile Hamner to William Zimmerman, 10 March 1936, CCF, 42774–35-Carson-720, RG 75, NA; Alida C. Bowler to Gilbert Ross, 12 March 1936, CCF, 42774–35-Carson-720, RG 75, NA; Bowler to CIA, 10 August 1935, CCF, 42774–35-Carson-720, RG 75, NA.

[17]Bowler to CIA, 3 August 1935, p. 4, CCF, 42774–35-Carson-720, RG 75, NA.

[18]Bowler to Ross, 12 March 1936, CCF, 42774–35-Carson-720, RG 75, NA.

[19]TC-BIA, "The Nye County Shoshone Project of Nevada," April–May 1937, p. 17, BIA, PAO, RG 75, FARC-LN; TC-BIA, "South Fork and Ruby Valley Projects for Shoshones of Northeastern Nevada," April–May 1937, p. 93, BIA, PAO, RG 75, FARC-LN; Bowler to Ross, 12 March 1936, CCF, 42774–35-Carson-720, RG 75, NA.

[20]"Rehabilitation Expenditures," Ely Colony, 1938; Elko Colony, 1936; Ruby Valley, 1936; all in 76006-P-1-a; Death Valley, 1938, in 76006-P-2; Rehabilitation Division (RD), Carson Agency, RG 75, NA. Interview with Pauline Esteves, 24 August 1989, Death Valley, Calif.

[21]Ray R. Parrett, "Landless Indian Report," Civil Works Administration (CWA) Survey, Walker River Agency, Records Relating to Social and Economic Survey, RG 75, NA.

[22]Bowler, "Report of the National Resources Board," September 1934, p. 20, BIA, PAO, RG 75, FARC-LN; "Report on Indian Land Unit of NRB . . . ," Walker River Agency, Records Relating to Land Use Survey, RG 75, NA.

[23]See the correspondence of Alida Bowler in *John Collier Papers, 1922–1968*, Yale University (microfilm ed.), ed. Andrew M. Patterson and Maureen Brodoff (Sanford, N.C.: Microfilming Corporation of America, 1980), Reel 1, FF 00327–43.

[24]"A Woman Superintendent," *Indians at Work* 3 (1 December 1935):36; Bowler to CIA, 1 November 1934, CCF, 9532–36-C-066, RG 75, NA.

[25]Bowler, "Report of the National Resources Board," September 1934, p. 20, BIA, PAO, RG 75, FARC-LN.

[26]This conclusion can be drawn from Bowler's writings, including "Report for National Resource Board," 1934, p. 26, BIA, PAO, RG 75, FARC-LN.

[27]Bowler, "Report of the National Resources Board," September 1934, pp. 20, 26–27, BIA, PAO, RG 75, FARC-LN.

[28]Bowler, "Report of the National Resources Board," September 1934, pp. 20–23, 25, BIA, PAO, RG 75, FARC-LN.

[29]*Newe: A Western Shoshone History*, p. 95

[30]"Ruby Valley Project, Carson Agency—Nevada, Project Plan, Schedule I," 12 January 1937, p. 3, BIA, PAO, RG 75, FARC-LN; Crum, "The Ruby Valley Indian Reservation," pp. 1–18.

[31]Committee to Collier, 15 December 1934, CCF, 39224–34-C-310, RG 75, NA; Committee to Pittman, 15 December 1934, Pittman Papers, LC.

[32]Bowler, "Report of the National Resources Board," September 1934, p. 26, BIA, PAO, RG 75, FARC-LN.

[33]Bowler to Mike, 21 August 1936, BIA, PAO, RG 75, FARC-LN.

[34]Leonard Ware, "Background Data on the South Fork Reservation, Nevada," 14 May 1959, CF, 11740–59-N-077, RG 75, WNRC; Philp, *John Collier's Crusade*, pp. 124–25; interview with Bert Tybo, 4 September 1983, Owyhee, Nev.; interview with Saggie and Gladys Williams, 26 August 1990, Battle Mountain, Nev.

[35]"Ruby Valley Project, Carson Agency—Nevada, Project Plan, Schedule I," 12 January 1937, p. 3, BIA, PAO, RG 75, FARC-LN.

[36]Leonard Ware, "Background Data on the Odgers Ranch, Nevada," CCF, 11740–59-Nevada(N)-077, RG 75, WNRC.

[37]Leonard Ware, "Data on the Yomba Reservation," 12 December 1958, RG 75, WNRC.

[38]"The Big Fandango at the Bowler Ranch," *RRR*, 14 August 1937, p. 6; "Reese River Indians Plan 5-Day Festival," *RRR*, 3 September 1938, p. 1; "Big Fandango at Yomba Reservation," *RRR*, 12 September 1942, p. 1.

[39]Jenkins to Woehlke, 19 June 1934, CCF, 48299–34-C-310, RG 75, NA; "Background Data Relating to the Duckwater Reservation, Nevada," CCF, N, 077, RG 75, WNRC, p. 2.

[40]E. M. Johnston, "Mountain City Project," Preliminary Report, 23 March 1937, BIA, PAO, RG 75, FARC-Seattle; Johnston, "Jarvis Ranch Project," 24 March 1937, CCF, 294–37-WS-310, RG 75, NA; E. J. Armstrong to Carl Beck, 29 November 1938, BIA, PAO, RG 75, FARC-LN.

[41]TC-BIA, "Survey of the Beatty-Pahrump Area Located in Southwestern Nevada," April 1937, pp. 4–6, CCF, 00-37-C-330, RG 75, NA.

[42]"Technical Reports regarding the Death Valley Timbi-sha Shoshone Band of Death Valley, California," 1982, p. 4, California Indian Legal Services (CILS), Bishop, Calif.; interview with Pauline Estes, 24 August 1989.

[43]Shoshone Leaders to Charles Kappler, 21 June 1939, p. 3, CCF, 51838–32-WS-174.1, RG 75, NA.

[44]Muchach Temoke to Collier, 20 December 1938, CF, 78468–38-WS-066, RG 75, NA.

[45]Interview with George P. LaVatta (Shoshone), Portland, Ore., 28 October 1981; "George LaVatta Wins Recognition as an Outstanding Indian," *Indians at Work* 9 (October 1941):14–15.

[46]McNeilly to CIA, 27 October 1934, Indian Organization Division (IOD), 9794–26-WS-066, RG 75, NA; Philp, *John Collier's Crusade*, p. 162; McNeilly to CIA, 24 March 1936, CCF, 9794-A-36-WS-068, RG 75, NA.

[47]LaVatta to CIA, 10 October 1935, CCF, 9794-A-36-WS-068, RG 75, NA; "Constitution and By-Laws of the Shoshone-Paiute Tribes of the Duck Valley Reservation," 20 April 1936, U.S. Department of the Interior, Office of Indian Affairs (Washington, D.C.: GPO, 1936).

[48]Report of Council Elections, 1936–47, CCF, 7206–41-WS-055, RG 75, NA.

[49]"Constitution and By-Laws of the Shoshone-Paiute Tribes of the Duck Valley Reservation."

[50]Ten-Year Program, 31 March 1944, p. 6, CCF, WS-031, RG 75, NA; "Self-Sufficiency Reflected in New Duck Valley Shoshone-Paiute Farm," *Free Press*, 21 August 1982, p. 5.

[51]Tribal Committee to CIA, 6 March 1939, Collier Office File, Peyote Papers, RG 75, NA.

[52]Shoshone-Paiute Business Council statement, 28 March 1951, BIA, PAO, RG 75, FARC-LN.

[53]"Constitution and By-Laws of the Shoshone-Paiute Tribes of the Duck Valley Reservation."

[54]Te-Moak Minutes, 8 March 1985, pp. 7–8, BIA, ENA; "Duck Valley Shoshone Group Considers Forming a New Band," *NN*, August 1984, p. 40; Willis Premo to Steven Crum, 12 May 1991, letter in possession of author.

[55]"Duck Valley Voting Districts?" *NN*, 25 July 1975, p. 9.

[56]"Laura Townsend Leads Duck Valley," *NN*, 2 July 1976, p. 4; see also Duck Valley Tribal Minutes, 1989, BIA, ENA.

[57]Bowler to CIA, 1 November 1934, CCF, 9532–36-C-066, RG 75, NA; see Rusco, "The Organization of the Te-Moak Bands."

[58]"Survey of Conditions of the Indians in the United States," pp. 14847–54.

[59]Bowler, "Report of the National Resources Board," September 1934, p. 20, BIA, PAO, RG 75, FARC-LN.

[60]Indian Reorganization Act Voting Returns, Carson Agency, 1935, CCF, 9532–36-C-066, RG 75, NA.

[61]"Indians in B.M. Camp Favor Act," *Scout*, 20 June 1935, p. 1; *Newe: A Western Shoshone History*, pp. 94–100.

[62]Johnnie Bill Antelop and others to Collier, 13 January 1936, CCF, 15804–25-WS-174.1, RG 74, NA.

[63]Bowler to CIA, 28 May 1936, IOD, 9571-A-36-C-068, RG 75, NA.

[64]Interview with George P. LaVatta (Shoshone), Portland, Ore., 28 October 1981.

[65]LaVatta to CIA, 27 July 1936, IOD, 9571-A-36-C-068, RG 75, NA; "Constitution and By-Laws of the Te-Moak Western Shoshone Bands of Nevada," 16 May 1936, IOD, 9571-A-36-C-068, RG 75, NA.

[66]Zimmerman to Bowler, 23 October 1936, IOD, 9571-A-36-C-068, RG 75, NA.

[67]Muchach Temoak and Tommy Wahne to CIA, 25 November 1919, CF, RG 75, NA.

[68]Bowler to CIA, 13 October 1936, IOD, 9571-A-36-C-068, RG 75, NA.

[69]Muchach Temoke to Collier, 20 December 1938, CCF, 78468–38-WS-066, RG 75, NA.

[70]Certification of Election, 31 May 1938, IOD, 9571-A-36-C-068, RG 75, NA.

[71]Council Minutes, 4 September 1940, CCF, 42673–39-WS-054, RG 74, NA; Council Minutes, 4 October 1940, CCF, 42673–39-WS-054, RG 75, NA; Council List, September 1943, CCF, 7206–41-WS-055, RG 75, NA; Sawyer to Malone, 31 March 1951, CCF, 44166–44-WS-362, RG 75, NA.

[72]A. C. Cooley to Collier, 23 January 1940, p. 5, CCF, 26199–40-WS-342, RG 75, NA; J. E. White, "Social and Economic Information for the Te-Moak Bands of Western Shoshone Indians," 10 April 1939, p. 19, CCF, 22444–39-WS-032, RG 75, NA; Pohland to CIA, 4 August 1944, CCF, 22444–39-WS-032, RG 75, NA; Minutes, 14 July 1943, CCF, 22444–39-WS-032, RG 75, NA; Loan Papers of the Te-Moak Livestock Association, 14 May 1942, CCF, 28994–42-WS-259, RG 75, NA.

[73]Te-Moak Minutes, 28 October 1966, BIA, ENA; Te-Moak Minutes, 16 September 1974, BIA, ENA; memorandum, CIA to Secretary of the Interior, 1977, BIA, ENA; "Constitution and By-Laws of the Ely Colony," 8 April 1966, BIA, ENA.

[74]"Chief Temoke Says Rubies 'Whitest' in His Lifetime," *Free Press*, 19 May 1975, p. 1.

[75]Bowler to LaVatta, 1 February 1939, Collier Office File, RG 75, NA; Carson Agency credit papers, 1936–37, BIA, PAO, RG 75, FARC-LN.

208 *Notes to Pages 108–112*

[76]Committee to Collier, 15 December 1934, CCF, 39224–34-C-310, RG 75, NA; Committee to Pittman, 15 December 1934, Pittman Papers, LC.

[77]See citations in note 76 above.

[78]Minutes of meeting, 18 January 1938, CCF, 9827-E-36-C-054, RG 75, NA; "Certification of Tentative Land Assignment, Yomba Reservation," 25 April 1939, CCF, 9827-A + B-36-C-068, RG 75, NA; Margold to Secretary of the Interior, 1 November 1938, BIA, PAO, RG 75, FARC-LN; interview with Bud and Isabel Decker, 24 August 1982, Battle Mountain, Nev.; letter from Ernest Hooper, Fallon, Nevada, 24 August 1993.

[79]Minutes, 24 April 1939, BIA, Western Nevada Agency (WNA); Minutes, 5 June 1938, CF, 9827-E-36-C-054, RG 75, NA; Minutes, 18 January 1938, CCF, 9827-E-36-C-054, RG 75, NA.

[80]Robert Bromert, "The Sioux and the Indian New Deal, 1933–1944," Ph.D. diss., University of Toledo, May 1980, p. 65; Bowler to Collier, 1 February 1939, Collier Office File, RG 75, NA; Minutes, 4 April 1939, BIA, WNA; Minutes, 24 April 1939, BIA, WNA; U.S. Department of the Interior, Office of Indian Affairs, *Constitution and By-Laws of the Yomba Shoshone Tribe of the Yomba Reservation, Nevada,* 22 December 1938 (Washington, D.C.: GPO, 1940).

[81]Clifford to Pittman, 24 January 1935, Pittman Papers, LC.

[82]Minutes, 13 February 1940, CCF, 9827-E-36-C-054, RG 75, NA.

[83]"Agricultural Extension Program of Work, Carson Indian Agency Jurisdiction, Yomba Reservation, 1941," CCF, 7764–42-C-031, RG 75, NA; Greenwood to Foster, 26 April 1940, CCF, 11746–40-C-031, Pt. 1, RG 75, NA; Clifford to Bowler, 11 July 1936, BIA, PAO, RG 75, FARC-LN; Summary, Cattle Count, 1 December 1944, Carson (C), RG 75, FARC-SB.

[84]Bowler to CIA, 24 July 1937, BIA, PAO, RG 75, FARC-LN; Committee to Scrugham, 18 July 1937, BIA, PAO, RG 75, FARC-LN; *Duckwater Shoshone History* (Duckwater, Nev.: Duckwater Shoshone School Board, 1986), p. 7.

[85]See citations in note 84 above.

[86]Committee to CIA, 7 February 1938, CCF, 3199–37-C-310, Pt. 1, RG 75, NA; Committee to Bowler, 19 March 1938, BIA, PAO, RG 75, FARC-LN; Committee to Scrugham, 5 November 1937, Pittman Papers, LC; Committee to Roosevelt, 27 August 1938, CCF, 3199–37-C-310, Pt. 1, RG 75, NA; Committee to Ickes, 14 March 1939, CCF, 9532–36-C-066, RG 75, NA; Committee to Collier, 22 December 1939, Pittman Papers, LC.

[87]Memorandum to Foster, 14 December 1940, BIA, PAO, RG 75, FARC-LN; "Social and Economic Information of the Duckwater Project," 28 February 1941, p. 7, BIA, PAO, FARC-LN; Minutes, 1 November 1940, CCF, 9829-E-36-C-054, RG 75, NA.

[88]U.S. Department of the Interior, Office of Indian Affairs, *Constitution and By-Laws of the Duckwater Shoshone Tribe of the Duckwater Reservation, Nevada,* 28 November 1940 (Washington, D.C.: GPO, 1941); Coulter to White, 9 January 1941, N, RG 75, FARC-SB; Foster to CIA, 11 January 1941, Nevada Agency (N), RG 75, FARC-SB.

[89]Bromert, "The Sioux and the Indian New Deal, 1933–1944," p. 72.

[90]F. H. Daiker to Collier, 14 November 1936, Collier Office File, RG 75, NA.

[91]"Minutes, Sixth Inter-Tribal Conference of Council Representatives, Carson Jurisdiction, on Council Procedures and Organization Activities," 6–8 November 1941, p. 12, N, BIA, RG 75, FARC-SB.

[92]Ibid.

[93]"Result of Indian Vote," 14 June 1935, File 076.0-Organization, Tribal Records: Indian Ranch, Sacramento Area Office, RG 75, FARC-SB.

[94]Fred Daiker to Alida Bowler, 4 February 1938, Federal Acknowledgement Papers, Timbisha Shoshone Tribe, CILS.

[95]Quoted in "Shoshones Want Aid from Whites," *Scout*, 25 December 1947, p. 1.

[96]"Indians in Elko Meet," *Inter-Tribal Council of Nevada, Inc.*, *Newsletter* 2:2 (April 1965):24.

[97]Quoted in *Newe Sogobia: The Western Shoshone People and Lands*, p. 13.

[98]Szasz, *Education and the American Indian*, chap. 8, "The Johnson–O'Malley Act: Indian Children and Public Schools, 1928–1945"; educational information, 30 September 1940, WS, RG 75, FARC-SB; Morgans to CIA, 15 August 1936, p. 1, WS, RG 75, FARC-SB.

[99]C. Leon Wall, "History of Indian Education in Nevada from 1861 to 1951," M.A. thesis, University of Nevada, 1952, pp. 156, 192, 200.

[100]"Five Year Report," Education Division, February 1940, CCF, 37969-40-C-800, RG 75, NA; "B.M. Indian Girl Is Graduated from University," *Scout*, 13 May 1937, p. 1.

[101]Zimmerman to Badt, 10 January 1936, BIA, ENA; contract, 27 July 1936, ENA; Badt to Bowler, 2 October 1936, BIA, ENA.

[102]See the following bills: H.R. 9035 (1934), S. 2510 (1935), H.R. 10665 (1936), S. 68 (1937), H.R. 5560 (1937), S. 2670 (1939), S. 12 (1941), S. 23 (1943), all in LC.

[103]Ibid.

[104]Temoke to Collier, 20 December 1938, CCF, 78468-38-WS-066, RG 75, NA.

[105]Lawrence C. Kelly, "Anthropology and Anthropologists in the Indian New Deal," *History of the Behavioral Sciences* 16 (January 1980):10–11.

[106]Ibid.; Bowler to Mekeel, 12 November 1936; Mekeel to Bowler, 16 December 1936; Mekeel to Bowler, 28 October 1936; Mekeel to Bowler, 18 November 1936; all in CCF, 9038-43-C-042, RG 75, NA.

[107]Steward, *Basin-Plateau Aboriginal Sociopolitical Groups*; Steward, *Culture Element Distributions*.

[108]See citations in note 107 above. Bowler to Mekeel, 12 November 1936; Mekeel to Bowler, 16 December 1936; Mekeel to Bowler, 28 October 1936; Mekeel to Bowler, 18 November 1936; all in CCF, 9038-43-C-042, RG 75, NA.

[109]Julian H. Steward, "Report of Shoshonean Tribes (Utah, Idaho, Nevada, Eastern California)," 1936, Papers of Julian Steward, University of Illinois at Urbana-Champaign Archives.

[110]Harris, "The White Knife Shoshoni of Nevada."

[111]Ware, "Data on the Yomba Reservation," 12 December 1958, p. 4, RG 75, WNRC; Bruce Bernstein, "Panamit-Shoshone Basketry, 1890–1960," *American Indian Basketry* 19 (n.d.):5–12.

[112]"Indians Hold Dance near Hercules Gap," *Ely Record*, 2 July 1937, p. 1; "Indians Holding Tribal Sun Dance Here for Sick," *Wells Progress*, 2 July 1937, p. 1; Steward, *Culture Element Distributions*, p. 266.

[113]"Use of Peyote Probed Here at Recent Inquest," *RRR*, 16 December 1939, p. 2; Omer C. Stewart and David F. Aberle, eds., "Peyotism in the West," *University of Utah Anthropological Papers* 108 (1984):279–91.

[114]"Annual Indian Fandango at Yomba Reservation on Reese River Big Success," *RRR*, 30 August 1947, p. 1.

Chapter 6: From the New Deal to Termination, 1941–1960

[1]Alison R. Bernstein, *American Indians and World War II: Toward a New Era in Indian Affairs* (Norman: University of Oklahoma Press, 1991), pp. 89, 98; Philp, *John Collier's Crusade*, p. 205.

[2]For information concerning the termination period, see the following: Prucha, *The Great Father*, 2:1013–84; Donald L. Fixico, *Termination and Relocation: Federal Indian Policy, 1945–1960* (Albuquerque: University of New Mexico Press, 1986); Larry Burt, *Tribalism in Crisis* (Albuquerque: University of New Mexico Press, 1982); S. Lyman Tyler, *A History of Indian Policy* (Washington, D.C.: GPO, 1973).

[3]Bernstein, *American Indians and World War II*, p. 23.

[4]"Shoshones Tell of Action against Draft," *Salt Lake Tribune*, 5 November 1940, p. 12.

[5]"Ruby Valley Shoshone Indians Want U.S. to Stay Out of War, But Will Take Up Arms in Event of Invasion," *Free Press*, 5 October 1940, p. 1.

[6]"Resolution," 24 October 1940, CCF, 75263–40-WS-125, RG 75, NA.

[7]Col. Horace F. Sykes to CIA, 12 November 1940; Henry H. Blood to Clark Draper, 7 November 1940; Fred H. Daiker to Carl W. Beck, 26 November 1940; Beck to CIA, 3 December 1940; all in CCF, 75263–40-WS-125, RG 75, NA.

[8]Folder 610.0, "Military Service Gen," Box 82, Carson Indian School, RG 75, FARC-SB.

[9]"Entire 1942 Stewart Football Team Fought in World War II," *NN*, April 1984, pp. 7–8.

[10]"Dick Birchum Writes from Belgium," *RRR*, 25 August 1945, p. 1.

[11]*Duck Valley News* 1:1 (1940):1, CCC-ID, 62375–40-WS-346, RG 75, NA; Tribal Minutes, 18 December 1941, CCC-ID, 76105–36–361, p. 2, RG 75, NA.

[12]Yomba Minutes, 10 April 1942, CCF, 9827-E-36-C-054, RG 75, NA.

[13]Agricultural Extension Program of Work, 1943, CCF, 23505–43-C-919.1, RG 75, NA; Yomba Minutes, 13 March 1942, 14 January 1944, BIA, WNA; Gelvin, "Carson Agency Ten-Year Program Report," pp. 218, 221, WNA.

[14]"F. Muncey Dies of Wound in Nazi War," *Scout*, 22 March 1945, p. 1; "Francis Muncey Buried with Military Honors," *Scout*, 13 May 1948, p. 1.

[15]Edna B. Patterson, "Mary Hall," *Northeastern Nevada Historical Society Quarterly* 85:4 (Fall 1985):107; "Indian Sun Dance Held near Wells," *Free Press*, 1 July 1946, p. 1.

[16]60 Stat. 1049–56. For a discussion of the Indian Claims Commission (ICC) and the Western Shoshone, see Elmer Rusco, "The MX Missile and Western Shoshone Land Claims," *Nevada Public Affairs Review* 2 (1982):45–54.

[17]Prucha, *The Great Father*, 2:1022–23.

[18]Ibid., 2:1018.

[19]See various bills, filed in LC: H.R. 9035 (1934), S. 2510 (1935), H.R. 10665 (1936), S. 68 (1937), H.R. 5560 (1937), S. 2670 (1939), S. 12 (1941), S. 23 (1943), H.R. 4394 (1944).

[20]*Newe Sogobia: The Western Shoshone People and Lands*.

[21]18 Stat. 689–92.

[22]J. Dean Woodruff and Glenn V. Bird, *Ernest L. Wilkinson: Indian Advocate and University President* (Provo, Utah: privately published, n.d.), pp. 157–69.

[23]E. J. Diehl to CIA, 13 February 1947, p. 1, WSA, Box 335, FARC-SB.

[24]Milton Badt to Diehl, 3 September 1946, Wilson and Barrows Law Firm (WBLF), Elko, Nev.

[25]Ernest L. Wilkinson to Badt, 22 August 1946, p. 1, WBLF.

[26]Diehl to Orville WIlson, 16 September 1946, WBLF.

[27]Diehl to CIA, 11 November 1947, pp. 1–2, WBLF.

[28]*Constitution and By-Laws of the Te-Moak Bands of Western Shoshone Indians*, Nevada (Washington, D.C.: GPO, 1938). For a study of the formation of the Te-Moak Bands organization, see Rusco, "The Organization of the Te-Moak Bands of Western Shoshone."

[29]Council List, September 1943, CCF, 7206–41-WS-055, RG 75, NA.

[30]Badt to Wilkinson, 4 February 1947, p. 1, WBLF.

[31]Committee to James Scurgham, 18 July 1937, BIA, PAO, RG 75, FARC-LN; Tribal Minutes, 13 May 1936, CCF, 9794-C-36-WS-057, RG 75, NA.

[32]"Special Meeting of the Te-Moak Western Shoshone Council of the Te-Moak Bands of Western Shoshones of Nevada," 10 February 1947, WBLF.

[33]Ibid., pp. 2–3.

[34]Badt to Muchuch Temoke, 18 January 1947, WBLF.

[35]Wilkinson to Muchuch Temoke, George McQueen, and Jacob Browning, 3 March 1947, WBLF; Wilkinson to Wilson, 3 March 1947, WBLF.

[36]Wilson to Wilkinson, 25 March 1947, WBLF.

[37]Wilkinson to Wilson, 28 February 1947, WBLF.

[38]Wilson to Diehl, 10 March 1947, WBLF.

[39]"Special Meeting of the Western Shoshone Indians of Nevada," 29 March 1947, WBLF.

[40]Diehl to Birchum, 14 April 1947, WBLF; "Important Notice to Western Shoshone Groups," 12 May 1947, WBLF.

[41]"General Meeting of the Western Shoshone Indians of Nevada and Vicinity Held at Elko, Nevada," 1 June 1947, WBLF.

[42]Dave Clifford to Sen. Key Pittman, 24 January 1935, Pittman Papers, LC.

[43]"General Meeting," 1 June 1947, p. 3, WBLF.

[44]Ibid., p. 5.

[45]Contract of 16 August 1947, WBLF.

[46]F. A. Magun, "Interview with Chief Te-Moak and Mr. George of Ruby Valley on June 11, 1947," CCF, 00–1940-WS-054, RG 75, NA.

[47]Agreement with George Wright, 29 August 1947, John O'Connell Papers, O'Connell and Yengich Law Office, Salt Lake City.

[48]George Wright to Interior Department, 24 December 1947, p. 3, WBLF.

[49]Too-Toaina Tribe to Interior Department, 8 December 1947, WSA, Box 335, FARC-SB.

[50]Western Shoshone Leaders, letter, 24 December 1949, in *Records of the Special Committee on Indian Affairs*, Sen. 83, A-F9, RG 46, NA.

[51]Muchuch Temoke to Sen. Hugh R. Butler, 7 February 1951, Sen. 83, A-F9, RG 46, NA.

[52]Minutes of the Battle Mountain Meeting, 16 December 1951, O'Connell Papers, Salt Lake City.

[53]Dave Pabawena to Clifton Young, 1 November 1953, CCF, 4552–57-N-308, RG 75, NA.

[54]"Minutes of Meeting of Delegates," 31 May 1950, WBLF.

[55]Robert Barker, report, 15 October 1957, p. 2, BIA, ENA.

[56]Ibid., p. 4; Omer C. Stewart, "The Western Shoshone of Nevada and the U.S. Government, 1863–1950," in *Selected Papers from the 14th Great Basin Anthropological Conferences*, ed. Donald R. Tuohy (Socorro, N.M.: Ballena Press, 1974), pp. 78–114.

[57]Woodruff and Bird, *Ernest Wilkinson*, pp. 249–51, 264–65.

[58]Minutes, 21 August 1959, separately recorded by Gloria Williams and June Tom, BIA, ENA; "Indian Meeting Dominated by Side Disputes: Shoshones Fail to Reach Main Decision," *Free Press*, 21 August 1959, pp. 1–6.

[59]Frank Temoke to Wayne Aspinall, 3 September 1959, O'Connell Papers, Salt Lake City.

[60]Statement of the Traditional Council, or the Western Shoshone Nation of Indians, 1970, Papers of Howard Cannon, University of Nevada at Las Vegas. For a study of the activities of this organization in the 1960s and early 1970s, see Richard Clemmer, "Directed Resistance to Acculturation: A Comparative Study of the Effects of Non-Indian Jurisdiction on Hopi and Western Shoshone Communities," Ph.D. diss., University of Illinois, Urbana-Champaign, 1972.

[61]Prucha, *The Great Father*, 2:1028.

[62]"Western Shoshone Indian Tribes Plan Conference in Elko," *Free Press*, 27 April 1949, pp. 1, 5.

[63]Duck Valley Minutes, 20 December 1948, BIA, ENA.

[64]Ibid., 22 April 1949, BIA, ENA.

[65]"Long Range Program Meeting Held at Elko, Nevada, 2 May 1949," CCF, 37678–47-WS-071, RG 75, NA.

[66]Ibid.

[67]"Long Range Program Meeting Held at Elko, Nevada, 22 June 1949," CCF, 37678–47-WS-071, RG 75, NA.

[68]Ibid.

[69]"Objection: By Muchuch Temoke and Groups of the Western Shoshone Indians of Ruby Valley," CCF, 37678–47-WS-071, RG 75, NA.

[70]"Statement from the Yomba Tribal Group," CCF, 37678–47-WS-071, RG 75, NA.

[71]Long Range Meeting, 22 June 1949, p. 6, CCF, 37678–47-WS-071, RG 75, NA.

[72]"Long Range Program Meeting," 1 September 1949, p. 1, CCF, 37678–47-WS-071, RG 75, NA.

[73]John Provinse to John E. White, 8 June 1948, and Bert Courtright to CIA, 14 November 1948, both in Battle Mountain File, BIA, PAO, RG 75, FARC-LN.

[74]E. Morgan Pryse, letter, 9 September 1949, BIA, PAO, RG 75, FARC-LN.

[75]"A Bill: To Promote the Rehabilitation of the Battle Mountain Tribe of Shoshone Indians, and for Other Purposes," 1949, BIA, PAO, RG 75, FARC-LN.

[76]"$20,000 Sought for Use at Elko Indian Colony," *Free Press*, 28 April 1950, p. 1; "Improvement of Indian Colonies' Facilities Looms," *Free Press*, 10 August 1950, pp. 1, 6.

[77]"City of Elko Has No Authority over Indian Colony," *Free Press*, 10 July 1954, p. 2; "City Takes Commendable Action," *Free Press*, 3 August 1954, p. 2; "Indian Colony Sanitation Scored in Health Report," *Free Press*, 4 August 1954, pp. 1, 6.

[78]"Progress on Indian Colony Project Told," *Free Press*, 14 March 1957, pp. 1, 7; "Cost Estimate Made on Indian Colony 'Cleanup'," *Free Press*, 29 March 1957, pp. 1, 6; "City, U.S. Representatives Meet on Colony Issues," *Free Press*, 20 April 1957, pp. 1, 6.

[79]See citations in note 78 above; "Colony Residents to Aid City, U.S. in 'Cleanup'," *Free Press*, 22 April 1958, p. 1.

[80]71 Stat. 353.

[81]"Sanitation Project Completed This Week at Indian Colony," *Free Press*, 21 February 1958, p. 1.

82Duck Valley Minutes, 30 September 1949, 23 December 1954, BIA, ENA.

83Report by Leonard Ware, 5 August 1959, p. 13, BIA, RG 75, Nevada Agency, WNRC.

84Prucha, *The Great Father*, 2:1026; Tyler, *A History of Indian Policy*, pp. 163–64.

85"Report with Respect to the House Resolution Authorizing the Committee on Interior and Insular Affairs to Conduct an Investigation of the Bureau of Indian Affairs," House Report 2053, 82nd Cong., 2nd sess., Ser. 11582.

86E. J. Diehl, "Western Shoshone Ten Year Report," 1944; "Ten Year Program for Carson Agency, 1944"; both in BIA, WNA.

87"Report with Respect to the House Resolution Authorizing Committee on Interior and Insular Affairs to Conduct an Investigation of the Bureau of Indian Affairs," H. Rep. 2680, 83rd Cong., 2nd sess., Ser. 11747.

88S.B. 2726, 81st Cong., 1st sess., 3 January 1949–19 October 1949.

89Te-Moak Bands Minutes, 18 February 1950, 31 January 1950, BIA, ENA.

90Joe Gibson, report, CCF, 28994-42-WS-259, RG 75, NA.

9167 Stat. B132.

92"Termination of Federal Supervision over Certain Tribes of Indians," joint hearing before the subcommittee of the committees on Interior and Insular Affairs, 83rd Cong., 2nd sess., Pt. 10, pp. 1207–11.

93Wesley Bobo to Burton Ladd, 4 February 1954, CCF, 1980–53-Nevada-013, Pt. 1, RG 75, NA.

94"Termination of Federal Supervision over Certain Tribes," pp. 1290–91.

95Ibid.

96Ibid., p. 1271.

97Ibid.

98Ibid., p. 1267; "Private Ownership Sought for Elko Indian Colony," *Free Press*, 24 February 1954, pp. 1, 6.

99Burton Ladd to Ralph Gelvin, 30 March 1954, CCF, 1980–53-Nevada-013, Pt. 1, RG 75, NA.

100"Termination of Federal Supervision over Certain Tribes," p. 1311.

101Ibid., p. 1267.

102Ibid., p. 1295.

103Ibid., pp. 1297–98.

104Ibid., p. 1303.

105Ibid., p. 1305.

106Ibid., pp. 1306–7.

107Duck Valley Minutes, 24 November 1954, p. 1, BIA, ENA.

108Duck Valley Resolution, 7 June 1955, BIA, ENA.

109H.R. 3239, 84th Cong., 1st sess.

110Fred Seaton to Chair Engle, 18 July 1956, p. 1, CCF, 1801–55-Nevada-013, RG 75, NA.

111Prucha, *The Great Father*, 2:1058.

112*Statutes of the State of Nevada*, 1960, pp. 504–5.

113Leonard Hill to CIA, 20 February 1960, File 308: Indian Ranch, Tribal Records, Box 14, Sacramento Area Office, RG 75, FARC-SB.

114Dugan Hanson to Clair Engle, 24 January 1957, 7 May 1957, and CIA to Engle, July 1957, Clair Engle Papers, Boxes 2, 58, California State Archives, Sacramento; Dugan Hanson to Leonard Hill, 1 February 1960, File 308: Indian Ranch, RG 75, FARC-SB; Richard Burcell to William Ketchum, 23 August 1977, Central California Agency, Sacramento.

[115]Prucha, *The Great Father*, 2:1044–45; "Owyhee Police Exemption Order Clarified Today," *Free Press*, 8 September 1955, p. 1.

[116]*Statutes of the State of Nevada*, 1954, p. 297.

[117]"Owyhee Police Exemption Order Clarified Today," *Free Press*, 8 September 1955, p. 1.

[118]Oscar Johnny, "Law and Order on Indian Reservations and Colonies," 12 March 1970, Papers of the Nevada Indian Commission, Reno.

[119]"Nevada Indians Vote on State or Federal Law," *Wassaja*, June 1974, p. 16; Paul Walker to Benson Gibson, 20 June 1974, Nevada Indian Commission.

[120]"Ely Indian Colony, NV: Acceptance of Retrocession of Jurisdiction," *Federal Register* 53:38 (26 February 1988):5837; "Swimmer Backs Down on Shoshone Decision," *Navajo Times*, 7 April 1988, p. 4.

[121]Prucha, *The Great Father*, 2:1079–84; Fixico, *Termination and Relocation*, pp. 134–57; Tyler, *A History of Indian Policy*, pp. 151–88.

[122]Duck Valley Minutes, 14 February 1956, 21 February 1956, BIA, ENA.

[123]John Bertrand, letter, 4 April 1955, Agricultural Extension Records (unprocessed), University Archives, University of Nevada at Reno.

[124]Duck Valley Minutes, 21 April 1954, BIA, ENA.

[125]Leonard Ware, memorandum, 12 December 1958, p. 5.; Ware, memorandum, 15 May 1959, p. 5, Nevada Agency, WNRC, RG 75, NA.

[126]"Annual Indian Fandango at Yomba Reservation on Reese River Big Success," *RRR*, 30 August 1947, p. 1.

[127]"Senator McCarran Is Honored at Fandango," *Scout*, 28 October 1948, p. 1; "Senator McCarran Will Attend Annual Shoshone Fandango Here," *Scout*, 25 August 1949, p. 1; "Indian Fall Festival Set," *Battle Mountain Scout*, 11 September 1958, p. 1; "Shoshones Are Hosts at Fandango," *Scout*, 1 September 1960, p. 1.

[128]Temoke to Wayne N. Aspinall, 23 September 1959, BIA, ENA.

[129]Temoke to Alan Bible, 29 March 1960, Alan Bible Papers (AB), University of Nevada at Reno.

[130]Blossom to Bible, 29 March 1960, AB, University of Nevada at Reno.

[131]I use words and phrases of historian Robert Berkhover who argues that scholars need to produce a new "Indian-centered history" in which the Indians are the principal "actors." See his "Cultural Pluralism versus Ethnocentrism in the New Indian History," in *The American Indian and the Problem of History*, ed. Calvin Martin (New York: Oxford University Press, 1987), p. 36.

Chapter 7: Recent Western Shoshone History, 1960–1990

[1]For information about Native Americans in the post-1960 period, see the following: Russell Lawrence Barsh and Katherine Diaz-Knauf, "The Structure of Federal Aid for Indian Programs in the Decade of Prosperity, 1970–1980," *American Indian Quarterly* 8 (Winter 1984):1–35; Barsh and Diaz-Knauf, "Federal Policies, American Indian Politics and the 'New Federalism'," *American Indian Culture and Research Journal* 10 (1986):1–13; Edward J. Danziger, Jr., "A New Beginning or the Last Hurrah: American Indian Response to Reform Legislation of the 1970s," *American Indian Culture and Research Journal* 7 (1984):69–84.

[2]Mark K. Ulmer, "The Legal Origin and Nature of Indian Housing Authorities and the HUD Indian Housing Programs," *American Indian Law Review* 13:2 (1986):109, 111.

[3]Ibid.

⁴Shoshone-Paiute Business Council Minutes, 8 October 1963, p. 1, BIA, ENA.

⁵"Owyhee Enjoys Self Help Project Homes," *Free Press*, 19 July 1966, p. 1; "Valley Roundup," *NN*, 26 September 1966, p. 5.

⁶"76 New Houses Go Up in Owyhee—More on the Way," *NN*, 6 August 1982, p. 20.

⁷Beverly Crum, "Young Indian Male Suicides," unpublished paper, 1971; Crum, "Duck Valley Indian Reservation Suicides," unpublished paper, 1971. Both of these papers focus on the Duck Valley Reservation.

⁸" 'Housecleaning' for Elko's Indian Colony . . . ," *Free Press*, 2 June 1964, p. 3.

⁹"Elko," *NN*, September 1970, p. 5; "New House Being Built for 109-Year-Old Woman," *Free Press*, 11 December 1970, p. 1.

¹⁰Te-Moak Council Minutes, 10 August 1966, BIA, ENA.

¹¹"Te-Moak Housing Coordinator Named," *Free Press*, 27 June 1977, p. 1; "Te-Moak Indians Complete Office Construction Contract," *Free Press*, 18 November 1977, p. 1.

¹²"Indian Housing Chairman Tells of New Development," *Free Press*, 6 February 1981, p. 1; "Work Begins This Month on 118 Te-Moak Houses," *NN*, 9 November 1980, p. 8.

¹³"Indian Representatives Attend City Council," *Wells Progress*, 26 March 1976, pp. 1, 4.

¹⁴*Newe: A Western Shoshone History*, p. 102; conversation with Gracie Begay and Alta McQueen, 16 September 1989.

¹⁵"Housing Project Set by Ely Indian Group," *Ely Daily Times*, 10 August 1966, p. 1.

¹⁶Ely Resolution, 8 April 1969, BIA, ENA.

¹⁷"Land Transfer," *Ely Daily Times*, 16 June 1977, p. 1; conversation with Alfred Stanton, 18 September 1989.

¹⁸*Newe: A Western Shoshone History*, pp. 88–89; conversation with Benny Reilly, 18 September 1989.

¹⁹Keith Honaker et al., *Duckwater Shoshone History* (Duckwater, Nev.: Duckwater Title III Project), pp. 19–20.

²⁰Conversation with Jerry Millett, 18 September 1989.

²¹"Duckwater," *NN*, February–March 1973, p. 3.

²²"A Housing Project, a New Tribal Building and Active Programs Keep Yomba Busy," *NN*, 8 December 1980, p. 10.

²³"New Yomba Houses Ready for Occupancy," *NN*, 11 September 1981, pp. 1–2.

²⁴Ulmer, "The Legal Origin and Nature of Indian Housing Authorities," p. 113.

²⁵"BIA Reneges on Hip Loans to Battle Mountain Colony," *NN*, January 1972, p. 3.

²⁶"Battle Mountain," *NN*, February–March 1972, p. 7.

²⁷Shoshone-Paiute Business Council Minutes, 26 September 1968, BIA, ENA, p. 1.

²⁸"Duckwater," *NN*, March 1972, p. 8; South Fork Minutes, 30 January 1971, 4 November 1975, Te-Moak Tribal Minutes, ENA.

²⁹Edward Marich to Sen. Alan Bible, 29 April 1966, Alan Bible Papers, University of Nevada at Reno.

³⁰BM Leaders to Sen. Howard Cannon, 23 September 1969, Cannon Papers, Special Collections, University of Nevada at Las Vegas.

[31]Allen J. Matusow, *The Unraveling of America: A History of Liberalism in the 1960s* (New York: Harper Torchbooks, 1986), pp. 103–5.

[32]"Review M.D.T.A. Program at Owyhee," *NN*, May 1965, p. 5.

[33]"Leather Craft Project," *NN*, April 1972, p. 6.

[34]Whitney McKinney, Interview, 7 September 1989.

[35]"Elko and South Fork News," *NN*, 2 February 1968, p. 6.

[36]"Elko News," *NN*, April 1971, p. 6.

[37]Matusow, *The Unraveling of America: A History of Liberalism in the 1960s*, p. 100.

[38]Ibid., pp. 100–102; Prucha, *The Great Father*, 2:1092.

[39]Robert L. Bee, *Crosscurrents along the Colorado: The Impact of Government Policy on the Quechan Indians* (Tucson: University of Arizona Press, 1981), p. 123; "10-Year Development Program" reports, 1966, for South Fork, Ely Colony, Duckwater Reservation, Elko Colony, Yomba Reservation, Duck Valley Reservation, Battle Mountain Colony, CCF, 7277-64-Nevada, 076, RG 75, WNRC.

[40]"Dedication Ceremonies . . ." *Free Press*, 3 September 1975, p. 1; conversation with Lillian Garcia, 15 September 1989; conversation with Jerry Millett, 18 September 1989; conversation with Jack Woods, 11 September 1989; conversation with Dolores Conklin, 12 September 1989; conversation with Benny Reilly, 18 September 1989.

[41]"Elko Colony Dedication of Four Projects May 13," *NN*, 5 May 1978, p. 1.

[42]"New Day Care Center Built on Old Ely Colony Will Serve 45 Kids," *NN*, June 1983, p. 29.

[43]"Elko Corporation Formed," *NN*, August 1971, p. 3; "El Shonie in Operation," *NN*, September 1971, pp. 6–7; "Elko," *NN*, March 1972, p. 5; "El-Shonie Corp," *NN*, April 1972, p. 5.

[44]"Duck Valley Shoshone-Paiute Tribe Sees Unlimited Potential in New Farm," *NN*, 6 August 1982, p. 14; "Self-Sufficiency Reflected in New Duck Valley Shoshone-Paiute Farm," *Free Press*, 21 August 1982, p. 5.

[45]*The Economic Opportunity Act of 1964: Implications for American Indians*, pamphlet published by BIA and the Department of the Interior (Washington, D.C.: GPO, September 1964).

[46]Ibid., pp. 2–4.

[47]James T. Patterson, *America's Struggle against Poverty, 1900–1985* (Cambridge: Harvard University Press, 1986), p. 142.

[48]"ITC Programs in Owyhee," *NN*, 27 November 1967, p. 5; recorded interview with Whitney McKinney, 7 September 1989.

[49]"Elko Indian Colony News Flash," *NN*, 21 December 1966, p. 4.

[50]"Elko," *NN*, January 1972, pp. 6–7.

[51]"Elko Colony and South Fork Reservation Hold Classes," *NN*, 31 July 1967, p. 5; South Fork Minutes, 5 December 1973, p. 2, ENA.

[52]Te-Moak Council Minutes, 20 February 1974, ENA.

[53]"Duckwater News," *NN*, 1 September 1967, p. 5; "Duckwater News Notes," *NN*, 3 August 1968, p. 4.

[54]"Ely Housing," *NN*, December 1973, p. 3.

[55]Recorded interview with Whitney McKinney, 7 September 1989; conversation with Lillian Garcia, 15 September 1989; conversation with Alfred Stanton, 18 September 1989.

[56]Recorded interview with Whitney McKinney, 7 September 1989.

[57]"Elko Indian Colony News Flash," *NN*, 21 December 1966, p. 4.

[58]"Nevada Indian Youth Convention," *NN*, August 1972, pp. 1, 3.

[59]"Local Indian to Attend Conference," *Free Press*, 25 April 1973, p. 1.

[60]"Elko," *NN*, November 1972, p. 7.

[61]See the neon sign outside the Elko High School, from the mid-1970s to the present.

[62]"Seventy-Five Indians Earn Better Grades," *Navajo Times*, 28 December 1967, p. 11.

[63]"Upward Bound," *NN*, 1 September 1967, p. 6.

[64]"Indian Students in College," *NN*, 22 October 1965, p. 3; "Students Furthering Education," *Independent*, 14 December 1988, p. 8.

[65]"Five Grads Get Awards from UNR," *NN*, 1 July 1977, p. 5.

[66]"Owyhee News . . . 36 Youngsters Attending Owyhee Head Start Classes," *NN*, 25 July 1966, p. 3.

[67]"Elko Indians Have 15 Children in H.S. Program," *NN*, 25 July 1966, p. 5; "Elko Indian Colony News Flash," *NN*, 21 December 1966, p. 4.

[68]Recorded interview with Whitney McKinney, 7 September 1989.

[69]"Elko Indian Colony Given Grant to Produce Film on Elko Indians," *Independent*, 10 April 1975; "Dedication Tomorrow for Colony Buildings," *Free Press*, 12 May 1978, p. 1.

[70]"Having Trouble in School?," *Camp Chronicle* 3:6 (1973):3; conversation with Lillian Garcia, 15 September 1989.

[71]Conversation with Alfred Stanton, 18 September 1989.

[72]Conversation with Jerry Millett, 18 September 1989.

[73]"ITC Programs in Owyhee," *NN*, 27 November 1967, p. 5; "Elko," *NN*, January 1972, p. 6.

[74]*NN*, March 1964. This was the first issue of the *Native Nevadan*.

[75]Recorded interview with Whitney McKinney, 7 September 1989.

[76]"Update of the Overall Economic Development Program of the Yomba Shoshone Tribe," July 1977, Inter-Tribal Council of Nevada (ITC-N) Records, p. 12; "Down Lonely Roads," *NN*, September 1986, p. 15.

[77]Patterson, *America's Struggle against Poverty, 1900–1985*, p. 148.

[78]Conversation with Jerry Millett, 18 September 1989.

[79]Elko Colony Minutes, 11 March 1975; "Overall Economic Development Program of the Elko Indian Colony, Progress Report, 1977," p. 1, ITC-N Records, Nevada State Historical Society (NSHS), Reno, Nevada.

[80]"Owyhee News," *Free Press*, 28 July 1980, p. 9.

[81]"Officials Criticize Revenue-Sharing," *Free Press*, 12 January 1972, p. 1; conversation with Jack Woods, 11 September 1989.

[82]Conversation with Lillian Garcia, 15 September 1989; conversation with Bennie Reilley, 18 September 1989; conversation with Jerry Millett, 18 September 1989; conversation with Glenn Holley, 13 September 1989.

[83]"Duckwater Report," *NN*, 2 March 1979, p. 14.

[84]"Update of the Overall Economic Development Program of the Yomba Shoshone Tribe," July 1977, pp. 4–5, 12, ITC-N Records, NSHS; "A Housing Project, a New Tribal Building and Active Programs Keep Yomba Busy," *NN*, 8 December 1980, pp. 10–11.

[85]"South Fork Indian Action Training Program Proposal, 1977–78," ITC-N Records, NSHS.

[86]Prucha, *The Great Father*, 2:1140; Timothy La France, *Handbook of Federal Education Laws* (Boulder, Colo.: Native American Rights Fund, August 1972), pp. 25, 32.

[87]La France, *Handbook of Federal Education Laws*, p. 32.

[88]"Duckwater School Board," *NN*, August–September 1973, p. 1; "Duckwater School Opens," *NN*, December 1973, p. 6.

[89]Honaker et al., *Duckwater Shoshone History*, p. 14.

[90]"Indians, Whites at War over Indian Children," *NN*, October–November 1973, p. 1; "Duckwater School Opens," *NN*, December 1973, p. 6; "Duckwater Graduates Four," *NN*, 19 June 1975, p. 4.

[91]"All These Kids Are Learning to Speak Shoshone in Duckwater," *NN*, June 1983, pp. 32–33.

[92]Honaker et al., *Duckwater Shoshone History*.

[93]Conversation with Glenn Holley, 13 September 1989; telephone conversation with Felix Ike, 22 March 1993; Prucha, *The Great Father*, 2:1157–60.

[94]Stephen Cornell, *The Return of the Native: American Indian Political Resurgence* (New York: Oxford University Press, 1988); Stan Steiner, *The New Indians* (New York: Dell, 1968).

[95]Rodolfo Acuña, *Occupied America: A History of Chicanos*, 2nd ed. (New York: Harper and Row, 1981), p. 394; Richard Polenberg, *One Nation Divisible* (New York: Penguin Books, 1980), p. 246.

[96]Vine Deloria, Jr., " 'Congress in Its Wisdom': The Course of Indian Legislation," in *The Aggressions of Civilization: Federal Indian Policy since the 1880s*, ed. Sandra L. Cadwalader and Vine Deloria, Jr. (Philadelphia: Temple University Press, 1984), p. 118.

[97]Wilcomb E. Washburn, "Indian Policy since the 1880s," in *The Aggressions of Civilization: Federal Indian Policy since the 1880s*, ed. Cadwalader and Deloria, p. 52.

[98]"Indian Fall Festival Set," *Scout*, 11 September 1958, p. 1; "Shoshone Indian Tribe to Hold Fandango Aug. 25," *Scout*, 25 August 1960, p. 1; "Indian Colony Holds Fandango," *Scout*, 31 August 1961, p. 1.

[99]"Shoshone Tribe Denies Tie with General," *Free Press*, 24 August 1966, p. 1; "Ruby Valley Fandango Scheduled," *Free Press*, 21 August 1971, p. 1; "Ruby Valley Fandango Next Week," *Free Press*, 16 August 1973, p. 1.

[100]"Elko Colony Plans Fair-Time Fandango," *Free Press*, 30 July 1976, p. 1; "Fandango under Way at Elko Colony," *Free Press*, 4 September 1976, p. 1.

[101]"Class on Indian Dialects Set," *Free Press*, 8 July 1971, p. 1.

[102]"Shoshone Language Class," *Camp Chronicle* 3:2 (22 February 1974):5.

[103]"Elko Indian Colony Opens History Project Museum," *Free Press*, 24 August 1976, p. 1.

[104]"Duckwater Gets First-Ever Bilingual Education Grant," *NN*, 8 January 1982, p. 14; "All These Kids Are Learning to Speak Shoshone in Duckwater," *NN*, June 1983, pp. 32–33.

[105]*Newe: A Western Shoshone History*.

[106]Ibid.

[107]Cheri Robertson, *After the Drying Up of the Water* (Fallon, Nev.: The Fallon Paiute-Shoshone, 1977).

[108]Resolution to Congress, 10 January 1936, CCF, 6212–36-Carson-066, RG 75, NA.

[109]McKinney, *A History of the Shoshone-Paiutes of the Duck Valley Indian Reservation*.

[110]Honaker et al., *Duckwater Shoshone History*.

[111]"Elko Indian Colony Opens History Project Museum," *Free Press*, 24 August 1976, p. 1.

[112]"First History of Duck Valley Is Undertaken," *NN*, 6 June 1980, pp. 18, 21; "Duck Valley Shoshone-Paiutes Publish Their Own Tribal History," *NN*, April 1983, pp. 3, 30.

[113]"Vets Honored," *Free Press*, 24 November 1990, p. 8.

[114]"Shoshone Artist's Work in Special Mt. Exhibition," *NN*, 2 November 1981, p. 28; "Shoshone/Washoe Artist Jack Malotte Receives State Award," *NN*, September 1982, p. 18; "Western Shoshone Artist Jack Malotte Sets New Show in Reno," *NN*, June 1983, p. 46.

[115]"Great Basin Indian Spiritual Conference Was a Good Model," *NN*, December 1982, pp. 24, 26; "Great Basin Tribes Plan Aug. Spiritual Conference," *NN*, 6 July 1982, p. 1.

[116]"3rd Annual Great Basin Spiritual Gathering Is Set for Aug. 22–26," *NN*, August 1984, p. 20.

[117]"Festival Offers Good Time," *NN*, June 1985, p. 5.

[118]Speech by Raymond Yowell, May 1985, Duckwater, Nev.

[119]"Western Shoshone Annual Gathering, *NN*, August 1988, p. 11; "Annual Gathering," *NN*, July 1989, p. 18.

[120]"Newe Commemorate Ruby Valley Treaty," *NN*, October 1988, pp. 13, 38; "Gov. Bryan Proclaims Western Shoshone Days," *Free Press*, 29 September 1988, p. 1; "Shoshone Indians Slate Ruby 'Treaty Days' Event," *Free Press*, 21 September 1988, p. 1.

[121]Te-Moak Minutes, 31 May 1962, BIA, ENA.

[122]Te-Moak Minutes, 7 April 1965, BIA, ENA.

[123]Te-Moak Minutes, 28 October 1966, BIA, ENA.

[124]Te-Moak Minutes, 16 September 1974, BIA, ENA.

[125]Memorandum, CIA to Secretary of the Interior, 1977, BIA, ENA.

[126]"Constitution and By-Laws of the Ely Colony," 8 April 1966, BIA, ENA.

[127]Te-Moak Minutes, 8 March 1985, pp. 7–8, BIA, ENA.

[128]Prucha, *The Great Father*, 2:1193–96.

[129]Susan D. Greenbaum, "In Search of Lost Tribes: Anthropology and the Federal Acknowledgement Process," *Human Organization* 44 (Winter 1985):361–67.

[130]John G. Herron, "Death Valley—Ethnohistorical Study of the Timbisha Band of Shoshones," Branch of History, Alaska/Pacific Northwest/Western Team, Denver Service Center, September 1981; memorandum, Deputy Assistant Secretary to Assistant Secretary of the Interior, 9 February 1982, CILS.

[131]"Timba-sha Alternatives Study," Death Valley National Monuments, California-Nevada, U.S. Department of the Interior, National Park Service, December 1984.

[132]C. Hart Merriam, "Vocabularies of North American Indians, Panamint Shoshone, Death Valley, California," Papers of C. Hart Merriam, Box 37, Library of Congress, Washington, D.C.

[133]"A National Council for Western Shoshones," *NN*, January 1984, p. 14; "Western Shoshone National Council Formed to Unite Groups," *NN*, February 1984, pp. 7–8.

[134]Ray Mills to Orville R. Wilson, 10 September 1963, and William Coffey, Sr., to all Shoshone Groups, 17 October 1963, both in WBLF.

[135]By-Laws of Western Shoshone Tribe (n.p., n.d.); "Shoshones Announce Officers," *Inter-Tribal Council of Nevada, Inc., Newsletter* (September 1964):18.

[136]"Indians in Elko Meet," *Inter-Tribal Council of Nevada, Inc., Newsletter* (April 1965):24.

[137]Unpublished paper, "Western Shoshone Indian Nation," and Chief Frank Temoke, Sub Chief Oscar Johnny, etc., to Raymond Yowell, 16 October 1965, both in O'Connell Papers, Salt Lake City.

[138]Oscar Johnny to Sen. Howard Cannon, etc., 1970, Cannon Papers, Special Collections, University of Nevada at Las Vegas.

[139]*Newe Sogobia: The Western Shoshone People and Lands*, p. 1.

[140]"Dann Sisters Win in Court—Judge Says Shoshone Title Is Still Valid," *NN*, June 1983, pp. 3, 47.

[141]Elmer Rusco, "Historic Change in Western Shoshone Country: The Establishment of the Western Shoshone Council and Traditionalist Land Claims," *American Indian Quarterly* 15 (1992):337–60.

[142]"Duckwater Chairman's Many Accomplishments Outlined," *NN*, March 1984, pp. 1, 39.

[143]Rusco, "Historic Change in Western Shoshone Country," pp. 337–60.

[144]Western Shoshone National Council (WSNC) Minutes, 17 March 1984, 8 September 1984, 4 May 1985, WSNC, Duckwater, Nevada.

[145]"Shoshone Elders Bring Dignity to Highest Court," *NN*, November 1984, p. 3.

[146]WSNC Minutes, 6 April 1985, 4 May 1985, 2 June 1984, WSNC.

[147]Rusco, "Historic Change in Western Shoshone Country," pp. 337–60; "Western Shoshones Arrested," *NN*, April 1988, p. 4; "Nuclear Waste Vitally Concerns Tribes," *NN*, June 1988, p. 3.

[148]Various WSNC Minutes, 1987, 1988, WSNC.

[149]Omer C. Stewart, "The Shoshone Claims Cases," in *Irredeemable America*, ed. Imre Sutton (Albuquerque: University of New Mexico Press, 1985), pp. 187–206.

[150]*Western Shoshone National Council Newsletter* (May 1986):9.

[151]WSNC Minutes, 7 March 1987, 22 November 1986, WSNC.

[152]"Report of Claims Attorneys to Claims Committee of Western Shoshone Identifiable Group," 26 June 1974, Wilkinson, Cragun, & Barker law firm (WCB), Washington, D.C.

[153]"Western Shoshone Claims Meeting, Elko, Nevada," 23 March 1963, BIA, ENA.

[154]Ibid.

[155]William Coffey, Sr., to all Shoshone groups, 17 October 1963, Ray Mills to Orville Wilson, 10 September 1963, WBLF.

[156]"Do Shoshones Know the Truth? Tribal Member Offers Thoughts," *Nevada State Journal* (16 February 1964):12.

[157]Statement by Chief Frank Temoke, 24 April 1965, p. 3, O'Connell Papers, Salt Lake City.

[158]"Indians Discuss Future of 'Nation' in Elko Meet," *Free Press*, 26 April 1965, p. 1.

[159]For more discussion about the "traditional council," see Clemmer, "Directed Resistance to Acculturation: A Comparative Study of the Effects of Non-Indian Jurisdiction on Hopi and Western Shoshone Communities."

[160]"Shoshones Argue Claims Case," *NN*, 17 July 1965, p. 2.

[161]Robert Barker to Raymond Yowell, 27 September 1965, O'Connell Papers, Salt Lake City.

[162]"Report on Western Shoshone Claims Meetings," September–October 1965, O'Connell Papers, Salt Lake City.

[163]Ibid.

[164]Rusco, "The MX Missile and Western Shoshone Land Claims," p. 49.

[165]Transcription of the movie *Broken Treaty at Battle Mountain*, Joel Freedman, producer (New York: Cinnamon Productions, 1975).

[166]18 Stat. 690.

[167]*Broken Treaty at Battle Mountain.*

[168]Richard O. Clemmer, "Pine Nuts, Cattle, and the Ely Chain: Rip-off Resource Replacement vs. Homeostatic Equilibrium," in *Selected Papers from the 14th Great Basin Anthropological Conference*, ed. Tuohy, pp. 61–75.

[169]*Newe Sogobia: The Western Shoshone People and Lands*, pp. 22–23.

[170]*U.S. Law Week*, 19 February 1985, p. 4171; Rusco, "The MX Missile and Western Shoshone Land Claims," p. 49.

[171]*Newe Sogobia: The Western Shoshone People and Lands*, pp. 1, 18.

[172]Ibid.

[173]"Te-Moaks Fire All Attorneys," *NN*, 4 February 1977, p. 13.

[174]*Newe Sogobia: The Western Shoshone People and Lands*, p. 18.

[175]"Shoshone Yowell Takes Issue with Barker," *NN*, 2 September 1977, p. 3.

[176]*Newe Sogobia: The Western Shoshone People and Lands*, pp. 19, 24.

[177]"85 People Testified at Western Shoshone Hearing of Record-Testimony of Congress," *NN*, 1 August 1980, pp. 16–17.

[178]Rusco, "Historic Change in Western Shoshone Country," pp. 337–60.

[179]Prucha, *The Great Father*, 2:1144–45.

[180]Rusco, "The MX Missile and Western Shoshone Land Claims," pp. 45–54; "Western Shoshone Oppose the Location of MX Missile System," *NN*, 2 November 1979, p. 1.

[181]See citations in note 180 above; Duckwater Minutes, 9 October 1974, ENA.

[182]"Is Sagebrush Rebellion a Threat to Nevada Indians?" *NN*, 7 December 1979, p. 7; "Sagebrush Rebellion: The Rape of the West," *NN*, 2 November 1979.

[183]"Dann Sisters Win in Court—Judge Says Shoshone Title Is Still Valid," *NN*, June 1983, pp. 3, 47; *U.S. vs. Mary Dann and Carrie Dann*, 19 May 1983, U.S. Court of Appeals for the Ninth Circuit.

[184]*105 Supreme Court Reporter*, 1058–68; "Court Bars Shoshone Claim," *Reno Gazette-Journal*, 21 February 1985, p. 1A; "U.S. Supreme Court Rules against Western Shoshone on Land Issue," *NN*, March 1985, pp. 3, 38.

[185]*Western Shoshone Newsletter* (Fall 1986), WSNC.

[186]"Vucanovich Considers Shoshone Money Bill," *NN*, August 1989, pp. 3, 42; "Vucanovich Introduces Shoshone Money Bill," *NN*, October 1898, p. 4; "Testimonies before the House of Representatives, Interior and Insular Affairs Committee on H.R. 3897," 30 April 1992, Te-Moak Tribe of Western Shoshone files, Elko, Nevada.

[187]"Shoshone Agree to Agree: Land and Money," *NN*, April 1989, p. 7.

[188]"Dann's Statement Eloquent," *NN*, February 1989, p. 38. In late 1992 the BLM started rounding up Carrie and Mary Dann's cattle, using the argument the sisters were illegally grazing their stock on federal land. The Western Shoshone claims case remains unresolved as of September 1993. See "BLM suspends roundup after 269 horses caught," *Free Press*, 25 November 1992, p. 2.

[189]"New Film Hits Hard on Shoshone Treaty Rights," *NN*, November 1989, pp. 4, 32.

Epilogue

[1]Helen S. Carlson, *Nevada Place Names: A Geographical Dictionary* (Reno: University of Nevada Press, 1974), pp. 148, 214, 233; Coca-Cola™ advertisement, *Nevada State Journal*, 6 March 1940, p. 3.

[2]"Election of Officers," *Independent*, 28 June 1873, p. 3; "Important Order of Red Man Organized," *Independent*, 15 February 1917, p. 1; "Big Annual Rabbit Hunt Announced," *Ely Record*, 21 December 1928, p. 9.

BIBLIOGRAPHY

Articles

Barsh, Russell, and Katherine Diaz-Knauf. "Federal Policies, American Indian Politics and the 'New Federalism'." *American Indian Culture and Research Journal* 10 (1986):1–13.

————. "The Structure of Federal Aid for Indian Programs in the Decade of Prosperity, 1970–1980." *American Indian Quarterly* 8 (Winter 1984):1–35.

Bromert, Roger. "The Sioux and the Indian-CCC." *South Dakota History* 8 (Fall 1978):340–56.

Bruner, Edward M. "Obituary on Julian H. Steward." *Journal of the Steward Anthropological Society* 3 (Spring 1972):108–10.

Christian, Howard A. "Open Hand and Mailed Fist: Mormon-Indian Relations in Utah, 1847–52." *Utah Historical Quarterly* 46 (Summer 1978):216–35.

Clemmer, Richard O. "Differential Leadership Patterns in Early Twentieth-Century Great Basin Societies." *Journal of California and Great Basin Anthropology* 11 (1989):35–49.

————. "Hopis, Western Shoshones and Southern Utes: Three Different Responses to the Indian Reorganization Act of 1934." *American Indian Culture and Research Journal* 10:2 (1986):15–40.

————. "Pine Nuts, Cattle, and the Ely Chain: Rip-off Resource Replacement vs. Homeostatic Equilibrium." In *Selected Papers from the 14th Great Basin Anthropological Conference,* ed. Donald Tuohy, pp. 61–75. Socorro, N.M.: Balena Press, 1978.

————. "The Piñon-Pine: Old Ally or New Pest? Western Shoshone Indians vs. the Bureau of Land Management in Nevada." *Environmental Review* 9 (1985):131–49.

Coates, Lawrence G. "Brigham Young and Mormon Indian Policies: The Formative Period, 1836–1859." *Brigham Young University Studies* 18 (Spring 1978):428–52.

Crum, Steven. "The Ruby Valley Indian Reservation of Northeastern Nevada: 'Six Miles Square'." *Nevada Historical Society Quarterly* 30 (Spring 1987):1–18.

————. "The Western Shoshone People and Their Attachment to the Land: A Twentieth-Century Perspective." *Nevada Public Affairs Review* 2 (1987):15–18.

223

———. "The 'White Pine War' of 1875: A Case of White Hysteria." *Utah Historical Quarterly* 59 (Summer 1991):286–99.

Danziger, Edmund, Jr. "A New Beginning or the Last Hurrah: American Indian Response to Reform Legislation of the 1970s." *American Indian Culture and Research Journal* 7 (1984):69–84.

Darrough, Hicks K. "All Western Shoshones Are Urged to Make Part in Solution." *Native Nevadan* 19 (November 1982):19.

Downes, Randolph C. "A Crusade for Indian Reform 1922–1934." *The Mississippi Valley Historical Review* 32 (December 1945):331–54.

Ellis, Richard N. "Indians of Ibapah in Revolt: Goshutes, the Draft and the Indian Bureau, 1917–1919." *Nevada Historical Society Quarterly* 19 (Fall 1976):163–70.

"George LaVatta Wins Recognition as an Outstanding Indian." *Indians at Work* 9 (October 1941):14–15.

Gower, Calvin W. "The CCC Indian Division: Aid for Depressed Americans, 1933–1942." *Minnesota History* 43 (1972):3–13.

Green, Elizabeth. "Indian Minorities under the American New Deal." *Pacific Affairs* 8 (December 1935): 420–27.

"Indians of Nevada Speak for Themselves." *Indians at Work* 9 (December 1941):13.

"In the Middle of Everything." *Indians at Work* 4 (15 February 1937):21.

Kelly, Lawrence C. "Anthropology and Anthropologists in the Indian New Deal." *History of the Behavioral Sciences* 16 (January 1980):6–24.

———. "The Indian Reorganization Act: The Dream and the Reality." *Pacific Historical Review* 46 (August 1975):291–317.

Koppes, Clayton R. "From New Deal to Termination: Liberal Indian Policy, 1933–1953." *Pacific Hisitorical Review* 46 (November 1977):543–66.

Kunitz, Stephen J. "The Social Philosophy of John Collier." *Ethnohistory* 18 (Summer 1971):213–29.

Lambert, C. Roger. "The Drought Cattle Purchase, 1934–1935: Problems and Complaints." *Agricultural History* 45 (April 1971):85–95.

Mander, Jerry. "This Is Not Air Force Land." *Western Shoshone Sacred Land Association* 1 (April 1980):2.

Manners, Robert A. "Julian Haynes Steward, 1902–1972." *American Anthropologist* 75 (June 1973):886–903.

Mekeel, Scudder. "An Appraisal of the Indian Reorganization Act." *American Anthropologist* 46 (1944):201–17.

O'Neil, Floyd A., and Stanford Layton. "Of Pride and Politics: Brigham Young as Indian Superitendent." *Utah Historical Quarterly* 46 (Summer 1978):236–50.

Parman, Donald L. "The Indian and the Civilian Conservation Corps." *Pacific Historical Review* 40 (February 1971):39–56.

Patterson, Edna B. "Mary Hall: Western Shoshone Basketmaker." *Quarterly: Northeastern Nevada Historical Society* 85:4 (Fall 1985):103–15.

Philp, Kenneth. "Herbert Hoover's New Era: A False Dawn for the American Indian, 1929–1932." *The Rocky Mountain Social Science Journal* 9 (April 1972):54–60.

———. "John Collier and the Crusade to Protect Indian Religious Freedom, 1920–1926." *Journal of Ethnic Studies* 1 (Spring 1973):22–38.

———. "The New Deal and Alaskan Natives, 1936–1945." *Pacific Historical Review* 50 (August 1981):309–27.

Rusco, Elmer R. "Historic Change in Western Shoshone Country: The Establishment of the Western Shoshone National Council and Traditionalist Land Claims." *American Indian Quarterly* (Summer 1992):337–60.

———. "The MX Missile and the Western Shoshone Land Claims." *Nevada Public Affairs Review* 2 (1982):45–54.

———. "The Organization of the Te-Moak Bands of Western Shoshones." *Nevada Historical Society Quarterly* 25 (Fall 1982):175–96.

———. "Purchasing Lands for Nevada Indian Colonies, 1916–1917." *Nevada Historical Society Quarterly* 32 (Spring 1989):1, 3, 17–19.

Sennett-Walker, Beth. "The Panamint Basketry of Scotty's Castle." *American Indian Basketry* 5 (n.d.):13–17.

Slater, Eva. "Panamint Shoshone Basketry, 1920–1940." *American Indian Art Magazine* (Winter 1985):58–63.

Smith, Michael T. "The Wheeler-Howard Act of 1934: The Indian New Deal." *Journal of the West* 10 (July 1971):521–34.

Stevens, Alden. "Whither the American Indian?" *Survey Graphic* 29 (March 1940):168–74.

Stewart, Omer C. "Temoke Band of Shoshone and the Oasis Concept." *Nevada Historical Society Quarterly* 23 (Winter 1980):246–61.

Taylor, Graham D. "Anthropologists, Reformers, and the Indian New Deal." *Prologue* 7 (Fall 1975):151–62.

———. "The Tribal Alternative to Bureaucracy: The Indian's New Deal, 1933–1945." *Journal of the West* 13 (January 1974):128–42.

Ulmer, Mark K. "The Legal Origin and Nature of Indian Housing Authorities and the HUD Indian Housing Programs." *American Indian Law Review* 13 (1986):109–174.

"Various Tribes Pass Resolution Affirming Faith in Indian Reorganization Act." *Indians at Work* 8 (1940):24.

Weeks, Charles J. "The Eastern Cherokee and the New Deal." *North Carolina Historical Review* 53 (July 1976):302–19.

"Western Shoshone Girls Rid Reservation of 2,000 Bushels of Mormon Crickets." *Indians at Work* 6 (November 1938):21.

"Western Shoshone Organizes Sports Program." *Indians at Work* (1 March 1938):34.

"A Woman Superintendent." *Indians at Work* 3 (1 December 1935):36.

Wood, David L. "Gosiute-Shoshone Draft Resistance, 1917–18." *Utah Historical Quarterly* 49 (Spring 1981):173–88.

Wright, Peter M. "John Collier and the Oklahoma Indian Welfare Act of 1936." *The Chronicles of Oklahoma* 50 (Summer 1972):347–71.

Books

Bee, Robert L. *Crosscurrents along the Colorado: The Impact of Government Policy on the Quechan Indians*. Tucson: University of Arizona Press, 1981.

Bernstein, Alison R. *American Indians and World War II: Toward a New Era in Indian Affairs*. Norman: University of Oklahoma Press, 1991.

Bowers, Martha H., and Muessig, Hans. *History of Central Nevada: An Overview of the Battle Mountain District*. Cultural Resource Series 4. Reno: Nevada State Office of the Bureau of Land Management, 1982.

Burt, Larry. *Tribalism in Crisis*. Albuquerque: University of New Mexico Press, 1982.

Collier, John. *From Every Zenith*. Denver: Sage Books, 1963.

Corless, Hank. *The Weiser Indians: Shoshoni Peacemakers*. Salt Lake City: University of Utah Press, 1990.

Cornell, Stephen. *The Return of the Native: American Indian Political Resurgence*. New York: Oxford University Press, 1988.

Crum, Beverly. *How To Read and Write Shoshoni: A Book of Spelling Lessons, Readings, and Glossary for Shoshoni Speakers*. Salt Lake City, Privately printed, 1987.

d'Azevedo, Warren L., ed. *Handbook of North American Indians*. Vol. 11, *Great Basin*. Washington, D.C.: Smithsonian Institution, 1986.

Fixico, Donald L. *Termination and Relocation: Federal Indian Policy, 1945–1960*. Albuquerque: University of New Mexico Press, 1986.

Fowler, Don D., and Fowler, Catherine S. (eds.). *Anthropology of the Numa*. Washington, D.C.: Smithsonian Institution Press, 1971.

Gibson, Arrell Morgan. *The American Indian: Prehistory to the Present*. Lexington, Mass.: D. C. Heath, 1980.

Gibson, Benson. *Survivors of the Bannock War*. Duck Valley Indian Reservation, Owyhee, Nev., Privately printed, 1990.

Harris, Jack S. "The White Knife Shoshoni of Nevada." In *Acculturation in Seven American Indian Tribes*, ed. Ralph Linton, pp. 39–116. New York: D. Appleton-Century, 1940.

Hauptman, Laurence M. *The Iroquois and the New Deal*. Syracuse: Syracuse University Press, 1981.

Honaker, Keith, et al. *Duckwater Shoshone History*. Duckwater Shoshone Tribe, Duckwater, Nev., 1986.

James, Steven R., ed. *Prehistory, Ethnohistory, and History of Eastern Nevada: A Cultural Resources Summary of the Elko and Ely Districts*. Cultural Resource Series 3. Reno: Nevada State Office of the Bureau of Land Management, 1982.

Leuchtenburg, William E. *Franklin D. Roosevelt and the New Deal, 1932–1940*. New York: Harper and Row, 1963.

Madsen, Brigham D. *The Northern Shoshoni*. Caldwell, Idaho: Caxton Printers, Ltd., 1980.

———. *The Shoshone Frontier and the Bear River Massacre*. Salt Lake City: University of Utah Press, 1985.

Martin, Calvin, ed. *The American Indian and the Problem of History*. New York: Oxford University Press, 1987.

Matusow, Allen J. *The Unraveling of America: A History of Liberalism in the 1960s*. New York: Harper Torchbooks, 1986.

McKinney, Whitney. *A History of the Shoshone-Paiutes of the Duck Valley Indian Reservation*. Salt Lake City: Howe Brothers, 1983.

Newe: A Western Shoshone History. Reno: Inter-Tribal Council of Nevada, 1976.

Newe Sogobia: The Western Shoshone People and the Lands. Battle Mountain, Nev.: Western Shoshone Sacred Lands Association, 1982.

Parman, Donald L. *The Navajos and the New Deal*. New Haven: Yale University Press, 1976.

Patterson, Edna B., Louise A. Ulph, and Victor Goodwin. *Nevada's Northeast Frontier*. Sparks, Nev.: Western Printing and Publishing, 1969.

Patterson, James T. *America's Struggle against Poverty, 1900–1985*. Cambridge: Harvard University Press, 1986.

Philp, Kenneth R. *John Collier's Crusade for Indian Reform, 1920–1954*. Tucson: University of Arizona Press, 1977.

Prucha, Francis Paul. *American Indian Policy in Crisis: Christian Reformers and the Indian, 1865–1900*. Norman: University of Oklahoma Press, 1976.
————. *The Great Father*. Lincoln: University of Nebraska Press, 1986.
Robertson, Cheri. *After the Drying of the Water*. Fallon-Paiute Shoshone Tribe. Fallon, Nev.: Duck Down Press, 1977.
Schlesinger, Arthur M., Jr. *The Coming of the New Deal*. Boston: Houghton Mifflin, 1958.
Steward, Julian H. *Basin-Plateau Aboriginal Sociopolitical Groups*. Smithsonian Institution, Bureau of American Ethnology, Bulletin 120. Washington, D.C.: Government Printing Office, 1938.
————. *Culture Element Distributions: XIII, Nevada Shoshone*. Anthropological Records 4. Berkeley and Los Angeles: University of California Press, 1941.
Stewart, Omer C. "The Western Shoshone of Nevada and the U.S. Government, 1863–1950." In *Selected Papers from the 14th Great Basin Anthropological Conference*, ed. Donald R. Tuohy, pp. 78–114. Socorro, N.M.: Ballena Press, 1974.
Szasz, Margaret Connell. *Education and the American Indian: The Road to Self-Determination since 1928*. 2nd ed. Albuquerque: University of New Mexico Press, 1977.
Taylor, Graham D. *The New Deal and American Indian Tribalism: The Administration of the Indian Reorganization Act, 1934–35*. Lincoln: University of Nebraska Press, 1980.
Thorpe, Dagmar. *Newe Sogobia: The Western Shoshone People and Lands*. Battle Mountain, Nev.: Western Shoshone Sacred Lands Association, 1982.
Tyler, S. Lyman. *A History of Indian Policy*. Washington, D.C.: Government Printing Office, 1973.
Utley, Robert. *The Indian Frontier of the American West, 1846–1890*. Albuquerque: University of New Mexico Press, 1984.
Woodruff, J. Dean, and Glenn V. Bird. *Ernest L. Wilkinson: Indian Advocate and University President*. Provo, Utah: Privately published, n.d.

Theses and Dissertations

Bromert, Roger. "The Sioux and the Indian New Deal, 1933–1944." Ph.D. diss., University of Toledo, 1980.
Clemmer, Richard O. "Directed Resistance to Acculturation: A Comparative Study of the Effects of Non-Indian Jurisdiction on Hopi and Western Shoshone Communities." Ph.D. diss., University of Illinois at Urbana-Champaign.
Crum, Steven. "The Western Shoshone and the Indian New Deal." Ph.D. diss., University of Utah, 1983.
Godfrey, Anthony. "Congressional-Indian Politics: Senate Survey of Conditions among the Indians of the United States." Ph.D. diss., University of Utah, 1985.
Hamlin, Alfred Stree. "The Federal Policy in Relation to the Nevada Indians." M.A. thesis, University of California at Berkeley, 1908.
Rosenthal, Harvey D. "Their Day in Court: A History of the Indian Claims Commission." Ph.D. diss., Kent State University, 1976.
Schrader, Robert Fay. "The Indian Arts and Crafts Board: An Aspect of New Deal Indian Policy." Ph.D. diss., Marquette University, 1981.
Wall, C. Leon. "History of Indian Education in Nevada from 1861 to 1951." M.A. thesis, University of Nevada at Reno, 1952.

Interviews and Informal Conversations

Adamson, Irene (Shoshone). Battle Mountain, Nev., 24 August 1993.
Allison, Marie (Shoshone). Fallon, Nev., 5 September 1991.
Begay, Gracie, and Alta McQueen (Shoshones). Wells, Nev., 16 September 1989.
Conklin, Delores (Shoshone). Battle Mountain, Nev., 4 September 1991.
Decker, Bud (Shoshone). Battle Mountain, Nev., 24 August 1982.
Esteves, Pauline (Shoshone). Death Valley, Calif., 24 August 1989.
Garcia, Lillian (Shoshone). Elko, Nev., 15 September 1989.
Holley, Glenn (Shoshone). Battle Mountain, Nev., 13 September 1989, 21 August 1991.
Ike, Felix (Shoshone). Elko, Nev., 22 March 1993.
LaVatta, George P. (Shoshone). Portland, Ore., 28 October 1981.
Main, Lew (Shoshone). Battle Mountain, Nev., 21 August 1991.
Millett, Jerry (Shoshone). Duckwater, Nev., 18 September 1989.
Pabawena, Rosie (Shoshone). Wells, Nev., 29 August 1979. Interviewed by Beverly Crum (Shoshone).
Reilly, Bennie (Shoshone). Ely, Nev., 18 September 1989.
Sam, Brownie (Shoshone). Elko, Nev., 28 August 1982.
Sam, Nelson (Shoshone). Elko, Nev., 3 September 1991.
Stanton, Alfred (Shoshone). Ely, Nev., 18 September 1991.
Tybo, Bert (Shoshone). Owyhee, Nev., August 1982.
Weeks, Pansy (Shoshone). Fallon, Nev., 5 September 1991.
Williams, Saggie, and Gladys Williams (Shoshones). Battle Mountain, Nev., 26 August 1990.
Woods, Jack (Shoshone). Elko, Nev., 11 Spetember 1989.

Published Government Documents

Bercaw, Louise O., A. M. Hannay, and Esther M. Colvin. *Bibliography on Land Settlement*. Agriculture Department Miscellaneous Publication 172. Washington, D.C.: Government Printing Office, 1934.
Executive Orders Relating to Indian Reservations, from May 14, 1855, to July 1, 1912. Washington, D.C.: Government Printing Office, 1912.
Executive Orders Relating to Indian Reservations, from July 1, 1912, to July 1, 1922. Washington, D.C.: Government Printing Office, 1922.
National Resources Board. *Indian Land Tenure, Economic Status, and Populations Trends of the Report on Land Planning*. Part 10. Washington, D.C.: Government Printing Office, 1935.
U.S. Congress. House. *Relief of Needy Indians*. Hearings before the Committee on Indian Affairs, 66th Cong., 1st sess., Part 28, 1940.
———. House. *Wheeler-Howard Act—Exempt Certain Indians*. Hearings before the Committee on Indian Affairs, 76th Cong., 1st sess., 1940.
———. Joint Hearing. *Termination of Federal Supervision over Certain Tribes of Indians*. Joint Hearings before the Subcommittee of the Committee on Interior and Insular Affairs, 83rd Cong., 2nd sess., Part 10, 1954.
———. Senate. *Survey of Conditions of the Indians in the United States*. Hearings before a Subcommittee of the Committee on Indian Affairs, 72nd Cong., 1st sess., Part 28, 1934.
U.S. Department of the Interior. Office of Indian Affairs. *Annual Report of the Commissioner of Indian Affairs to the Secretary of the Department of the*

Interior, for the Years 1850–1920. Washington, D.C.: Government Printing Office, various years.

———. Office of Indian Affairs. *Annual Report of the Commissioner of Indian Affairs to the Secretary of the Department of the Interior, for the Fiscal Year Ended 30 June 1874.* "Report of J. W. Powell and G. W. Ingalls," 18 December 1873. Washington, D.C.: Government Printing Office, 1874.

———. Office of Indian Affairs. *Constitution and By-Laws of the Shoshone-Paiute Tribes of the Duck Valley Reservation, Idaho and Nevada.* August 1936. Washington, D.C.: Government Printing Office, 1936.

———. Office of Indian Affairs. *Corporate Charter of the Shoshone-Paiute Tribes of the Duck Valley Reservation, Idaho and Nevada.* 22 August 1936. Washington, D.C.: Government Printing Office, 1936.

———. Office of Indian Affairs. *Constitution and By-Laws of the Te-Moak Bands of Western Shoshone Indians, Nevada.* 24 August 1938. Washington, D.C.: Government Printing Office, 1938.

———. Office of Indian Affairs. *Corporate Charter of the Te-Moak Bands of Western Shoshone Indians of the State of Nevada.* 12 December 1938. Washington, D.C.: Government Printing Office, 1938.

———. Office of Indian Affairs. *Constitution and By-Laws of the Yomba Shoshone Tribe of the Yomba Reservation, Nevada.* 22 December 1939. Washington, D.C.: Government Printing Office, 1940.

———. Office of Indian Affairs. *Corporate Charter of the Yomba Shoshone Tribe of the Yomba Reservation, Nevada.* 22 December 1939. Washington, D.C.: Government Printing Office, 1940.

———. Office of Indian Affairs. *Constitution and By-Laws of the Duckwater Shoshone Tribe of the Duckwater Reservation, Nevada.* 28 November 1940. Washington, D.C.: Government Printing Office, 1941.

———. Office of Indian Affairs. *Corporate Charter of the Duckwater Shoshone Tribe of the Duckwater Reservation, Nevada.* 30 November 1940. Washington, D.C.: Government Printing Office, 1941.

U.S. Department of War. *The War of the Rebellion: A Compilation of the Official Records of the Union and Confederate Armies.* Washington, D.C.: Government Printing Office, 1897.

U.S. Statutes at Large. Vol. 18, pt. 3 (December 1873–March 1875). "Treaty with Western Bands of Shoshonee Indians." 1 October 1863.

U.S. Statutes at Large. Vol. 36, pt. 1 (March 1909–March 1911). Chap. 431. 25 June 1910.

U.S. Statutes at Large. Vol. 48, pt. l (March 1933–June 1934). Chap. 576. 18 June 1934. *U.S. Statutes at Large.* Vol. 60, pt. 1 (1946). Chap. 959. 13 August 1946.

Unpublished Government Documents

Federal Archives and Records Center, Laguna Niguel, Calif.
Records of the Phoenix Area Office, Bureau of Indian Affairs, Record Group 75.
Federal Archives and Records Center, San Bruno, Calif.
Records of the Farmer-in-Charge of the Western Shoshone Indians, Nevada, Record Group 75.
Records of the Western Shoshone Agency and School, 1878–1952, Record Group 75.
Records of the Reno Indian Agency, 1913–1925, Record Group 75.
Records of the Carson Indian Agency, 1900–1925, Record Group 75.

Records of the Nevada Indian Agency, post-1952, Record Group 75.
Federal Archives and Records Center, Seattle, Wash.
  Records of the Portland Area Office, Bureau of Indian Affairs, Record Group
  75.
National Archives, Washington, D.C.
  Records of the Bureau of Indian Affairs, Record Group 75
    Central Classified Files
    Records of the Irrigation Division
    Records of the Inspection Division
    Records of the Construction Division
    Records of the Civilian Conservation Corps, Indian Division
    Records of the Rehabilitation Division
    Records of the Indian Organization Division
    Office File of John Collier
    Letters Received by the Office of Indian Affairs, 1824–1880. Microcopy No.
      234, Rolls 538–45 (Nevada Superintendency); Rolls 897–901 (Utah Super-
      intendency).
    Report of Inspection of the Field Jurisdictions of the Office of Indian
      Affairs, 1873–1900. Microcopy No. 1070, Roll 56 (Western Shoshoni).
    Superintendents' Annual Narrative and Statistical Reports from Field Juris-
      dictions of the Bureau of Indian Affairs, 1907–1938. Microcopy No.
      1011, Rolls 167–68 (Western Shoshoni), Rolls 9–11 (Carson School).
  Old Military Records, Record Group 398
    Records of Camp Ruby, Nevada
    Returns from U.S. Military Posts, 1800–1916. Microcopy 617, Roll 439,
      Fort Halleck (June 1867–December 1875).

Manuscript Collections

Badt, Milton B. "An Interview with Milton Badt." NC217, Oral History, Depart-
  ment of Special Collections, Getchell Library, University of Nevada, Reno.
Bible, Alan, MSS. Special Collections, University of Nevada, Reno.
Cannon, Howard, MSS. Special Collections, University of Nevada, Las Vegas.
Collier, John, MSS. Sterling Library, Yale University, New Haven, Conn. Micro-
  film edition, ed. Andrew M. Patterson and Maureen Brodoff. Sanford, N.C.:
  Microfilming Corp. of America, 1980.
Creel, Lorenzo, MSS. Special Collections, University of Nevada-Reno.
Engle, Clair, MSS. California State Archives, Sacramento.
Oddie, Tasker, MSS. Nevada Historical Society, Reno.
Pittman, Key, MSS. Library of Congress, Washington, D.C.
Steward, Julian H., MSS. University Archives, University of Illinois at Urbana-
  Champaign.

Newspapers

Battle Mountain Bugle (Battle Mountain, Nev.)
Battle Mountain Scout (Scout) (Battle Mountain, Nev.)
Central Nevadan (Battle Mountain, Nev.)
Elko Daily Free Press (Free Press) (Elko, Nev.)
Elko Independent (Independent) (Elko, Nev.)
Ely Record (Ely, Nev.)
Humboldt Star (Winnemucca, Nev.)

Manhattan Post (Manhattan, Nev.)
Native Nevadan (NN) (Reno, Nev.)
Reese River Reveille (RRR) (Austin, Nev.)
Salt Lake Tribune (Salt Lake City, Utah)
White Pine News (Ely, Nev.)

INDEX

Aadneson, Grand, 131
Acculturation studies, 116
Adams, Richard C., 81
Adams, Tom, 111
Adams–Onis Treaty (1819), 12
Agricultural Adjustment Act (AAA), 89
Agriculture, Shoshone: antipoverty programs and, 157; cooperative extension and termination policy, 146; establishment of reservations and, 36–37; on Duck Valley Reservation from 1880 to 1933, 52–54; practice of in 1850s and 1860s, 21–22, 30–31
Alcohol and alcoholism, 41, 55–56
American Baptist Home Mission Society, 74
American Indian Defense Association, 92
American Indian Religious Freedom Act (1978), 164
Annuity payments, 31, 38–40, 44, 82
Antelope, Bill, 83
Anthropology, study of, 115–16
Antipoverty programs (1960–1990), 149–63
Archuleta, Nick, 157
Area Redevelopment Administration (ARA), 155–56
Arts, 167. See also Basketweaving; Crafts
Asbury, Calvin, 44, 45–46, 72, 82
Assimilation, government policy of: and Duck Valley Reservation, 43, 51–57; and nonreservation Shoshone, 67–75; termination policy and, 146–47
Austin, Nevada, 30

Badt, Milton, 103, 114–15, 126, 132
Bancroft, Hubert Howe, 12
Band organizations, 18–19, 35. See also

Paddy Cap Bands; Te-Moak Bands;
White knife (Tosa wihi) Shoshones
Bannock War of 1878, 29, 47
Baring, Sen. Walter, 137
Barker, Robert, 176, 178
Barnes, A. J., 37
Basketweaving, 8–9, 52, 63, 116
Battle Mountain Colony: creation of by presidential executive order, 73–74; and formation of Te-Moak Bands under IRA, 104; housing assistance programs at, 153–54; Long Range Program and, 136; New Deal assistance to, 91; termination policy and, 140–43, 146–47
Beeler, Dick, 60, 77
Benson, Todd, vii
Berkhofer, Robert, vii-viii
Bible, Alan, 137
Biddle, James, 27
Bidwell-Bartleson party of 1841, 14
Bilingual Education Act of 1968, 164
Billie, John, 121
Birchum, Bobby, 121
Birchum, Jim, 78
Birchum, Richard, 111, 122, 126, 130
Bird, Doc, 72
Blackeye, Chief, 60, 111
Blossom, Clancy, 177
Blossom, Clarence and Renee, 132, 141, 147
Blossom, Doc, 130
Blossom, Ida, 130
Blossom, Leslie, 169, 180
Boarding schools, 54–55
Bob, Captain, 60, 62
Bobb, James, 110
Bobb, Willie, 109, 110

Bobo, Wesley, 141
Boulden, Lottie, 104, 114
Bowler, Alida, 89, 92–93, 94–95, 97, 98, 103, 105, 108, 111
Brady, George, 100
Brady, Leah, 159
Brady, LeRoy, 178
Brigham, Charlie, 121
Brotherhood of North American Indians, 81
Browning, Jacob, 127
Bryden, W. S., 69
Buck, Captain (band leader in Ruby Valley), 22–23, 27, 36, 37, 48, 49, 55
Buffalo Horn, 29
Bullcreek, Bert, 123
Bureau of Indian Affairs (BIA): Applied Anthropology Unit (AAU), 115–16; Battle Mountain Colony and termination policy, 140–41; creation of in 1824, 19; Federal Acknowledgement Program and recognition of tribes, 170; land claims controversy and ICC, 179; management of Ruby Valley reservation in 1850s, 22; native leaders on Duck Valley Reservation, 48–49; New Deal programs, 90–91; Operation Relocation, 145–46; policy of neglect toward nonreservation Shoshone, 59; refusal of Ruby Valley Shoshone to move to Duck Valley, 46; reservation policy in 1860s and 1870s, 33–41; self-determination program, 149–63; tribal constitutions, by-laws, and charters, 112. *See also* Federal government
Bureau of Land Management (BLM), 98
Butterfield Overland mail company, 24
Byers, Willie and Iola, 165

California gold rush, 17–18
Call, B. C., 131
Calloway, Colin, ix
Campbell, Franklin, 27, 32
Carlin Farms Reservation, 36–37
Carlisle Indian School (Pennsylvania), 50, 55, 67
Carpenter, W. S., 39
Carson, Willie and Josie, 67
Carson Agency (Indian Bureau), 116
Cattle industry, 30, 31, 50–51, 53–54
Central Pacific Railroad, 30
Central Route, 23–24
Charles, Frances, 55
Charles, Winona, 102
Charley, Captain, 48, 49
Charley, Jim, 121
Charley, Wixon, 110
Church of Jesus Christ of Latter-day Saints, 19

Citizenship, U.S., 69
Civil War, 24
Civil Works Administration (CWA), 91
Civilian Conservation Corps (CCC), 86–89
Clifford, Dave (Kawich), 64, 65, 109
Collier, John, 85, 101, 115, 117
Collins, Frank and Truman, 64
"Colony" program, 73–75
Community Action Programs (CAP), 157
Community centers, 156
Comprehensive Employment and Training Act (CETA), 161
Connor, Patrick E., 23
Constitutions, tribal, 50, 112
Couchum, John, 84
Courtright, Bert, 101, 134, 135
Courts, Sam, 60
Coyote, in folklore, 1, 10, 11–12
Coyote, Fred, 167
Cradle boards, 9
Crafts, 52. *See also* Arts; Basketweaving
Creation myth, 1
Creel, Lorenzo, 73
Criminal law, 48, 69–70, 145
Crum, Beverly, 164
Crum, Dick and Emma, viii
Crum, Earl, 121
Crum, Jim, viii
Cultural pluralism, government policy of, 43, 86, 103, 164
Culture, Shoshone: active efforts to preserve, viii; and assimilation policy on Duck Valley Reservation, 51–57; Bureau of Indian Affairs in 1930s and, 116–17; continuation of traditions in 1860s and 1870s, 40–41; in early period of contact, 14–15; maintenance of native ways in present, 187; resurgence of in post-1960s period, 163–68; and Shoshone-Paiute Business Council, 101
Curran, Frank, 68
Cushing Academy, 68

Dances, 4–5, 8. *See also* Fandangos
Dann, Carrie, 167, 176–77, 179–80
Dann, Dewey, 128, 129
Dann, Mary, 179–80
Darrough, James, 64, 109
Davies, Benjamin, 22
Dawes Act of 1887, 44–46, 72, 185
Death Valley National Monument, 98
Death Valley Shoshones, 98, 113, 170–72
Decker, Bud, 64, 109, 110
Deere, Phillip, 167
Deforestation, 30
Delano, Charles, 33–34

Department of Housing and Urban Development (HUD), 150, 152–53
Dick, Sylvia, 181
Diet. *See* Foods; Natural resources
Dixon, George, 141
Dixon, Harry, 60, 77–78
Dorsey, Willie and Nora, 48
Doty, James, 25
Douglas, Henry, 33
Downing, Roger, 160
Draft, military, 71, 120–23
Duck Valley Housing Authority, 150
Duck Valley Reservation: acceptance of site by Shoshone groups, 37–38; additions to under IRA, 96; and assimilation policy from 1880 to 1933, 51–57; creation of by presidential executive order, 43; and Dawes Act of 1887, 185; federal housing programs on, 150, 152; land claims controversy and ICC, 125–26; Long Range Program and, 137; native leadership of from 1880 to 1933, 48–51; and New Deal programs, 86–89; political activism in post-1960 period, 170; political reorganization under IRA, 99–103; Powell-Ingalls Commission and, 35–36; settlement on in 1880–1933 period, 43–48; termination policy and, 143, 145–46; tribal histories of, 166
Duckwater Festival, 168
Duckwater Reservation, 96, 111–12, 153, 166, 168
Duckwater Tribal Council, 112

Eagle (Pia kwi'naa), 9
Earth Mother, 1, 10, 12
Economic development, antipoverty programs, 154–62
Economic Development Administration (EDA), 155–57
Education: antipoverty programs and, 159, 162–63; assimilation policy and, 54–55, 67–68; New Deal and changes in, 113–14; termination policy and, 146–47
Egan, Chief, 29
Egan, Howard, 23
Elections, 60, 75–76. *See also* Political organization; Voting rights
Elko Colony: establishment of by executive order, 74–75; federal housing programs at, 152; and formation of Te-Moak Bands under IRA, 104, 107; local tribal history projects at, 166; Long Range Program and, 136–37; New Deal assistance to, 91; Te-Moak Bands and HR 7552, 141–42
Elko Indian Youth Club, 158

El-Shonie Corporation, 156–57
Ely Colony, 91, 104–105, 169–70
Ely Colony Council, 170
Engle, Charles, 46
Environmental Protection Committee, 174
Esteves, Pauline, 171
Ethnic Heritage Studies Act of 1972, 164
Ethnohistory, viii

Fallon Reservation, 64, 65
Family organization, 2, 18
Fandangos: and assimilation policy on Duck Valley Reservation, 52; Bureau of Indian Affairs and practice of in 1930s, 117; to celebrate creation of Yomba Reservation, 95–96; and cultural resurgence in post-1960 period, 164; as expression of culture in late nineteenth and early twentieth centuries, 60–62; and termination policy in 1940s and 1950s, 146–47; and traditional culture in 1860s and 1870s, 40–41
Federal Acknowledgement Program, 170–72
Federal Emergency Relief Administration (FERA), 90
Federal government, Western Shoshone and: antipoverty programs in post-1960 period and, 149–63; assimilation policy and, 51–57, 67–75; beginnings of relations between, 19; land claims controversy in post-1960 period and, 176–83; policy of neglect toward nonreservation Shoshones, 59; relations between after signing of Ruby Valley Treaty, 26–41; termination policy (1945–1960) and, 119–20, 123–33, 137–38. *See also* Bureau of Indian Affairs; New Deal
Fisherman, John, 65
Folklore: creation myth, 1; and hunting, 7–8; pine nut in, 4–6; and role of women, 10–11; transmission of tribal knowledge and tradition, 10, 11–12. *See also* Culture
Foods, 2–8, 15, 30. *See also* Hunting; Natural resources
Forney, Jacob, 21
Fort Bridger Treaty (1868), 29
Fort Hall Reservation, 34, 44
Foster, Don, 111
Fourth of July celebrations, 52
Frank, Amos, 71
Frank, Harry, 110
Frazier, Lynn, 84
Freedman, Joel, 168, 179, 183
Fur trade, 13–14

Gammick, John, 137
Garity, Gus, 57
George, Captain, 48
George, Johnnie, 112
George, Oren, 129
Gheen, Levi, 27, 29, 33, 35–36, 37, 39, 41
Ghost Dance religion, 56, 62–63
Gibson, Bill, 67–68, 83, 84, 93, 97, 104, 105
Gibson, Joe, 133–34, 136, 139–40
Gilbert, Alex, 78, 106–107
Gilbert, Joe, 60, 77, 78
Gonzales, Davis, 156
Goshute Reservation, 73
Goshutes, 27, 28, 128
Goshute Treaty of 1863, 71
Government. *See* Federal government; Nevada
Graham, Bodie, 65, 165
Graham, Raymond, 111, 112, 178
Grand Junction Indian School (Colorado), 55
Grass Valley, 33
Great Basin: natural resources of and precontact way of life, 1–2; place names and Shoshone language, 186; Shoshones as active force in region, 187; as U.S. territory, 17
Great Basin Indian Spiritual Conference, 167–68
Great Depression, 85. *See also* New Deal
"Great Society" (1964–1968), 149
Greeley, Horace, 65
Grorud, Albert, 74

Haggett, George, 49, 52
Hall, Bill, 60, 77
Hall, Dick, 60, 77
Hall, Mary, 63, 123
Hanks, Clarence, 123
Hanson, Dugan, 144
Hanson, George, 75, 112, 144
Hanson, Isabel, 144
Harney, Corbin, 167
Harney, Willie, 120
Harris, Jack S., 116
Haskell Institute (Kansas), 55
Hauke, C. F., 46
Head Start program, 159
Healey, Ralph, 107
Health: alcohol and alcoholism, 41, 55–56; assimilation policy at Duck Valley Reservation, 52; impact of epidemic diseases on, 41, 44
Herron, John, 171
Hicks, Albert, Sr., 65, 165
Histories, tribal, viii, ix–x, 165–67

Historiography, Native American, vii–x
Holeman, Jacob, 19–20
Holley, Glenn, 164, 169, 173, 180, 183
Holly, Sam, 130
Hooper, Alice (Kawich), 109
Hospitals, 52
House Concurrent Resolution (HCR) 108 of 1953, 139–40, 147
House Resolution (HR) 3239 (1955), 143–44
House Resolution (HR) 7552 (1953), 140–43
House Resolution (HR) 7833 (1957), 144
Housing, antipoverty programs, 149–50, 152–54
Housing Improvement Program (HIP), 153–54
How, John, 48
Humboldt River, 13, 14–15, 18
Hunting: adoption by whites of native methods, 186–87; off-reservation Shoshones and state regulation of, 64, 65–66; precontact way of life, 6–9; Shoshone leaders on treaty rights and, 83; traditional in 1860s and 1870s, 40; Western Shoshone National Council and state regulation of, 175
Hurt, Garland, 20, 21

Ike, Felix, 167
Ike, Pug and Juanita, 165
Improved Order of Red Men, 186
Indian Action Teams (IAT), 162
Indian Bill, 60
Indian Citizenship Act of 1924, 69, 77
Indian Civil Rights Act of 1968, 164
Indian Claims Commission (ICC) Act of 1946, 123, 176
Indian council, Duck Valley Reservation, 49–51
Indian Education Act of 1972, 162–63
Indian Ranch (California), 75, 112–13, 144
Indian Reorganization Act (IRA) of 1934: as aspect of New Deal, 85–86; formation of Te-Moak Bands, 103–108; formation of Yomba and Duckwater Shoshone tribes, 108–13; land provisions of, 91–99
Indian Self-Determination and Education Act of 1975, 163
Indians, use of term, x
Ingalls, G. W., 34
Inter-Tribal Council of Nevada (ITC-N), 160
Irrigation, 45–46, 54, 88. *See also* Agriculture; Water rights
Iverson, Peter, ix

Jack, Andrew, 123
Jackson, Alice, 129, 134, 135
Jackson, Dimmie, 65

Jackson, James, 129, 134
Jackson, Lloyd, 167
James, Jimmy, 84, 107
Jarvis, Robert, 21
Jenkins, James E., 74, 96
Jim, Charlotte, 129
Joaquin, Willie, Jr., 68
Job Corps, 157
Johnnie, Wagon, 111, 112
Johnny, Harry, 74, 84, 130
Johnny, Oscar, 145, 164, 172
Johnson, Johnny, 120, 130
Johnson, Lyndon, 149
Johnson-O'Malley Act (JOM) of 1934, 114

Kawich, Chief, 34, 35, 106
Kennedy, John F., 149
Kennedy, John Paul, 183

Labor, 31, 54, 63, 187
Ladd, Burton, 132
Land allotments, 44–46, 72–75
Land claims controversy, 176–83
Language, Shoshone: acculturation versus
    assimilation at Duck Valley, 43, 54; cul-
    tural resurgence in post-1960 period,
    164–65; early period of contact, 15;
    place names in Great Basin, 186; pre-
    contact way of life, 2
Lauritzen, Ed, 142
LaVatta, George, 99, 111–12, 135
Leach, Jim, 60, 77
Limerick, Patricia, vii
Lockhart, Jacob, 25–26, 32
Lone Bear, Sam, 117
Long, Johnny, 130
Long, Sam, 129
Long Range Program (LRP), 133–37
Luebben, Thomas, 174

McCarran, Patrick, 136
McDade, Edward, 113, 172, 177
McKinney, Whitney, 166
McQueen, George, 127
McQueen, William, 178
Major Crimes Act (1885), 69
Malheur Reservation, 47
Malone, George, 139, 143
Malotte, Charles, Sr., 107, 129, 135
Malotte, Jack, 167
Manning, Arthur, 132, 178
Manpower Development Training Act
    (MDTA), 154–55
Marriage, precontact patterns of, 2
Mayhugh, John, 47, 49, 53, 60
Medicine persons, 7, 9, 52

Menstruation, isolation of women during,
    52
Meritt, Edgar, 80–81
Mexico, control of Great Basin by, 12–13
Military service, 57, 72
Millett, Danny, 61–62, 94, 163
Millett, Jerry, 173
Millett, Mike, 111
Mining industry, 30, 63, 64
Moapa River Reservation, 34–35
Mormons, 19
Mose (Ruby Valley band leader), 35
Mose, George, 130
Muncey, Francis, 122
Muncey, Jack, 84
Munsey, Jay A., 167
Mutual Help Homeowners Program, 150
MX missile system, 182
Myers, Billy, 98, 121, 127
Mythology. *See* Folklore

National Indian Youth Council (NIYC), 158
National parks, 98
National Resources Board (NRB), 91
Native Americans, use of term, x. *See also*
    Goshutes; Paiutes; Western Shoshones
Native Nevadans for Political Education and
    Action, 167
Natural resources: emigrant groups and de-
    pletion of on Humboldt River, 14–15,
    18; and establishment of white settle-
    ments in Nevada, 30; fur trade and de-
    pletion of, 14; precontact organization
    of family groups and, 2. *See also* Foods;
    Hunting
Neighborhood Youth Corps (NYC), 157–58
Ne-me-te-kalt (Neme tekkate), 19–20
Nevada, Western Shoshone and: affairs of in
    Ruby Valley, 22; criminal law and juris-
    diction of, 145; establishment of perma-
    nent white settlements, 30; Indian labor
    as part of historical development, 187;
    regulation of hunting and fishing, 64,
    65–66, 175; termination policy, 144
Nevada Emergency Relief Administration
    (NERA), 90
New Deal: and changes in education, 113–
    14; general programs of, 86–91; and
    land provisions of Indian Reorganization
    Act, 91–99. *See also* Indian Reorganiza-
    tion Act (IRA)
"New Frontier" (1961–1963), 149
Newe (Shoshones). *See* Western Shoshones
Numa (Northern Paiute). *See* Paiutes
Nye, James, 23, 24, 27, 31–32
Nye County Shoshone Committee, 93–94

Oddie, Tasker, 74
Office of Economic Opportunity (OEO), 157–62
Office of Indian Affairs. *See* Bureau of Indian Affairs
Ogden, Peter Skene, 13–14
O-haga, 33
Operation Relocation, 145–46
Oral tradition. *See* Culture; Folklore
Ottogary, Willie, 77
Overland Route, 18
Owens Valley, 66
Owyhee River, 45, 46–47, 53

Pabawena, David, 127, 130–31
Pabawena, James, 67, 77, 127, 130
Pabawena, Thomas, 105, 121, 123, 127
Pacific Railway Act (1862), 24
Paddy Cap Band, 49, 102
Paharagosam, George, 77, 121
Paiutes: and Bannock War of 1878, 29; and Duck Valley Reservation, 47–48; influx of in 1860s and 1870s, 41; intermarriage with Shoshones in Owens Valley, 66; native leadership of Duck Valley Reservation and, 49; precontact political organization of, 8; precontact relations with Shoshones, 2
Palmer, John, 36, 37
Pa-mo-tao, 48
Parrett, Ray, 64, 91
Paternalism, government, 49
Patterson, Hank, 113
Peavine, Johnnie and Minnie, 64
Penoli, Nevada, 181
Peyote religion, 56–57, 101, 117
Pia Sokopia (Earth Mother), 1, 10, 12
Piffero, Eva, 123
Piffero, Larry, 166
Pine nuts, 4–6, 30
Plants, spiritual and medicinal uses, 9–10. *See also* Foods; Natural resources
Plumb, William, 56
Police, Reservation, 48
Political organization: activism in post-1960 period, 169–75; Indian Reorganization Act (IRA) and, 99–103, 111–12; precontact way of life, 8
Pony Express, 24
Pope, John, 132
Powell, John Wesley, 34
Powell-Ingalls Commission, 34–35
Preacher, Harry, 62, 75–76
Premo, Anna, viii
Premo, Thomas, viii, 51, 55, 100, 112, 128, 133, 135
Premo, Willis, 178

Pryce, Colonel E. Morgan, 135
Public Law (PL) 85–671 (1958), 144
Public Law (PL) 93–638, 163
Public Law (PL) 95–133, 152
Public Law (PL) 95–191, 153
Public Law (PL) 280 (1953), 144–45
Public Works Administration (PWA), 86, 88–89, 90
Puccinelli, Leo, 142–43
Pyramid Lake Reservation, 32

Racism, 68, 90, 162
Railroads, transcontinental, 24, 30
Rancherias, 75, 144
Red Power movement, 163
Reese River Valley Shoshones, 40
Rehabilitation Division, 90–91
Religions, native: practice of in 1930s, 116–17; precontact way of life and, 9; as response to government assimilationist policies, 56–57. *See also* Ghost Dance religion; Peyote religion; Sun Dance religion
Reservations, 21–22, 31–41. *See also* Duck Valley Reservation; Ruby Valley Shoshones; Treaty of Ruby Valley
Revenue sharing, federal, 162
Richards, Dick, 107
Robertson, Cheri, 165
Rocky Mountain Fur Company, 13
Rogers, Benjamin, 21–22
Rogers, Frank, 72
Roosevelt, Franklin D., 85
Rosse, Emmett, 178
Rosse, William, 174
Ruby Valley (Nevada) Shoshones: and Duck Valley Reservation, 46; establishment of "six miles square" reservation in 1859, 21–22, 32–33; land allotments for, 72–73, 79–84, 94–95; and opposition to HR 7552, 142–43. *See also* Treaty of Ruby Valley
Ruby Valley Treaty Days, 168
Rusco, Elmer, 73
Rutabaga Bob, 65

Sagebrush rebellion (1970s-1980s), 182
Sam, Brownie, 111, 112
Sam, Captain, 35, 36, 44, 47, 48
Sam, Henry, 111
Sam, Wilfred, 167
Sante Fe School (New Mexico), 55
Santos, Addie Hanson, 144
Schofield, John M., 27
Seaton, Fred, 144
Selective Service Acts, 71, 120

Self determination, government policy of, 149, 162–63
Sells, Cato, 79–80
Senate Subcommittee of Committee on Indian Affairs, 51, 83–84
Shamans. *See* Medicine persons
Sho-kub (Tsokkope), 22
Shontnezt, Pheban, 123
Shoshone Mike, 70
Shoshone-Paiute Business Council, 100–103, 143
Shosohones. *See* Newe; Western Shoshones
Shoshone treaty council, 83–84
Shoshoni-Goship Treaty (1866), 26
Silva, Eunice, 68
Simpson, James, 23
Skull Valley Reservation, 73
Smallpox epidemics, 41
Smith, Edward, 34
Smith, Fitz, 55
Smith, Jedediah, 13
Smith, Willie, 111
Social Security Administration, 89
South Fork Indian Reservation, 94
Spain, and Great Basin, 12
Spanish Jim, 69
Stanton, Albert, 98, 105, 121, 127, 130, 142
Stanton, Harry, 83, 84
Stanton, Mary, 123
Steele family (Goshute Reservation), 66, 71
Steward, Julian, 115–16
Stewart, Omer C., 131, 175
Stewart Indian School (Nevada), 55, 65, 67
Street, Jim, 117, 142
Strikes, labor, 63
Sun Dance religion, 116–17, 123
Supreme Court, 19. *See also United States v. Mary and Carrie Dann*

Taipo (white), 14
Task Force on Urban and Rural Non-Reservation Indians of the American Indian Policy Review Commission, 170
Taylor Grazing Act of 1934, 98
Te-Moak Bands, 103–108, 125, 141–42, 169–70
Te-Moak Bands Council, 180
Te-Moak Western Shoshone Housing Authority, 152
Temoke: and Powell-Ingalls Commission, 35; and practice of agriculture, 31; refusal to leave Ruby Valley, 36, 37–38, 78–79; relations with whites, 23, 27; Te-Moak Bands organization and, 104
Temoke, Frank, Jr., 132, 147, 169

Temoke, Frank, Sr., 130, 132, 164, 168, 172, 177, 180
Temoke, Gordon, 168
Temoke, Jack, 71, 84
Temoke, Joe, 79
Temoke, John, 129
Temoke, Muchach: creation of IRA reservations, 93, 97, 98–99; formation of To-Moak Bands under IRA, 105, 107; land claims under Ruby Valley treaty, 115, 127, 129, 135; land titles in Ruby Valley, 79–81; Long Range Program, 135; Shoshone participation in World War II, 120; Shoshone treaty council, 83, 84; World War I and white hysteria, 71
Termination, government policy of, 119–20, 123–47
Territory, Shoshone tribal, 8, 26
Thacker, Charlie and Nellie, 48
Thacker, Harry, 100
Thomas, Senator Elmer, 83–84
Thompson, Bruce, 179, 181, 182–83
Thompson, Fred, 113
Thompson, Johnny, 83
Thurston, George, 39
Tiller, Veronica E. Velarde, ix-x
Timbisha Shoshones, 98, 171–72
Toiyabe National Forest, 65, 72
Tommy, Annie, 121
Tootiaina, Harry Dixon, 105
Tosa wihi. *See* White Knife
Tourtellotte, J. E., 33
Townsend, Laura, 102
Treaties, 20, 24. *See also* Treaty of Ruby Valley (1863)
Treaty goods, 38–40. *See also* Annuity payments
Treaty of Guadalupe Hidalgo (1848), 17
Treaty of Ruby Valley (1863): creation of IRA reservations, 93, 98–99; education of Shoshones and advocacy of rights under, 67–68, 114–15; end of annuity distributions, 44; establishment of Duck Valley Reservation, 46; formation of Te-Moak Bands, 104, 105; formation of Yomba Shoshone Tribes, 110; groups participating in, 26; ICC act and land claims controversy, 124–47, 176–83; and land title controversy in Ruby Valley, 79–81; negotiation of, 24–25; and new era in relations with government after signing of, 26–41; provisions of, 25–26; revival of Shoshone treaty council in 1912, 82–84; status of Western Shoshones as sovereign nation, 69; World War II and draft, 120, 121
Trickster, in folklore, 11

Turner, Frederick Jackson, ix
Tu-tu-wa (Toi-Toi), Chief, 24, 76, 106
Tu-tu-wa, Tom, 76–77
Tu-tu-wa Band, 113
Tuukkwasu'unneen (cavalry), 23

Uintah-Ouray Reservation, 34
Unaffiliated Western Shoshone, Inc., 172, 177
Unemployment, 156, 161
United States v. Mary and Carrie Dann (1983), 173, 179–80, 181, 182–83
University of Nevada, 159
Upward Bound program, 159
Utah Territory, 19
Uteen Taikwahni, 1

Vietnam War, 167
Vigilante justice, 70
Volunteers in Service to America (VISTA), 157, 159–60
Voting rights, 69. *See also* Elections; Political organization
Vucanovich, Barbara, 183

Wahne, Thomas, 80, 83
Wai-Pai-Shoshone Craftsmen, Inc., 116
Walker, Joseph Reddeford, 14
Walker River Reservation, 32, 64–65, 93
Warfare: formation of band organizations, 18–20; and water rights after 1863, 27; white hysteria in 1860s and 1870s, 28–30
Washington, George (Shoshone leader), 47, 48, 49
Wasson, Warren, 24
Water rights, 27. *See also* Agriculture; Irrigation
Wells Colony, 152
Western Shoshones: as active force in shaping own history, viii; chaos and warfare in 1848–1863 era, 17–26; contact with European culture, 12–15; experiences of compared to other tribes, 185; influence of on white culture, 186–87; precontact way of life, 1–12; present way of life, 185–86; relations with government after signing of Ruby Valley Treaty, 26–41. *See also* Duck Valley Reservation; specific topics
—Nonreservation: formation of Te-Moak Bands organization, 103–108; and land allotments, 72–75; life of from 1880 to 1933, 59–72; native leadership of, 75–84; and New Deal programs, 89–91
Western Shoshone Business Council, 170

Western Shoshone Council, 50
Western Shoshone Elders Council, 183
Western Shoshone National Council (WSNC), 168, 172–75
Western Shoshone Reservation. *See* Duck Valley Reservation
Western Shoshone Sacred Lands Association (WSSLA), 173, 180
Western Shoshone Stock Association, 51
White Knife (Tosa wihi) Shoshones: agricultural interests and Carlin Farms Reservation, 36; organization of as band, 18–19; relations with whites after Ruby Valley Treaty, 27; settlement on Duck Valley Reservation, 43; Temoke Band relations with, 38; use of firearms, 21
White Pine War (1875), 27–28
Wild Horse Dam, 54, 88
Wilkinson, Ernest L., 124–25, 126, 127, 131
Williams, Saggie, 113, 141
Williams, Willie, 110
Wilson, Orville, 124, 126, 129
Wilson, Tom, 113
Wines, Stanley, 79, 81
Wines, Willie, 55
Wolf, in folklore, 10, 11
Women: and basketweaving, 63, 116; election of to Shoshone-Paiute Business Council, 102; employment of by Civilian Conservation Corps, 88; practice of isolation during menstruation, 52; role of in folklore, 10–11
Woods, William Jack, 169, 178
Woods, Willie, 112, 142
Woodson, Clara, 142
Worden, Dr. John, 74
Work Incentive Program, 160
Works Progress Administration (WPA), 90
World War I, 57, 71–72
World War II, 120–23
Wounded Knee Massacre, ix, 56
Wovoka, 56
Wright, George, 129, 130

Yakima Reservation, 47
Yomba Reservation, 95–96, 108–10, 117, 153
Yomba Tribal Business Committee, 109–10
Young, Brigham, 19
Young, Clifton, 140, 143–44
Yowell, Raymond, 168, 173–74, 178, 180–81

Zepeda, Ofelia, 165
Zimmerman, William, Jr., 106, 137–38